Laid Waste!

EARLY AMERICAN STUDIES

Series editors:
Daniel K. Richter, Kathleen M. Brown, Max Cavitch, and David Waldstreicher

Exploring neglected aspects of our colonial, revolutionary, and early national history and culture, Early American Studies reinterprets familiar themes and events in fresh ways. Interdisciplinary in character, and with a special emphasis on the period from about 1600 to 1850, the series is published in partnership with the McNeil Center for Early American Studies.

A complete list of books in the series is available from the publisher.

Laid Waste!

The Culture of Exploitation in Early America

John Lauritz Larson

PENN

UNIVERSITY OF PENNSYLVANIA PRESS

PHILADELPHIA

Published by
University of Pennsylvania Press
Philadelphia, Pennsylvania 19104-4112
www.upenn.edu/pennpress

Printed in the United States of America
on acid-free paper

10 9 8 7 6 5 4 3 2 1

A Cataloging-in-Publication record is available from the Library of Congress
ISBN 978-0-8122-5184-5

For KJ,
whose world we must preserve

CONTENTS

Introduction

AFTER HUMBLE BEGINNINGS AS faltering British colonies, by 1900 the United States acquired astonishing wealth and power as a result of a process we call modernization.[1] Originating in England and Western Europe, transplanted to the Americas, then copied around the world in the nineteenth and twentieth centuries, this process locked together science and technology, political democracy, economic freedom, and competitive capitalism in what I am calling a "culture of exploitation." In this culture of exploitation, the resources of nature, first seen as gifts from God, became mere commodities for industry, while greed, once proscribed as sin, was naturalized and elevated to a virtue. This process of modernization has produced for some populations unimagined wealth and material comforts. The same process, however, now has brought the global environment to a tipping point beyond which life as we know it may not be sustainable. Since 1971 our children and grandchildren learned as much from the story of *The Lorax* by Dr. Seuss; still, many intelligent adults refuse to reflect historically on the ideas and practices that have made us rich and powerful.

In the twenty-first century we confront more urgent global challenges arising from cumulative degradation, resource depletion, and global warming. Scientists of every stripe have made the case abundantly that greater change will be required. The current rates of resource use, carbon consumption, habitat destruction, and population growth are not sustainable. The standard of living enjoyed by the rich cannot be shared with billions of the world's poor. The global food supply is imperiled by industrial monocultures, while free market distribution systems impose hunger on at least a quarter of the world's population.[2] Many people—especially in the richest countries—fear that any move toward sustainability will threaten their claim on life's necessities. They think that the way we have lived is the only way we *can* live; that more sustainable ways must radically curtail our comfort and our happiness. This fear is rooted in assumptions at the heart of popular culture. Some years ago an aging friend shared a bit of wisdom on the challenge of retirement: "There are two ways to make ends meet," he said. "You can try to get more, or you can learn to need less." We can learn to need less, but we must first *unlearn* the compulsion to get more.

All people understand the world through stories we tell about who we are, how we came to be, and how we know what we "know." In the United States our stories have focused relentlessly on liberty and progress while mostly dismissing the negative consequences that accumulated over time. Americans in particular tend to believe (are encouraged to believe) that freedom and prosperity depend absolutely on our current social and economic systems. As popularly understood, the story of modernization—of democracy powered by capitalism—presents itself as an unfolding natural phenomenon, as inevitable as sunset. Actually, the modern world came together in historical time. *We* created, through cumulative choices, a matrix of ideas and assumptions that shape our understanding of the world as we know it. The resulting framework is not nature itself but a narrative we *chose* to embrace because of rewards it promised. It constitutes a culture of exploitation that was constructed gradually from commitments to individual liberty, private property, Enlightenment-era reasoning, certain religious and scientific dogmas, human greed and arrogance, European imperialism, and the enslavement of people of color.

According to this narrative, in the sixteenth and seventeenth centuries heroic and creative Europeans seized the initiative to develop the "underused" resources of the Western Hemisphere. The resulting plunder of the "New World" was not recorded as a conquest but simply as the natural result of human ingenuity turned loose in an environment of riches. The systems of colonization fed agricultural, commercial, and industrial developments in the eighteenth and nineteenth centuries that, in turn, touched off patterns of social and economic change that we embrace as natural and (mostly) benevolent. Over four centuries Western Europeans and their colonial offspring became enormously rich and powerful thanks, they said, to their own creativity, virtue, initiative, and hard work—that is, to modernization. If people elsewhere around the world suffered poverty and stagnation, it was not because of Western modernization but because they failed to work hard and embrace their opportunities in the same way. Because modernization made the rich rich, those recipients of riches prefer to believe that present-day maldistribution of wealth, intractable poverty, or shortages of natural resources should be blamed, not on modernization itself but the failure of others to modernize according to plan.[3]

This simply is not true. Modernization generated Western wealth and power, but it did so at a price that was paid by environmental ecosystems and by the rest of the global population. Exploitation, through wind-powered sailing ships, state-sponsored commerce (what historian Sven Beckert calls "war capitalism"), staple crop plantation agriculture, and a tragically brutal form of racial slave labor, set the stage for industrialization. Empowered by the use of fossil fuels to drive big machines, industrialization radically transformed material life as well as the cultures of Western societies, resulting in the modern capitalist world order. The story told by the victors *naturalized* these patterns of exploitation and established what economists call "free market forces" as laws of nature akin to gravity and mechanics. In truth these "natural" forces rely on axioms every bit as arbitrary as the bases of decimal arithmetic, Euclidian geometry, and modern particle physics. As famously explained by Thomas Kuhn half a century ago, "normal science" makes sense within a paradigm of assumptions which scientists agree support their working hypotheses. But sometimes anomalies persist that force the analysts to step outside the paradigm and entertain radically different axioms to accommodate real time problems and data.[4]

History abounds with examples of axiomatic assumptions we have managed to revise or abandon in pursuit of more satisfying ways to understand the world. For example, early generations of smart people believed in divine right monarchy as an essential foundation for political legitimacy and national independence. We have learned to believe otherwise. After 1500 African slavery became universally accepted among Western European people who found their access to wealth and power dependent on commodified human property. For nearly three hundred years this conviction reigned supreme and yet, within about fifty years, it fell from favor in much of Europe and America. By 1863 chattel slavery had lost its legal props in most of the modern world (although its shadow long persists in forms of racial and worker exploitation). To accommodate new realities in the twenty-first century we in the West—especially in the United States—must imagine a paradigm shift of similar magnitude. We must learn to celebrate intelligent resource management and a planetwide sense of the common good. Sustainability and optimization must replace individual profit maximization as the fundamental measures of economic value. Holistic concerns for human populations and their neighborhood ecosystems (once common among some "primitive" cultures) must supersede narrow atomistic claims about private rights and gains, as if the advantage of any individual outweighs the common good of the planet.[5]

My goal in the book that follows is not to map out the details of such a paradigm shift: that is a complex task that must stand at the top of the political agenda in the twenty-first century. My less ambitious purpose is to show that such a paradigm shift is as possible—and as survivable—as many other major changes that have rocked our world from time to time. What I here call the culture of exploitation is no less susceptible to amendment than so many historical "truths" we have abandoned since the medieval era. Every piece of this cultural construct was once new and disbelieved —starting with the astonishing tales told by voyagers who first encountered the American continents. Religious and civil authorities scrambled to account for indigenous people, flora, and fauna not catalogued in Christian scriptures. Terms like "liberty," "equality," "ambition," even "natural law" seemed dangerous and disruptive until they found their way into common thought and discourse. Free markets were denounced as dangerously antisocial until they were embraced gradually in the nineteenth century as ideal and incorruptible. Tribal groupings—the English, Dutch, French, Spanish, Portuguese "races"—seemed fixed and immutable until intermingling and intermarriage diminished their peculiarities.

This book does not pretend to offer a comprehensive narrative or even a balanced synthesis of all we have learned about the past four hundred years from an outpouring of modern scholarship. Historians have complicated richly our understanding of the colonial experience, by forcing the thirteen British mainland colonies composing the new United States back into the context of a multicultural Atlantic world teeming with Spanish, Portuguese, French, Danish, Dutch, Swedish, German, English, African, and Native American actors. Recent narratives, such as Alan Taylor's masterful *American Colonies*, help shift the center of our attention away from Puritan New England and into the polyglot chaos of the Caribbean, where most of the players interacted, where most of the money was made, and where arguably the worst of the crimes against humanity and nature were committed in the seventeenth and eighteenth centuries. Colonial history involved so much more than the prehistory of the United States.[6]

But for my purposes most of this complexity will not be repeated because the American culture of exploitation (the object of my meditations) was not built on an accurate platform of historical developments. The true foundations and buttresses supporting the culture of exploitation will be found, not in the critical histories of our past, but in the triumphal stories that emerged from that past to shape a master narrative about the rising "glory of America." Willful distortions and selective memorialization shaped the building blocks of this constructed "history" in ways that dismissed as irrelevant much of the chaos of the early Atlantic world and silenced most of those non-English voices as contributing nothing significant to the emerging United States.

For example, our English forebears *told us* that they conquered an empty "howling wilderness," unaided by anyone and mostly impeded by other colonial actors. Although the eastern woodland Natives had been farmers for generations, they were set down in memory as irredeemable hunters and gatherers (addicted to the chase, said Jefferson). We could seize their lands with impunity because they did not "use and improve" them according to European standards (except, of course, when they did). English planters in the Carolina low country earned their fortunes cultivating rice, about which they knew nothing until taught by their African slaves, who by definition knew nothing of value. In 1776 intrepid patriots snatched independence from "corrupt" and "grasping" imperial rulers, to the wild cheering of Americans, two-thirds of whom did not actually support independence until bullied into it by radical neighbors. Once liberated, however, those Americans declared themselves a chosen people, special instruments of world-historical forces that moved the center of civilization westward across the Atlantic, and then west across the continent, in a process not of conquest or aggression but of "destiny."

The culture of exploitation grew out of the convergence of ideas, discoveries, innovations, lofty ideals, and base transgressions. It drew from evolving political, economic, religious, and scientific understandings. At times these chapters will seem to be about environmental history, economic history, intellectual, social, or political trends; it is all of these, but not in equal parts at every turn. There is however an arc of evolution, away from reverence for God's Creation and toward the exploitation of natural resources; away from narrow, truncated expectations and toward the liberation of expansive individualism; away from stewardship of the commons and toward growth through competition; away from embeddedness in the environment and toward the control through knowledge of nature's mysteries; away from community and toward isolating private acquisitiveness. At different points along the way complaints were raised about this trajectory, but it was the genius of the culture of exploitation to proclaim itself a thing of nature—not of choice—and thus persuade the ever-growing mass of people disserved by its performance that nothing could be done short of repealing natural laws. Each chapter in what follows is built as a meditation on a central idea that became a building block of the culture of exploitation.

The book opens with a chapter on "Stability." What the early modern English called the natural order—the Great Chain of Being—doubled as a framework protecting inequality and imposing material scarcity on the vast majority of people. Christian doctrines tempered market-based transactions, set prices, and regulated lending. English common rights and traditions bound lords, tenants, and servants with reciprocal promises that emphasized obligation and discouraged excessive self-love. Never completely honored, such values nevertheless attached to transgressive behavior a moral hazard not to be ignored. Inequality may have been the norm in early modern England, but it did not quench a thirst for gain that was triggered by the reports of "Abundance" (Chapter 2) of riches pouring in from the New World. Colonizers saw these resources not as the property of others (requiring seizure) but as lost parts of the original "Creation," the gift of God to His Christian people. In the process of getting established, colonists embraced aspects of individualism, liberty, and ambition that solved their immediate problems but gradually transformed their provincial societies in ways they did not intend or expect.

By the 1700s, the application of labor (their own and that of coerced slaves) and the development of markets yielded viable communities and fostered a sense of power and pride in the "Achievement" (Chapter 3) of colonization. This pride of accomplishment blended congenially with Enlightenment ideas about civilization, moral philosophy, natural theology, and social evolution to lay the foundations for a culture of exploitation that would replace the old culture of stability. Pleased with their own achievements, colonial Americans began to imagine themselves as agents of world-historical developments. After 1750, growing out of speculative philosophy as well as Renaissance humanism, a new science of politics laid the foundations for "Liberation" (Chapter 4) as the American Revolution rejected Europe's authority traditions. Decrying metaphorical "enslavement" to British designs (if not the actual enslavement of African workers), colonial radicals such as John Adams crafted an ideology of liberation with which they organized their independence movement. In the same generation Adam Smith proposed as "natural" a competitive free-market model for economic activity to replace the corrupt and "erroneous" policies of mercantilist governments. In fact, "natural laws" appeared everywhere to structure the dreams and expectations of the coming generation and help create the optimism that buoyed Americans into believing they could erect "a new order for the ages."

Armed with liberation and a new confidence in their own potential, assured that their path represented the very arc of civilization, citizens of the new United States set out to take "Inventory" (Chapter 5) of the untapped riches at their disposal. In some of the hard-used older places (Virginia, New England, the Delaware Valley), declining fertility, deforestation, and resource depletion sparked critical calls for reform, but spectacular reports of great riches in western lands suggested an easier solution. Great schemers imagined themselves as impresarios opening "virgin lands" to civilization; ordinary farmers simply laid claim to Indian land and set about improving their private fortunes. Apparently limitless natural resources allowed all kinds of white Americans to entertain dreams more expansive than ever before. Chapter 6, "Improvement," zeroes in on the word that best captures the "spirit" of the times at the turn of the nineteenth century. If husbandry and stewardship implied lowered expectations, improvement promised more and better things through science, enterprise, and innovation. The "conquest" of space and time through innovations in transportation and communication boosted American optimism to intoxicating levels. Knowledge itself seemed to explode as the "useful arts" unleashed waves of invention unlike anything seen before. Problems mechanical, material, organic, even spiritual, all would be solved by the contriving brains and skillful hands of nineteenth-century Americans. The original Adam was charged with tending the Garden and harvesting its fruits, but this new Adam added invention, design, and fabrication to the list of human obligations.

Soon it was thought to be the manifest "Destiny" (Chapter 7) of the United States to transform the continent (and later the world?) through its signature blend of personal liberty and technical prowess. This phrase "manifest destiny" applied narrowly at first to campaigns of territorial expansion, but it contributed as well to Americans' materialistic notions of entitlement that energized the next wave of modernization. Here two visions of political economy competed for their attention: one aimed at maintaining a "harmony of interests" within a national economy while the other encouraged relentless competition and individual freedom. Armed with railroads, steamships, and electromagnetic telegraphs, the advocates of competition and freedom conjured up artificial networks with which to subdue the continent. Scientific and technical solutions promised to usher in America's grandeur. Tragically, the "problem" of slavery lurked like a dragon guarding the entrance to the bountiful universe of continental riches and Oriental commerce on view from the shores of California.

Chapter 8 opens with a scene of the mighty Corliss engine that powered the Centennial Exhibition in Philadelphia in 1876 and closes with a look at the monumental "White City" of the Columbian Exhibition in Chicago in 1893. Here Americans laid claim to a sense of "Mastery" and reached for a leadership role in the century ahead. By removing the "stain" of slavery (now redefined by the victors as a "barbarous" antiquated system incompatible with "civilized" ways), the Civil War had purified the American progress machinery. Heavy industry took off and technological innovations multiplied exponentially. Unprecedented urbanization, immigration, and rising aggregate prosperity followed. Liberal economists lectured on the "natural laws" of trade; popular preachers spoke of "acres of diamonds" waiting to be collected; and steel baron Andrew Carnegie set down his own "Gospel of Wealth." Confronted with the arid regions of the American West, the masters of modernization labored to "fix" nature's faulty landscapes and make deserts bloom. Still, negative feedback accumulated everywhere—in ragged pauperized workers, filthy cities, industrial wastelands, ruined mining landscapes, cut-over washed-out forest lands, and localized shortages of water, fuel, and sometimes breathable air. Cue the age of reform, including environmental awareness and the conservation movement. By 1900 the culture of exploitation was fully formed, but articulate critics were gaining traction at last.

Chapter 9, "Prophecy," reaches back to pick up some critical voices that had been raised (without much effect) against the boisterous enthusiasts of modernization. Writers like Emerson, Thoreau, and George Perkins Marsh suggested counternarratives to a generation that refused to listen; later in the century John Muir and John Wesley Powell sharpened such critical perspectives. Gradually these voices of prophecy aligned with the concerns of more "practical conservationists," who worried about dwindling stocks of timber, minerals, and virgin land. Theodore Roosevelt braided the threads together, hiking in Yosemite with John Muir while pushing to establish a science-based forestry department under the direction of Gifford Pinchot. The culture of exploitation came under attack from many directions, yet its central place in the popular mind would prove to be surprisingly secure. This chapter will end with the battle over Hetch Hetchy Canyon, in which the civic boosters of San Francisco took on the romantic idealists of the newly formed Sierra Club. The city won, and the canyon filled with water.

I make no attempt in these chapters at comprehensive or photographic representation. Like icons in an Orthodox church, these chapters strive to focus the reader's attention on elemental claims that sometimes are conveyed best through symbolic emphasis on perspective, composition, or color. I offer concrete evidence and authentic voices, and I try to let them take their place in the larger gallery that is the argument. For every "witness" called here to testify there are many more who told the same tale—and some whose stories differed. One could select those pieces of evidence that would affirm, not contradict, the heroism of the past, but that of course is what sustains the errors of our ways. By design I have interrogated some of the most familiar actors from the standard narrative in order to deflect the charge that mine is a twisted record drawn only from disaffected players. Finally, through the reference notes I mean to invite readers to question further and challenge these assertions by digging into the extraordinary library of scholarship on which my argument and understanding rest.

There must be an Epilogue stitching these historical meditations (ending as they do around 1900) to the urgent questions facing our present generation. The past does not dictate the future, but our narratives about the past do inform the questions we ask and the answers we can imagine. Twentieth-century actors saw the modern world as a given—natural, appropriate, inevitable—and thus were led to analyze problems inside the framework of assumptions I have called here the culture of exploitation. Over the course of the twentieth century a conservation impulse gained enormous traction, but the "greening" of America primarily has aimed at cleaning up our systems of exploitation. The existing literature on American environmental history for the twentieth century richly documents these gradual awakenings that finally resulted, by the 1970s, in landmark legislation including the creation of an Environmental Protection Agency.[7] Surprisingly, what looked like a steady unfolding of environmental awareness and policy adjustments was thrown into reverse in the 1980s by a "neo-liberal" revolution. Capitalizing on disruptions caused by the Arab oil embargo and the sharp rise in fuel prices that followed, advocates of unrestricted economic liberty announced that we cannot afford to worry about smog, acid rain, or polar bears. Deregulation, tax cuts, and economic growth incentives promised to restore the prosperity machinery: more growth, more freedom, more exploitation. Over the next two decades incomes of the wealthiest half percent of Americans spiked like never before in history, but the benefits largely disappeared into private fortunes while the exploitation of labor, consumers, and natural resources lurched back toward the standards of the Gilded Age.

At the level of popular culture and political discourse, the old matrix still enjoys a scriptural force that can be tapped (and is) to disqualify voices critical of modernization. We are told that talk of restraint is "unmanly," that we are "losing ground" because others in the world's population are squeezing more wealth from the global capitalist system. Progress alone can keep us happy; anything else must *by nature* result in slavery to foreign rivals. This perspective cripples serious talk of major, long-term solutions to global inequality, resource depletion, pollution, or climate change on a global scale. But progress—the culture of exploitation—is not a law of nature and it is not the only framework that could guide our collective behavior. Historically, Americans collectively chose extravagance over sufficiency, competition over cooperation, individual gain over community welfare, dominion over stewardship. That we did so *then* does not invalidate those alternative values or preclude the construction *now* of a culture of sustainability with its own deep roots in the American experience. To begin creating a culture of sustainability we must first acknowledge the framework we already inhabit, recognize it *as* a framework, and evaluate the work that it does to perpetuate old habits, reward longtime beneficiaries, and silence the critical voices that have been there all along.

The key words in my title, *Laid Waste!*, introduce a grammatical ambivalence that is fortuitous if not wholly intentional. We often deflect collective responsibility for a destructive impact: the planet was "laid waste" by unanticipated consequences, by unnamed actors, or perhaps by a natural disaster. Alternatively, we sometimes delight in rewarding heroic actors who "laid waste" the tyrant and his minions. The ambivalence has given us the choice, over the centuries, of accepting or denying our collective role as purposeful actors in history. Similarly, the word "waste," used as a noun, refers to land or resources not yet seen as fit for human development *or* to the detritus left when raw materials are transformed into "useful" objects. Used as a verb, "waste" refers to the reckless or willful misuse of valuable things. These subtle differences of meaning reverberate through the chapters below because the culture of exploitation was forged by the confluence of conscious and unconscious actions, willful and reckless behaviors, active transgressions and passive acceptance of benefits bestowed by our failure to act. If there were less at stake we might debate this as a problem in understanding historical causation; but the fat is in the fire, and our urge to protect our innocence does not contribute to needed reforms.

In the end I have three objectives in mind for this project. First, I hope to provoke readers who may suspect that something is wrong but do not know where to turn to investigate their options. I hope to transform their nascent discomfort into curiosity. Next, I would invite them to take up the simple tools of historical inquiry that have led me to these alternative conclusions. The historical record is readily at hand. Both scholarship and source material are more available now than at any time since the invention of printing, and these meditations may serve as a primer on how to read deeply into that which appears familiar on the surface. Finally, I hope that readers, so provoked and so invited, will engage in the difficult work of reimagining our modern world in more sustainable ways. Americans like to think of ourselves as leaders, and we clearly have led the way down the path of modernization. Now we are in position to lead in new directions and model new assumptions in pursuit of an alternative relationship with the globe and its people. I am inclined to believe that course corrections small enough to be endured can start the process. The cumulative effect of doing a little more good and a little less harm—like savings in a retirement plan—can make a big difference a century out. Nature itself is resilient and the Earth will prevail, but we also would like to preserve the possibility of human life on this planet. This is a goal about which nature is utterly indifferent, but it was one of three in the hearts of the American founders. In Thomas Jefferson's hands the Lockean triad of "life, liberty, and property" was recast as "life, liberty, and the pursuit of happiness." That subtle difference implies so much more than mere survival or brutal domination; it suggests that wealth and power are not ends in themselves but means to something greater and deeply humane.

CHAPTER 1

Stability

THEY OBSESSED ABOUT ORDER: God in His heavens, a monarch on the throne, and every man, woman, and child secure in a proper niche. The English who colonized British North America—more especially their immediate forebears—imagined a universe structured in fine, orderly gradations. In their mind's eye they saw a Great Chain of Being, descending from the hand of their Creator God, angels and archangels linking the deity with the crown of earthly creation, the human man (gendered male), and on down the natural hierarchy through the lowest earthly creatures. Inequality stood as an essential fact of this early modern European worldview; everyone belonged on a vertical axis, above some inferior person but in peaceful subjugation to greater ones. Dominion marked relations viewed from the top—God over all, angels over men, men over lesser creatures and the firmament itself. Among humans, great men stood over the lower orders, white men over persons of color (however subtle the shade), and individual men over females and their minor offspring. Obligation characterized the opposite vector. The potential for abuse at every step was tempered by expectations of mutual care and reciprocity. Equality—the horizontal axis—meant relatively little on earth (perhaps more in heaven); one's vertical obligations of obedience and responsibility took clear precedence. When order prevailed, harmony followed. As historian David Underdown once summed it up, "the authority of the monarch corresponded with that of the patriarchal father over his household: undermine discipline and obedience in one sphere, and it would inevitably collapse in the other." According to all accounts, this well-ordered array reflected not just human design but the natural order of things, laid down by the Creator when the universe was born. It was all explained for the curious in the first three chapters of the Christian scripture.[1]

They obsessed about order because resources were scarce—or appeared to be—or this is what they were led to believe by those who controlled the resources. Land of course was in finite supply, owned by a tiny minority, time out of mind, and parceled out in leases that could be bought and sold only under fairly controlled circumstances. Food supplies turned on the local harvest, itself dependent on natural conditions and the choices made by the few who controlled the land. Fuel grew scarcer each year as those woodlots not locked up in royal forests or deer parks failed to meet demand. Cottages, jobs, partners for marriage—everything came in short supply, meted out by others whose interest it was to perpetuate this culture of stability. Reciprocal obligations required privileged elites to sustain the welfare of their many dependents, while dependents obeyed, performed their expected roles, and affected gratitude for the ministrations of their governors. Good order assured a satisfactory distribution of life's essentials, at least most of the time. Ambition, novelty, and innovation introduced elements of unpredictability that could upset the system, and the resulting disorder might threaten the whole community. Safety and sustainability derived from the maintenance of order and the perpetuation of customary ways of administering scarce resources.[2]

Reality never truly resembled the satisfying images by which writers captured this timeless ideal. True stability was threatened often by disruptions and disappointments. Resources were not so much scarce as ill-distributed. The social hierarchy never was really static; individuals and whole families rose and fell, but they did so behind a curtain of deniability. In the fourteenth century visitations from the "Black Death" (bubonic plague) cut down over a third of Europe's people. In England in 1520 the population stood at roughly 2.4 million—barely half the number alive in 1300. Badly shaken survivors temporarily enjoyed greater prospects for an adequate living, but no one could be sure another outbreak was not on the horizon. Dynastic struggles among nobles trying to erect and control enduring national governments, such as the fifteenth-century Wars of the Roses, unavoidably scattered collateral damage among innocent country people. As change and confusion settled over each generation there appeared in memory, always receding, a golden age when all was in order; but in fact there was no true "beginning" from which to measure triumph or decay.[3]

There was one disruption, however, that seemed to mark for the people of Europe an epochal break in the passage of ordinary time: they called it the "discovery" of the New World. Starting with the voyages of Columbus in 1492, Spanish and Portuguese, then French, Dutch, and finally English explorers ventured westward, laying claim to worlds not imagined by their fathers. They introduced into commerce and popular expectations new sources of land, produce, treasure, and opportunity. The orderly systems that propped up a culture of stability in Old Europe shuddered from the sudden prospect of places and things unknown. All over Europe in the sixteenth century people struggled to absorb and contain the impact of new knowledge, new resources, new ideas, new foods, and new technologies that shook conventional realities to the core. This traumatic era (one that we benignly remember as the "age of discovery") alone did not cause the upheavals that persisted through the seventeenth century, but the prospect of a New World to conquer and possess surely marked the start of the experience for those who lived to tell. John Locke famously wrote, "In the beginning all was America."[4] He employed the New World as a trope for the "state of nature" on top of which his (and all subsequent) conjectural schemes would be erected. But Locke wrote in 1690, two hundred years after Columbus's arrival in Hispaniola. During those two hundred years the New World operated not just as a metaphor but as an active, destabilizing force in an Atlantic world of emerging empires, cultural conflicts, cruel subjugations, and competitive exploitation. Here were the roots of modern American history.[5]

A Tree of Commonwealth

In 1509, confined to a cell in the Tower of London, Sir Edmund Dudley allowed his thoughts to play with the ideal shape and structure of a proper commonwealth. He framed his treatise as "advice to a young prince"— ineffective advice, apparently, since his new king, Henry VIII, soon ordered his execution. Nevertheless, Dudley felt compelled to set down in allegorical form his ideas of how the parts of a well-ordered society ought to relate to one another. He chose an organic metaphor, a "mighty tree growing in a fair field or pasture, under the cover or shade whereof all beasts, both fat and lean, are protected and comforted from the heat and cold as the time requireth." Such a great tree sheltered "all the subjects of that realm," but its growth and endurance relied upon "diverse strong roots . . . fastened surely in the ground."[6]

The "chief" or tap root of Dudley's tree was the "love of God," without which nothing thrived and whose ordinance bound "all kings" to their subjects "by the commandment . . . to maintain and support them." People might be subjects of the king, Dudley explained, but they also were "the people of god, and god hath ordained their prince to protect them and they to obey their prince." Contained in this simple statement lay the central organizing principle of the early modern social and political order: reciprocal obligation linking obedience to protection, binding the powerful few to the vulnerable many in a mutual but unequal relationship. To further anchor his tree of commonwealth, Dudley identified four more essential roots: justice, truth, concord, and peace. In the balance of the work he spelled out the nature of these four roots, the fruits borne of each, and the poisonous cores hidden in those fruits that delivered not nourishment but disaster to any who would eat of them heedlessly. Suspended throughout Dudley's allegory was a cosmic tension between salvific order and the chaos that surely followed the vices known to tempt mankind: gluttony, avarice, tyranny, envy, dishonesty, and faithlessness. The harmonious vision of order and tranquility painted by Dudley's words barely concealed an underlying sense of foreboding—the awareness of disturbing forces in the world as he knew it—that must have driven Dudley's literary enterprise.[7]

For the prince, Dudley's advice returned again and again to the obligations of justice and protection, that his subjects "not be oppressed by great men and their superiors." The king must model law, not raw power, and truth above all. On the other hand, the people must commit themselves to "concord," a third root which Dudley defined as the agreement that every man "be content to do his duty in the office, room, or condition that he is set in, and not to malign or disdain any other." English nobles, he feared, did not properly model this contentment. Because of the promotion of "poor men and mean folk" to positions of authority, English aristocrats stood out, in Dudley's view, as the "worst brought up" in Christendom. For the "commonality of this realm"—the merchants, craftsmen, "graziers," toilers, and others who did not "murmur to live in labor and pain," Dudley counseled contentment. Do not "presume above" your "own degree" or "counterfeit the state" of your betters. Beware political operatives who dress up in the "Liverie of lords." Eschew gaming halls and taverns, hawking and hunting (unless of noble birth). Let not substantial merchants and farmers squeeze "great lucre" from their dependents, "but be unto their underlings loving and charitable." Tradesmen must not cheat in measures, artificers avoid "sloth," and plowmen "delight" in their labors.[8]

Order and stability—happiness—depended absolutely on the maintenance of ranks and assignments up and down the ladder of dependencies. In Dudley's ideal commonwealth "Idleness" was proscribed, but so too was ambition and reaching for advancement. Concord came with equilibrium, and the whole framework came from God, who had: "set an order by grace between himself and Angell, and between Angell and Angell; and by reason between Angell and man, and between man and man, man and beast; and by nature only between beast and beast; which order, from the highest point to the lowest, god willeth us firmly to keep without any enterprise to the contrary."[9]

Tragically immune to his own advice, Dudley himself had risen to wealth and power as a heavy-handed debt collector for Henry VII. When the old king died Dudley's enemies pushed Henry VIII to charge him with treason, and *The Tree of Commonwealth* may have been intended to flatter the incoming monarch rather than school him in traditions. Either way, the treatise stands as an eloquent statement of the "Great Chain of Being" clearly invoked as a shield against the winds of change and confusion that threatened the peace at the accession of Henry VIII.

Material Life

Land supported material life in early modern England, and the land belonged to a tiny minority of noble and aristocratic families who monopolized political power and restricted access to economic opportunity. In the year 1500 the crown claimed the largest holdings of any individual, with estates totaling perhaps 5 percent of the whole kingdom. Another 25 percent belonged to the church and its various orders. Some two hundred families—the nobles—owned another 20 percent, followed in rank by gentry who numbered several thousand and claimed 30 percent of the land. Consider all of these proprietors "gentlemen"—leisured individuals who did not work with their hands for economic gain. They depended for their income on rents and fees paid by tenants who were bound by a bewildering array of traditional tenures, some reaching back hundreds of years. At the top of this agricultural class came the "freeholders," substantial yeoman farmers who controlled their own land (owned it outright or paid a nominal rent that conferred all the privileges of ownership otherwise). These working farmers controlled the remaining 20 percent of England's land. If their landed rents met the annual forty-shilling threshold (£2) they could vote in parliamentary elections; some earned far more and employed many of their village neighbors. Their economic freedom was limited less by the rights of the lords above than by the customary expectations of commoners below.[10]

Smaller tenant farmers (husbandmen and cottagers) with less secure and complicated leases, artisans and craftsmen, and unskilled laborers filled out the ranks of the "lower orders." Constituting a vast majority of the whole population, this class of persons depended ever more completely (moving down the scale) on their "betters" who owned and controlled the means of production. Softening their desperation were customary rights to the ancient "commons," where even the poorest individual might succor a pig or chicken, or himself scratch for food and fuel. These were the people that the "natural order" promised to sustain, for whom proprietors in theory were responsible in times of crisis, and for whom any winds of change raised the greatest anxiety and genuine distress. Because of fierce battles that eventually erupted over tenant and common rights, historians have scoured the archives to understand the structure of rural life at the start of the sixteenth century. As a result, we now know that, while land *ownership* was highly concentrated, landless people as a whole probably enjoyed *access* to land or the use of land through lease arrangements or common rights. Historian Keith Wrightson claims that "even the laboring poor enjoyed such access to considerable extent." Unlike conditions in 1750, on the eve of industrialization, in the early 1500s "complete dependence upon agricultural wages was still exceptional in most areas." If so, there was a shred of truth behind the memory of harmony and reciprocity in the "golden age."[11]

Traditional farming in England wore a different aspect from one location to another, but in general common farmers produced cereal grains (wheat, rye, and barley) in two- or three-field rotations. Hay was gathered from natural meadows while livestock grazed on village commons or nearby waste (nonarable lands). Most grain found its way to the miller for bread or the brewer for malting in the process of making ale. Cattle supplied meat and milk, the latter converted to butter and cheese. Poultry furnished the eggs that often constituted the best poor man's protein. Pigs recycled kitchen and garden wastes before retiring to the smokehouse in the form of hams and sausages. Substantial yeomen typically employed a small number of paid hands while smaller husbandmen relied on family labor. Poor cottagers might still plant a garden patch and tether a "milch cow" on the common while a few chickens scratched in the yard. The medieval open-field system, where village residents all worked together on common fields had been giving way in England, replaced by discrete holdings, set off by hedges, and farmed to best advantage by the leaseholder and his employees. In scale, rural life remained compact and local, with most residents clustered in ancient villages. Fat times or lean, whole communities experienced both together; inequality prevailed, but deprivation appeared to fall on neighbors proportionally, reinforcing the prevailing assumptions about social relations and the vicissitudes of fortune.[12]

Nonfarm employment occupied a small fragment of the rural population. Blacksmiths, millers, weavers, and workers of wood and leather could be found in many rural villages and all market towns. Teamsters, cartmen, and wagoners plied the roads, gathering country produce into market towns and distributing to the fringes things not produced by local hands. The wealthier gentry shopped in distant towns or cities—Devizes, Bristol, even London—forging a tentative connection between the semisubsistence world of the common people and the wider emporia of material delights. Artisans learned their trade and passed along its mysteries to the coming generation by a system of apprenticeship that already was ancient. Masters engaged young boys in the shop (or girls in household service) for a term of years expected to culminate in a skillful competency. Then followed a wage-earning journey in search of a permanent opening usually not far away. Like their agricultural neighbors, village people sought to reproduce in future the ways and means they had known since time immemorial. Find your place in the order of things, make your appointed contribution, and draw from the common stock the living you deserve.[13]

Finding your place was the most important task facing young adults in the early modern English countryside, but seldom did the search carry them far from home. Most children of farmers stayed in farming; artisan's sons generally took up a skilled trade (apprenticed under a different master). Young women learned domestic arts from mothers, grandmothers, aunts, and female neighbors, often going into paid service for some years between childhood and marriage. Courtship began late for the middling and lower orders because married couples needed a cottage in which to live and a source of income to live on. Early English households typically comprised parents and minor offspring—nuclear families rather than extended networks of kin. Most youths found marriage partners within the parish of their birth; all but a tiny fraction found spouses within fifteen or twenty miles of home. That may have been the radius of the circle in which many people lived their entire lives. Marriage for men took place at an average age of twenty-seven, for women twenty-four, which left married women about twenty childbearing years. Women usually conceived shortly after (or just before) the wedding, and subsequent pregnancies followed every two or three years until their early forties. Such fertility notwithstanding, infant or child mortality and maternal death kept most families surprisingly small: household size at one data point in 1523 averaged less than four. Life expectancy at birth stood at thirty-four years; survivors to adulthood gained fifteen or twenty years. Viewed from the modern era, rural life in 1500 seems to have been short and fragile, marked by waiting, loss, uncertainty, and deprivation.[14]

Metropolitan London presented a special case, echoed but never reproduced in smaller cities such as Bristol, York, or Canterbury. Here trade and politics, not the agricultural seasons, set the tempo and purpose of life, while a majority of denizens focused on meeting the day-to-day needs of maybe 70,000 persons living one atop the other. Goldsmiths, hatters, tailors, milliners, jewelers, apothecaries spiced up the retail menu; provisioners of comestibles, together with tavern-keepers, hackney drivers, messenger boys, laundresses, chimney-sweeps, pickpockets, actresses, and prostitutes rounded out the occupational rosters. Clerks scratched in account books and government servants scurried back and forth between Whitehall and Westminster, the taverns on Fleet Street, the nearby inns of court, and the private in-town estates of the ruling elite. Aristocrats were drawn to London by the twin magnets of power and luxury. At court they displayed their wealth, their achievements, their evidence of favor with the sovereign. In town they vied with one another, staged lavish entertainments, sought conjugal matches for their offspring, and indulged their private vices, spending freely of the revenues wrung from estates by the sweat of "their" country people. Their servants and the thousands of lower-class men, women, and children who made up the working population of the metropolis divided their time between waiting on the elites, scratching out a subsistence, and snatching scraps of indulgence in coarse imitation of "their betters." In London finding your place was a dangerous game. If not more exploitative in absolute terms, inequality in London *looked* crass, illegitimate, and profoundly at odds with the rural ideal and the Great Chain of Being.[15]

Economic Assumptions

As in most of Europe at the time, the English economy in 1500 was built around markets but it was not yet a market economy. Market *places* facilitated all kinds of exchanges without which the simplest specialization or division of labor would not have been possible. The myriad farmers brought surplus grain to markets where townsfolk, millers, and bakers bought it for their own consumption or for manufacture into flour and bread. Cheese, butter, eggs, bundles of firewood, and other country produce found buyers in regional market towns or the smallest of local villages. Households with greater means imported wine, spices, and luxury consumables from larger vendors farther from home, although more common folk might sometimes find small lots of fancy goods for sale in local shops. Handicraft artisans mostly produced their wares "bespoke" for a particular buyer with whom they struck a bargain directly. It is important to distinguish these early modern networks of exchange from a more mature, cash-based market economy, but it would be wrong to exaggerate the self-sufficiency of country people or project back onto them a naive innocence of commercial temptations and the disruptive power of market forces. Self-provisioning—supplying most household needs at home or from local exchanges—remained almost universal in 1500, but in the next generation market forces were seen and felt in volatile prices for food and fodder. The time had arrived when substantial profits *could be* made by raising surplus grain for distant markets, and that opportunity would not be ignored forever.[16]

What constitutes the difference between markets and a market economy is the degree of penetration by market forces into the system of values that governed social relations. When people persisted in traditional ways of planting, spending, and investing regardless of changing prices or short-term opportunities, they appeared to be pursuing a risk-averse "safety first" strategy intended to deflect disaster and protect what they knew as "normal." Individuals who embraced innovation and changed their ways in rhythm with prices and distant demand clearly were paying more attention to short-term opportunities. The evidence is sketchy and often difficult to interpret, but apparently before 1500 "safety-first" governed most behavior while during the sixteenth century—as a result of the challenges discussed below—more individuals responded more often to market signals. Traditionalists stridently condemned such innovations, producing the documentary outcry that calls our attention to the problem in the first place.[17]

Early modern markets still carried a web of constraints and regulations designed in feudal times to blunt shocks and damp down fluctuations in a world of imperfect transport and communication. Statutes fixed markets to specific days of the week, so that sellers could do business in more than one town or village. Laws prohibited the transport of grain except on designated market days to prevent forestallers from locking up the local supply and withholding it from actual consumers. Additional restrictions gave commoners the first hours of the morning (perhaps 9:00 to 11:00) to purchase grain for household use, forcing bakers, brewers, and "badgers" (speculators) to wait. Laws proscribed other speculative actions such as engrossing (cornering supplies) and regrating (buying purely for resale). Supporting all these elaborations was the Assize of Bread and Ale (51 Henry III), the thirteenth-century statute by which local authorities set the size, weight, and price of a common loaf to serve as a floor in behalf of the weakest consumers. How well these prescriptions worked in practice remains debatable, but in the early sixteenth century local magistrates enjoyed significant authority to interfere in market transactions. Prices *did* fluctuate in relation to market forces, some of which people apparently respected as legitimate; but the *stated* goal of local markets—especially in foodstuffs—remained the maintenance of order and welfare, neither of which prevailed if selfish operators succeeded in producing artificial dearth or bounty for the sake of short-term profits.[18]

This ambivalence about market forces found deep roots in Christian culture and feudal traditions. Between the collapse of serfdom in the wake of the Black Death and the rise of more authoritative state governments by the seventeenth century, both churchmen and secular lords had depended on keeping in health and harmony a local population to work the land—and shoulder the pike if needed. Technically free, such peasants were rooted practically in place by custom and kinship. In the past occasional fairs and itinerant merchants had acquainted them with exotic goods and cash money, scattering in the process news, disease, and desires. Local princes across Europe and England had exercised the right to encourage, prohibit, or regulate commercial activity according to their sense of how it disrupted the local community. The Roman church weighed in with teachings that condemned avarice, gluttony, and covetous desire, all of which contradicted Christian charity and inflamed self-love, one chief source of sin. As early as the ninth century Charlemagne had set the precedent by banning usury among Christians, claiming that lending exploited the hardship of persons who better deserved benevolence. The acquisitive impulse triggered in many people a deep revulsion, one regularly endorsed and fortified in sermons and proclamations—and yet, in markets restless men and women found energy, advantage, and excitement.[19]

By the thirteenth century scholastic thinkers, trying to analyze commerce theoretically, had encountered a fundamental contradiction in their economic ideology. Commercial exchanges commonly exploited the many while enriching a few; at the same time market transactions tended to flatten the verticality of their ideal "natural" order. Vendors charged the same price for any buyer. Albertus Magnus saw that in commerce it mattered not if seller or buyer was an "emperor, farmer, or priest," which made cash money a powerful leveler of men. In many jurisdictions sumptuary laws tried to counteract this tendency by fixing who was entitled to carry swords, display silver buckles, or embroider their cloaks with gold. More ominous was the possibility that men with cash might dominate the market and starve into submission the great mass of the population. To counteract these disorderly tendencies, Thomas Aquinas insisted that *indigentia*— need—should be established as the true measure of inherent values, at least for the staples of life. There must be a "just price" of things, he concluded, and it must be determined "according to how much men need them because of their usefulness." Otherwise supply and demand threatened to subvert good order and reward immoral or unethical behaviors with secular power and privilege. Scholastic price theory sought to reconcile the egalitarian ethics of Jesus's teaching with the sharply hierarchical social order of medieval Europe and England. The result was that state of ambiguous tension, still visible in Dudley's "Tree of Commonwealth," between the selfish prerogatives of wealth and power and obligations to the people preserved in law, custom, and Christian teaching.[20]

Taken together, at the start of the sixteenth century these elements yielded in England a patchy mosaic of manors and markets, governed by laws, customs, and traditions but also by market forces. Landed elites stood with one foot planted in manorial traditions and the other stepping experimentally on the new ground of agricultural improvement, economic rationalization, and personal advancement. The century of contraction just past had forced landlords to convert some arable land into pasture for want of tenants to farm it, while clothiers had moved to the country in search of under-employed hands. The wealthier yeomanry pulled at the traces of customary farming systems. Relatively secure in their tenures, freehold farmers found themselves drawn to potential rewards from innovation and commerce despite the risk that accompanied novel departures. The great majority of landless commoners, however, clung to traditional rights and expectations for want of any more tangible means of ensuring their survival. The Great Chain of Being with its reciprocal obligations and vertical stability—proclaimed by everyone to be the very natural order or things—embodied their entitlement. The lure of markets and commercial exchange fostered hope for advancement *up* the chain and so triggered ambitions that could generate wealth and support the advance of "new men." But mobility could run in both directions, and slipping *down* the hierarchy appealed to no class of people. Two codes of conduct vied for preeminence: one celebrated everywhere as timeless, legitimate, and supposedly natural, called for order, faithfulness, and obligation; the other, tinged with scandal, promised tangible rewards to men and women bold enough to risk censure and loss in the hope of realizing gain.

Challenges of the Times

The unacknowledged tensions in early modern English culture broke into the light during the second quarter of the sixteenth century as a result of serious pressures no one at the time could explain or fully understand. The first and most significant such pressure came from a surge in population. The postplague generations had taken advantage of abandoned farms and underused resources throughout the fifteenth century, but now the increasing number of mouths began to crowd the food supply. After a century of remarkable stability (long enough for three generations to know no other reality), English food prices rose dramatically, beginning in the 1520s and accelerating after mid-century. Incomes failed to keep pace, and little could be heard in the countryside except complaints about the price of "victuals," steeply rising rents, and the distress this was causing for the rural poor. Population pressure alone did not account for this inflation; possible other vectors included royal currency manipulations, New World silver, the steady rise of rural woolen manufacturing, and a structural shift of rural households away from self-provisioning toward greater reliance on market purchases. Whatever the technical causes, contemporaries never understood them; instead they saw bakers demanding more for bread and landlords squeezing tenants for higher rents and fees. Habitually "price takers," poor consumers assumed that their superiors enjoyed real freedom of action and they blamed hard times on willful, selfish, greedy behaviors that flouted the traditional social compact.[21]

If spiking prices were not distressing enough, the universal structure of Christendom exploded after 1517 with the schismatic movements of Luther and Calvin. On the Continent the Reformation sparked a decades-long series of confrontations, wars, and repressions. In England, Henry VIII seized the precedent suggested by Protestant rebels and abolished the link between the English church and the pope of Rome. Although the Henrician reformation served Henry's private marital convenience as much as issues of piety and conscience (he gained a divorce from Catherine of Aragon), it nevertheless shook one enormously important pillar of traditional order. The introduction of choice and human volition in spiritual matters damaged irreparably the confidence with which medieval common people had imagined their salvation. Violent confrontations, purges, heresy prosecutions, and the burning of martyrs proved incredibly disorienting, especially to illiterate persons who lacked the skills or inclination to parse out fine distinctions of doctrine and ecclesiology. Faithful Roman Catholics laid in wait, hoping to overturn the Anglican pretension; zealous Puritans clamored in the other direction, demanding far more thorough reforms in dogma, style, and praxis. Henry's death in 1547 set off succession struggles that restored briefly the Roman hegemony under the furious hand of Mary Tudor. Mary's restoration did not survive her death in 1558, but it did energize Puritan radicals who rallied their supporters behind John Foxe's "Book of Martyrs." Elizabeth I artfully constructed a truce of sorts on a platform combining moderately Protestant Anglican principles with less-than-zealous enforcement of religious conformity. Nevertheless, both public and private wars of religion simmered on and would explode again in the century to come. It is hard to overstate the impact of this turmoil on the first generations of people to be driven from the comfortable arms of a single, universal, and unquestioned religious establishment.[22]

One material consequence of Henry's reformation was the "dissolution of the monasteries"—the seizure by the crown of church lands, which constituted a fifth of the whole of England and as much as a third of the acreage in some locales. Large quantities of these new crown lands Henry bestowed on friends and political supporters; even more were sold to fill the coffers of an ever more expensive and belligerent government. The landed classes swelled with newly minted "gentlemen" while acquisitions and consolidations reshuffled the rank order of existing landholding families. Lawrence Stone estimates that between the accession of Henry VIII and the Puritan Revolution in 1641, somewhere between 5,000 and 15,000 families joined the ranks of the ruling class while some 2,000 advanced to the rank of squire, 800 became knights or baronets, and 100 families acquired peerages. Much of this was done by the early Stuarts after 1603, but dramatic changes first appeared during Henry's reformation. This much seems clear: the wholesale redistribution of land and titles flagrantly contradicted the pretense that power belonged to the gentry by some ancient God-given right. The surging real estate market helped launder money from commerce, industry, and patronage, making it possible for more and more men with "mean" or common roots to acquire estates (and a title to legitimate them) and pass into the landed class. Historian Wrightson cites this example: Nicholas Bacon, son of a Suffolk sheep-reeve, grew rich in London practicing law and serving the crown. Between 1540 and 1562 he spent £10,000 buying church property and died a knight and a landed gentleman.[23]

More often than not buyers in this booming land market intended "enclosure"—that is, taking out of production fields that once had been farmed in common by the whole village workforce. Enclosers set off their parcels with hedges, converted arable land to pasture, kept livestock and manure, dug ditches, and made other improvements to increase productivity. Such innovations displaced rural hands that depended on open-field farming for their living. The resulting profits accrued to enclosing farmers whose private fortunes visibly rose. Landlords—especially new owners not bound by old feudal tenures—demanded higher rents, shorter leases, and closer attention to market production. Successful (innovative) yeomen often found the capital and energy required to take advantage of these changes, but higher rents drove poor husbandmen and cottagers off the land and into a growing class of rural wage-seeking laborers. Additionally, since at least the 1470s overseas demand for English woolens had encouraged the raising of sheep and a corresponding increase in spinning and handloom weaving, all of which caused sixteenth-century households to grow less food and depend more on purchased victuals. Such dependency in turn fueled the price inflation that rose dramatically in the two middle decades of the sixteenth century. No doubt in the long run enclosure increased productivity and "modernized" English agriculture, but at the time it was *perceived* by many (rural laborers, common yeomen, and less ambitious gentry) to be abusive and unjust. Viewed from below, enclosure appeared as an attack on the welfare of the common people. As early as 1516 Sir Thomas More condemned the enclosure of arable for pasture with the chilling claim that mild-mannered sheep did "eat up" men, devouring down "whole fields, houses, and cities." At that time his *Utopia* was available only in Latin, but the sentiments were found in the vernacular.[24]

Precisely because the traditional vertical order assigned agency to proprietors and obedience to their dependents, common people (those without power) naturally assumed that what came to pass was orchestrated by the men with power, money, and the freedom to act. Investigators charged with exposing the causes of rural distress blamed the grasping selfishness of newly minted landlords who forgot their obligations. One such critic, John Hales, drafted legislation designed to outlaw most enclosures, but landlords in Parliament charged him instead with inciting disorder by giving voice to the angry peasants. After 1550 complaints and unrest surged as inflation spiked; necessities cost more than twice what they had fifty years back, and opportunities to earn declined throughout the rural economy. Rural people poached game and firewood and sometimes plowed up parks belonging to their leisured masters. Others simply took to the roads as wandering beggars, the dreaded vagrants known as "masterless men." "Dearth in the face of plenty": that was the riddle of the day, for it was recognized widely that food itself was not scarce but rather money with which to buy.[25]

Mid-century chaos forced the Tudor monarchs to raise a more active hand in the maintenance of social order and economic justice. Queen Mary took small steps to revalue the coinage, protect rural weavers from exploitation, and prevent the overseas export of grain. In 1562 Elizabeth established a licensure for corn badgers (speculators), and the next year she signed a sweeping Statute of Artificers designed to guarantee that "the hired person" would receive "both in the time of scarcity and in the time of plenty a convenient proportion of wages." Time and again authorities stated the ideal goal: "the quiet of the good and the correction of the bad, the stay of the rich and the relief of the poor, the advancement of public profit and the restraint of injurious and private gain." Year after year the goal proved elusive. Vagrancy, unemployment, and poverty persisted, and the entrepreneurial urges of innovating farmers, cloth merchants, and enclosing landlords did not abate no matter how ardently proscribed. Finally, with "An Act for the Relief of the Poor" (1598), the Elizabethan government acknowledged the right of the "worthy poor" to subsistence at public expense if all else failed. Local "Overseers of the Poor" were charged to procure stocks of "flax, hemp, wool, thread, iron and other necessary ware and stuff" on which to "set the poor to work." "Sturdy beggars" and other vagrants were excluded harshly from entitlements, unemployed persons found themselves practically incarcerated in their home parish, and the recipients of public relief were in no way coddled by their benefits. Refined in 1601, this novel Elizabethan system provided a bridge between earlier social obligations, propped up by tradition and the fear of God, and the heartless liberalism of the Victorian future. In the effort to do right by her subjects *and* harvest the benefits of modernization, Elizabeth shouldered, however imperfectly, the burden of dealing with the unanticipated consequences of life in a freer, competitive, market-oriented world.[26]

Into a Whirling Future

Elizabethan England struggled in the sixteenth century because it was caught in something not of its own devising and so much bigger than little England. The God-given order of the medieval worldview promised peace and widespread happiness, but wealth and power increasingly flowed from commerce, development, and overseas trade. Part of the problem, of course, could be traced to the long-standing failure of social, political, and economic realities to match the elegant ideals by which they were described and often judged. Over time transgressions by ruling elites, by enclosing landlords, by ambitious yeomen and entrepreneurs had shaken the imagined framework of stability until it seemed ready to collapse. By the end of the sixteenth century the strength of the English monarchy within the realm, and of the kingdom among rivals, depended on careful but steady advancement into modern ways of getting, spending, and governing. Innovation triggered energy and risk engendered reward, but both threatened to uproot the tree of commonwealth so lovingly described by Dudley in 1509. Back when Dudley wrote, Spain had just begun its conquest of Mexico and South America. Soon France started exploring American lands as well. The shock of discovery, the presence of mystery and potential, and (especially in Spain) the flow of New World riches back to Europe altered the architecture of expectations everywhere and energized markets as never before. In Spain, France, and later the Dutch Republic, state and empire grew up together, with national governments and colonial systems building on each other. Even if it was not on the minds of most Englishmen in the sixteenth century, the so-called discovery of the New World and its colonization by Europeans profoundly influenced all the turmoil they endured.[27]

The Tudor state building project itself contributed to social instability in sixteenth-century England while it set the stage for the rise of empire. The monarch's demands for loyalty, defense, and revenue stimulated profit seeking by rural landlords. In the 1530s Henry's reformation upset the universal religious culture and placed the kingdom at odds with Catholic Europe. The dissolution of the monasteries shook the whole hierarchy of property and place for a generation. After 1558 Elizabeth proudly charted an independent course and encouraged private adventures against Spanish treasure ships lumbering home, stuffed to the gunwales with American silver. The famous Elizabethan "Sea Dogs" (John Hawkins, Francis Drake, Walter Raleigh, and others) curried favor at court through their piracy, and their names stood at the head of colonial projects in both Ireland and the Americas. Raleigh, Humphrey Gilbert, and Ralph Lane all shared in the Irish campaigns of 1579–83 and showed up later in schemes to plant a colony on Roanoke Island off the North American coast. Martin Frobisher, Hawkins, and Drake conducted early reconnaissance of American shores. These extravagant English characters prowling the seas in Elizabeth's day apparently saw the Atlantic rim as one common arena of adventure and opportunity.[28]

Elizabeth famously kept her distance from colonial projectors such as Raleigh and Drake, encouraging them to "annoy the King of Spain," yet preserving her right to disavow any knowledge or involvement in their international exploits. Joint-stock companies proved to be convenient instruments for launching such adventures. Private investors secured a charter from the Crown permitting them to engage in exploration and trade with the subjects of foreign powers. Mary Tudor chartered the earliest examples: the Company of Merchant Adventurers (1553) and the Muscovy Company (1555). Such consortia of private investors stood behind nearly all the efforts of English explorers and gave a limited color of sanction to their activities. Elizabeth chartered the Levant Company (1582) for trade with Turkey and the East India Company (1600) that eventually would dominate the subcontinent of India. By such charters in the next century the early Stuarts would enable the first successful English colonies in the western Atlantic: Virginia (1607), Somers Island (1615), Plymouth (1620), Massachusetts Bay (1629), and Providence Island (1630). In striking contrast to Spain's formal colonial administrative structures, the English process of colonization would display significant variations and an element of chaos for the better part of a century.[29]

What connected the rise of state and empire with the erosion of stability in rural England was the impulse to seize for profit and power new opportunities not rooted in ancient traditions or the theoretical ideals of the Great Chain of Being. The emerging central state necessarily abridged the freedom of local notables and gradually transformed "their people" more directly into subjects of the king. Successful innovations pursued at Court could not help but encourage a taste for the same among the lesser lords and gentry who otherwise were caught between old-fashioned obligations, diminishing authority, and changing economic realities. Novel sources of wealth and power both sustained the emerging state and encouraged the spread of market interactions that further destabilized life among the lower orders. No amount of preaching, proclaiming, and threatening sanctions in the name of ancient rights could stay the force of these encroachments as long as leading actors at the center of the story—monarchs, ministers, and wealthy farmers and merchants—pursued their own advantages. As a result, England came to the threshold of colonization torn by the appeal of its long traditions and the logic of new competitive realities in rural villages, in regional market towns, in London, at Whitehall, and around an Atlantic lake already crowded with travelers and settlers, merchants and pirates, warriors, explorers, and refugees. Many Englishmen still craved stability, but there was a "new" and wider world out there filled with promise and possibilities. The ideal of stability in Old Europe had been upset forever.[30]

CHAPTER 2

Abundance

IN 1516, LONG BEFORE any Englishman had seen America, Thomas
More had named it "Utopia." Imagining the newfound land, More conjured up a witness to a place of infinite abundance, where greed was banished along with private property and pride—the tragic flaws that
corrupted the world as he knew it. Some twenty years before, sailing under
a Spanish flag, Christopher Columbus had "discovered" a New World to
the west—an actual physical place not expected or accounted for by Christian thinkers. That discovery shook the foundations of European culture. It
challenged the limits of Christian cosmology and sent scholars scrambling
through scripture to explain the apparent anomalies. Its inhabitants, clearly
human, could not be paired with known "facts" about the origins of human
beings, nor did its flora and fauna correspond to the universe of things
already neatly tucked into the Great Chain of Being. Finally, its very presence outside the known world introduced the prospect of abundance into
a cultural framework designed to administer scarcity according to timeless
traditions. The windfall profits that colonization first showered on Spain
fueled a scramble for empires that soon drove France, Holland, and
England to explore American lands. The very existence of new resources
whetted acquisitive appetites and encouraged risky new adventures.[1]

During most of the sixteenth century Spanish exploration and plunder
focused on Central and South America and the Caribbean Islands. North
America remained largely a mystery until French and English explorers
began in earnest to search for a northern passage to China. A joint-stock
enterprise, The Company of Merchant Adventurers to New Lands (1553),
led the way for English-speaking explorers—first Hugh Willoughby, then

John Hawkins, Francis Drake, Martin Frobisher, and others well known in both the Elizabethan Court and the public houses of London. Out of their reports enthusiasts and promoters (two of them named Richard Hakluyt) pieced together briefs for colonizing northern regions of the Americas. Some of these colonial "projectors" cherished the hope of finding gold and silver riches, exotic raw materials, and tractable Indians to provide extractive labor. Others recognized the promise of abundance in more prosaic resources such as timber, fish, furs, dyestuffs, and agricultural products.[2]

As they struggled to understand the places they discovered, Englishmen quickly took up the language of Eden or New Canaan to describe lands flowing with *potential* milk and honey. Writing of Florida, for example, as early as 1564, John Hawkins claimed "the commodities of this land are more than are yet known to any man . . . it flourisheth with meadow, pasture ground, with woods of Cedar and Cypress, and other sorts, as better can not be in the world." Philip Amadas and Arthur Barlow reported to Walter Raleigh in 1584 that the soil of Virginia was the "most plentiful, sweet, fruitful and wholesome of all the world." Thomas Hariot listed among Virginia's "Merchantable commodities" grass silk, worm silk, flax, hemp, alum, pitch, tar, rosin, turpentine, sassafras, cedar, wine, oil, furs, skins, civet cats, iron, copper, pearl, sweet gum, and dyestuffs. So generous was the land (he claimed) that a man could in twenty-four hours plant corn (maize) enough to sustain him for the year—on a plot no more than twenty-five yards square! The air was "so temperate and wholesome" and the soil "so fertile and yielding such commodities," that Hariot could not imagine how planters, properly supplied the first year, could fail to prosper. Repeated tirelessly in London by the younger Richard Hakluyt and other New World projectors, such reports became dogma and put stars in the eyes of those who would venture to Virginia—or hazard their fortunes on behalf of surrogates. American soil appeared so "propitious to the nature and use of man" that no place was "more convenient" for his "pleasure, profit, and . . . sustenance." In a word, to Englishmen raised in a world of limited, hard-used resources, America represented abundance.[3]

Virginia

Real experience with colonization produced contrapuntal narratives soon enough. By 1590 Sir Walter Raleigh's fledgling settlement at Roanoke had disappeared mysteriously. Next, early reports from Jamestown (1607) described an unimaginable disaster: according to George Percy, never were "Englishmen left in a foreign Country in such misery as we were in this new discovered Virginia." In 1608, as the death toll rose alarmingly, John Smith blamed an obsession with "private trade" that prevented settlers from serving the common welfare. From the company store axes, chisels, and hoes apparently disappeared, traded to the "Salvages" for furs, food, and sexual favors. Each arriving ship brought more useless persons—"poor Gentlemen, Tradesmen, Serving-men, libertines, and such like, ten times more fit to spoil a Common-wealth, than . . . help to maintain one." Fantastic visions of gold mines, orange groves, and easy riches persisted in Virginia for years against the more sober realization that only permanent occupancy and development would make Virginia valuable. In an oft-quoted summary (later picked up by Smith, a relentless plagiarist), William Simmonds first gave voice to the disappointment:

It was the Spaniards good hap to happen in those parts where were infinite numbers of people, who had manured the ground with that providence that it afforded victual at all times; and time had brought them to that perfection [that] they had the use of gold and silver, and [of] the most of such commodities as their countries afforded. . . . But we chanced on a land, even as God made it. Where we found only an idle, improvident, scattered people, ignorant of the knowledge of gold, or silver, or any commodities; . . . nothing to encourage us but what accidentally we found nature afforded.[4]

Nearby Indian communities did succor the desperate English, but the newcomers bungled early commercial interactions. Christopher Newport, trying to impress (said Smith) the "idle, improvident" Natives, let them "truckle and trade at their pleasure," until they demanded more for their corn than it was worth set down in Spain! Trading swords for turkeys, Newport supposedly left the Indians "so insolent there was no rule." John Smith preferred a regimen of whipping, beating, and intimidation topped with the occasional execution to demonstrate superiority. His approach did not work much better, and soon Smith found himself exchanging tools and weapons for food with Indians farther up the Chesapeake shoreline. In the short run Jamestown survived, but the resulting arms race, in which Euro-American agents tried to exploit intertribal rivalries, set up a power dynamic that would poison cross-cultural relations for two centuries to come.[5]

John Smith's confidence rested on his faith in a cosmic destiny. As early as 1608 Powhatan, the political head of the local Natives, accused the English of coming to "invade" and "possess" his country. The charge essentially was true, but Smith denied it in part because he could not imagine that Virginia "belonged" in any meaningful sense to the Indians: "God did make the world to be inhabited with mankind, and to have his name known to all Nations, and from generation to generation: as the people increased they dispersed themselves into such Countries as they found most convenient. And here in *Florida, Virginia, New-England,* and *Canada,* is more land than all the people of Christendom can manure, and yet more to spare than all the natives of those Countries can use and culturate [*sic*]." If this logic did not satisfy men of "tender consciences," Smith added that the Indians were suckers: "for a copper kettle and a few toys, as beads and hatchets, they will sell you a whole Country." Whoever planted a colony in America, so far from "wronging any" persons, should be remembered and honored "with praise."[6]

John Smith labored the rest of his life to vindicate the bountiful prospects of greater Virginia. In 1623 he told the king's commissioners to blame what "we called the starving time" entirely on human error "and not the barrenness and defect of the Country." In the Chesapeake, a servant could, in four or five years, live as well "as his master" in England, and for Smith this fact would drive the project's success. Were it not so, any man would be "double mad" to leave England for America. No, the land had not starved the English; colonists had done it to themselves. Fill the colony with sensible men, give them "as much freedom in reason as may be," and Virginia will thrive.[7]

This apparent endorsement of freedom, advancement, and the profit motive invites us to credit Smith as a harbinger of modernization. He was not. He framed colonization not as plunder but a great commission, like the work of Adam and Eve, "to plant the earth to remain to posterity, but not without labour, trouble, and industry." In the wake of the Flood, Noah and the patriarchs effected a "second Plantation," and now it fell to Smith's own generation to plant the "unplanted" parts of God's world and redeem the "poor Salvages." He found models not in Roman or Spanish imperialism but in Abraham, Jesus, and the Apostles: "Riches were their Servants, not their Masters." They ruled "their people as Children, not as Slaves."

America made it possible to right the wrongs and relieve the strains that burdened old Europe. Smith's hopes in part would be accomplished: in time America would become something like a "best poor man's country." But Virginia would not long be restrained by the higher purposes Smith desired.[8]

Jamestown survived the starving times, the subsequent tobacco boom, a devastating Indian uprising, and a royal takeover, before things stabilized in the third decade of the colony's existence. In the late 1610s, while still governed by directors in London, the company began granting land in fee simple, giving headrights to planters, and allowing tobacco-mad settlers to spread all over the Chesapeake. Policy made it possible, tobacco made it worthwhile. A man with land and laborers could realize a fortune in just a few years if he concentrated on tobacco. Almost immediately a shortage of labor became the central concern of the planter class, who quickly assumed local political control. Self-made Virginia grandees devised a system of indentured servitude that soon grew oppressive while it "graduated" every year a new class of would-be planters who then dumped more tobacco on saturated markets. After 1630 prices fell sharply. By the middle decades of the 1600s Virginia boasted a volatile but thriving society with large planters claiming authority over a restive class of small landholding tobacco farmers (hungry for advancement), and a larger class of bound servants and landless laborers (ambitious for the privileges of freemen). Natural abundance had been bent to the needs of the colonizers, but it had been a surprising struggle. During the next century, Virginia's planter elite embarked on a fateful project that finally secured stability and wealth by substituting African slaves for free or term-bound laborers. Thus was Smith's vision perverted, and Virginia became not a yeoman's paradise but a slave-based oligarchy resembling after all the imperialism of Rome and Spain more than the benevolent reign of Jesus.[9]

Plymouth

Much of the northwestern Atlantic rim had been known to Europeans longer than the Chesapeake and points south. The Vikings of legend had settled Greenland once, and since the 1400s fishermen—mostly Norman, Breton, and Basque—had been tapping the cod stocks off Newfoundland. As early as 1497 John Cabot, sailing for England's Henry VII, reported that

Newfoundland, while barren, was full of "white bears," giant stags, and "plenty of fish." Dreams of English profits on the cod banks, coupled with the continued search for a northwest passage to China, fed the interest of British schemers. In 1614 Virginia's John Smith reported (with a characteristic disregard for reality) that a person was "worthy . . . to starve" who could not flourish in such bountiful environs. National honor plus the "assurance of wealth" awaited his countrymen on the American shore, where even a "very bad Fisher" with a hook and line could pull in "one, two, or three hundred Cods" a day. Accordingly, when a clutch of Calvinist Separatists approached the Merchant Adventurers for help in relocating from Leiden to New England, the London investors struck a deal.[10]

Less influenced by Smith's frothy literary visions, the Reverend William Bradford on board the *Mayflower* first gazed at the shores of Cape Cod with a heavy heart. It was November 1620. His wife had just thrown herself into the sea rather than face the trials of the coming winter, and none of the Leiden Separatists was well prepared for what came next. Never really party to the grand designs of Hakluyt, Raleigh, or Smith, Bradford's Pilgrims were bound on an altogether different mission. Now, having passed "the vast ocean, and a sea of troubles," Bradford set down his first impressions of a place where the Pilgrims had "no friends to welcome them nor inns to . . . refresh their weatherbeaten bodies; no houses or much less town to repair to, to seek for succor." The Natives stood ready to "fill their sides with arrows," while the winter weather threatened life and inhibited travel with "cruel and fierce storms." All he could see was "a hideous and desolate wilderness, full of wild beasts and wild men."[11]

Not surprisingly, given the worldview of these zealous Calvinists, every turn of events was recorded by them as resulting from God's intervention. As they cautiously explored the sandy shores Bradford's men found caches of corn, which they took for their own use. This they understood as borrowing not stealing, because they searched under God's direction and the owners of the grain could not be found. Without this bounty the Pilgrims "might have starved." They came across towns and fields, apparently once the homes of "thousands" but now eerily abandoned. At one such site—a fine high place (Patuxet), well-watered by a "sweet brook," and surrounded by "much corn-ground cleared"—the Pilgrims chose to build their town. When finally they learned that an "extraordinary plague" had carried off the Natives "four years ago," they embraced the Indians' misfortune as a gift to themselves from a gracious Providence.[12]

In fact the Pilgrims were on two missions simultaneously: one to hive off and live, by the grace of God, according to his holy ordinances; the other to scrounge up a surplus with which to repay the Merchant Adventurers who had bankrolled their arrival. From the beginning tensions built between sacred and profane opportunities. In 1621 Robert Cushman explained, in a sermon to the Plymouth community, that New England was no place to seek "great riches, ease, pleasures, dainties, and jollity in this world." What they needed instead were people who would work hard now "for the benefit of them that shall come after." Cushman spoke on behalf of the colony's creditors, and he adopted the cautionary tone precisely because New England *was* a place to seek riches, ease, and pleasure. The current Pilgrims, Cushman warned, would be sorely tempted to forget their debts—as the settlers in Virginia clearly had done—and go chasing after vain profits, "hoping for office, place, dignity, or fleshly liberty." Now was no time for self-love and "particularizing"—that wicked concern for personal aggrandizement first taught to man by the serpent in the Garden. God required that they cleave fast to one another, "laboring to make each other's burden lighter."[13]

"Particularizing" is a terrific word no longer used to identify that selfish impulse that seemed to threaten the better motives of English colonizers in America. In Virginia John Smith had blamed it on the bad character of pampered elites. The Calvinists at Plymouth traced the cause to "original sin," a central stirring of desire and disobedience that according to St. Paul dwelled in the heart of all people. And if the wilderness itself was not inherently corrupt (no verdict yet on this), it offered up fertile ground for seeds of self-love that could overwhelm any godly mission. In addition to the "Salvages," English agents of corruption surrounded Bradford's fragile community: the blasphemous Thomas Morton of Merry Mount and Thomas Weston's non-Pilgrim settlers at Weymouth, who lived and dreamed more like the early Virginians. Impressed by the "lusty trees" overburdened with fruit, Morton focused squarely on pleasure and indulgence, luring people into "quaffing and drinking," "dancing and frisking" with Indian women "like so many fairies, or furies" (or so reported Bradford). He corrupted the Natives by selling them firearms and setting them "to hunt and fowl for him." In Bradford's mind the quick returns from either the fur trade or commercial fishing only tempted men away from the serious long-run task of developing a pious farming community.[14]

Fair dealing with the native Wampanoag people appears to have played a crucial part in the Pilgrims' understanding of their right to take and develop the Indians' land. Their salvific goal of preserving servants of the Gospel gave them every moral right to take what was required, but plundering for profit they condemned. The assertion of "emptiness" that later erased the claims of all native peoples, at first was deployed with surprising precision. The site of Plymouth, for example, had no one "living *near by eight or ten miles*"—hardly a vast and empty continent. Writing for an English audience this time, Robert Cushman pointed (as would John Winthrop a decade later) to the Indians' lack of industry, art, science, skill, or inclination to use their land and commodities appropriately; but even this did not authorize expropriation. To shore up their justification, the Pilgrims referenced their good relations with the native people and the consent of their "imperial governor," Massasoit, who invited the desperate little band to make good use of abandoned villages.[15]

Eventually the Plymouth colony stabilized. In 1625 Bradford reported that the Lord had given his Plantation "peace and health and contented minds" and so blessed "their labors as they had corn sufficient, and some to spare to others." The surplus they quickly traded up the Kennebec River for seven hundred pounds of beaver furs, making a dent at last in what they owed their creditors.[16] If Massasoit really had invited them to take as much land as they wanted (as Cushman claimed), he clearly never imagined the magnitude of the invasion that was coming. Neither did the Pilgrims experience the future for which they prayed so desperately. Their "vendible" stocks increased, but community cohesion disintegrated: "there was no longer any holding them together."[17] Once again it seemed that abundance and scarcity came yoked together, the one whetting appetites while the other forced colonists to scramble for solutions outside their original vision.

What were the proximate causes of the gathering troubles? Bradford identified three. First, original sin was at work: "wherever the Lord sows good seed, envious man will sow tares." Second, labor in New England was so scarce that many "untoward servants" were brought over, who, when their indentures expired, stayed on and reproduced. Third, English agents took up emigration as a business and "cared not who the persons were" as long as "they had money to pay." By this means the country "became pestered" with "unworthy persons" who "crept into one place or another." The perennial scarcity of labor coupled with relentless demands for profits from investors back in England undermined community spirit, while the urgent need for farms and food encouraged dispersal and enlarged the settlers' demands on the Wampanoags' homeland. At Plymouth, an unholy mix of markets and abundant resources nursed a "particularizing" impulse that weakened cultural restraints and rewarded more exploitative behavior toward the Indians, each other, and the environment itself.[18]

Massachusetts Bay

Founded in 1630, the colony at Massachusetts Bay, as every textbook relates, unfolded as a roaring success compared to Jamestown or even Plymouth. Two closely related advantages smoothed the way for the Boston-area settlements. First, hundreds of substantial families in England stood ready to hurl themselves and their fortunes into the colonizing enterprise. Second, these self-financing missionaries faced less urgent demands to return a profit at the expense of settling in. Furthermore, ten years of prior effort by the settlers north and south of Boston already had established a local agricultural surplus (albeit small) and a network of trading connections that served the newcomers right from the start. The Puritans credited little of this and assumed their blessings flowed directly from God's marvelous interventions. Do justly, love mercy, and walk humbly with our God, John Winthrop told his followers before they disembarked. Eyes fixed on their "Commission," hands pledged to the "work" of their "community," these colonists would be "as a City upon a Hill, the eyes of all people" upon them. If they dealt falsely with their God he would withdraw "his present help," and they would fail.[19]

Like the Pilgrims before them, leaders of the Bay Colony felt compelled to explain their taking of "heathen" land, and the language of their justifications offers more clues to their thoughts about the earth and the natural environment. The "Lord's Garden," argued Winthrop, was given to the "sons of men" on the condition that they properly subdue it. Bluntly repeated to Noah after the flood, this bequest created a "moral & natural" right in man to enjoy "the fruits of the earth" that "god might have his due glory from the creature." Land that never was "replenished or subdued" was free to men who would "possess and improve it." Why should Englishmen, faced with shortages at home, "suffer a whole Continent, as fruitful & convenient" as America "to lie waste without any improvement"? As long as they left the Indians "sufficient for their use," the English might "lawfully take the rest." The theory implied a first right of refusal for the Natives, but, as luck would have it, God's hand smote the Indians so that few remained alive: "If we had no right to this land, yet our God hath right to it, and if he be pleased to give it us (taking it from a people who had so long usurped upon him, and abused his Creatures) who shall control him or his terms?"[20]

Comfortably assured of his right to inhabit the place, Winthrop proceeded to outline a process by which he hoped to erect in New England sacred versions of the English rural village: communal, hierarchical, practical, patriarchal, paternalistic, exclusionary, and wrapped in the sweet communion of religious love.[21] In a 1635 essay on the "Ordering of Towns," he tried to blend dynamic New World potential with a stable hierarchical result that somehow tapped into private ambition and abundance before screeching to a halt in a fully developed community. Start with a parcel of land six miles square, put the meeting house right in the center, and assign lots close in until such time as growth and improvement required further distributions. Winthrop tried to harness the energy of market forces in behalf of the traditional commonwealth outcomes of order, stability, and plenty. A little competition was a good thing. Take a large farm, for example, lease one-fourth each to different farmers, and one of the four shall "in the ordinary ways of Gods providence produce more benefit to the Common wealth" than if the whole had been cultivated by servants in common fields. The industrious farmer, Winthrop argued, would make the "best employment of his known proportion" while others would follow, "drawn on by his good example." Common lands should be held temporarily in trust by the "richer men" of the town; but the private enclosure of freehold estates did not alarm the governor.[22]

Winthrop recognized self-interest as an engine of "speedy Improvement," and improvement was "one of the principal clauses of that grand Charter" given to Adam: "Replenish the earth and subdue it." At the same time his endgame was not a modern, permanent state of entrepreneurial competition but rather a balanced, hierarchical, steady-state system that would achieve mature equilibrium and then replicate itself by an orderly process rather like cell division. Apparently because of the open frontier, enclosure in America was not expected to trigger the symptoms of scarcity, greed, and exploitation so much complained about in England. Instead, drawn by the promise of gain, ambitious husbandmen would transform the wilderness and then retire in peaceful communion for generations to come. In reality, such encouragement of "industry" and enterprise inflamed the acquisitive impulse, scattered the population, accelerated encroachment on Indian lands, and placed mounting demands on the resource base. The benevolent framework of the Puritan covenant could not check the corrosive effects of self-interest ("self-love") in the New England countryside.[23]

An early example can be seen in the siting of Boston itself on the Shawmut peninsula. Blessed with safe harbors and surrounded by wooded islands and salt marshes for grazing, fodder, and fuel, the peninsula boasted little arable land and no room for seating new families as they arrived. They could move, but unlike Bradford's congregation at Plymouth, Winthrop's Puritans in 1630 found Englishmen already living around the bay. After months of debate and negotiation no single place suited the various groups and by the end of the year seven separate towns (including Boston) had been established. The Puritans' "city on a hill" now occupied many hills, divided by tidal rivers and saltwater inlets that made communication on land especially awkward. The General Court meeting at Boston aspired to govern the whole community, and it kept control of the company's land; but the distribution of land to the towns and the dispersal of settlers into diverse communities soon gave rise to calls for local autonomy to satisfy particular demands.[24]

Particular demands multiplied quickly. For example, grants of rocky farmland, no matter how generous, sometimes forced petitioners back to the court to beg for more arable parcels. Such questions were handled best by selectmen in the towns who knew the territory and the virtue of the claims. Towns that faced the sea often found their inland development cramped by claims of adjoining towns, forcing individual settlers— including the sons and daughters of the founders—to seek promising situations outside their town of origin. As free land grew scarce some towns tried granting smaller allotments to tradesmen and fishermen who did little farming, but this further penalized the interests of their offspring. Ambitious town leaders—selectmen chosen for their wealth, piety, and virtue— allotted to themselves large grants and choice parcels and sometimes conspired to sponsor townsite promotions, which made them rich while encouraging even more geographical diffusion. Shortages of firewood plagued nearly every community within a few years: wrote Winthrop in 1638, "We at Boston were almost ready to break up for want of wood." Several towns outlawed the sale to outside buyers of firewood, lumber, or ship's timbers cut from the common town lands. In the midst of extravagant abundance, local resource depletion sparked conflicts reminiscent of old England.[25]

The scarcity of labor in the 1630s created severe upward pressure on wages, giving skilled workers a novel advantage and causing employers (men of property) to wonder who controlled negotiations with their "servants." Similar market pressures hit scarce imported commodities—especially housewares, hardware, and consumer goods not produced locally. Authorities responded with price controls and blistering sermons against taking advantage in trade, but no regime of market regulation seems to have endured or produced the desired effect. Market forces threatened to make wealthy gentlemen out of crooks, gamblers, and common tradesmen—just as they had done in Virginia. The imposition of restrictions even by "visible saints" seemed to discredit authority itself, while abundance fostered a thirst for self-interest and independence—"particularizing" Robert Cushman called it—that undermined stability and good order. Real flesh-and-blood Puritans found their vision of sweet communion challenged by the need to deflect vulgar competition—or the temptation to indulge in it.[26]

Massachusetts Bay caught the rising slope of English colonizers' learning curve, and a remarkable convergence of spiritual self-righteousness and material prosperity stamped the project with a cosmic seal of approval. As the Great Migration ended and the first generation of American-born Englishmen came of age, Edward Johnson gathered all the stories of the Massachusetts "genesis" into his *Wonder-Working Providence of Sion's Saviour in New England* (1654), concluding that the Lord was "pleased . . . to complete this Commonwealth abundantly beyond all expectations" by turning "every thing in the country" into a "staple-commodity, wheat, rye, oats, peas, barley, beef, pork, fish, butter, cheese, timber, mast, tar, soap, plankboard, frames of houses, clapboard, and pipestaves, iron and lead." And so the wilderness did "turn a mart," for the Lord "had been pleased to turn one of the most hideous, boundless, and unknown Wildernesses in the world in an instant, as 'twere (in comparison of other work) to a well-ordered Commonwealth, and all to serve his Churches."[27]

The profligate abundance of the New World environment was both the promise *and* the problem for early seventeenth-century Englishmen in North America. Such easy abundance tempted people to wallow in leisure or founder in licentious consumption. Bradford, Winthrop, and Johnson all paused to reflect upon the hazards of a world where "nature and liberty" afforded too generous a living.[28] And the evidence stood right before their eyes, both in the free-for-all at Jamestown and at scandalous Merry Mount, where Thomas Morton made no effort to hide his hedonistic delight:

> Which made the Land to me seem paradise:
> for in mine eye 'twas Nature's Masterpiece;
> Her chiefest Magazine of all where lives her store;
> If this Land be not rich, then is the whole world poor.[29]

Thus did the "Lord of Misrule" articulate the problem (and no doubt nail it fast upon his maypole). Watching farmers "over eager" for wealth move beyond the reach of the meeting house, Johnson fretted that "plenty and liberty" would mar their prosperity. More fateful yet was the impact of the "Merchants and traders" who, bedazzled by the promise of "a large profit," would "willingly have had the Commonwealth tolerate divers [sic] kinds of sinful opinions" and "incite men to come and sit down with us, that their purses might be filled with coin." Thomas Shepard, pastor of First Church, Cambridge, warned his flock against the allure of material prosperity—their "fleshly ends and lusts" he called it. Nothing else so threatened the good order of towns and commonwealths, and the danger was greatest in "places of liberty" such as Massachusetts Bay.[30]

Two Contrasting Islands

These three familiar stories have stood for generations at the center of the dominant narrative sustaining popular United States history. Recent histor-ies of American colonization emphasize the broader sweep of European settlements ranging from Newfoundland through the Caribbean and South America. My focus on English dreams and frustrations is not intended to privilege the small slice of the colonial experience that became the United States but rather to explore where appropriate the larger context in which British colonialism took place. The Atlantic in the seventeenth century teemed with colonists and traders from Portugal, Spain, France, Ireland, Denmark, Sweden, German principalities, and the Netherlands. Colonists in Virginia and Massachusetts understood this better than readers do today, and to sketch in that background we need to consider briefly this bigger picture. In nearly every case, for the first fifty years Native American actors played an important role in the progress of all these European colonies, until treachery and growth triggered violent confrontations that proved devastating to the Indians. Similarly, Africans made steadily increasing contributions to settler fortunes, whether as trading partners or commodified unfree laborers. No doubt guided by the ethnic chauvinism of the time, most European colonizers perceived their world through narrow cultural lenses, filtering out the influence of "others" on the achievements of their countrymen. Easily lost to memory is the complex polyglot nature of colonial networks binding Africa, South America, the Caribbean islands, North America, and the North Atlantic rim. Two contrasting British islands help locate the mainland stories within the larger context that was known to colonial peoples throughout the western Atlantic. At the same time, these Caribbean stories introduce the worst features of the incipient culture of exploitation.

At precisely the same time John Winthrop was trying to shape the settlement at Boston, a second company of Puritan colonizers set foot on Providence Island. Organized in London in 1629 by aristocratic Puritan adventurers (including John Pym and other future leaders in the revolutionary Long Parliament), the Providence Island project combined in equal measure the religious idealism of Massachusetts Bay with the geopolitical ambitions of earlier Elizabethan colonizers who sought to build up England (and pull down Spain) by exploiting the American tropics. Located deep in the Spanish Caribbean—a thousand miles west of Barbados and just a hundred miles from the Central American isthmus—their new colony stood as a clear insult to Spanish hegemony and a kind of test of the Puritan God, whether He would protect and preserve "His people" so near the mouth of the Catholic "beast."

Like the corporate sponsors of Jamestown, the Providence Island investors first projected a community of servants working company land on shares, pursuing company-defined objectives, and taking direction from the investors back home. Unlike Virginia or Massachusetts Bay, these directors discouraged the dispersal of economic free agents. They demanded compact settlement, even if this prevented first-comers from scattering to capture choice parcels. They stocked the magazine with provisions and arms as well as seeds and slips for well-known tropical plants with instructions on how to grow them. They insisted that attention be paid to food crops, livestock, and essential infrastructure. They tried (with little success) to forbid the raising of tobacco. Claiming to prize "honor more than profit," the directors ordered Governor Phillip Bell to report individuals found planting "that Scurvy weed" to the neglect of better staples such as vineyards, olives, sugarcane, citrus, and dyestuffs.[31]

By the middle of the first full year in residence, Providence Island settlers were praising the land for its "excessive fertility" and extravagant natural abundance; they seemed to have escaped the "starving time" drama that plagued most other English projects. If the land itself seemed promising however, discontent mounted among the settlers over the work of their corporate lords. The magazine charged too much, they complained, for provisions of poor quality. The obligation to pay half their produce back to the company store (per their original contracts) now struck them as horribly unjust. Dangling like a bait in the mouth of the Spanish empire, settlers feared military invasion. The questions about land tenure festered as settlers worried they would not secure title to acres painstakingly cleared by their own hands. Authoritarian controls rested heavily and English tenants demanded relief from obligations to labor on common fortifications and public works. Where both John Smith and John Winthrop wound up embracing (perhaps reluctantly) the wider distribution of property and political power, the directors of Providence Island held fast to the original corporate model. Discounting the settlers' rebellious temper, the company principals reaffirmed their own prerogative and directed the governor to set aside twenty parcels of the "most commodious and Fertile places of the Island" for their private use should they decide to emigrate or send over their kin.[32]

The Providence Island leaders seem not to have worked out how their initial vision would grow and mature. Indentured servants, on whom all planters depended for labor, expected land and servants of their own once their contracts expired. Such a proliferation of small farmers quickly ran through the finite land of an island settlement while exacerbating the chronic scarcity of labor. African slavery (introduced in 1633) offered an obvious alternative, but the presence of an alien enslaved population undermined hopes for creating a godly English Protestant commonwealth. Both established planters and newly minted freemen turned to slavery as a labor solution they could control with money (not requiring favor with the directors). Through this back door, market forces further challenged the designs of the governing elites. Everything on Providence Island seems to have happened in a foreshortened frame: the descent into slavery that unfolded over several decades on the Chesapeake mainland here could be seen in a quick-time preview of less than five years.[33]

Focused on how to bring a tropical colony into production to the benefit of themselves and their home markets, the promoters of Providence Island rebuffed the complaints of settlers who found their security and agency *reduced* rather than enlarged in their New World situation. Ironically, for Providence Island planters, the surest way to escape service to masters of the company was to acquire servile labor and exploit the proceeds to secure their own liberty and independence. Consequently, instead of scattering family farms across the countryside, as in Massachusetts, these Puritans erected a slave-based plantation society. Far from disappointed by the divergence, in 1640 John Pym challenged Massachusetts Puritans to abandon their comfort and help claim for Protestant England the fabled riches of the Spanish Caribbean. While seizing power at home in the Long Parliament, the Providence Island directors entertained dreams of finally dislodging popery from the treasury of the New World—that is until May 1641, when a Spanish force invaded Providence Island, driving off some 350 English residents and confiscating their 381 African slaves.[34]

As this *Puritan* dream of tropical riches exploded, a more successful combination of sugar and slaves was just giving rise to a new model of wealth and exploitation on the opposite edge of the Caribbean Sea. The island of Barbados in the 1620s presented itself to colonizers as a lush tropical paradise, dangerously fecund but lacking any human population to turn its riches into commodities. Island flora bore fruit, not in seasons like respectable English plants, but promiscuously all year long because of the steady equatorial climate. In 1625 an English voyager, Captain John Powell, touched at Barbados, found it literally begging for cultivation, and returned home to organize a company of eighty colonists willing to risk all for the promise of extraordinary gain. In February 1627, they arrived and put their shoulders to the wheel. King Charles I later gave a patent for Barbados to the Earl of Carlisle (and another by mistake to the Earl of Pembroke), which at a stroke turned Powell's settlers into squatters and set the island on a course of proprietary management by rent-seeking absentee owners.[35]

For a full decade the planters on Barbados tried to make their fortunes growing tobacco and other standard tropical commodities. John Winthrop's son Henry, one of the first settlers, expected tobacco to bring him wealth and power despite his father's warnings that no man should expect to grow rich who did not invest substantial capital of his own. The son's hopes were dashed because Barbadian tobacco proved "foul" compared to Virginia's weed. The relentless scarcity of servants threatened all, and planters on Barbados showed no scruple in employing black slaves except that the price of African hands remained comparatively high. Then in 1638 Archibald Hay planted the first canes, and over the next fifteen years Barbados was transformed completely by the sugar culture. Within five years Thomas Robinson declared Barbados "the most flourishing island in those American parts, and I verily believe in all the world for the producing of sugar." Land values soared as did the number of African laborers. Common white servants who survived their indentures found themselves priced out of the market for plantation lands. By 1652 great planters had consolidated most of the island's acreage into some 2,000 huge estates fitted out with a full complement of expensive sugar-making equipment and staffed by 20,000 enslaved black Africans.[36]

Richard Ligon published our best contemporary account of early Barbados based on his own observations starting in 1647. Like most Englishmen in the tropics, Ligon found the heat and humidity oppressive—and dangerous for those who drank strong spirits. Iron tools rusted as fast as one could brighten them, and food spoiled almost before it could be eaten. The strangeness of the environment sometimes proved costly, as when one planter turned his cattle out to graze a new pasture only to find all fifty of them dead the next morning. Nevertheless, sugar profits dazzled all. Sugar (Ligon claimed) kept men from improving their houses to catch the breeze or harvesting abundant fish to improve their wretched diet. He reckoned that £14,000 was required to outfit a sugar plantation, and he captured in fine detail the entire system of equipment required to produce a marketable product. The high price of admission suggested to Ligon that men with such a fortune in hand might better stay in England and enjoy their leisure. Still they came, accepting great risk in pursuit of even greater gain. Rampant materialism so characterized Barbados after 1650 that visitors repeatedly noticed the presence of "tricks" and "cheats," of "ten thousand knaves" for every "honest man," of an "acquisitiveness" among the people that knew "no moral boundary."[37]

Seen as the "jewel" of the first British empire, Barbados rose to fame through a system of exploitation that delivered extravagant returns to a small planter class who in turn locked everyone else in a state of dependency or chattel slavery. Here abundance, engrossed and controlled by acquisitive *resident* elites, delivered the wealth that eluded absentee Puritan directors on Providence Island. But success came at dramatic cost to the social order. Barbados rewarded the least attractive aspects of early modern English restlessness and produced the most rapacious and unfree extractive society found in the British Atlantic. If the Massachusetts settlements seemed driven toward liberal, competitive, decentralized, and democratic ways, Barbados stood for the opposite extreme. Yet both were sides of the same coin in the emerging culture of exploitation.

Loosening Constraints

Through the lens of culture provided by their Old World experience, British colonizers in the western Atlantic saw before them an unprecedented blend of opportunity and risk. At first they were astonished at the richness of a place that, compared with the hard-used English countryside, seemed barely touched by the resident populations.[38] New World abundance stood poised to reward ambitious settlers with proprietary independence—with a competence, as it was known. At the same time, English colonizers experienced crippling instances of scarcity and "starving times," especially at the start of a new plantation. Plentiful land without adequate labor, capital, and knowledge refused to sustain the newcomers. The English were unnerved by the harshness of the weather and the wildness of the landscape. Reluctant to learn from the "savages" how best to draw a living from the local environment, they clung to familiar habits and worried that the chaos of the place might strip away whatever gloss of civilization separated Christians from the brutes. In grave danger they grasped at expedient solutions— trading arms to rival Indians for food and furs, spreading out on dispersed semisubsistence farmsteads, slashing recklessly at the forest for fuel and arable land—all of which subverted good order and made the project of cultural replication nearly impossible.[39]

In the end the English survived—and eventually prospered—by tapping the reservoir of private ambition (long constrained by the culture of stability) and transforming American resources into "merchantable" commodities. Wealth and power flowed to individuals with courage and ambition to seize them. But New World abundance also rewarded transgressive behavior in ways that disrupted the social order and threatened its ideological underpinnings. Common people sought land—and got it. Families grew large and did not suffer for it. Planters became more rapacious and their abuses went unchecked. Britons in North America found that they could profit, but not without bending (or breaking) the rules. The resulting tension between good order and successful exploitation complicated the experience of colonization from Newfoundland to the Caribbean islands.[40]

It is one of the conceits of the modern understanding of the culture of exploitation that it reflects nothing more than human nature—impulses of greed and violence that are written on the hearts of all persons. Embrace that claim and critics appear to be tilting at so many windmills: how far can we change human nature? It seems clear in history that ideas and social institutions in every time and place strive to blunt and channel such primal urges in behalf of peace, order, and community values. The idealized claims of the early modern English worldview, about stability, entitlement, and obligation, never had been realized fully; but they offered a rubric by which transgressions might be called out, and they had not yet been replaced by alternative cultural objectives. New World abundance loosened these constraints and rewarded ambition, but it did not neutralize British expectations. In the colonies, actors on the ground reached for outcomes that improved their individual stations without intending to revolutionize the world. Gentlemen and commoners alike sought what they had—or aspired to have—back home in England: a landed estate, a competent living, secure proprietary tenure, a reasonable chance to launch successful offspring. Despite the chaos of the sixteenth century, with its religious conflicts, agrarian crises, economic disruptions, social and political upheavals, Englishmen had not yet abandoned their confidence in natural distinctions between rich and poor, gentle and common, master and servant. A porous fiction had sustained English aristocratic culture, keeping gentlemen at their leisure and commoners in their place, absorbing a few rising and falling families without losing its timeless credibility. Believing that their customs and traditions reflected the natural order, Englishmen welcomed the discovery of New World riches as a bonus distribution from the generous Creator.[41]

The British experience with New World abundance was not unique, but particular expectations and habits of thought shaped their responses and accommodations as their colonies matured. Two patterns of consequence emerged from the experiences of the 1600s. First, a competitive, individualistic, market-oriented social order encouraged middling free agents to pursue their private interests more or less regardless of the impact on communal objectives or received cultural assumptions. Such a restless awakening of interests challenged Englishmen at home as well, but in the colonies its impact was magnified by the abundance of resources, the urgency of needs, and the relative weakness of institutions of control that might have policed private behaviors. Persons in authority in the colonies *did try* to resist these trends; but often as not they were guilty of the same behavior, and this liberalizing tendency prevailed wherever access to resources rewarded ambition and initiative.

Second, a slave-based plantation system in the Chesapeake and points south raised up a class of grandees in British America who managed to engross the profits of staple-crop agriculture. Unlike gentry in England, such slaveholding gentlemen tried to suppress completely the agency of their work force (never as fully as they would like). Scooping up political authority as well as arable land, colonial planters took pains to blunt the ambitions of middling competitors, newcomers, and innovators lest their entrepreneurial activities threaten the critical systems of power that enslaved the Africans and protected the master class. Chesapeake gentry arrogated to themselves traditional roles as magistrates and legislators; they tried to establish unchallenged authority over their neighbors. Stability proved elusive however, especially in the mainland colonies. Yeoman farmers and backcountry settlers with easy access to frontier acres constantly reminded the tidewater grandees that their pedigrees were thin and their authority rested not on hereditary titles but the ownership of African workers and stolen Indian land.

Economic liberty proved to be corrosive to hierarchical structures and assumptions, but before 1700 this could not be seen clearly; what *was* visible might be dismissed as artifacts of chaotic beginnings. In the same way the pernicious trap of African slavery no doubt appeared a happy expedient until, in the next century, its systems of legal and racial control profoundly distorted the social order. Where environments presented the most alien discomforts—as in Barbados and the other sugar islands—the English toyed with the thought that they had wandered into places where they did not belong. Still they soldiered on, venturing forth, claiming estates, rewarding themselves with offices, and hoping they could control the process of development that would bring their New World settlements to perfection. They did not—would not for a generation—recognize the existential changes that accompanied the changes they managed to impose on the land. The siren appeal of abundance that lured colonizers to their fate subverted purposeful actions and shaped the surprising consequences of colonization.

In *Utopia* Thomas More had imagined America as the setting for a parable in which a race of people shared a perfect communion without the pride, envy, and greed that seemed to flow from an obsession with private property. Whether his intention was didactic or only heuristic we cannot be sure, but no such utopia grew out of English colonization. Quite the opposite prevailed. If the discovery represented a chance to reform the world—a third planting (Smith) like Noah after the flood, or a beacon (Winthrop) from a "city on a hill"—the colonizers failed to establish any such new covenant. Rather they planted in their newfound land the same seeds of deceit and decay that were undermining order at home, and in profligate America these flourished beyond all imagining. Instead of innocence and love the new Americans cultivated greed and competition in their wondrous land. Released from the scarcities maintained by the Old World culture of stability, the English in America prepared the way for a new culture of exploitation that actually accelerated the social and economic changes already taking place in early modern England.

CHAPTER 3

Achievement

BY THE EARLY 1700S, England's New World colonizers began to relax and celebrate their achievements in this perilous enterprise. Through the application of labor (their own and that of coerced slaves) and the development of markets (their own and those of merchant capitalists around the Atlantic), they had established viable communities and secured for themselves more than adequate livings. They could see the outlines of a prosperous future. Tobacco plantations covered the tidewater region around Chesapeake Bay while prosperous farms dotted the landscape north and east all the way to the province of Maine. The harbors at Boston, New York, and Philadelphia sheltered hundreds of ships and even a few shipyards; workshops, warehouses, homes, taverns, churches, and public buildings filled out the urban landscapes. Despite treacherous difficulties in the early years, for many the promise of "abundance" had been fulfilled. More importantly, a sense of purposeful action and competence began to replace original fears of being lost to the fates in a howling wilderness. Both the hand of God and the accidents of fortune that seemed so imminent in the seventeenth century receded in the face of the colonizers' growing confidence in their own achievements.

Colonists' pride in this accomplishment blended congenially with new intellectual trends that are known to history as the Enlightenment. New discussions of "natural theology," science, moral philosophy, and social evolution laid the foundations for a culture of exploitation that would sweep away the confusions of the settler generation and replace the old culture of stability. Ways of "knowing" shifted away from scripture and toward scientific observation, experimentation, and reason. Nature was seen to display an exquisite order and regularity, apparently obeying universal rules that, once known, reduced the need for guesswork, mysteries, or perhaps even prayer. Philosophers and naturalists searched for patterns and "natural laws" in astronomy, physics, botany, anatomy, social development, and economics. Taking their cue from John Locke ("In the beginning all was America") people studied North America both as a source of great curiosities and an example of a universal process of historical development.[1]

Anxieties remained, of course: about being marginalized and forgotten; about the social disruptions encouraged by excessive individualism; about the security of social regimes based on violence and slavery; about being backward and out-of-touch. The quickening circulation of goods and information around the Atlantic brought the provinces into closer contact with ideas, trends, and fashions in London. As a result, American provincials followed the course of the Enlightenment (if always at a distance) and began to measure their achievements not just against the original environment of "wilderness" but also the rapidly changing English metropolis. Some of their anxieties were quieted by new assertions that commerce was good and that America was on the rise even as Old World systems shuddered in probable decline. Most Americans layered new ideas on top of older convictions such that their thoughts on religion and science became tangled together. Pleased with their own achievements, colonial Americans began to imagine themselves not as refugees in need of divine blessing but as participants and agents of the great world-historical developments of the age.[2]

Success in Virginia

In July 1726, William Byrd II of Virginia penned some arresting lines that provide an overture to this rising sense of colonial achievement. Byrd was just back in Virginia after a long and dissipating stay in London. To Charles Boyle, Earl of Orrery (an acquaintance whose favor he was cultivating) he wrote the following about his American home: "Besides the advantages of pure air, we abound in all kinds of provisions, without expence [sic] (I mean we who have plantations). I have a large family of my own, and my doors are open to everybody, yet I have no bills to pay, and half-a-crown will rest undisturbed in my pocket for many moons together. Like one of the patriarchs, I have my flocks and my herds, my bondsmen, and bond-women, and every soart [sic] of trade amongst my own servants, so that I live in a kind of independence on everyone but Providence."³

Such boasting in behalf of New World environmental riches had become routine in American descriptions, but what was new was the playful use of language from the King James Bible in a jocular and lighthearted context. Soon after, Byrd wrote a second epistle fairly dripping with subtle, urbane impiety:

> Were your Lordship to see or smell our ground, you would think it almost as fresh, as if it came out of it's [sic] makers hands. . . . Our waters too have a spirit and a sweetness, far beyond those of your island. . . . Nay our very fire, besides being clearer, and more kindly for respiration, receives force and vigour from the neighbourhood of the sun, and casts its heat to a wider distance. . . . Our plants have juices more refined and better digested, our fruits are more sprightly flavoured, our meats are more savoury, and I doubt not but when we come to find them, our metals will prove all ripened into gold and silver. Our men evade the original curse of hard labour, and sweat as much with eating their bread, as with getting it.

Warming to his blasphemy, Byrd plunged ahead. Colonial women, he claimed, brought forth children "with little sorrow." The land grew no thorns or thistles, and even Virginia's "poor Negroes" were "free-men in comparison of the slaves who till your ungenerous soil." Blessed with "all the fine things of Paradise, except innocence and the tree of life," Byrd thought Virginians would live forever, were it not for their sinful habits.⁴

In this playful account of a New Eden the curse of Adam and Eve had been modified significantly. Byrd seems to have recovered a sense of the entitlement first enjoyed by the original tenants of the Garden. Compared with the urgent reverence and fear that characterized English providential language through much of the previous century, Byrd here sounded more like the libertine Thomas Morton of Merry Mount. His God had backed several steps away from the affairs of the Creation, allowing creatures space to imagine themselves, with pride, irony, and humor, as partners in the bounty of this world. Here was an enlargement of human confidence and a decline of Reformation piety, without which the exploitation of the New World's treasures surely would have been less gleeful, more subdued.

Byrd himself was something of a cipher. Randy, crass, and sensual, he also cultivated genteel habits (reading Greek and Hebrew before dawn), corresponded with scientific fellows of the Royal Society (such as Boyle), collected a formidable library of 3,600 volumes, enjoyed coffee-house repartee as well as bawdy tavern banter. Byrd indulged his sexual appetites freely, then reported faithfully in his secret diary either the proud domination of his wife or his abuse of serving girls—black or white—for which he *always* asked God's forgiveness. In the same book he recorded his daily religious devotions; he attended church with regularity, and he studied theology with care. A moral hypocrite to be sure, it nevertheless is safe to treat him as a thoughtful Christian, most at home among Anglican latitudinarians of the very late seventeenth century, led by Archbishop of Canterbury John Tillotson, whose many volumes of sermons Byrd owned and read. Tillotson preached tirelessly about the reasonableness of Christianity and labored for three decades to demonstrate how faith and logic, revelation and reason reinforced each other.[5]

One thing in Tillotson stood in sharp contrast to the sterner tone of Calvinist divines: his God wanted people to be *happy*. Self-interest, he believed, lay in the heart of human nature, not as sin but a great human motivator.[6] God did not command us to deny what is good, pleasing, and convenient but called us to the wise and virtuous use of Creation to gratify our "natural" desires. Moderation seemed to be the key to the "use and enjoyment of worldly comforts, that there shall be no bitterness in them." For Tillotson, one glorified God by the vigorous pursuit of one's natural calling, and the stewards of great estates enjoyed opportunities for superior benevolence: "those of meaner condition can only be *men* to one another . . . but he that is highly raised and advanced above others, hath the happy opportunity in his hands, if he have but the heart to make use of it, to be *a kind of God to men*." Doubtless this was good news to William Byrd, who managed a great estate and enjoyed playing God to his wife and daughters, bondsmen and bondswomen, neighbors, rivals, and friends. There seemed room enough in Tillotson's commandments for lavish wealth, comfort, privilege, expropriation, and the frequent lapse into lechery and indulgence. Religion, according to Archbishop Tillotson, tamed the passions of men, suppressed lust, comforted the poor, and drove the industrious to perform good works of benevolence. Unless the "the lusts of men" blinded their eyes, it was impossible "so long as men love themselves, and desire their own happiness, to keep them from being religious."[7]

Tillotson's assurances were seconded by William Wollaston's *Religion of Nature Delineated* (1722), another popular treatise with which Byrd was heartily familiar. For Wollaston the first law of nature was respect for truth, out of which all happiness flowed, and toward which human reason inclined. Desperate to avoid a head-on collision with the emerging scientific worldviews, Wollaston threw down a standard that few eighteenth-century skeptics could fail to welcome: whatever was "inconsistent with the general peace and welfare (or good) of mankind" contradicted "the laws of human nature."[8] While it clearly was not his intention to unleash mankind's basest ambitions, Wollaston's artful blending of divine purpose, natural law, and human happiness scarcely could be read as anything *but* an invitation to relax the tension between an omnipotent God and God's self-interested creatures.

Here we see neither the triumphal hand of Providence, laying waste the Cape Cod Natives to make way for Bradford's Pilgrims, nor the jealous landlord of Eden lashing to the shoulders of disobedient humans a perpetual yoke of labor. Instead we see benevolence and harmony in nature, available at bargain prices, for all who would repent, believe, and modulate their gluttony within reasonable limits. The Creation was good, and the "Crown of Creation"—humans—though fallen, were not so sinful and unclean that their nature automatically drove them into the arms of Satan. The stage was set, by the early eighteenth century, for the parallel embrace of religion, science, and worldly success by a generation of Anglo-Americans who proceeded to enrich themselves from nature's bounty through slavery, commerce, and development. On that stage men and women were encouraged to perceive themselves as agents of the natural order, cocreators of prosperity, and inventors of that thing called "progress" that would so thoroughly energize and transform ambitions in the century to come.

However impressed with his own good fortune in this new earthly paradise, William Byrd warned against taking one's providential blessings for granted. The "more highly" a man was exalted, he wrote in his Commonplace Book, "the more lowly" should be "his behavior." A man should never forget: "the good things of this world [were] only lent, and not given him by Providence, because he must be accountable for the right employment & disposition of them."[9] The charge of stewardship accompanied material blessings: be not just a user but an improver also. Byrd began to see himself as something of an impresario to the natural riches of interior Virginia, especially after his commission to survey the dividing line between that colony and North Carolina (1728), a venture that took him deep into the frontier. In his journal of that expedition he noted with great pleasure the potential of the country—matched only by the disgusting indolence of its feckless inhabitants: "I am sorry to say it, but idleness is the general character of the men in the southern part of this colony as well as in North Carolina. The air is so mild and the soil so fruitful that very little labor is required to fill their bellies, especially where the woods afford such plenty of game. These advantages discharge the men from the necessity of killing themselves with work."[10]

Keenly aware of the winning formula in tidewater Virginia—seize Indian land and develop it with enslaved African labor—Byrd thought such backcountry "slothfulness" threatened to subvert the progress of the colonies. He wrote tirelessly to friends in England of schemes to promote new settlements and propagate coffee trees, wine grapes, tea, cinnamon, oranges, olives, and the insect from which to make cochineal. If word of New World potential ever became common knowledge in England, he teased one correspondent, "your island would quickly be dispeopled." He purchased a vast tract of land (twenty thousand acres) on the upper Dan River, "as fertile as the lands . . . about Babylon," where he intended to settle a thousand families of Swiss immigrants.[11] This urge to plant industrious settlers and develop the wilderness spread widely among his fellow tidewater planters. Whatever religious dimension may have graced the motivations of the founders of the Jamestown Colony, it had atrophied severely by William Byrd's day. His social vision and these latter-day planting schemes were all about resource development, wealth extraction, and the "progress" of civilization. Never fully committed to collective religious reformation, Virginians in the eighteenth century worried more about market saturation, soil exhaustion, access to African slaves and undeveloped lands, and the pacification of the remaining Native population.

Success in New England

In New England the eighteenth-century celebration of achievement ushered in a more wrenching change in religious orientation. In addition to fish and forest products, New Englanders found that their greatest product was food, which enabled English settlements to thrive and grow at rates never seen in Britain. Whatever had been their original mission—whether to spread the Gospel among the "savages" or create a model "city on a hill" for reformed Christianity—their tangible achievement clearly was anchored in this world of farms, food, and family formation. Their steady success as settlers ramped up the pressure on their Indian neighbors. Families with four or more offspring quickly overwhelmed the original towns and eventually swarmed all over New England—north and east into New Hampshire and Maine, west and south into the Connecticut River valley and all around Narragansett Bay. Unavoidably, diffusion fostered diversity while material comfort encouraged men and women to think more about things of this world than the next.

What had marked the original Puritan "errand" into the Massachusetts wilderness was the imminence of God in the consciousness of the settlers. Increase Mather (*Illustrious Providences*, 1684) catalogued dozens of in-breakings in the lives of his people, and in all the churches regular sermons tracked the progress (and decay) of their holy experiment. These colonizers inhabited stories at once sacred and profane, and they struggled to understand their suffering and deliverance in both registers. At first they tried to exclude the influence of the unregenerate; over time, however, doctrinal factions emerged, church membership and political interests diverged, and dissenters hived off (or were driven) into separate enclaves in search of purity or toleration.[12] As each offshoot community prospered, claims of unique providential favor became harder to believe. As children and grandchildren burned with less religious zeal, theological innovations softened the interface between a strict Calvinist God and the utilitarian world of property, marriage, and inheritance. From the frontier pulpit of Northampton, Massachusetts, Solomon Stoddard introduced the "halfway covenant" for persons who could not yet document a conversion experience, and he opened the communion table to all professing Christians. Relentlessly the clergy harangued their people with "jeremiads" detailing how Satan tempted fallen humans with promises of comfort and prosperity; relentlessly the dissonance persisted.[13]

Political chaos in England badly disrupted seventeenth-century New England. In 1640 the Parliamentary Revolution put the Puritans at home suddenly in charge. The great migration to America paused, ending a steady transfer of private wealth. Then in 1660 Parliament restored the monarchy to Charles II, who promptly imposed on the colonies a degree of religious toleration (protecting Quakers, for example), and vacated Massachusetts's charter. In 1686 King James II gathered everyone east of New York into a viceroyalty called the Dominion of New England; the same year Anglican services first were held in Old South Church, Boston. Excluders were threatened with exclusion, and the new power structure clouded not only their churches but the deeds to their farms. Then the "Glorious Revolution" of 1688 reversed all that, replacing the Catholic James with Protestant (but not Puritan) monarchs, William of Orange and Mary Stuart. Massachusetts got a new charter, but religious pluralism remained and confusion persisted into 1692, when hysterical accusations of witchcraft fueled a series of trials in Salem. Guided by the thesis that no omniscient God would allow an innocent person to appear as a specter in someone's dreams, the special Court of Oyer and Terminer meted out death to defendants who would not confess their alliance with demons. Twenty executions resulted. Increase Mather put an end to the madness in October 1692, denouncing the court's reliance on so-called spectral evidence. Peace and legitimate government returned, some of the prosecutors apologized to families of the victims, and the New Englanders entered the eighteenth century chastened and seeking a new way of reconciling faith, reason, law, Gospel, and temporal experience.[14]

Over the next fifty years the religious culture of New England fractured. In 1698, the new Brattle Street Church in Boston offered prosperous families a more generous theology of grace served up from the evangelical pulpit of Benjamin Colman. In protest, Increase Mather published *The Order of the Gospel, Professed and Practised by the Churches of New England* (1700), reasserting the covenant theology with its focus on exposing the visible saints and excluding the unregenerate. Colman answered with a devastating countercharge calling Mather's covenant itself a non-biblical invention—the very thing Puritans by definition raged *against.* Colman offered a more relaxed approach to church discipline, limiting the use of exclusion and offering infant baptism to all who promised to raise the child in the Christian faith. During worship he allowed what Mather called the "dumb reading" of scripture without inserting the didactic comments by which Puritan clergy typically quashed all possibilities of error. Preaching itself—and a more accessible, persuasive style of preaching at that—constituted explication of the Word, and Colman trusted his auditors to comprehend, with the grace of God, the import of his homilies.[15]

Colman's church became a gathering place within the temporal community where persons might hear the Word and receive the gift of grace that made it possible to reconcile with the Creator. Not fully Arminian yet (unwilling to entertain the possibility of earning salvation with good works), the Brattle Street theology, like Stoddard's Northampton variation, rendered Calvinism more welcoming, more evangelical, more open to a comforting prospect of salvation than the earlier Boston churches. Colman profoundly softened "original sin" and set the stage for thoughtful individuals to approach religion not in shame but with confidence that their natural faculties might facilitate sanctification. He once characterized Adam's "fall" as an irrational mistake that deranged the God-given faculties of human reason. Scripture (revelation) then was offered as the route to reconciliation. "God deals with us *as with rational Creatures*," Colman proclaimed. The gift of grace restored "the Exercise of reason" and brought "Sinners to repent." Reason was "the rule and Law of the Eternal and perfect *Infinite Mind* inscribed *on* us and *for* us." Christians ought to "reverence it as the *Wisdom of God*."[16]

This softening of Reformation piety in New England had the effect (intended or not) of legitimizing religious pluralism and supporting a certain freedom of conscience at least for similar strains of reformed Protestantism. As they agreed to disagree about the fine points of dogma, these Americans pulled their religious impulses in a more private direction. Spiritual welfare and personal salvation became less a concern of others or the state. Such moves made it easier for people to interact in the present, temporal world—a more secular world—guided by rational sense, common law, and a kind of generic morality toward a goal of worldly progress and prosperity. Secular achievements could be seen as marks of good conduct, pleasing in the eyes of God. Few went so far as to sanctify wealth and accomplishment as direct proof of divine favor, but the goals of happiness in this world and salvation in the next coexisted in the minds of third-generation New Englanders who saw their collective accomplishment maturing.[17]

Of course some churchmen continued to sound the alarm as they saw the centrality of religion slipping. Jonathan Edwards, for example, Solomon Stoddard's grandson and successor in Northampton, coupled reason with experience (emotion) to spark an outbreak of religious enthusiasm that eventually scorched the Protestant landscape in what was called the Great Awakening. Although not an enemy of scientific inquiry, Edwards never wavered in his conviction that God actively directed the universe; no laws of nature worked out by men could stay the Creator's hand. The end for which God created the world was happiness to be sure, but not the happiness William Byrd craved. Edwards's rapture would come in a spiritual reconciliation that owed nothing to sensual or material realities. "Man's chief end," he insisted bluntly, was "the business of religion." Even the carnal indulgences of Northampton's teens (the proximate cause for Edwards's first revival) bothered him mostly because lust distracted the youths' attention from spiritual work (imagine that!).[18]

Edwards's Northampton revival (1734–35) intersected with similar eruptions in New Jersey, where William and Gilbert Tenant stirred an enthusiastic fever among local Presbyterians. Then in the fall of 1739 an extraordinary itinerant evangelist from England, George Whitefield, returned to the colonies and began welding discrete antecedents into an intercolonial trans-Atlantic event. Blending charismatic preaching with savvy advance promotional efforts, Whitefield launched a crusade along the entire Atlantic coast. At every stop he peddled sacred merchandise (printed sermons and journals, T-shirts not having been invented yet), giving participants tangible souvenirs of the experience. Reaching directly into the hearts of individual sinners and stirring the sensation of receiving grace in what he called "experimental religion," Whitefield unintentionally loosened their ties to local religious institutions. In his wake he left congregations divided and fighting over style and clerical authority, which had the effect of further privatizing the search for salvation in the minds of many colonists. For all its heat and energy, the impact of revival was ambivalent. Evangelists intended to focus attention on the presence of the Holy Spirit, but when Whitefield preached in Philadelphia, Benjamin Franklin noticed instead the size of the crowd. Driven by his own "experimental" curiosity, he began stepping off the distance at which the great man could be heard.[19]

The Tree of Knowledge

In the eighteenth century the retreat of revelation as a source of practical knowledge was matched by a corresponding rise in empirical study and human reason as reliable ways of knowing about the natural world. Since time immemorial a thirst for knowledge had served as a metaphor for human overreach, and at least since St. Paul's letter to the Romans the concept of "sin" defined human beings as corrupt by nature and at odds with divine pleasure. During the seventeenth century, however, speculative inquiries began identifying patterns and "laws" in nature that gave rise, after 1650, to the notion that the material world was morally good and human reason might someday comprehend it. The craving for knowledge that once had signaled disobedience to God took on a positive moral attribute. The resulting "scientific revolution" was launched by pious churchmen following the lead of Francis Bacon; well into the eighteenth century, men of science comfortably harmonized religion and empirical inquiry.[20] This process of gathering data, rooted in Bacon, Locke, and Newton, captured the imagination of genteel English intellectuals who began to explore, collect, and categorize things in the natural world. The very existence of the Americas played a central role in this impulse to study nature. Novel plants and animals, celestial and meteorological observations, fossils, artifacts, information about Native Americans and their languages all fascinated English "virtuosi," as these self-trained empiricists were called.[21]

Seventeenth-century English science found its institutional home in the Royal Society of London, chartered in 1662. Collecting specimens, descriptions, and explanations of all kinds of things, the Royal Society set itself up as official custodian of Baconian inquiry. Fellows scrutinized reports from a rapidly growing network of correspondents worldwide, and if the information proved credible in their eyes, they published it in their *Philosophical Transactions*. That imprimatur transformed mere rumor into knowledge. Sifting through the cumulative "heap" of "nature's particulars," members in turn developed theoretical frameworks, taxonomic matrices, and rational explanations, fitting more and more details into comprehensive systems. Eventually synthetic volumes appeared. In 1690 Robert Boyle published *The Christian Virtuoso: Shewing that by being addicted to Experimental Philosophy, a Man is rather assisted, than Indisposed, to be a Good Christian*. The next year John Ray published an even more popular treatise, *The Wisdom of God Manifested in the Works of Creation*. With such promotional works, fellows of the Royal Society recruited and mentored intellectual disciples (especially in the New World) who dreamed of being useful to the cause of Enlightenment by delivering into these august hands the raw "stuff" of knowledge.[22]

The Royal Society listed one resident of North America among its original fellows: John Winthrop Jr. The eldest son of the Massachusetts founder, an accomplished chemist, metallurgist, astronomer, medical doctor, and alchemist (as well as governor of Connecticut), Winthrop shipped over various specimens and observations and served as western correspondent for the society. Rhode Island's dissident founder, Roger Williams, gained election for his pioneering work on the languages of Native Americans. In

1692 Virginia's William Byrd delivered a live rattlesnake and female opossum to the society's London meeting rooms, to the astonishment and delight of the fellows. Byrd served on the governing council for several years, contributed one formal paper on the dappled skin of an African boy, and remained devoted all his life to the work (and the prestige) of the organization. (Accidentally dropped from the rolls in 1737, Byrd protested in anguish that he was not dead and hoped "to survive some years longer.")[23] By the middle of the eighteenth century the Royal Society had admitted nearly forty resident colonials into their fellowship and sustained an extensive correspondence with other individuals never offered membership. Jamaica, Antigua, Barbados, Massachusetts, Virginia, Connecticut, New York, Maryland, Pennsylvania, Georgia, all were represented by one or more fellows. Beginning in 1712 Cotton Mather (whose intellectual reach and energy knew no bounds) filed dozens of letters with the Royal Society on everything from plants and animals, to weather events, comets, smallpox, monstrous births, antediluvian giants, and Indian herbal cures.[24]

Elected a fellow in 1713, Cotton Mather redoubled his studies and produced the massive *Christian Philosopher* (1721), the first comprehensive scientific textbook written by a North American scholar. Mather's opus captured the curious transition in worldview that characterized eighteenth-century Americans. He devoured (and freely plagiarized) the leading treatises coming out of England on natural history and natural theology. His mastery of technical details truly was phenomenal; still, at every turn Mather flushed out the creeping atheism inherent in "experimental" materialism and inserted instead the hand of his trusted, traditional, Calvinist God. Gravity, for example, he described as "an Effect insolvable by any *philosophical Hypothesis.*" It depended on "the *immediate Will* of our most wise CREATOR, who, by appointing this *Law*, throughout the material World" kept "all Bodies in their proper Places." The progress of human understanding itself was not strictly a secular achievement: no rational argument accounted for why some things were discovered while others remained "lock'd up from Human Understanding, till God, *in whose hand are our Times*, is pleased to make them understood by the Children of Men."[25]

Some New England intellectuals encountered modern science at college, but most early American empiricists trained themselves in the field. Cadwallader Colden studied medicine in Scotland before moving to the colonies in 1710, but his curiosity ranged in many directions and his major contributions to *new* knowledge lay in extensive descriptions of the Iroquois Confederacy as well as the land, soil, climate, and natural resources of New York.[26] The amateur, self-taught character of these early American investigators limited their credibility and impact in European scientific circles. Dozens of letters from Peter Collinson to Pennsylvanian John Bartram exhibited an air of quiet condescension. In 1730 Philadelphia instrument maker Thomas Godfrey invented an astronomical "octant" belatedly reported to the Royal Society in 1732, only to find an English inventor had acquired a patent and denied Godfrey's claim. When Cadwallader Colden published ambitious theoretical treatises on matter, motion, and gravity, attempting to extend and complete the work of Sir Isaac Newton, European readers scoffed. One thought it "remarkable" that something "incomprehensible to a Newton should now be cleared up, by a countryman from the New World." Colden earnestly believed he could not gain an honest hearing because of who he was, and his friend Benjamin Franklin tended to agree.[27]

In addition to being self-trained, American naturalists commonly relied on knowledge gained from women, Native Americans, and Africans, which further worried the men of the Royal Society. Jane Colden, Cadwallader's daughter, became an accomplished naturalist in her own right, as did a number of other colonial women; but their admission to the transatlantic scientific conversation always came through fathers, husbands, or brothers. They never were considered for Royal Society membership. Information gleaned from African and Native American collectors, who often knew the specimens and contexts better than whites, depended even more on endorsement from white, elite, male sponsors. Eyewitness accounts in theory ought to have helped validate the claims of distant correspondents, but popular travelers' narratives were known to include fables, fantasies, and outright fabrications. Still in need of a common language, taxonomic systems, established institutions, laboratories, methods, or even reigning theoretical paradigms with which to test the claims of strangers, science in the age of reason was forced in a way to invent its own credibility.[28]

Benjamin Franklin, of course, remains the ultimate example of a self-made American scientist who finally did dazzle the best minds of Europe. Schooled as a printer's apprentice in Boston, the young Franklin kicked away the traces of conventional education, ran away to Philadelphia, set himself up as an independent printer, and began crafting his persona out of whole cloth. An incredible polymath who educated himself reading books as they took shape in compositor's frames before him (letters marching backwards from right to left) his curiosity was extraordinary. Tirelessly he promoted intellectual inquiry and scientific correspondence (and Benjamin Franklin). In 1727 he organized a club in Philadelphia, called the "leather apron club" or "the Junto," intended to promote and discuss scientific speculations. In 1743 he published a call for an organization of "Virtuosi or ingenious Men, residing in the several Colonies, to be called *The American Philosophical Society.*" Not much came of it for another twenty years, although Franklin's many other initiatives, including founding the Library Company of Philadelphia (1731), fed the growing climate of Enlightenment inquiry in and around Philadelphia.[29]

Franklin began his own career as a scientific researcher with studies of household heating, smoke, and problems of fuel efficiency, which resulted in the "Pennsylvania Fire-Place" design (1744). Questions about fluid mechanics of all kinds followed, and it was through fluids he developed the theories about electricity that secured forever his place in the pantheon of scientific innovators. In the late 1740s scientists all over Europe were debating the nature of "Electrical Fire." Retiring from his print shop, and using apparatus sent by Peter Collinson (plus his famous kite and key), Franklin dedicated all his energy to electricity experiments, discovering the role of conductors, insulators, and most importantly, the existence of positive and negative charges. In 1749 his first letters on the subject were read before the Royal Society of London; by 1751 *Experiments and Observations of Electricity, Made at Philadelphia in America* appeared in London, edited and introduced by the Royal Society's John Fothergill, and translated into French the next year. Harvard and Yale both awarded Franklin honorary degrees, and in 1753 he won the Royal Society's Copley Medal. Elected a fellow in 1756, Franklin's fame opened doors to drawing rooms all over Europe, celebrity on which he would capitalize the rest of his days.[30]

By the middle of the eighteenth century many of the residents of British North America had managed to incorporate inquiry and reason with surviving elements of a Christian worldview that had cast them as terrestrial agents in a work of redemption. As they devoured treatises on "natural theology," sin retreated into the realm of private ethics and morality. New knowledge was found to correspond with scripture and reflect, not prideful arrogance but the respectful exercise of faculties bestowed on humans by the Creator. As a result, colonial Americans warmly embraced the Enlightenment culture of inquiry and began to imagine their world as a laboratory for the advance of scientific knowledge. Then as now, many people doubtless lived their lives without pondering in any conscious fashion the shifting foundations of their moral and ethical frameworks, but with historical perspective we can see there was a tipping point where the values of one world fell away and the values of another moved into place. At stake was nothing less than the purpose of a human life. Clinging to an older ideal, Jonathan Edwards still preached against a world of "pride and malice and contention" where "self-interest governs." Who, he asked, would lay up a store "in such a world as this?" His skeptical friend, Ben Franklin, writes historian Daniel Walker Howe, might have responded cheerfully, "I would."[31]

Gathering Better Evidence

Enlightenment science played a crucial role in reforming for contemporary eyes both the nature of the New World itself and the virtues of material progress of which the colonists justly were proud. One persistent concern about the New World had been the fear that wilderness itself was cursed and somehow *caused* the primitive conditions, monstrous animals and plants, wild chaotic weather, and the "savage" ways of the indigenous population. Extravagant claims by early colonial projectors such as the Hakluyts or John Smith had tarnished the credibility of information flowing back from America, leaving critics at home quick to believe the worst and doubt reports of success. Over time, better information about the Americas— especially regarding natural history, weather conditions, indigenous people, health, and trade statistics—displaced hysterical impressions. Hyperbole fell away as promoters sought to convey a tone of disinterested reportage. Advertising for immigrants to Pennsylvania and New Jersey in the 1680s, William Penn pioneered the use of frank representation to overcome widespread skepticism. In *The History and Present State of Virginia* (1705), provincial author Robert Beverly likewise begged the readers to see his book as real history, not a fancy-filled travel narrative.[32]

In 1708 English writer John Oldmixon published a massive two-volume history of the "discovery, settlement, progress, and state" of all the British plantations in America, the first of its kind that stands fairly well as a primary source. Objectivity was still as much a pose as a point of view: Oldmixon favored the empire, especially Barbados, where his patron, John Bromley, owned a sugar plantation. Together with the newly formed Board of Trade in London, he represented an interest group at Court promoting a form of imperialism that owed nothing to Christian missions and every-thing to British commercial supremacy. Nevertheless, his claims for credi-bility document the shifting universe of understanding. Critics of British plantations, he argued, based their specious objections on lies and slander collected from faulty or dishonest accounts. Far from *costing* Great Britain money (as some members of Parliament claimed), plantations relieved the English of their surplus population and generated wealth through trade. Marshalling elaborate calculations proving that a "hand" employed in the provinces was worth twenty times the value of a workman at home, Old-mixon crafted one of the earliest economic arguments that valued colonies not just as sources of exotic staples but also markets for the products of the mother country.[33]

Oldmixon's hundreds of pages quickly were joined by a stream of reports from interested tourists eager to see what the colonists had done. In 1724 Anglican clergyman Hugh Jones reported impressive advances in Virginia even while he faulted the obsession with tobacco and the tendency of slavery to limit opportunities for common white men and women. Mary-land physician Alexander Hamilton, a recent immigrant from Scotland, toured New York and New England in 1744, recording his general satisfac-tion with the places he visited (complaining only that very lowborn Ameri-cans easily acquired luxury goods from abroad). Swedish naturalist Peter Kalm visited Pennsylvania in 1748 and saw a bountiful environment, pros-perous settlements, large families, rich diets, and a thriving trade with the sugar islands—but also expensive firewood, scarce manure, and exceedingly careless farming habits: "The great richness of the soil which the first Euro-pean colonists found," reported Kalm, gave rise to slash-and-burn abuses, heedless of the time and expense that would be required one day "when the earth is quite exhausted." Traveling northward in 1760, another English visitor, Andrew Burnaby, labeled Philadelphia a place of "wonder and admiration," New Jersey the "garden of North America," and New York City "flourishing." Massachusetts impressed Burnaby as already showing signs of decay; Rhode Island was in a "wretched state," filled with "cunning, deceitful, and selfish" people, corrupt and ungovernable.[34]

Descriptions of Native Americans took a marked turn in the eighteenth century as a result of scientific curiosity. The Puritans still struggled to see Indians as anything but minions of the Devil, but elsewhere colonial writers began to notice customs and beliefs that, while different from English norms, did not disqualify Natives from the human family. Virginia's Robert

Beverley wistfully acknowledged that contact with Europeans had cost them their "Felicity" and "Innocence," and left them "desiring a thousand things, they never dreamt of before." Oldmixon thought it might be "Vanity in any one People to call another barbarous, because their Customs differ." Prefacing his history of the Five Indian Nations in colonial New York, Cadwallader Colden scolded his countrymen for mistreating these people. Possessed of a "bright and noble genius," the Iroquois, depending on their treatment, might "add honor to the British Nation"—or be turned into "faithless thieves and robbers." Many writers were struck by the freedom with which Indians shared material possessions with one another. Of course such generous perspectives gained traction only where the Native American threat to colonial welfare had been extinguished. Colonizers—especially the owners of proprietary claims in Pennsylvania or Carolina—exhibited no such scruples when angling for more Indian land, and vulnerable frontier communities showed little interest in understanding their indigenous neighbors.[35]

A sharp rise after 1700 in the use of enslaved black labor introduced a question that would fester and grow over the decades ahead: how did racialized chattel slavery affect the health of the whole society? In Barbados and the other sugar islands, slave populations had ballooned while the middle ranks of white laborers, yeomen, and servants disappeared. Between 1650 and 1750, the white population of Barbados fell by half (to 15,400) while the number of blacks mushroomed to over 75,000. In the Chesapeake tobacco region the number of black slaves doubled between 1700 and 1720 (to about 30,600) then jumped to five times that number in the next thirty years. Early critics worried that the long-term interests of the province might be ruined by the plantation system; later observers affirmed that it was so.[36] Tobacco culture as practiced in the Chesapeake favored men of enormous fortune, drove out small cultivators, encouraged wide residential dispersal, and undercut the development of towns. Rich forest resources went unharvested, potential new crops and domestic manufactures never materialized, and the worst sort of indolent white immigrants (most recently, hordes of English felons) scratched out a lazy subsistence in the backcountry, contributing nothing to the common weal. Every commentator from Beverley on recognized the trend, but resident Virginians preferred to blame the low character of the whites rather than the impact of slave-based staple crop agriculture. One Anglican clergyman in 1759 did offer up a shrewd—in fact a scathing—portrait. Enormous wealth coupled with unchecked power over slaves had left the richest planters "vain and imperious," ignorant, vicious toward "Indians and Negroes," haughty, "jealous of their liberties," and unwilling to acknowledge any "superior power." On a positive note, he admitted they *were* "exceedingly fond" of race horses and "spared no expense or trouble to improve the breed of them."[37]

By any material measure, the British American colonies by 1750 must be considered profoundly successful. Nearly 1.2 million colonists lived in continental provinces of North American, about one-fifth black (mostly enslaved), the balance white (free or indentured), mostly British, but including rising numbers of European immigrants as well. Another 330,000 settlers lived in the British sugar islands, where African descendants outnumbered whites eight to one. Two things undeniably were true: colonization by Englishmen was possible, and life in the wilderness did not necessarily degrade the bodies or the minds of the adventurers. The standard of living for white colonists in British America everywhere exceeded that in England and Europe. For this result historian Alan Taylor credits the combination of natural resources and coerced African labor. Ironically, the patterns of success favored slavery over free labor: as Taylor notes "West Indian planters lived in the greatest luxury because they conducted the harshest labor system with the greatest number of slaves." Next came South Carolina, the Chesapeake, and the Middle Colonies. Inverting experience from the previous century, eighteenth-century New England, where independent family farms covered the landscape, posted the lowest standard of living. Using physical stature as a proxy for material prosperity, Taylor concludes: "On average, the tallest colonists were southern planters—those who profited most from African slavery and Indian land." Taylor's point cannot be overstressed: the achievement for which English colonizers in America credited themselves so proudly, rested more than anything on the expropriation of Native land and African labor. The abundance of effectively free land (ignoring the expense of settler violence that was charged to "defense against savages") and unpaid labor (not really free but barely compensated from the fruits of production) "explain" colonial American history (to echo a claim made famous by Frederick Jackson Turner).[38]

The Progress of Civilization

All this observing, describing, and assessing of progress in the New World colonies took place within the framework of a new social science. Since the early seventeenth century natural philosophers had been studying human society as if it were an organism. How was society born? Did it pass through developmental stages like a human youth? Which variations were natural and which foretold disease or malformation? Among creatures, individuals grew up, thrived, and died, while the species endured unchanged: was it also true that nations rose and fell while civilization endured—or even improved? Were there natural laws guiding the development of nations just like the laws that regulated every other aspect of the material universe? The works of Thomas Hobbes (*Leviathan*, 1651) and John Locke *(Two Treatises of Government*, 1689) called particular attention to New World examples and began to shift focus from organic "ages" to developmental "stages" more closely keyed to material conditions and the means of production than the mere passage of time.

America, of course, struck all of these thinkers as a perfect museum of social evolution. Perceived alternately by early Europeans as wholly undeveloped *and* as home to human communities at primitive stages, New World examples fed this speculative enterprise just as specimens of plants and animals nourished the rise of natural history. Montesquieu developed an overtly environmental framework in *Spirit of the Laws* (1748), mapping social and moral characteristics onto the peoples of the world based on hot or cold, wet or dry conditions and the pastoral or agricultural habits of the people. French "Physiocrats" mounted a new theory of national wealth centered not on commerce and money but the products of the soil, drawing positive attention back to the countryside. Gradually a rough consensus emerged around "stages of development" theories found in the works of many comparative historians, including Henry Home Lord Kames, David Hume, Adam Ferguson, and Adam Smith. At the lowest stage, hunting and gathering yielded a bare subsistence with no discernable social organization. Nomadic herdsmen displaced such primitives in the second stage, followed in sequence by even more organized communities of settled farmers. Agriculture produced a material surplus, fostered the division of labor, and made possible urban centers where governance and trade developed. Eventually society entered the highest stage marked by extensive specialization, international commerce, fine manufactures, refinement of habits, and luxury consumption, at least for the better class of people. Not surprisingly this highest stage described the commercial societies of England and Continental Europe, where extensive manufactures flowed out to supply colonists around the world who paid in foodstuffs or luxury consumables such as sugar and tobacco.[39]

Debates raged among theorists about the moral valance of these stages and advancement from one to another. Moral and civic virtue long had been associated with farmers and country living, where subsistence was generated close to home and dependency on distant others kept to a minimum, but the complex "arts and sciences" only advanced in urban commercial environments where gentlemen of learning and leisure could dedicate their energies to abstract thought. At the same time, refinement, leisure, and luxury encouraged vulgar indulgence and dissipation that could eat the heart out of a great people, leading (as in the example of Rome) to decadence and tragic conquest by grossly inferior "barbarians." Clinging to civic virtue, Spartan values, and Renaissance humanist traditions, bitter critics of courtly extravagance heaped scorn on those who valued profit and interest over honor and tradition. Anchoring the counterposition, Bernard Mandeville, in *Fable of the Bees* (1714), launched a blatant defense of selfish material interest that, while scandalous at first, became in time a central tenet of Adam Smith's political economy.[40]

Americans watched these debates with interest as they pondered their own achievements and considered the shape of the future. The contrast between the opulence of London and the modesty of even successful American estates had been a source of embarrassment for many in the eighteenth century (recall William Byrd's peculiar boasting). Imports of luxury appointments—wallpaper, mirrors, clothing, carpets, carriages, fancy race horses for breeding—soared in the middle decades as provincials scrambled to "perform" their sense of accomplishment. At the same time, country critics of the Georgian Court—the Tory Viscount Bolingbroke, and "real Whigs" Joseph Addison, Richard Steele, John Trenchard, and Thomas Gordon—found eager readers in America, giving rise to a counternarrative in which Great Britain was said to be advancing toward destruction. Society depended, according to this theory, on a civic commitment among the political classes to suppress private interest and keep service to the commonwealth foremost in mind. Unfortunately late-stage commercial riches fostered dangerous indulgences that enervated physical and moral virtue. Georgian England by the 1740s (so the criticism went) already was awash in such decadence, and the vaunted British Constitution was in danger of final destruction.[41]

Benjamin Franklin took up the question of social evolution in the midst of his electrical experiments. "Observations Concerning the Increase of Mankind," written in 1751, approached development as a problem of "political arithmetic"—what we would call demography. Nations advanced,

Franklin argued, from the agricultural to the commercial stage, only when population outran available land, forcing people into towns and manufacturing employment. Although a good thing in moderation, intensive manufacturing glutted markets, depressed prices, forced employers to curb wages and seek a "vent" for their manufactures through foreign trade. Lacking open land, England necessarily advanced into unchecked industrialization, but Franklin saw no danger at home despite a booming population that doubled every twenty years. The America that Franklin knew (Pennsylvania) had reached the happiest stage of moderate development, mostly agricultural with adequate domestic manufacturing, and possessed of a seemingly infinite store of western lands on which to seat the growing population. Simply by turning around and facing west, and dispossessing the Natives they found there, Americans might balance indefinitely at the edge of stage three, enjoying agricultural riches without triggering the forces of inevitable decay.[42]

These standard models of social evolution failed, however, to explain a glaring anomaly that confronted every student of the eighteenth-century American achievement: great agricultural wealth squeezed by violence from enslaved Africans. American slavery produced an unstable social order with a tiny reckless elite enjoying total control over a vast laboring population, dehumanized by chattel status and racial ideology, excluded from the social contract, and subjected to the most licentious private tyranny. The great mass of middle-rank people disappeared from the areas of staple crop wealth, fleeing altogether (in the case of the islands) or escaping to the margins in the mainland colonies, where they found a subsistence and nursed a growing resentment toward their resident grandees. Where did such a pattern leave such colonies on the evolutionary time scale? This question soon would intersect with moral qualms about racial slavery, opening the door to an antislavery argument that would complicate American development into the Revolution and long after.

Worried about this and other aspects of the emerging American society, Anglican clergyman William Smith of New York published very candid remarks in 1752 (addressed to the colonial assembly) about luxury, corruption, and the inevitable "death" of the British monarchy. Citing writers at home (he meant Bolingbroke), Smith declared Great Britain already mortally poisoned by corruption. He was no advocate of independence; the provinces, he said, were far too enmeshed in luxury consumption, and if the mother country fell now the colonies must perish as well. What he hoped for was to establish in New York a great university and help prepare the colonies to become the new seat of civilization. In stilted verse he argued that "Empire, Liberty and Arts" moved around the globe from east to west. When "by the sad vicissitudes of Things" the Old World had "sunk back to its pristine Sloth and *Barbarism*," the New World would be "the last Retreat of *Arts*, imperial *Liberty* and *Truth*." The government of New York was not moved, but Benjamin Franklin caught sight of Smith's treatise and brought him down to Philadelphia as provost of a new College of Philadelphia. Together the theologian and the electrician worked to make Philadelphia a refuge for the migrating muses.[43]

Lest we think Smith's analysis was idiosyncratic, Andrew Burnaby reported several years later that "an idea, strange as it is visionary, has entered into the minds of the generality of mankind, that empire is traveling westward." "With eager and impatient expectation" people looked forward "to that destined moment" when America would "give law to the rest of the world." Burnaby himself thought the idea "illusory and fallacious." America was formed, he countered, "for happiness, but not for empire." Too many private ambitions directed the course of events to produce a coherent nation. In the North "different nations, different manners, different religions, and different languages" subverted all hope of union in a common destiny. In the South, the insurmountable weakness was slavery. The climate rendered whites "indolent, inactive, and unenterprising." Rather than take up labor themselves, southern men retired "westward" to settle on fresh lands where, "by the servitude of a Negroe [*sic*] or two, they may enjoy" an easy "independency." Burnaby doubted the mainland colonies ever could unite in common cause: civil war he thought more likely, in which the "Indians and Negroes" would seize the "opportunity of exterminating them all together."[44]

In the end, in 1760, at the accession of George III, Great Britain seemed either to be mired in fatal corruption or charging ahead as the world's model commercial empire. His majesty's subjects in America looked forward to imperial glory—or harbored dark fears that world-historical forces were about to do them in. The shape of the empire under George III soon would become the central question: would the colonies continue to enjoy relative freedom to chart their own way and enjoy their own prosperity, or would they be forced into systems of control that serviced only the yawning appetites of London? Most Americans doubtless kept their day-to-day attention on immediate tangible things such as making a living, raising a family, keeping dangers at bay, whether from the warring armies and navies that perpetually roiled the Atlantic world, embittered Native Americans relentlessly pressed to surrender their homes, or African slaves stripped of all hope in life or even in death. At least for whites, the challenges of "starving times" lay now securely in the past and the prospects for the future seemed reasonably secure. No longer on a mission from God, but neither wholly released from a sense that providential blessings once factored into their history, and newly armed with scientific tools and confidence in human ingenuity, Americans on the eve of the imperial crisis celebrated their achievements. Many components of their sense of progress and modernization could be seen, but tradition and history still cast doubts on its virtues as well as their right to embrace it heartily. It required one more link—liberation—to lock in the canopy that supported the culture of exploitation for generations to come.

CHAPTER 4

Liberation

BRITAIN'S KING GEORGE III came to the throne in the middle of a great war for Atlantic empire that, by 1763, left him in control of French Canada as well as the English sugar islands and coastal settlements from Maine south to Spanish Florida. By that time well over a million Englishmen (plus assorted Germans and Scots) made their homes in what would become the United States. Another 326,000 people of African descent provided slave labor that fueled a staple-crop economy south of Delaware. Most other white residents owed their prosperity one way or another to the circulation of goods, money, and people around the Atlantic basin. Despite their different origin stories, the North American colonies had acquired certain common characteristics. Each now had a charter of some sort and a legislative assembly. In most cases governors and other imperial officials had learned to keep their distance. Commercial regulations from London protected and encouraged colonial enterprise; when they proved inconvenient they likely were ignored. Americans gloried in the British governing tradition binding King, Lords, and Commons together with a "Constitution" (unwritten) that included ancient customary rights. The sons of provincial elites finished their educations with tours at London's Inns of Court, and their parents grasped after the latest fashions available from England. By many measures, provincial Americans were wealthier, more self-governing, more mobile and privately ambitious, and more "free" than they would have been anywhere else in the Atlantic world. And yet, in just a few short years they were clamoring for liberation from the iron grip of a "tyrant king" who they said was determined to enslave them.[1]

What prompted this impulse among colonial Americans to liberate themselves? In a surprisingly short period of time a new common narrative charged British authorities with mounting a conspiracy against the fundamental rights of Englishmen—first in the colonies, where they could operate with impunity, but doubtless aimed at snuffing out freedom at home in England as well. This narrative once had flowed from the pens of radical "country" critics in England, then was picked up by elite Americans who argued that the government of George III was bent on oppressing the colonists. Had such a monstrous conspiracy existed we would not wonder at the spread of rebellion, for the settlers in British North America always had been jealous of their relative freedom and presumed constitutional rights. But not everyone saw the oppression complained of, and many questioned for years whether British designs really threatened American peace and happiness. The evidence for British tyranny had to be exposed and explained, and even then a substantial minority of people questioned the need for revolution right up to the eve of independence and beyond.

Fifty years ago historian Bernard Bailyn urged students of the American Revolution to "suspend" their "disbelief" and listen to the rhetoric itself. American revolutionaries told a coherent tale of liberties lost and tyranny's encroachment that somehow struck a nerve with enough individuals after 1763 to launch a rebellion that eventually shattered the empire. What Bailyn called a new "grammar of thought" fit hand in glove with enough popular fears, ambitions, and expectations to mobilize a people into armed rebellion.[2] True slavery never was a threat, but the metaphor of powerlessness energized persons who understood bondage because they were the masters of enslaved Africans. That it kindled a widespread urge among the colonists to liberate themselves from tyranny cannot be doubted; whether the source of discomfort was Whitehall or something else remains a puzzle. Justified or not, the invitation to rebel produced many different uprisings that barely were contained within a complex new political creation that would be called the United States. The regime that emerged from the chaos promised liberty and equality to the citizens of new republics, who then would graft that dispensation onto the culture of exploitation they had been building since the seventeenth century.

The Revelation

It came to John Adams as a revelation. The flowering of New England was not just a private human achievement but an essential turn in a world-historical drama pitting truth and virtue against the dark eternal forces of tyranny and corruption. Adams alone did not start the American Revolution, but his path to revelation can illustrate the process. As the British government pondered its postwar options for colonial reorganization and urgent revenue enhancement, Adams began composing his thoughts on colonial rights. Through the lens of his own experiences, his reading in classical and contemporary political science, his passion for the law and the British constitution, Adams saw a great conspiracy taking shape. The course of history seemed clear at last, and vague discomforts Americans had begun to experience stood out in Adams's mind as markers of great portent. Let those with eyes see.[3]

In a series of essays on "Canon and Feudal Law," published in 1765, Adams first roughed out the germ of an argument he would polish until Independence Day. By nature and design, he began, the Creator endowed mankind with unalienable rights, but for generations an unholy "confederation" of Roman priests and feudal princes had trapped the people of Europe in ignorance and servility. Eventually Protestant reform and constitutional restraints (especially in England) loosened the grip of these oppressors, but not without a century of turmoil during which the English people manfully defended their ancient rights against Stuart pretensions and papist resurgence. In the early 1600s this desperate struggle with tyranny drove the Puritans to New England: "it was a love of *universal Liberty*," explained Adams, and a "dread" of "the infernal confederacy" of Catholicism and feudalism "that projected, conducted, and accomplished the settlement of America."[4]

To preserve their essential freedoms, Adams's American forebears (the story continues) remodeled both church and state and chartered schools to perpetuate learning, so that ignorance might never again blind people to the work of usurpers. They banished hereditary titles and lordly prerogatives and carefully distinguished religious from civil government. Nevertheless, wealth and power threatened to corrupt men of all classes and temperaments. As communities prospered the dangers reappeared. A famous trio of innovations—the Proclamation of 1763, the Sugar Act of 1764, and the Stamp Act of 1765—signaled new intentions in Whitehall to regulate settlers who until now had done pretty much whatever they liked. The first two struck at habits of transgression—against Indian lands and against the revenue system that sustained the empire. The third placed a tax on paper documents, not oppressive but potentially annoying and the first ever levy imposed directly by the Parliament in England. These "reforms" marked a dangerous new campaign by power against freedom. Thus did Adams embed the transient complaints of postwar merchants and lawyers in a Whiggish tale about the cosmic struggle of good against evil.[5]

We might ask, why on earth would imperial authorities initiate a war against freedom in colonies that had become such a source of pride and wealth for the British nation? Great Britain's staggering war debt along with the acquisition of the former French possessions in North America presented the Grenville ministry both an opportunity and a motive to restructure a sprawling empire that never had been governed coherently. Projected costs for defense and administration proved daunting, and English taxpayers demanded relief. Massachusetts governor Francis Bernard tried to articulate the theory of imperial interdependence that would pacify everyone: primary products from America would pay for imported British manufactures, and everyone would share the cost of governance and defense. Regulations, he admitted, at first would "appear disagreeable," but experience would show the benefits to all. In the meantime, he lectured the Massachusetts assembly, "a respectful submission to the decrees of the parliament" was their "interest, as well as their duty."[6]

Few people shared Bernard's transatlantic perspective. Members of Parliament thought the provincials had been "riding free" for a generation. At the same time colonial elites told counternarratives of how they had created without help the profitable networks of trade that now fattened the empire. Once confident in their birthright protections under Britain's constitutional monarchy, nervous colonists began to worry. They studied scathing attacks on ministerial corruption from a generation earlier, blaming Robert Walpole's patronage machine for empowering the "court" party and corrupting members of Parliament with fees and favors doled out by the King's ministers. Extravagant living in Georgian London had corrupted the independence of English political elites (as well as the sons of wealthy Americans sent there for "refinement"). Addicted to luxury, the ruling class was said by their critics to be "wallowing" in one great "puddle of voluptuousness." Austerity and virtue might keep this urge in check, but not even the perfectly balanced structure of King-in-Parliament could stand if people lacked the will or fortitude to check their baser impulses. Given our natural human "Love of Pleasure and Aversion to Pain," John Adams believed, "all Men would be Tyrants if they could."[7]

Page after painstaking page, for the next ten years, Adams recorded in letters, essays, and diary entries the march of events, refracting them through his interpretive lens, always finding new and compelling proof that tyranny was on the march. Conscious at times of the importance of his own role (his "vanity" he called it), Adams never saw himself as a player advancing an interest. Like the Old Testament prophets, he imagined himself trapped in a calling that would prove his own undoing. Still he soldiered on. When at last the Continental Congress finally voted to declare independence, he pronounced it "the most memorable Epocha, in the History of America." The greatest question "which ever was debated in America" (perhaps "among Men") at last had been settled—correctly: "It is the Will of Heaven, that the two Countries should be sundered forever." Then, characteristically, Adams's excitement turned to foreboding: "It may be the Will of Heaven that America will suffer Calamities still more wasting and Distresses yet more dreadful. . . . The Furnace of Affliction produces Refinement, in States as well as Individuals. And the new Governments we are assuming . . . will require Purification from our Vices, and an Augmentation of our Virtues or they will be no Blessings. The People have unbounded Power. And the People are extreamly [sic] addicted to Corruption and Venality, as well as the Great. I am not without Apprehensions from this Quarter."[8]

Invitations to Rebellion

The road to revolution in America was paved with documents, all of them inviting the people to stand up and defend their liberties—or suffer enslavement at the hands of relentless masters across the sea.[9] The story that follows is complicated, and it will take some time to unravel the threads and tie them back into the culture of exploitation that is our purpose in the end. Pick up the record in April 1765. Rumors about the Stamp Act swept American taverns and coffee houses. "The Folly of England, and Ruin of America," ran a New York headline, soon followed by complaints in Boston, Providence, Philadelphia, and Virginia. Patrick Henry introduced in Virginia's House of Burgesses the first official protest, building his case on the claim that Virginia's first settlers brought with them intact all the "Liberties, Privileges, Franchises, and Immunities" possessed by the British people. Reprinted throughout the summer, Henry's rhetoric provided a theme on which others worked variations. Pennsylvania added the "natural Rights of Mankind" to the "noble Principles of *English* Liberty."[10]

Up and down the coast crowds chanted "Liberty and property! No stamps." Protests devolved into riots; houses were ransacked, furnishings burned, and officials were threatened personally. Quickly the standard argument took shape. First, without consent of the American assemblies the new taxes were unlawful. Americans acknowledged the "burthen of debt" under which Great Britain groaned and claimed they gladly would pay a fair assessment if they were asked. (Easily said, likely untrue.) Second, paying the tax in specie (as required) proved virtually impossible. Third, enforcement in admiralty courts without juries violated English rights reaching back to Magna Carta. The freeholders of Plymouth, Massachusetts, declared their town the "first asylum of liberty" in the wilderness and begged their representatives to record a "full and explicit assertion of our rights," so that generations to come will know that they never would be "slaves to any power on earth."[11]

November 1765 brought the official implementation of the hated stamp tax and a general campaign of nonimportation by which the Americans sought to starve their British partners into repealing the law. Astonishing even themselves, Americans rallied behind the boycotts. Wrote one wag, "Don't imagine your acts of parliament have no power here: They have had the power of working miracles"—of turning a million "good, faithful, and affectionate subjects, as any government ever had, into little less than downright rebels."[12] The Stamp Act crisis had precipitated a general recognition among the colonists that their achievement in creating a prosperous community impressed nobody back home, and that their rights as Englishmen —rights they claimed by history and by nature—*might* be trampled by ambitious new managers of a centralizing empire.

In his careful reconstruction of Boston's response to the Stamp Act, historian Dirk Hoerder portrayed a dangerous game in which elite radical operatives tried (with limited success) to choreograph the violence of angry crowds. Traditional "Pope's Day" companies of working-class men and boys, long accustomed to "rioting" against the popish plot on Guy Fawkes Day, had been groomed and feted by John Hancock to stage the protest on August 14. Led by Ebenezer Mackintosh, "Captain of the Liberty Tree," the mob burned effigies and then pulled down stamp vendor Andrew Oliver's office. Twelve days later a similar crowd destroyed Lieutenant Governor Thomas Hutchinson's new house. Then on November 1 some two thousand angry men turned out to stop the distribution of stamped paper. On December 17 Mackintosh's troops forced Oliver to resign his commission. Operating just beyond the reach of controlling elites, such plebeian operatives poured into talk about "rights" their own resentment of haughty wealth and social pretension aimed primarily—but not exclusively—at imperial officials.[13] In the ears of such recruits promises of "liberty" and "equality" rang true in different registers than those intended by John Adams or John Hancock. The progress of the movement depended on that resonance, blending raw energies from below with sophisticated logic and damage control.

In May 1766 Parliament backed down and replaced the Stamp Act with traditional trade-based revenue duties. Nevertheless, members of Parliament bristled at the idea that the provinces would dictate terms and appended a "Declaratory Act" bluntly asserting their authority over the colonists. What happened next depends on where we look—in Boston, New York, Philadelphia, or the plantation South. In Virginia, nonimportation sparked austerity campaigns intended to encourage self-sufficiency and relieve the burden of consumer debt. In New York, protests blurred in the public mind with anti-impressment actions as well as tenant-landlord conflicts on the great Hudson River estates. In North Carolina, revolutionary politics pitted notorious local magistrates ("courthouse rings") against royal officials, and common persons sometimes found that their would-be liberators posed the greater danger. In Pennsylvania, factional divisions between proprietary elites and conservative Quaker merchants neutralized the voice of the governing class, while radical sentiments among the artisans of Philadelphia simmered in the background.[14] Through it all committed radicals (the "seers" who embraced the original revelation) worked to persuade their neighbors of the persisting monstrous conspiracy against them. Writing as "Rusticus," Pennsylvania's John Dickinson characterized the 1773 Tea Act as a shameless gift to the East India Company, that "corporate" "engine" of "Asian despotism" (three inflammatory tropes in one phrase), now in league with the ministry in Whitehall, that would exercise its "Talents of Rapine, Oppression and Cruelty" to "strip us of our Property." Here again was the image of evil-on-the-march, deployed to frighten the innocent who might see nothing more than trade regulation.[15]

Nothing moved the argument more quickly than British responses to Americans' escalating acts of rebellion. In August 1766 the King's troops cut down New York's "liberty pole," and a crowd of two or three thousand gathered in protest. In March 1770 the presence of "redcoats" in Boston contributed directly to the so-called Boston Massacre, a signal atrocity "proving" the malevolent intentions of royal authorities. In 1772 somebody in Rhode Island attacked the revenue cutter *Gaspee,* burning it to the waterline. Because American juries refused to convict the parties charged with these crimes, Parliament transferred more criminal prosecutions to English courts. This in turn gave constitutional purists such as Adams further proof of an expanding conspiracy. For audacity nothing matched the Boston Tea Party, December 1773, at which "Sons of Liberty" in disguise destroyed 90,000 pounds of East India Company tea (valued at £9,659—nearly $1.7 million today). King George himself condemned the Bostonians. Parliament closed the port in March and then in May suspended local government for all of Massachusetts.[16]

At this point "committees of correspondence" sprang up everywhere, distributing accounts of the brutal repression in Boston and coordinating local responses. An emerging narrative was canonized by Thomas Jefferson's *A Summary View of the Rights of British America* (1774). To the usual list of God-given rights Jefferson added a natural right to colonize "new habitations." Under this "universal law" the Saxon ancestors had taken possession of Britain and by the same process private settlers had seized America from the Indians. England had spent "not a shilling" for "their assistance" in well over a hundred years. Turning to the Boston Tea Party, Jefferson reported that "a number" of Bostonians "threw the tea into the ocean" to register their frustration. If "they did wrong, they were known [untrue] and amenable to the laws of the land." Instead, on the word of "a few worthless ministerial dependents," authorities closed the port of Boston, reducing "in a moment" the whole town from "opulence to beggary." As final proof of imperial abuse, the king sent armed troops to enforce his will, sacrificing "the rights of one part of the empire to the inordinate desires of another." The colonists welcomed "union" with the mother country, but they would not be excluded from the markets of the world nor allow their property to be taxed by any power but their own.[17]

Jefferson's *Summary View* neatly synthesized theoretical claims about liberty while eliding specific, interest-based arguments on which no consensus existed. Were homegrown elites, for example, any more deserving of respect than the "placemen" sent out from London? If the absence of Americans in Parliament nullified that body's authority, did the scarcity of yeomen and tradesmen in local assemblies imply the same? And nothing taxes our tolerance for hypocrisy quite like the persistent complaint about "enslavement" by rebellious Americans who owned, abused, and squeezed labor from Africans by the hundreds of thousands. In this complicated climate of opinions and interests, any mass movement in behalf of liberty had to finesse staggering inconsistencies before it could succeed.[18]

In response to the crisis in Boston, a "Continental Congress" assembled to "consult" on colonial "grievances." Petitions poured in filled with hyperbolic rhetoric: the "fate of this new world, and of unborn millions" hung in the balance, cried the self-styled "guiltless children" of the Puritan fathers from Dedham, Massachusetts.[19] A new agreement called upon colonists not to consume or purchase British goods nor sell to British exporters and placed enforcement of these decrees in the hands of local (self-created) Committees of Observation. By the end of October the Continental Congress had sent declarations to the people of Britain and a formal petition to His Majesty, George III. Through the long weeks required for communications to pass to England and back again, people waited, boycotts continued, radical committees assumed the functions of local government, and militia companies drilled. For safe keeping, colonists stored munitions in country towns, barns, and cellars. In April 1775, on a mission to search for such caches of military stores, British soldiers exchanged fire with the Minutemen near Lexington and Concord. Hostilities began, and nothing so thoroughly justified violence as violence already committed.[20]

A Second Continental Congress convened in haste, and another declaration appeared July 6 explaining the causes for "taking up arms" against the empire. Backs against the wall, delegates now "resolved to die Freemen, rather than to live Slaves."[21] King George declared the American "rebels" out of his protection. Parliament stiffened its demands. The British gave up on Boston and recentered their presence in New York. Individuals of all ranks worked and reworked the private calculus required by revolutionary turmoil: Where am I better off? What is at stake? Whose accounts do I believe? In January 1776 *Common Sense* appeared, in which Thomas Paine focused his attack on monarchy itself. This self-styled "Englishman" found the very idea of royal prerogative absurd, at odds with liberty in every way. Left alone the King would be the "ruin of the Continent." Then came the famous challenge: "Oh ye that love mankind! Ye that dare oppose not only the tyranny but the tyrant, stand forth! Every spot of the old world is over-run with oppression. Freedom hath been hunted round the globe. Asia and Africa have long expelled her.—Europe regards her like a stranger, and England hath given her warning to depart. O receive the fugitive, and pre-pare in time an asylum for mankind."[22]

By May 1776 all hope of reconciliation evaporated and Congress ordered the colonies to create new governments. Then followed the most famous of declarations that laid out "for a candid world" the logical formula delegates had rehearsed a dozen times: "When in the course of human events" it became "necessary" for a people to assume "the separate and equal station to which the Laws of Nature and Nature's God entitle them," the human community deserved an explanation. Boldly centered on a world-historical stage that John Adams had described a full decade before, the Americans now proclaimed the "self-evident" truths that "all men" were "created equal" and "endowed by their Creator" with "unalienable Rights," includ-ing "Life, Liberty and the pursuit of Happiness." Government existed for no other purpose than "to secure" these rights, and when it failed to do so the people had a "duty" to "abolish it" and institute another more likely "to effect their Safety and Happiness."

The Declaration of Independence stood as the pivot on which the creation of the new United States would turn. It ripped the fabric of history, over-turned custom and tradition, and stripped from the powers of the sovereign all purposes other than the liberty and happiness of "the people." The ancient prerogatives of power, birth, class, and station collapsed before the universal claims of liberty, equality, and happiness.[23] Deeply rooted in high-toned aca-demic discourses, these claims nevertheless seemed suddenly transparent, straightforward, approachable by men and women without experience or for-mal schooling. The hierarchical orientation of the early modern British cul-ture, built around inequality, privilege, obligation, patronage, and servitude, *potentially* was laid on its side by these "self-evident" truths. Whether or not the Declaration of Independence intended to establish democracy and economic liberalism, it surely could be read that way.

Popular Initiatives

Freedom or slavery? The rhetoric of protest crafted by the literate elites invited endorsement by less bookish people. Late colonial Americans witnessed every day several forms of bondage that shaped their under-standing of freedom: apprenticeship, indentured servitude, convict labor, imprisonment for debt, and permanent chattel slavery. At stake was inde-pendence, autonomy, and hope for any chance to participate in the material progress of which these settlements were proud. As recalled by Captain Levi Preston, a veteran of the initial Concord confrontation, the core complaint was simple: "We always had been free, and we meant to be free always. They [the Redcoats] didn't mean we should."[24] The resonance of words like "liberty," "equality," and "freedom" mobilized working-class crowds into the ranks of the amorphous "Sons of Liberty." The dialogue of protest and reaction produced dangerous polarization. The call for nonimportation spawned local committees of enforcement that bullied the noncompliant—often by threats of violence. In Falmouth (now Portland, Maine), a gang of insurgents forced a man to dig his own grave and threatened others with firing squads and drownings. Were these men patriots or thugs?[25] Self-appointed actors moved in to guide events, and in the process they helped shape the character and purpose of the movement that culminated in independence.

Consider, for example, Philadelphia. Egged on by the firebrand Thomas Paine, that city's artisans and shopkeepers struggled to advance the cause against conservative Quaker merchants *and* a proprietary party whose paci-fist convictions blocked any movement toward war. At Fourth and Chest-nut, in the Continental Congress, John and Samuel Adams dragged their colleagues toward independence; but Pennsylvania's official delegates mounted a fierce resistance. A radical caucus took to the streets, seizing control of the movement. In May 1776 they quickly elected a constitutional convention. By granting suffrage to all adult males who paid taxes—but disfranchising voters not pledged to independence—the process empaneled an unusually democratic body of ninety-six delegates, mostly farmers, to craft the new frame of government. Entirely unschooled (so said their detractors), this body produced by far the most democratic constitution to come out of the Revolution. Their new government reflected the central conviction that the people should govern themselves.[26]

In Virginia, class and racial stratification created a more treacherous seedbed for the rhetoric of liberation. Long-standing tensions existed between the large landholders and small farmers; between evangelical Bap-tists, straitlaced Presbyterians, and more latitudinarian Anglican worship-pers; between cash-strapped tobacco producers and wheat growers in the

Northern Neck (where slavery's importance was starting to wane). Webs of debt, credit, and patronage knit these disparate interests together in a camaraderie of distress, but the difficulties involved in making war while preaching liberty set them easily at odds with one another. The Continental Congress offered generous cash bounties and land warrants to men who would enlist for the duration of the war, forcing state recruiters to make similar deals to fill regiments at home. In the eyes of governing elites, poor men without slaves and plantations were "most fit" to serve in the army, but compensating such persons with money and land threatened to upset the balance of power. As the war ground on resentments mounted, recruitment faltered, and conscription riots erupted. The promise of liberation conjured up hopes of debt relief, legislative reapportionment, economic progress, the expansion of slavery—or perhaps its elimination? The great planters, whose rebellion could not prevail without these soldiers, faced real prospects of losing control of the movement intended to empower them. And in every gentleman's household where talk turned to "liberty" and "rights," enslaved blacks waited on the orators with open ears.[27]

Farther south the conflicts grew even more pronounced between great wealth and poverty, the virtues of slavery, religious allegiance, taxation, representation, and the fair administration of justice. Local government in North Carolina looked nothing like New England town meetings. Self-important tidewater planters monopolized the patronage and privileges that passed for governance. In the 1760s thousands of so-called Regulators begged imperial authorities for protection from abuses by local magistrates and sheriffs. When the same leading rogues seized the reins of Revolution, common people tried to stay out of the way or sought refuge in loyalty to the Crown—turning on its head the rhetoric of liberty by seeking freedom in the arms of the British. The Revolution in the Carolina backcountry raged for years as a vicious civil war in which the residents were ravished in turn by patriot and loyalist militias. "In few other colonies," concludes historian Roger Ekirch, "did revolutionaries go to war with so little popular support."[28]

Nowhere was the language of liberation more meaningful and confusing than among the African Americans. In April 1775, just days after the Minutemen squared off with the British at Lexington Green, Virginia's royal governor, Lord Dunmore, seized the powder magazine at Williamsburg in order to disarm the patriot insurgency. When the radical planters persisted, Dunmore threatened to free their slaves "and reduce the City of Williamsburg to Ashes." The situation represented two things white southern rebels feared most: enslavement for themselves and freedom for their bondsmen and women. In November 1775 Dunmore made good half his threat by proclaiming freedom for "servants, Negroes, or others" who would take up arms against the rebels. At least six thousand Virginia slaves liberated themselves by running away (contemporary estimates ran wildly higher); about one-third died, one-third fled with the British after Yorktown, and one-third were returned to their masters. Nationwide perhaps twenty thousand persons took up arms with the British while thousands more just ran away, forcefully reminding the master class that their "hands" were people with good reason to hate the violent plantation economy. At the same time free blacks and even some slaves also heard the rhetoric of liberation as an invitation to advance their position, not by running away, but by joining the American cause. Nearly every state saw black soldiers fighting on the patriot side. Most were offered freedom—and many such promises were broken when the emergency passed. In Rhode Island, New Hampshire, Massachusetts, and Vermont the process of abolition began during the war, suggesting possibilities for a more open society under new republican regimes. And even in Virginia, blacks with an ear to the ground (such as Gabriel Prosser) might have believed that liberation would extend to them in the end.[29]

During the War for Independence women stepped up to manage farms, shops, and counting houses on behalf of their absent fathers, husbands, and sons. Despite a legal and cultural framework that supposedly buried women in "civil death" inside the households of men, such flexible transgressions had been common for generations; the question now arose, would equality extend fully to women? In politics the answer primarily was "no," but in the marketplace women often found more room for independent action. Household production of butter and eggs, clothing, and textiles supplied demands created by war and nonimportation, and these contributions would swell in the postwar years. On the cultural level, republicanism required virtuous citizens, and women were thought to be the natural mentors of the coming generation. John Adams may have dodged Abigail's famous warning to "remember the Ladies," but the question of women's rights could not be dismissed forever.[30]

Loyalists, of course, were branded as the enemies of freedom and traitors to their country, but until at least 1774 most Americans were loyal British subjects, and even after independence was declared between a third and a half remained uncommitted. Some loyalists doubtless shared liberal and republican leanings but did not see the current rebellion as just or necessary. Harsh treatment of "Tories" (including bodily violence and property destruction) sometimes convinced other persons that the rebels cared more for personal gain than for justice, which did not bode well for the long term. In many places—especially New York and Philadelphia—the nearness of British troops, simultaneously threatening reprisals and spending gold and silver coin for sustenance, turned the heads of Americans who doubted if the patriot cause could prevail. Over twenty thousand colonists took up arms to serve the Crown, and one estimate puts the general proportion of true loyalists at 20 percent of white adults. Blacks and Indians favored imperial authorities whenever they offered better prospects for freedom and security.[31]

Long before these issues could be clarified, before the goals and objectives of revolutionaries could be ascertained, before realistic prospects for success could be measured, most individuals in the colonies faced the necessity of choosing—for or against—the promise of liberation. What they were getting they could not know. Staging a revolt against the world's most powerful empire surely was a fool's bet; but what if it were true, that history and justice and nature were on the side of the revolutionaries? Sooner or later most Americans confronted the intimidations of a radical committee, or the demands of British troops, or the forced "requisitions" of supplies by patriot forces (who may or may not have paid for them). There were many wars within the War for Independence, and few Americans experienced the conflict as a whole. In the end, faced with a choice framed starkly as "freedom or slavery," most Americans embraced freedom in the fervent hope that it meant *some* of what they thought it might mean. The status quo ante already was gone. At least the revolutionaries promised self-government dedicated (they said) to securing the rights and fostering the happiness of people.

The Magic of Self-Creation

War and rebellion forced the colonists to seek convergence, but the process of state making passed into many hands in thirteen different capitals (fourteen counting Vermont). Independence created, not a nation, but a federation of sovereign states, each determined to preserve its own interests, and many leaders at the time (including Jefferson) saw the work in the states as the most important. Written constitutions—novelties in British political experience—proved to be the instruments by which Americans hoped to establish durable governing structures. Ad hoc committees could disrupt the old order well enough, but for revolution to transcend mere rebellion they must perform extraordinary acts of self-creation, produce workable new regimes, and then close the window of revolution. They were building an asylum for liberty: it had better appear to be legitimate.

In November 1775 Richard Henry Lee asked John Adams for advice as Virginia prepared to craft a new constitution, and Adams's response eventually developed into a pamphlet, "Thoughts on Government" (1776). The goal, he began, was to create an "Empire of laws and not of Men." Right structures alone could check the natural human tendency to abuse power. Into the republican ideal of representative self-government Adams poured ideas familiar to English political science: checks and balances, separation of powers, bicameralism. Assign legislation to an elected representative assembly: it must be "in Miniature, an exact Portrait of the People at large. It should think, feel, reason, and act like them." To minimize the "fits" of caprice and "absurd Judgments" to which such bodies were prone, erect a small upper house or council. Add independent judges, appointed for life, and a governor elected by the popular assembly. Allow the governor a veto over legislation but return him to the electors annually and limit his tenure in office. Expect amendments to supply "Defects which Experience may point out."[32]

By styling his house of representatives "an exact Portrait of the People at large," Adams opened the door to radical interpretations of republicanism that courted both majority rule and interest-based politics. Nothing could be farther from his personal ideal, for he surely was the least sanguine of the founders about the stock of popular virtue. For republics to work, he argued, people must be happy "to sacrifice their private Pleasures, Passions, and Interests" whenever these competed with "the Rights of society." But where he looked for virtue he saw mostly greed: his neighbors were "addicted to Commerce." On the eve of independence, Adams's confidence in popular rule all but collapsed: "The most difficult and dangerous Part" of this business, he concluded, was "to contrive some Method for the Colonies to glide insensibly from under the old Government, into a peaceful and contented submission to new ones."[33]

To glide insensibly into submission? Adams never succeeded in squaring the rhetoric of self-empowerment with his ardent desire for order, deference, and control. His assessment was correct: having called the people to violence, it would be hard to restore order. Men of property surely expected to guide the process, but for the "lower orders" the stench of corruption hung about colonial elites as well as British lackeys. Given the chance, some Americans expected to dismantle the barriers to wealth and power that typified the old regime. In their eyes, liberty meant freedom, and self-government meant governing on behalf of yourself! In the past what had "governors" done but advance their own interests and those of their friends? The objective of government was happiness, and nothing made people happier than wealth and personal autonomy.

To begin this extraordinary business the Continental Congress charged provincial assemblies to write their own new constitutions. These state constitutions varied widely in detail but shared important features. Most declared the sole purpose of government to be the "benefit, protection, and security" of the people. Most constitutions outlawed hereditary emoluments, arbitrary executive actions, the suspension of laws or courts, and the awarding of special class privileges. Jury trials were guaranteed in criminal causes and often for property disputes as well. Most bills of rights protected free speech, assembly, protest, and shielded citizens from arbitrary arrest. North Carolina went out of its way to state that "property in the soil" was an "essential right" of the people—and then laid claim to a vast frontier region based on their charter from Charles II. Pennsylvania's framers considered but rejected a plank denouncing vast accumulations of land as "destructive of the Common Happiness." Each new government claimed for itself exclusive control over internal affairs, police, and taxation.[34]

Every state constitution called for "free" and frequent (usually annual) elections for lower-house representatives and sometimes for the whole roster of government offices. Persons without property—tenants, servants, employees, women, and children—were thought to lack civic independence; as a result most states set property requirements for voting and holding office. In Virginia, "evidence of permanent common interest" meant twenty-five acres and a house. More commonly the bar was set at fifty acres, or total estates of £20, £30, or £50. Pennsylvania chose to throw open the franchise to taxpaying white male adults (and their adult sons), while Vermont dropped the bar altogether. Determined to disfranchise the idle and profligate, Massachusetts's framers in 1780 reversed the broad "taxpayer" suffrage of 1776 and set the threshold at £3 annual income or £60 estate, barring in some towns nearly half the population.[35]

Who should stand for election in these new self-governing republics? In every case residency topped the list of candidate qualifications: no absentee placemen. John Adams's charge that assemblies resemble an "exact portrait of the people at large" suggested literal, actual representation—farmer for farmer, merchant for merchant; but Adams and others also wanted assemblies comprising the "most wise, sensible, and discreet" people. Pennsylvania said so but trusted broad suffrage and annual elections to guarantee it. Maryland said so and erected barriers, ensuring that only men of property would occupy high offices: £500 to stand for House, £1,000 for Senate, and £5,000 for governor! Common men had risen to prominence during the Revolution, which threatened old habits of deference. In Massachusetts, the wealthy John Hancock, sitting in the governor's chair, tried to silence Concord representative Joseph Hosmer, only to be schooled by the cabinetmaker-turned-legislator on the rights of the people to be heard. In South Carolina, tavern keeper William Thompson found himself expelled from the assembly for insulting the lordly John Rutledge. Instead of deferring to his "betters," Thompson campaigned for reelection, insisting that Rutledge and his kind, by their "pride, influence, ambition, connections, wealth and political principles" ought to be "excluded" from "*public confidence*."[36]

Finally, where was sovereignty—that indivisible wellspring of power that maintained order in society by curbing the autonomy of rogue individuals? Traditionally vested in government itself, sovereignty found its first postwar home in legislative assemblies. Governors enjoyed nothing like traditional Old World executive prerogatives, and judges found themselves checked by the presence of a jury. Further structural reforms suggested that real sovereignty resided outdoors in the hands of "the people." One thing that made this clear was a unique new approach to state making that helped to limit the disruptive impact of revolutionary self-creation: constitutions would be made by extraordinary conventions and then approved by plebiscite or special ratifying conference. First seen in Massachusetts in 1780, the process soon defined the difference between ordinary governance and the extraordinary exercise of sovereignty implied by the right of revolution.[37]

If sovereignty rested with the people in their states, what was the status of the union of those states? Agonizing as it was to arrive at independence, the forging of a framework for the union proved even more vexing for the Continental Congress. States like Delaware, New Jersey, and Rhode Island understandably feared the enormous weight of Virginia, Massachusetts, and

New York. From the start they had demanded that each state cast one vote. On the other hand, the large states controlled most of the wealth and population, which might be pillaged by demands of the smaller states. Apportionment by population raised the thorny question of how to count black slaves—as property or residents? Virginia, North Carolina, Connecticut, and New York claimed vast interior lands based on "sea-to-sea" language in their charters, a patrimony not shared by Massachusetts, Pennsylvania, and the smaller coastal states. Any power lodged in the Congress over the union as a whole threatened to "nationalize" unique advantages cherished by the states.[38]

The charter that finally emerged in late 1777—the Articles of Confederation—granted Congress power over little more than war and diplomacy. The new "league of friendship" could not lay taxes or command the people except through agencies of the states. Congress gained control of foreign policy, coinage, weights and measures, armed forces, and the post office. Comity protected the property and civil rights of citizens passing from state to state. No executive administered the union; instead, a "Committee of the States" could be assigned such recess powers as "from time to time" were deemed "expedient." Nothing could be altered in this plan of union without the consent of every state. Finally, no one could miss the significance of Article II: "Each state retains its sovereignty, freedom, and independence, and every power, jurisdiction, and right, which is not by this Confederation expressly delegated to the United States, in Congress assembled."[39]

Implementations

Depending on who you ask, the so-called critical period that followed the peace in 1783 saw either the flowering of freedom and self-government or proof of the folly of democracy. Thirteen sovereign states (plus Vermont) struggled to govern while keeping at bay the radical impulse to impose outcomes by decree. To finance the rebellion, American states together with the Congress had spent millions in borrowed money, issued mountains of paper securities, and promised their creditors, their neighbors, and themselves to make it all good at the end. Among the traditional duties of the sovereign, now placed in popular hands, were the power to tax, to create money, and to maintain courts of law to administer justice and protect private property. Nothing would test these new self-created regimes so painfully in the 1780s as the intersection of these three obligations on the question of public finance. The credibility of newly minted republican states left much to be desired, and the value of American securities had depreciated wildly during the war. With peace came the acid test of America's potential: could these new self-governing republics restart their economies and collect enough taxes to service their debts? If they could they might expect, in time, to enjoy all the benefits of independence they had imagined at the outset; if not, they would sink into disgraceful poverty and be reabsorbed into one of the great empires that still dominated their world.[40]

Three postwar economic realities pressed hard on the new states. First, local economies had been deranged by wartime spending, destruction, and neglect as thousands of farmers and tradesmen spent years in military service. Simply rebuilding the prewar farms, workshops, and markets, and replacing runaway slaves required significant infusions of capital. Second, Great Britain closed to America's merchants their lucrative Caribbean markets, at least until such time as American debtors settled accounts with their British creditors. Third, the circulation of gold and silver coin, never sufficient under colonial rule, proved utterly inadequate to the multiple demands of the American import-export trade, domestic investment, taxation, and debt service. In the harsh morning-after light of peace, the Americans faced the loss of many advantages and an additional new burden of debts that would require far greater levels of taxation than George III ever imagined.[41]

By the mid-1780s, this combination of high taxes and bad money threatened the viability of common rural households in every state. If freeholders lost their farms the whole purpose of the revolution was subverted. This left new regimes scrambling to find solutions. In several states the demand for inflationary currencies grew irresistible.[42] Another relief strategy centered on restructuring the debt. The total bill, both state and continental, including face value of fiat currency, stood around £165,000,000, (in dollars nearly $500,000,000) but the practical value of much of this paper had fallen between 50 and 99 percent. Mustering out soldiers took home pay that bought only pennies' worth of the tools, livestock, and seed they required to restart their family economies. Local shopkeepers hurriedly dumped such paper (at another discount) to restock their shelves. Eventually the interest-bearing part of the public debt drifted into the hands of a tiny class of "speculators" whose £100 bond may have cost them only £20, £30, or £50. If they drew 5 percent interest in gold on face value they earned an effective yield between 10 and 25 percent plus double their money or more when the bonds eventually matured.[43] Proposals abounded for minimizing this windfall transfer of wealth from "the people" to the "speculators." Some offered redemption at market value rather than face; some paid interest on the purchase price instead of face; one scheme proposed using tax money not to pay interest but to purchase the paper and retire it. Such proposals appealed to hard-pressed taxpayers, but creditors howled at every whiff of default. To common people caught in the squeeze it seemed profoundly unjust, but to the owners of capital the prospect of repudiation threatened another sacred aspect of liberty—the right to property.[44]

Whether we blame these conditions on bad government or not, the impression developed by the mid-1780s—in England and Europe and among American gentlemen of property and "vision"—that America was falling apart. Every year more seats in state government were filled by individuals whose experience in politics began with revolutionary committees or militia service and whose interests and perspectives seemed narrow and cramped. The simplest things could not get done—like signing an agreement between Virginia and Maryland to share improvements in the river that marked their boundary. In early 1785, five delegates from those two states gathered at George Washington's home, Mount Vernon, to hammer out a deal for the Potomac River. Free to negotiate, away from the suspicious gaze of every popular faction, these confident gentlemen crafted an agreement—and rediscovered the joy of deliberating in private. Buoyed by the experience, James Madison pressed for a wider convention in Annapolis where a similar process might yield further interstate cooperation.[45]

On the eve of the Annapolis Convention, armed rebellion broke out in rural Massachusetts, proving (at least for nervous elites) that violence still might endanger legitimate government. Massachusetts tax delinquents watched as sheriffs auctioned off their meagre estates to urban gentlemen who picked up land for dimes on the dollar. None of this was technically illegal (the same might be said of the Tea Act), but it struck the victims as clearly wrong! Protests fell on deaf ears in the state assembly in Boston. Finally, in August 1786, with cries about taxation and representation, these veterans of the earlier rebellion, now led by militia captain Daniel Shays, closed the courts to stop what they saw as abuses as bad as anything done by British authorities. To their astonishment, even Sam Adams denounced them. A *Massachusetts* army put down their rebellion. Reflecting on the news in Paris, Thomas Jefferson famously dismissed it as a dustup: "a little rebellion now and then is a good thing." Madison found it rather more worrisome. George Washington was "mortified beyond expression" by the chaos that darkened "the brightest morn that ever dawned upon any country." He wanted power to fix it.[46]

That power would come from a third convention, called by the Congress, that gathered the following May in Philadelphia. Almost before anybody could see what was happening, these delegates closed their doors, locked out the press, swore each other to secrecy, and embarked on a total restructuring of national power.[47] James Madison arrived at Philadelphia with a formal plan in hand. The gift of self-government he thought was being squandered in the states on narrow, selfish, local concerns. He wanted a super republic laid over the top of the states, creating a continental stage where the impulse to govern was focused on the great and pressing issues, not petty class envy. In substantial agreement were Washington, John Adams, Alexander Hamilton, John Jay, and John Dickinson. Bitterly opposed were friends of decentralized control—including such original radicals as Richard Henry Lee and Patrick Henry (who reportedly said he smelt a rat).[48]

Throughout the long hot summer formal debates occupied the delegates' days and boardinghouse scheming filled their nights. Madison's call for a national Congress based on population triggered the opposition of smaller states. Apportionment raised the intractable question of how to count slaves, until the bizarre "three-fifths compromise" broke that deadlock. Key provisions strengthened national control over money and shielded property and contracts from encroachment by the states. Federal courts gained authority to review statutes and rulings in states that strayed outside the bounds of "law and justice" (Madison's words). Through it all George Washington sat in stony silence, sanctioning the process by his presence but expressing no opinion. By August, tired and disgusted, the delegates sent a draft to the "committee on style" which inserted a preamble shedding light on the framer's ambitions: "We the people" (not the states) intended by this new Constitution to "establish justice," "insure domestic tranquility," "promote the General Welfare" and "secure the Blessings of Liberty." What followed was a charter that placed custody of these things squarely in the hands of a national republic. If you believed that the blessings of liberty were being wasted in democratic pandering, a "more perfect

Union" promised welcome relief. However, if you did not share the elites' concerns the new Constitution marked a breathtaking retreat from popular government and local control.[49]

The ratification of the Federal Constitution generated one more torrent of printed debate. Friends of the Constitution seized the high ground by calling themselves "Federalists" and insisting (against all evidence) that the new regime was *not* a national government. Opponents—and their numbers were formidable—denounced the work of the convention as illegal and unwarranted. The Anti-Federalists attacked the strong bias in the Constitution toward commerce and contracts and against legislative interference with markets. Had there been a single class division separating men of commerce from farmers and artisans this factor might have doomed the Federalist cause; but the Atlantic economy touched so many Americans in different ways that no such simple distinction obtained. Seen in prospect (with no real experience yet to test the claims), freer trade and market forces appealed to many whose experience to date had been tarnished by the corruption and distortions of mercantilist policies. In the end the promise of better government, stability, and maybe prosperity carried the day (aided by skillful political management). In 1789 the First Federal Congress assembled to launch another new United States.[50]

Novus Ordo Seclorum

In the minds of its admirers, the American Revolution was *supposed* to usher in a new order for the ages. After Christianity, proclaimed the English radical scientist/philosopher Richard Price, the American Revolution was "the most important step in the progressive course of human improvement." It had planted a "refuge" for the oppressed of the world and laid the foundation for the "seat of liberty, science and virtue," from which "these sacred blessings" might spread until the time "when kings and priests" had no more "power to oppress." Happily poised in a stage of development between "the *savage* and the *refined*," America's sturdy yeomen enjoyed the perfect balance.[51] Price captured well the magnitude of the experiment. Would the Americans build a utopian republic based on harmony, virtue, and community interest? Or would they foster a liberal democracy, freeing without limit the self-interested ambitions of the people? Was there safety enough in democratic procedures, or must the new regimes promote specific outcomes as well? How elastic was the promise of equality? Did it mean only equality before the law? Or did it extend to matters of wealth and station? Did it undermine the social and cultural divides that for centuries had separated gentlemen from commoners, governors from the governed? Was the promise of equality flexible enough to include adult men without property? (Pennsylvania and Vermont said yes.) Women? (New Jersey briefly allowed them to vote.) African or Native Americans?[52]

And what of property, the third leg of the Lockean triad along with life and liberty? Price referenced with approval the assault on private property implied in Sir Thomas More's *Utopia*, but Locke and others treated property as central to liberty itself. The "spirit of Commerce," said Philadelphia banker Robert Morris, required that "Property be sacred." In a popular republic, if "safety and happiness" (Jefferson's words) were slipping away, could the people restore them by legislation? Could they do so by expropriation? Did the founding generation think of markets as neutral alternatives to corrupt old networks of power and influence? Two new systems of power lay before them—popular government and incipient capitalism. Both claimed to be rooted in "nature," both celebrated "liberty" and "equality," both promised relief from whatever discomforts had plagued the cultures of the Old World. And in 1789 both remained in embryonic stages of development so that only the vaguest contours of their promise could be seen by men and women forced in real time to make decisions in this moment of liberation.[53]

A great menu of possibilities set the agenda for American politics after independence. As early as 1778 Charleston's David Ramsay gave voice to the most persistent vision of where America was heading: "Our Independence will naturally fill our country with inhabitants. Where life, liberty, and property are well secured, and where land is easily and cheaply obtained, the natural increase of people will much exceed" all calculations. Lured by "our excellent forms of government . . . thousands and millions of the virtuous peasants, who now groan beneath tyranny and oppression in three quarters of the globe" would now flock to "Happy America."[54] Thomas Jefferson shared the same vision, imagining a yeoman's paradise spreading across the continent for centuries to come. Jefferson saw no advantage in promoting capitalist development, commerce, and especially manufacturing. Let the workshops remain in Europe.[55]

James Madison approached this agrarian goal from a slightly different angle. He believed it was Great Britain, not the infant United States that faced a dangerous dependency in the new Atlantic economy. Americans could do without "luxuries" and "superfluities" imported from England, but the former mother country absolutely *needed* American food and resources. On this logic Madison tried to secure reciprocal trade agreements that favored cooperative partners (like France) and punished the British with their mercantilist system of domination and control. His ultimate goal was free trade and international division of labor, not integrated development and national competition. Prosperity for agrarian Americans would flow from exploiting their role as primary producers and eschewing the temptation to compete with the Old World as equals.[56]

Alexander Hamilton saw the agrarian model as a recipe for permanent dependency, even recolonization. *Real* nations paid their debts, protected their commerce, and developed their own industrial potential. As Washington's treasury secretary, Hamilton drew up aggressive plans to repair public credit and restart the domestic economy. His intention to fund public debts at par immediately split the Congress and the country into warring factions. Madison wanted to discriminate between "worthy" original creditors and the claims of latter-day speculators who stood to gain an astonishing windfall. Impractical, countered Hamilton; world markets would respect only dollar-for-dollar payments. By funding at par, and by assuming the debts of the states as well, Hamilton could soak up all the depreciated paper and disable forever the speculators' games that had originated in the states. To complement the impact of his funding plan, Hamilton proposed a national bank through which this mountain of debt could be transformed into money and provide the economy with much needed circulating banknotes. Economic growth would follow, prosperity would spread, taxes could be paid, interest payments made, bondholders would exchange their gold-bearing paper for more profitable shares in the national bank (dividends payable in banknotes), and gold would be freed up for international commerce. Thus the republic could be launched as a respectable trading partner that nobody could ignore.[57]

Partisans quickly realigned themselves from Federalists and Anti-Federalists to supporters or opponents of Hamilton's program, especially his national bank. Opponents saw the funding scheme as a conscious fraud (made worse by rumors of treasury officials scooping up bargain securities). The assumption of state debts simply enlarged the scope of the swindle. The proposed national bank—controlled by private investors—reproduced in the heart of liberty's republic that hated engine of the British fiscal-military state, the Bank of England. In 1792, a hysterical Jefferson pleaded with President Washington to block these stockjobbing harbingers of monarchy. Rebuffed with a presidential scolding, Jefferson fled, convinced that Washington had joined with the enemies of freedom. But funding, assumption, and the bank were not merely tools of selfish class interest. Urban artisans, many farmers, exporters of food and commodities, all depended to some degree on commerce, and many welcomed the prospect of stability and reentry into Atlantic markets.[58]

The limits of Hamilton's modern capitalist credentials can be seen in his capstone proposal to promote industrial development. Hamilton believed that only by erecting their own enterprises could Americans meet their former masters as equals in the Atlantic marketplace, but he envisioned no liberal free-for-all. Intentional public investment and control must guide the development of manufacturing, shipping, and financial services. Some of America's cities already were "pretty fully peopled," and in such places idle children, women, and paupers might be set to work immediately in manufacturing establishments. Hamilton proposed a Society for Establishing Useful Manufactures, a chartered corporation in Paterson, New Jersey, closely tied to the political leaders in the national government and capitalized with federal bonds and United States Bank stock. Controlled by the governing elites, this kind of intentional, hothouse development might stimulate growth without unleashing the reckless competitive forces that in England made industrialization so distasteful. In short, Hamilton proposed a republican neo-mercantilism that promised liberty, stability, *and* economic progress.[59]

Here we begin to see the importance of liberation to the emerging culture of exploitation. Liberty bestowed on the corporate body of the people—directed by statesmen duly elected—promised collective progress without dissolving the hierarchical bonds that held people together in harmonious interdependence. Some elite revolutionary leaders, especially among the nationalists (Washington, Hamilton, and Madison chief among them), imagined an orderly process that threw off the stultifying influence of British mercantile objectives and channeled the energies of a restless people into new paths of national development. Other postwar statesmen, rising from the middle ranks in state and local politics, envisioned a more thoroughgoing flattening of rank and privilege together with a general liberation that encouraged citizens to set the political agenda and pursue their own economic interests. It remained to be seen how deeply liberation would revolutionize society itself.

With the new government in place after 1789, Washington and Hamilton moved to close the window of revolution and secure the fledgling new Union. Their success created a rupture among the nationalists that Madison and Jefferson quickly transformed into a partisan movement they liked to call "Republican." Everyone insisted that organized parties threatened legitimate government, but Jefferson excused his own movement as distinguishing his group of "honest men" from the "roques" and "monarchists" supporting Hamilton's measures. Meanwhile, back in Philadelphia and other centers of popular democracy, political clubs sprang up to nominate candidates and mobilize voters in ways that reminded elites too much of Committees of Observation, Correspondence, and Safety. In his 1796 "Farewell Address," George Washington called on such "self-created societies" to cease their agitations and retire, safe in the knowledge that republican institutions already were in good hands. Self-creation could stand down. But it was not to be. Washington's successor, John Adams, experienced more bitter partisan rancor, and even after his electoral victory in 1800, Thomas Jefferson proved unable to control the unwieldy political game by which he had unseated the Federalists.[60]

By the turn of the nineteenth century, the Americans' "new world order" showed promise, but nobody knew if they could manage the flow of consequences from liberation. If they agreed on nothing else, ordinary Americans now saw themselves as authors of their own achievements. They had learned that private or small-scale collective actions held the key to getting what they wanted. In the past when authorities exerted control—from the courthouse, provincial capital, or Whitehall itself—the experience had not been positive. Authority lodged in American hands did not automatically seem more reliable or benign. Talk of liberty and independence drifted toward a libertarian sense of the term: freedom *from* government more than freedom to govern well. As rebels they had drawn on old community values—Pope's Day rhetoric and the strategies of "misrule" by which their English ancestors called to account neglectful governors. But in the early American republic the logic of freedom, the language of nature and natural rights, the abundance of resources, the habits of the people to seek, demand, or take what they wanted, pulled such traditional impulses away from collective class or village attachments and toward acquisitive individualism. Liberation, it seemed, could be corrosive of virtue and the common good.[61]

CHAPTER 5

Inventory

EXTRAVAGANT PRETENSIONS ACCOMPANIED THE thrill of liberation and helped propel America's founding generation through the process
of rebellion and into an unscripted future made possible by Independence.
Two college bards started very early to celebrate (in epic verse) the "Rising
Glory of America." Hugh Henry Breckenridge thought he saw unfolding
"the final stage where time shall introduce . . . glorious works of high invention and of wond'rous art." Philip Freneau piled on visions of a paradise
renewed: no "dangerous tree with deadly fruit" to tempt the "second
Adam"; no thistle, thorn, or brier to curse the husbandman; no fevers or
disease. Timothy Dwight proclaimed all science, art, philosophy, religion,
and history would be fulfilled in an empire blessed with earth's "richest
treasures," knit together with roads and canals, where war, rage, and discord would expire. Celebrating ratification of the Constitution in 1788,
Aaron Hall of Keene, New Hampshire, hailed the Federal Union as the
"cap-stone of the great American Empire." Providential blessings—the land
itself and "Liberty"—marked a moment when Americans could turn
the course of history. In the midst of perpetual fetes, argues historian
David Waldstreicher, Americans found no shortage of overwrought sentiments, both sacred and profane, with which to define their collective good
fortune.[1]

Such hyperventilating verses soon gave way to more prosaic treatments
of the tasks facing the new United States. In order to facilitate the "rising"
of this empire, Americans needed better information than anybody yet possessed about the extent of the country and its natural resources. This quest

for information continued a process that had blossomed near the end of the colonial era, but now the point of view had changed completely. The achievement of liberation energized the impulse to catalog environmental riches and profoundly advanced the pace and scope of the process of commodification. Possessed of clear title (in European terms) to everything east of the Mississippi (between Canada and Spanish Florida), Americans approached their material bounty with a providential sense of mission and a burgeoning confidence in science and the "progress of the arts." Restless citizens believed what lay before them belonged, not to a vengeful God, nor to the bitter remnants of indigenous peoples, nor to the monarchs of Europe whose claims until now had justified their presence on the continent. No, it belonged to "We the People," neither subjects nor servants, but sovereigns one and all, entitled (so they believed) to seize, possess, develop, extract, transform, improve, and market whatever their new country offered. This they understood both as a personal, private *right* to seek their fortunes and simultaneously a collective obligation to do so. No longer interested in Winthrop's holy "city on a hill," these Americans set out to develop an altogether different prototype, an "empire of liberty."[2]

An American Geography

Literally before the ink was dry on the Treaty of Paris (1783) Americans were taking inventory, sizing up the storehouse of things they had to work with as they embarked on a grand experiment in freedom and self-government. In 1780, a French diplomat in Philadelphia sent a questionnaire to correspondents in each of the thirteen states, the fruits of which he hoped would facilitate his own projected "history" of the infant republic. Thomas Jefferson responded with his book-length "Notes on the State of Virginia." Jeremy Belknap launched a massive three-volume history of New Hampshire, and James Sullivan wrote a smaller work on the district of Maine. Jedediah Morse moved as quickly as anyone to inventory all that was "known" about for the new nation. This Yale-trained clergyman and educator set to work on *The American Geography* (1789), an expanded second edition of which appeared in 1792. Drawing on his own travels as well as correspondence with government officials, colleagues in the ministry, and learned gentlemen of science, Morse assembled over four hundred pages on the United States (plus one hundred thirty more on the rest of the globe and the cosmos). The book followed a well-worn pattern, laying down boundaries and terrestrial locations, describing climate, soil, and natural resources, Native and settler populations, government, economic productions, history, and commerce. It came with decent maps—always in demand and hard to find.[3]

Starting with New England, Morse worked his way down the coastline listing (as had been done since the voyages of discovery) the "merchantable commodities" found in the undeveloped landscape. Valuable timber, especially mast trees, topped the list in New Hampshire and Maine. Another critical topic was climate, and Morse denied that New England was dangerously cold. Many inhabitants of Maine lived "ninety years," while in New Hampshire "the cold" braced the human constitution, rendering "the laboring people healthful and robust." Noting other advantageous features, such as rivers and harbors, Morse quickly turned to the fruits of settler enterprise, such as rich valleys cleared and sown to pasture, grain, or potatoes, livestock raised, fish stocks harvested and dried, naval stores processed from forest resources. Massachusetts, Rhode Island, and Connecticut stood out for their rising commercial importance, venting country produce (especially foodstuffs and livestock bound for the island economies of the Caribbean), converting West Indian molasses into rum, and trading that rum for the slaves, manufactures, and bills of exchange that powered the Atlantic economy. Accolades went to Boston for societies promoting "useful knowledge and human happiness," to Rhode Island for "fine women," cattle, and race horses, and to Connecticut for its "industrious sagacious husbandmen." Excellent prospects and comfortable subsistence induced the Connecticut yeoman to "marry young," toil "cheerfully through the day," eat the "fruit of his own labour with a gladsome heart," thank God for "his daily blessings," retire to bed, and while there contribute to the "amazing increase of inhabitants in this state."[4]

Agriculture preoccupied the geographer because well over 90 percent of Americans earned their living directly from the land. Grazing struck Morse as the ideal husbandry for rocky northern New England, while grain and dairy flourished wherever topography allowed. New York came in for heavy criticism as being "half a century behind" its neighboring states. Repeating slanders published earlier by Swedish naturalist Peter Kalm, Morse blamed the Dutch founders of New York, first for locking up huge estates against the enterprise of common farmers, second, for a narrow "avarice" that kept Dutch farmers from embracing innovations, and third because an adequate subsistence came so easily where land was cheap and plentiful that industry did not develop. This last point, echoing complaints made famous by William Byrd's tales from frontier North Carolina, grew more important as one moved south and west, where rich new lands and a temperate climate rewarded men of little ambition. Kalm had called out Pennsylvania farmers for their abusive waste of natural fertility, and Morse repeated the charge. Virginia and points south came in for far harsher assessments due to slavery and tobacco culture, both of which impressed this Yankee clergyman as disgusting and immoral. As heat, swamps, and pine-barrens replaced the rolling hills of the Mid-Atlantic, Morse found ever-greater fault with the progress and prospects of the southern states.[5]

Progress in terms of manufactures and the useful arts represented a second marker indicating the health of American communities. Again, Boston and Philadelphia clearly led the nation in both, but New York City showed sudden promise since "the dawn of our empire" (meaning Independence). Never a simple agrarian, Morse balanced his appreciation for the sustainability of rural virtues with a keen recognition that progress gathered energy from industry and innovation. Reflecting the popular "stages-of-growth" perspective of his era, Morse reprinted a schematic description from Benjamin Rush in which the first two waves of primitive pioneers were displaced by a third group of inveterate improvers who perfected their own farms and farming habits, then turned their attention to schools, churches, and social institutions. This was the ideal process of colonization; its "weapons" would be the "implements of husbandry," and its virtues "industry and oeconomy." Happy would it be for mankind, Morse opined, "if the kings of Europe would adopt this mode of extending their territories," putting an end to the "dreadful connection" between "war and poverty," between "conquest and desolation."[6]

Not surprisingly, given the northern bias of this geographer, tobacco culture came in for heavy criticism, much of it grounded in assessments made by planters themselves that their crop could not be sustained into the distant future. Demanding, fussy, and labor intensive, tobacco bound the planters in tight dependency on slave labor while the plant's ruinous impact on land forced them perpetually to seek fresh soil. Virginia's output had peaked, by one report, in 1758 and had been in decline ever since. Stagnant prices did not reward any program of manuring that might rejuvenate hard-used fields. Yet oversupply persisted because planters snapped up windfall profits on rich new acres in North Carolina, Georgia, and across the western country. Parts of Kentucky appeared to be fertile beyond belief, certain to flood markets with more tobacco. Savvy husbandmen, said many a critic in the postwar Chesapeake, would shift to wheat production and grazing, which practiced together might preserve the fertility of arable lands. Such mixed farming promised modest, not extravagant, returns that favored smaller producers and rendered large gangs of slaves uneconomical. This might have marked a moment of fundamental change for farming in the Chesapeake, but most planters chose to work within the systems of wealth, social status, and political power that had grown up with the slave-based economy.[7]

Slavery itself was seen by many as a blight on the rising glory of America. Not just Quakers and New England moralists but also planters (such as Washington, Jefferson, or young James Madison) thought that colonial system of exploitation fit poorly with republican values. The shortage of towns and commercial services, the scattered nature of rural settlements, the yawning gap between the rich and the poor in southern societies, and the lack of attention to cultivating progress in the useful arts—all readily was blamed on the slave-based path to colonial riches. Morse roundly condemned the influence of slavery on both the enslaved and the whites in whose interests they suffered. Everywhere that slavery prevailed, pride infected the spirit of the master race, fostering sloth, ignorance, "luxury, dissipation, and extravagance." "The absolute authority which is exercised" by masters over the enslaved "too much favours a haughty supercilious behavior." Slaveholders wallowed in leisure, neglected learning, and squandered their days in "drinking, or gaming at cards or dice," cockfighting, horse racing, boxing, and "memorable feats of gouging." Away from tobacco plantations, up-country farmers, forest workers, turpentine boilers, and other whites too poor to own slaves nursed their personal sense of disadvantage in a world completely governed by tidewater grandees. Unfortunately, the worst sort of slave-based slash-and-grab agriculture continued to reward planters on the underdeveloped fringe—especially in South Carolina and Georgia. Their fierce defense of slavery at the Constitutional Convention proved once for all that dreams of a slave-free American republic were premature.[8]

For Jedediah Morse—and this would be true for nearly every commentator from the 1780s into the early 1800s—the *real* hope of the United States lay in the trans-Appalachian West. Already American pioneers streamed into the far western counties of Virginia and North Carolina—soon to be admitted as the states of Kentucky and Tennessee. According to John Filson's *History* (1784), Kentucky had achieved in a decade "progress in improvements and cultivation" unlike any before in history. North of the Ohio River, not yet purchased from the Native nations, lay 220,000,000 acres "belonging to the federal government" (the contradiction went unnoticed). Geographers, surveyors, travelers all reported that no region united "so many advantages, in point of health, fertility, variety of production, and foreign intercourse," as the Ohio country. Given the encouragement laid down by Congress for orderly frontier development (the Northwest Ordinance), Ohio surely would become, as predicted by so many tourists, "the garden of the world, the seat of wealth, and the centre [*sic*] of a great empire."[9]

Once again a westward "course of empire" seemed the only vision adequate to capture the potential of the new United States. Morse had catalogued the types of extraction, cultivation, industry, and trade by which the Atlantic colonies achieved stability, wealth, and independence. Turning west with the new Constitution in hand, he found himself swept up in the vision of a rising glory, an empire of liberty and progress, unlike anything known to history. Civilization's "last and broadest feat" would be America. Here "the sciences, the arts of civilized life," would reach "their highest improvement." Liberty would flourish "unchecked" by "civil or ecclesiastical tyranny." Genius, "aided by all the improvements of former ages," would humanize mankind, expanding and enriching people's minds. The Mississippi would not remain the nation's western boundary: "the God of nature never intended" that the "best part of his earth" should be inhabited by subjects of a monarch four thousand miles away. The new American republic was "calculated to protect and unite, in a manner consistent with the natural rights of mankind, the largest empire that ever existed."[10]

A Plea for Husbandry

Jedediah Morse's *American Geography* can stand as an inaugural inventory proclaiming, for the record, the past achievements and future dreams of the American republic. Euphoria infected them all, but sometimes patterns from colonial experience cast a shadow of doubt on the otherwise prevailing optimism. Reckless extraction, resource depletion, and neglect of proper husbandry had left many older parts of the coastal states badly worn.

The anonymous author of *American Husbandry* (1775) laid the blame on colonial shortcuts. Cities such as Boston, Philadelphia, and New York had struggled to find firewood because the first settlers "destroyed the timber, as if it was impossible they should ever want any." "Seduced" by the "fertility of the soil," coastal farmers and planters had exhausted it as quickly as possible. Succeeding generations kept "ravaging" the landscape despite the visible effects all around them. (Relentlessly these gendered sexual metaphors framed this discourse.) Such "blindness" to the evidence of waste led one critic to conclude that "American planters and farmers" were "the greatest slovens in Christendom." Caught up in the excitement of achievement and liberation, colonists had dismissed such charges as slander, but now with independence secured some Americans wondered if the habits and excuses of their struggling forebears should be modified for the long-term health of the new nation.[11]

Public discussion of husbandry swelled in American periodicals and bookshops in the years after Independence. Learned societies—the American Philosophical Society, the American Academy of Arts and Sciences, the new Philadelphia Society for the Promotion of Agriculture—invited commentary and offered prizes for experimenters. Samuel Deane's *New England Farmer* (1790) linked the subject directly to the urgent business of nation building: "Our holding the rank of a free and independent nation allows us to consider the country as indisputably our own, and ourselves as monarchs over our farms." As a result Americans might "have reason to hope" that improvements made now would "benefit" them "through life, and that posterity would not be deprived of them." Traditionally poor farmers resisted innovation for fear of losing what little they had, but if the "richer sort" would do it for "love of their country," the United States might "become an opulent, respectable, and very powerful nation."[12]

George Washington agreed completely, but events in the 1780s did not overwhelm him with optimism. Having seen the Ohio country (where he owned some twenty thousand acres), and having studied the maps of rivers, roads, and mountain ranges, Washington saw the importance of extraordinary natural endowments. Both liberty and the land itself represented providential gifts of world-historical importance, but would we "have wisdom enough to improve them"? Like John Adams, he worried that liberation might unleash the meanest of Americans' popular impulses. The gift of political liberty already seemed to foster licentiousness; the physical landscape might just as easily be squandered in reckless assaults on the storehouse of riches now just coming into reach. On the Ohio frontier, squatters invaded Washington's lands, stole his timber, and refused to pay rents. Back on his own farm, Mount Vernon, he tried to demonstrate the virtues of improvement in crops, implements, livestock, and management techniques. To the English agricultural writer Arthur Young, Washington vented his frustration: "The system of agriculture (if the epithet of system can be applied to it), which is in use in this part of the United States, is as unproductive to the practitioners as it is ruinous to the landholders. Yet it is perniciously adhered to." Five years later his critique had not softened: "The aim of farmers of this country (if they can be called farmers) is not to make the most they can from the land, which is . . . cheap, but the most of the labour, which is dear." Young tried to publish this thoughtful plea for husbandry from the most revered of Americans, but ever-mindful of his own reputation, Washington demurred for fear it would be seen "as a piece of ostentation."[13]

In a nutshell Washington identified the American temptation—and the standard excuse for "perniciously" clinging to wasteful practices: everything about the American experience favored quick-and-dirty exploitation if it saved expensive labor and capital investment. But the Englishman was having none of it: Americans made bad choices. After Washington's death Young published the whole of their correspondence including Young's letters blasting American claims that their shortcuts brought them success. Washington had given the Englishman data on inputs and outputs from several estates, and Young found the evidence appalling. "Is it possible," he wrote, "that the inhabitants of a great continent . . . can carry on farming and planting as a business, and yet never calculate the profit they make by *per centage* [*sic*] on their capital?" One Bucks County farm of two hundred acres produced, by Young's calculation, a considerable "dead loss" after swallowing whole the labor of a family of five. Thomas Jefferson proudly reported raising five thousand bushels of wheat at Monticello, but Young condemned him for overcropping his land while keeping far too little livestock. Raising wheat Jefferson's way, without adequate animal manure, "would reduce the finest farm in the world to a *caput mortuum*." In his own defense the master of Monticello pleaded that wolves made it hard to keep sheep in Virginia.[14]

In 1801 another English agricultural specialist, William Strickland, published *Observations on the Agriculture of the United States*, filled with similar critical assessments. Americans, he wrote, paid no attention to return on capital. Possessed of the finest land on earth they practiced the worst husbandry. Refusing to rent land where they might earn 8 percent or better, they purchased freehold farms and earned half that rate or less. Farms growing wheat produced less than ten bushels per acre after the first year or two, barely covering the cost of inputs. Nobody bothered with manure. New England soils were badly worn, and Virginia had reached "the lowest state of degradation." Stung by such slander, John Taylor of Caroline took up the banner of reform in 1813 with a series of essays under the title of *Arator*. He acknowledged that planters ruined their lands, while their children fled to the West. Farmers pretended tobacco required virgin land, but everyone knew it grew even better on fields that were properly fertilized. Taylor directed his slaves to spread roughly fifty cartloads of barnyard litter per acre, at which rate he could dress each year two acres per hand ("including women and boys"). Best done in the winter months, nothing stood in the way of planters following suit except indifference. But here Taylor offered an excuse: perhaps it was anxiety caused by the antislavery rantings of northern Quaker fanatics that paralyzed his neighbors.[15]

Taylor's impressive command of agricultural science came packaged with a libertarian preference for unfettered markets and proprietary freedom. In front of any practical advice about farming he placed nine essays (forty-six pages) of political scorn for government policies—specifically Hamilton's strong-state fiscal program. All his advice about crop rotation, livestock keeping, and proper manuring disappeared beneath this diatribe against banking, industry, and tariff protection (the last was not yet even in force when Taylor wrote his essays). Readers inclined to neglect agricultural improvement found more comfort than shame in the early pages of *Arator*.[16]

The solid platform of domestic opinion on which a reform movement finally took shape was built by James Madison in a famous address in 1818 to the Albemarle Agricultural Society. Widely thought of as the best farmer in the world (Thomas Jefferson and John Quincy Adams both said so), Madison regaled this organization with a sweeping overture followed by seven concrete principles for creating sustainable farming regimes. The chief error of his countrymen lay in continuing to squander land in the name of conserving labor. The inevitable result was ruined acres that could not produce enough to feed "the ploughman and his horse." Better to give up on truly hopeless fields, invest in fields that can be recovered, and abandon tobacco "which gives the blow most mortal to the soil." As a rule, he said, whatever made a "rich farm poor" or failed to make a "poor farm rich" was bad for the owner. Whatever profit accrued did not balance the damage done to the land: "The goose is killed without even obtaining the coveted egg." Shallow plowing, neglect of manures and irrigation, improper management of livestock all came in for specific rebuke. Finally, Madison broadened his view and condemned the "excessive destruction of timber and firewood" that had characterized American habits since the earliest starving times. Finding the original forests a "great obstacle" to settlement, the colonizers developed an "antipathy" toward trees; apparently it never occurred to them that "the fund was not inexhaustible" or that trees "could not be raised as quickly as . . . wheat or corn."[17]

Madison's paper quickly was published as a pamphlet and reprinted in the Baltimore *American Farmer* and Albany *Plough Boy*. Not everyone approved, of course, but in the decades after 1819 agricultural societies, specialty periodicals, and critical American voices multiplied dramatically. Historian Steven Stoll suggests that the Panic of 1819, which burst a huge bubble in western land speculation, gave a prominent boost to the advocates of husbandry. The sudden collapse of prices for cotton, grain, and livestock, coupled with the nation's first experience with peacetime urban unemployment approaching 50 percent gave everyone cause to reflect on national economic development.[18] But strategies of husbandry contradicted the hope and excitement that energized so many Americans coming out of the Revolution. Husbandry conjured up limits, restraint, moderated expectations; it suggested (as had Madison in so many words) that America was on the path to becoming just like Europe. Like the classical strains of republicanism that called for submerging the interested "self" in pursuit of the common good, husbandry implied an ethic of self-denial, an image of equipoise rather than boundlessness. Who could stand on Virginia's Blue Ridge looking West and believe that the future belonged to the husbandman patiently scattering dung on the tired acres from which his ancestors once had wrung fantastic profits?

The Land Before Them

In truth nearly everybody saw western land as holding the key to the rising American empire. Washington made it central to his geopolitical vision: "I wish to see the sons and daughters of the world in Peace and busily employed in the more agreeable amusement of fulfilling the first and great commandment, *Increase and Multiply*: as an encouragement to which we have opened the fertile plains of the Ohio to the poor, the needy and the oppressed of the Earth." During the stormy 1780s, Washington worried that ineffective government, the lack of commercial connections, and the independent spirit of westering pioneers would dissolve the fragile bonds of Union forged in the Revolution. The "western waters" converged naturally to carry trade to the Mississippi River, but the port of New Orleans, by some accident of history, still belonged to Spain. Geography lured the settlers away from the Atlantic Union, just as the profligate environment lulled them into indulgence and easy living. Mere liberation guaranteed none of the structure, restraint, and best practices that assured the prosperity of the country (or the farm) into the coming generations. Washington hoped a strong government promoting quick and accurate surveys, compact settlement, orderly courts and markets, and artificial roads and canals would shepherd the western country through the chaos of colonization and bind them to the republic with chains of commerce.[19]

The process of bringing frontier land to market had been the work of promoters and speculators since the beginning of colonization. The sponsors of colonial "projects" (whether joint-stock companies or proprietors) divided vast grants of land into smaller tracts (still thousands of acres) to be offered for sale to groups of immigrants or individual settlers. Control of such real estate represented one of the primary ways to profit from colonization, and land barons guarded their privileges jealously. The Revolution complicated this traditional process. First, titles granted by European "owners" did not extinguish Native claims to American land. Rival negotiations with multiple authorities among the Indians produced incredible confusion which in turn encouraged pioneers to seize what looked like vacant land and make good their claim by settling there. Right after the Revolution individual states issued grants to favored speculators and warrants for frontier land as reward for unpaid soldiers. Congress coveted the same property to pay its own war debts. Daring promoters in Maine, upstate New York, far western Virginia and North Carolina engrossed huge swaths of land from which they hoped to squeeze fortunes by seating immigrants. Large tracts north of the Ohio River belonged to private developers such as Washington and John Cleves Symmes; another huge grant was purchased with war debt by Manasseh Cutler and his partners in the Ohio Company of Associates. Like promoters of seventeenth-century colonial projects, these impresarios sought to direct with their wealth and legal authority the course of events in which lesser men would live out their dreams.[20]

At this point an alternative idea took the stage, largely the work of Thomas Jefferson. Jefferson usually distanced himself from the distasteful game of land speculation. He preferred a system where primary settlers purchased their farms directly from the government. No grandees, no middle men, no swindlers required. Temperamentally more radical and democratic than Washington (or any other of the leading founders), Jefferson welcomed the liberation of individual citizens. He saw rambunctious squatters, not as lawless thieves and scavengers, but as the energizing agents of the empire of liberty. Land was the key to their independence, and in Jefferson's mind the impulse of pioneers to strike out into the wilderness fueled the hope of the republic. Nothing could stop or restrain them, but nature would bind them together if the republic guaranteed their freedom. He laid out his theory for Madison's benefit: whenever there were "uncultivated lands and unemployed poor," the system of land tenure violated "natural right." The earth was "given as a common stock for man to labour and live on," he explained. Not quite ready to condone squatter rights, Jefferson believed it was time "to provide by every possible means" that few men should be "without a little portion of land."[21]

In Congress Jefferson planted the seeds of policy that would accelerate and democratize the commodification of American land in ways even he did not anticipate. First, the states relinquished their claims to most western land, creating one vast public domain controlled by Congress. A 1784 ordinance called for the sale of such land to settlers and guaranteed statehood to purchasers after a period of temporary government largely controlled by the resident settlers. The statehood threshold in this first instance was set at twenty thousand free inhabitants. The next year a Land Ordinance set up the federal survey using a system of numbered squares. Beginning with the First Seven Ranges in Ohio, surveyors created townships of six miles square, entering them in plat books along with field notes noticing salt licks, mill seats, minerals, and other valuable anomalies. The system attached to every parcel of public land a unique numerical tag by which that parcel could be traded without ever even seeing it. At first whole townships were offered for sale, but after disappointing returns Congress altered the law to include smaller as well as much larger transactions, effectively pursuing both underlying strategies at once. After lots were offered at auction they could be purchased for a minimum price by private entry.[22]

In theory this process satisfied the frustration of men such as Washington, tired of squatters poaching their valuable property, as well as legitimate settlers hoping to gain clear title without long and expensive proceedings in distant, ineffective courts. In 1787 the Northwest Ordinance remodeled the territorial process, greatly reducing self-government in the early stages and giving the appointed governor (and presumably his friends in Congress) far greater authority. At this point the expansible Union was ready to grow to its western boundary on the Mississippi River. Admittedly the system never worked exactly as envisioned: squatters illegally settled on Indian lands, only to demand compensation for improvements when institutions finally caught up with them. Washington's fears and Jefferson's hopes remained locked in conflict for most of the next century; nevertheless, pioneering and land acquisition in the United States became cheaper, easier, quicker, and less contestable than probably anywhere in the world.[23]

Armed with these new policy regimes, the friends of American empire renewed their enthusiasm for building the nation by booming western lands. In 1792 Gilbert Imlay, a one-time Kentucky speculator and agent for the dishonest Scioto Land Company, put out an infinitely more detailed inventory of the Ohio Valley. Disguised as letters from a Kentucky native, Imlay's essays combined settlement history with close descriptions of the landscape on both sides of the Ohio from Pittsburgh to Natchez. Kentucky, he reported, had blossomed in one generation and was just now admitted to the Union as a state. Tennessee would be close behind. "Nature in her pride" gave this whole region "astonishing" fertility. "The bottoms on the Ohio are every where extensive and luxurious." All kinds of produce thrived there: grains, hemp, tobacco, livestock, the surplus of which found a ready market among the incoming settlers. Environmental riches coupled with a human reproductive prowess unmatched in the known world was certain to double the American population every fifteen years for generations to come. "The immense extent of the American empire," he concluded "abounds with all climates, with every kind of soil, and with rivers so various and extensive," that it seemed certain to rival "half the globe in trade and riches."[24]

Two obstacles stood perversely in the way of these altogether "natural" developments. First, north of the river Native Americans stubbornly clung to the idea (reinforced by the terms of the federal Constitution) that they rightfully owned the land on which they resided. As white settlements flourished in Kentucky, Natives redoubled efforts to stop that invasion from spreading north. Still enjoying trade with the older British and French networks via the Great Lakes, Shawnee, Delaware, and Miami people banded together to mount a resistance that made life treacherous for squatters and turned back American armies sent out to intimidate them. Official federal policy prohibited trespass on Indian lands, but early efforts to punish the squatters had shown the limits of Washington's control. Scenes of "American" (European) troops removing "American" (European) pioneers on behalf of "Indian" (American) rights contradicted popular expectations. Instead, the Washington administration focused on trying to intimidate the Natives into making "voluntary" concessions. Despite the very recent defeat of Arthur St. Clair's latest military campaign (1791), Gilbert Imlay predicted within a decade federal supremacy would be established. And so it was.[25]

The second barrier to the rising American empire lay at New Orleans, where Spain persisted in threatening commercial use of the Mississippi without which nothing raised in Kentucky could find its way to market. George Washington tried to spin this as an advantage, forcing settlers to focus their commerce eastward over the mountains. Most people thought that it flew in the face of the natural order of things. Leading Virginians as early as 1780 were pushing for rights to the Mississippi in whatever treaties ended the Revolution. The movement of tobacco farmers to the "western waters," wrote Madison, would prove as irrepressible as the flow "of the river itself." As secretary of state, Thomas Jefferson claimed the right of navigation "by nature" and "by treaty." Kentucky settlers asked Congress in 1788: "Can the God of WISDOM and NATURE have created that vast country in vain? Was it for nothing that he blessed it with a fertility so astonishing? Did he not provide those great streams which enter into the Mississippi, and by it communicate with the Atlantic, that other nations might enjoy the blessings of our prolific soil? View the country, and you will answer for yourselves. But can the presumptuous madness of man imagine a policy inconsistent with the immense designs of the DEITY? Americans cannot."[26]

Nature, nature, nature! Faced with this litany of claims about natural rights, natural forces, natural progress and destinies, how could calls for husbandry and restraint survive in the American consciousness? President Washington's preference for compact settlement and top-down restrictions on the impulse of pioneering appealed to coastal elites but not to common voters whose influence steadily grew in the coming decades. A United States military victory at Fallen Timbers (1794) finally brought Ohio's Natives to terms. The subsequent Treaty of Greenville (1795), which gained for the settlers most of Ohio, also guaranteed *forever* Indian rights over the rest of their land—the very country promised as future states by the Northwest Ordinance. American offspring poured into the Ohio Valley—following the river from Pittsburgh or down the Great Valley of Virginia and up through Kentucky—spreading out into the fertile bottoms and rich forests of Ohio, raising Indian corn and livestock, or making hemp, tobacco, and cotton farms in Kentucky, Tennessee, and Mississippi Territory.[27]

Whatever ideal template one might have embraced in 1783, the expansible republic by 1800 had charted irrevocably a course of rapid, reckless expansion into the rich interior, leaving to governing institutions the task of making it work and cleaning up the consequences. Aggressive and masculine, white "pioneers" drafted a script for a "westward movement" (another passive construction) that in the nineteenth century captured the imagination of settlers and their descendants. Celebrated in song and story, frontiersmen challenged the savages, tamed wild beasts, felled ancient forests, plowed up the prairies, and erected the framework of civilization from the Blue Ridge to the California coast. As in many good legendary sagas, violent details slipped from memory, as did the enormous contributions of women and enslaved Africans and the crimes against indigenous people who disappeared more readily in song than in reality. Armed only with his ax and his gun—and his wife, his children, and perhaps a dozen Africans—the mythic American pioneer in the nineteenth century brought the continent to heel.

To the Oregon Coast

The problem of the port of New Orleans set the stage for a famous round of inventories, the reconnaissance of the Far West. At one time the southern segment of a vast French corridor linking the Gulf of Mexico with the Great Lakes and North Atlantic, in 1762 Louisiana passed to Spanish control during the Seven Years' War. Spanish threats to the river trade and the "right of deposit" for American exports had been quieted by treaty in 1795, but in 1801 Spain promised to return Louisiana to Napoleon. A far stronger player, Napoleon's imperial pretensions might appeal to American settlers whose allegiance to the Union already was fragile. Jefferson, now president, threw down the gauntlet: New Orleans was the "one single spot" on the globe "the possessor of which" was a "natural and habitual enemy" of the United States. He tried to purchase New Orleans (including, he hoped, West Florida), but complications resulted in an offer from the French to sell the whole of the territory—close to nine hundred thousand square miles—for fifteen million dollars.[28]

This idea bristled with problems. The Constitution nowhere permitted a president to buy extensive new territory (and Jefferson *said* that nothing was lawful if not spelled out in the Constitution). At a stroke it literally doubled the size of the United States and more than doubled the size of the public domain. Different histories, laws, religion, and racial codes governed the eight thousand residents of New Orleans, adding to the cultural diversity that already destabilized the Union. The move guaranteed that Atlantic states would be overwhelmed in time by a multitude of western upstarts: New Englanders charged that Virginians intended to create in their own image a dozen new states to cement their control of the federal government. The expansion of slavery, delicately handled by a ban on its spread into the Old Northwest, charged back into the public mind—just as the cotton revolution fostered enormous new excitement behind the idea of slave-based plantation farming. Nevertheless, Jefferson "knew" that the great nation he imagined in the future required secure control in the West.[29]

Little truly was known about Louisiana in 1803. Fierce critics of the purchase said it was a barren waste filled with "wolves and wandering Indians." More numerous but no better informed, advocates of expansion declared it a perfect continuation of the fertile garden landscape already known. Rumor and theory posited great drainages such as those that cut through the eastern landscape: surely the Missouri River reached far into the "Stony Mountains," practically touching the source of the great Columbia or "Oregon" River that poured into the Pacific. On an almost blank geographical canvas full-throated friends of empire sketched in whatever they hoped to find. No one was more excited to see what real knowledge could be discovered than Jefferson, who already had launched Lewis and Clark's legendary "Corp of Discovery."[30]

Jefferson's interest in such a reconnaissance predated the Louisiana Purchase probably by a full year. Months before he learned of that deal he had chosen his private secretary, Meriwether Lewis, to head a secret expedition up the Missouri and down whatever drainages brought the Columbia to the sea. The object of the mission was to find a practical link to Pacific waterways. Detailed instructions drafted in June 1803 called for carefully mapping the rivers and all remarkable features of topography. They were to catalog the resident Natives, their numbers, territory, language, traditions, moral and physical circumstances, and gather such information as might enable outsiders "to civilize & instruct them." Other "objects worthy of notice" included the soil and its vegetable productions, animals, minerals, fossils, "volcanic appearances," and climate. Expecting wariness or outright hostility, Jefferson urged his explorers to be "conciliatory" with any people they met, to be "friendly & useful to them" and offer to bring back some of their children for instruction in civilized ways. Notwithstanding the total absence of conveyances, Jefferson ordered Lewis and Clark to generate multiple copies of written reports and ship specimens back to Washington or Monticello via whatever Pacific port they could find.[31]

More than three years later Lewis and Clark arrived back in St. Louis. They had reached the Pacific shore, filled hundreds of pages with journal entries, mapped the astonishing landscape, collected boxes of artifacts, seeds, roots, bones, and specimens. They learned, among many other things, that between the upper Missouri and the upper Columbia there lay several hundred miles of the most labyrinthine mountain country Anglo-Americans ever had seen. The fact that there was no easy path to the coast must have disappointed Jefferson, but he took delight in the treasure trove of geographical data, stories, and artifacts that eventually came to hand. (The mounted head of a bighorn sheep glares down on visitors to Monticello even today.) Among the headline findings: astonishing herds of bison on the plains; grizzlies that would not die when shot; the incredible Great Falls of the Missouri; all kinds of Indian nations, some surprisingly friendly, others equally hostile; boiling sulfur springs in Montana; and trees near the coast (Sitka spruce) that towered 230 feet above the forest floor. Tragically, Lewis's deteriorating mental health and eventual suicide delayed until 1814 any decent public report of this magnificent adventure. Most of the scientific data languished for generations in manuscript journals—fortunately stored at the American Philosophical Society.[32]

Useful reconnaissance depended on accurate information, which is why Jefferson sent a trusted individual like Meriwether Lewis with detailed instructions to gather not just impressions but "objective" data such as temperature readings, latitude, longitude, compass headings, drawings, specimens, and samples. Existing works of description and travel notoriously favored bizarre and outlandish findings. Too many such books absorbed and repeated every rumor of gold mines, lush meadows, wild vineyards, and hundred-pound catfish. West of the Missouri River the credibility of information deteriorated further. Everyone out there was driven by powerful private interests. The British in Oregon worked for the well-heeled Hudson's Bay Company, on whose business John Jacob Astor was hoping to encroach. French, Spanish, and Mexican "rascals" (such as Manuel Lisa out of St. Louis) plus later American "mountain men" (Jedediah Smith, James Clyman, Jim Bridger) generated networks of trade among Native people that threatened to lock up the mountain West in nonstate systems of organization. Even state actors sometimes betrayed their official commitments to stir up opportunities for profit and glory: the treasonous governor of Louisiana, James Wilkinson, who conspired to create his own separatist southwestern empire, stands as the most notorious example.[33]

Jefferson craved the kind of knowledge that could stand empirical testing. In 1805 he sent Zebulon Pike up the Mississippi, but before he reached its head Wilkinson ordered him off to the Rocky Mountains. There he discovered the towering peak that bears his name and the startling sandy dunes of southeastern Colorado. The report of Pike's expedition contained the first hints of an arid region; twenty years later Stephen Long would confirm it and write on the map for the first time, "Great American Desert."[34] In further pursuit of such information Jefferson started the military academy at West Point to train army engineers not just for war but for peacetime reconnaissance, and the United States Coastal Survey to generate accurate navigational charts for vessels plying the coastal waters. Neither institution flourished until after the War of 1812, when the internal improvement craze suddenly focused popular attention on public works. In the late 1810s Secretary of War John C. Calhoun led the way in using army engineers for building and laying out roads. In 1824 the General Survey Bill allowed federal engineers to provide "unbiased" studies of possible routes to be developed by other units of state or private enterprise. In the next decade some individual states created geological survey departments, effectively claiming public ownership of information about the landscape even as the land itself and its natural resources passed into private hands.[35]

The Tenor of the Vision

Taken all together this gathering flood of information could have produced a critical sense of the probable limits, benefits, and costs of the kind of development that took place in the nineteenth century. Indeed some skeptics and doubters weighed in from different quarters, but like the advocates of husbandry in old Virginia, their messages gained little traction. Human vision is an ambivalent phenomenon: it can gather and record information, or it can project onto external realities the images desired in the mind of the person who is "viewing." A seriously biased reading of the facts in early America fed a mounting vision of boundlessness and entitlement. Wrote one enthusiast in 1818, "no circumstance *can* prevent" the United States from "influencing and controlling the other sovereignties of the world." Secure from the "dread of powerful neighbours," possessed of a bountiful country, "free as the air they breathe," "prodigal of life; brave, enterprising, intelligent, and persevering," Americans were destined for "national greatness, prosperity, and influence."[36] Modern scholarship challenges the mythic core of this American sense of mission, calling attention to the plight of Native peoples, African Americans, non-Anglo resident nationals, even the plants, animals, and landscapes that made up the natural environment. But seen only in prospect by a generation filled with excitement, coming out of the Revolution, steeped in narratives that placed them on the leading edge of the process of civilization itself, the projected vision muted most negative signals.

This intoxicating sense of entitlement and destiny was partial and distorted in several important ways. First, most Americans saw the world through what historian Mary Louise Pratt calls "imperial eyes." European culture posited a matrix of signifiers by which New World adventurers perceived and explained what they "saw." Steeped in a Christian story of the "one true God," a single creation, and a natural order in which Europeans stood as the "crown" of that creation, colonizing people automatically coded "difference" as inferiority. The concept of "savagery" quickly evolved to incorporate indigenous people, beliefs, behaviors, even plants and animals that were strange and somehow threatening. Some colonists came with a clear intention to advance their interests and "empire"; others arrived as dissenters bent on escaping aspects of Old World culture that marginalized their convictions. It mattered very little. Bradford's humble Plymouth separatists relied no less on "imperial eyes" than did their more self-righteous Boston neighbors or the cutthroat tobacco boomers of early Jamestown. It is not that they *could not* see otherwise. Thomas Morton at Merry Mount published hundreds of perceptive pages about the Natives of Massachusetts Bay, an ethnographic tour-de-force that nobody at the time would credit as containing any truth. Jamestown's 1609 legal code punished by death any running away to live with the "savages," for the very good reason that running away to live with the savages made very good sense to starving Englishmen.[37]

"Imperial eyes" exist not in nature but in culture; one *could* filter out the distortions they promised, but typically distortions proved comforting, handy, and self-reinforcing. Probably nobody escaped completely from such cultural projections or wishful thinking, but some observers did better than others. Women and blacks probably saw more because they suffered more from white men's delusions. Compared to bounders like John Cleves Symmes or Gilbert Imlay, Meriwether Lewis and William Clark had little to gain from misrepresenting their findings even though they shared the American enthusiasm for conquest. Army explorers Zebulon Pike and Stephen Long as well as mountain men Jim Bridger and James Clyman probably took in reality better than later California dreamers such as Lansford Hastings and John C. Fremont. Projections became filtering lenses, editing the flow of information, creating a feedback loop that must have been intoxicating in the extreme.

Second, this vision was unabashedly exceptionalist. Starting with John Adams's comments on Feudal and Canon Law, founding-era Americans had cast themselves as people chosen to carry the torch of civilization into the future. The cause of liberty itself devolved upon them. The hand of Providence appeared in every type of panegyric, and the shores of the Pacific were mentioned as the natural boundary of this rising American empire. Morse had said as much in 1789. Jefferson implied it in 1801 as he assumed the presidency. The project of empire lay upon their shoulders as a sacred charge, not just a privilege but an obligation, a world-historical challenge. In defense of the Louisiana purchase in 1803, Senator John Quincy Adams proclaimed the republic "destined by God and nature" to bring all of North America into the hands of a "powerful people . . . speaking one language, professing one general system of religious and political principles, and accustomed to one general tenor of social usages and customs." This chosen people had been given a raw continent, original and unspoiled, waiting for development by men worthy of its plenty. Such projections successfully erased the presence of the Natives and the early dependence of colonists on Indian help, knowledge, and resources. They also neatly suppressed the memory of desperate urges to be more like England that had marked provincial culture during the middle years of the eighteenth century.[38]

Third, the vision was racially white and Anglo-American. At the founding of the republic native people by the thousands still inhabited parts of western New York and Pennsylvania, eastern Massachusetts (Maine), western Georgia, Kentucky, and Tennessee. State and federal negotiations for concessions of Indian land preoccupied authorities well into the nineteenth century, punctuated by violent conflicts caused most often by the trespass of white Americans onto Indian lands. Iroquois holdings complicated "progress" in western New York. Cherokees struggled to retain their homes in western Georgia and North Carolina by embracing Anglo-American customs, building fancy brick houses, growing cotton, and exploiting the labor of enslaved African Americans. Along the Gulf coast before the Transcontinental Treaty of 1819, Anglo-American settlers trespassed on Creek and Choctaw lands in actions that cannot be distinguished historically from simple invasion and seizure. "Indian removal," as it came to be known, topped the popular agenda for incoming settlers and their governing authorities. A fiction evolved that the retreat of the Natives resulted from "voluntary" compensated deals that were seen by tribal leaders as better than violence and forced removal. But when the "civilized" Cherokees sued to protect their rights—and won—the result was a campaign of ethnic cleansing against the Cherokees, Chickasaws, and Choctaws. By the 1840s nearly all of the Natives east of the Mississippi had been forced onto "trails of tears" by what was called the "westward movement." White pioneers saw neither violence nor injustice but only the progress of civilization displacing irrational savagery.[39]

Africans fared no better in the unfolding vision of a rising American empire. The northern states eliminated slavery per se, but servitude and exclusion survived intact and probably grew more severe as the number of free blacks rose. Many founding-era planters (Washington famously among them) freed some or all of their slaves in their wills, causing Virginia in 1806 to encumber such charitable acts with a requirement that the freedmen leave the state. Spanish Florida became a refuge for runaway slaves who set up wilderness "maroon" communities and mingled freely with local Natives. Much of the "security threat" posed by this foreign territory derived from the need to police America's racial caste system, which could not be accomplished until Spain relinquished the country (1819) and the Creek and Seminole Indians gave up their long and frustrating wars. Finally, cotton—the new staple crop tailor-made for slave production on rich southern soils—turned slavery back into a "positive good" in the eyes of a new generation of free and ambitious white planters. In the Southern mind, the empire of liberty was more an "empire for liberty" (Jefferson's alternate wording); the mantle of freedom draped the shoulders of Anglo-American white men only.[40]

Territorial expansion—Louisiana and Florida for now, Cuba, Canada, maybe parts of Mexico some day in the future—raised thorny questions of how to incorporate people who did not share the "story" of American liberation. Jefferson often spoke of his country as the natural home for *all* people who love liberty; but in fact even natural-born "Americans" flirted quite freely with expatriation and adventures outside the United States. The loyalty of early frontiersmen worried everyone in Congress. Time and again separatist movements threatened to declare independence or join an alternate empire—most scandalously the 1806 conspiracy headed by Aaron Burr, former vice president of the United States, and James Wilkinson, governor of Louisiana Territory. Patriotic hindsight revised the story of Texas to read like a part of the "westward movement," but in truth the settlers who went there with Stephen Austin in 1825 knew they were *leaving* the United States, possibly for good. If this was a "chosen country," the particular receptacle for liberty and civilization, how could we share the future with men and women who were not a part of the creation story, or worse yet, had worked against it? Race and rapacious behavior became the reliable markers by which Americans knew who to trust. The people most likely to own this new unwritten covenant were white men willing to displace Indians, enslave Africans, and ravage the land in front of them.[41]

Finally, the vision of rising empire was powerfully shaped by masculine gender codes. Women rarely were noticed by those who recorded the progress and virtues of the expanding republic—and this became more true over time. Eighteenth-century chroniclers even as late as Morse sometimes acknowledged the presence of women (not always to flatter them); but the sexualized language used to describe the "fertile" and "fecund" country, its "seductive" effect on the settlers, the "lustful" ways in which frontiersmen penetrated "virgin land"—all this was too universal not to be meaningful. Women's narratives of pioneering seldom reflected the heroic qualities found in the stories told by their men. More often they recorded deep ambivalence about the settler enterprise. Pioneer women found themselves cut off from the networks of female friends and relatives who for generations had made marriage, childbirth, and parenting tolerable. A primary issue for women remained invisibility. In February 1805, Sacagawea, the young Shoshone woman without whom Lewis and Clark would not have found their way through the Snake River country, gave birth in the Mandan villages, then set out on the expedition, carrying her newborn son through exploits that frightened hardened soldiers. Almost none of this shows up in the journals except a report of a serious illness sixteen months later, which could have been the miscarriage of another pregnancy. Sacagawea, the record states, "had a cold." Feminist scholars, first in literature and then in history, have brought these perspectives to light and forced us all to consider the impact of male privilege, obstructed vision, and violently gendered values that filtered perceptions through which so much of the continent was seen and assessed. Would the outcome have been different if guided by feminine values? We can only wonder; but the fact that masculine codes *did* reward aggressive, violent, and self-centered ways must stand as solid fact.[42]

In the end, these early inventories assured the newly liberated citizens of the United States—at least white men with land or the means to purchase land—that an inexhaustible storehouse of environmental riches lay at their feet: given by Providence, won in the Revolution, deserved because of their special dispensation as the carriers of civilization. The impact of New World abundance was no less impressive in 1800 than it had been two hundred years before, but now the culture of exploitation brought to bear powerful elements that made the commodification of nature positively normative. A new science of politics promised that republican self-government would rescue the world from age-old tyranny and oppression. The progress of science and "the useful arts" guaranteed that the mysteries of nature would be understood, encouraging people to see any barriers not as warnings but as challenges to be overcome. The privatization of religion made it possible for individuals to compartmentalize their sins and insulate their spiritual lives from their material ambitions. All the drivers of history converged on the popular impulse of ordinary (white) men to seize these natural resources, turn them to private advantage, and worry not a whit about any long-term downside consequences. Washington said it succinctly in 1783: Providence had dealt us "her favors" with a "profuse" hand. What was left was for man to improve them.[43]

CHAPTER 6

Improvement

NOBODY COULD MISS THE fact that the new United States was awash in abundant and undeveloped natural resources. The newly liberated Americans enjoyed a unique combination, not seen before, of staggering material abundance and widespread personal freedom to exploit it with impunity. Having taken inventory and concluded their endowment was limitless, Americans in the early republic focused with renewed vigor on the habits of development and exploitation they had been perfecting since the early days of colonization. There was no question that they would tackle this storehouse of potential, but how would they go about it? At whose direction? To what end? For whose advantage? "Improvement" as a concept embraced goals and objectives that transcended petty greed and thoughtless consumption. In a word, it captured the imagination of the first generation after Independence. It comprised all imaginable elements of material, intellectual, and spiritual growth for a people whose world was not yet divided sharply into economic, political, and moral realms. Improvement was growth, but growth toward greatness; development, but development on behalf of the common good; innovation, but innovation designed to enlarge happiness; progress, but progress with a distinctly upward moral trajectory.

Improvement as a goal would shape and direct the activities of early Americans as they launched their experiment in freedom; but like "liberty" itself, "improvement" could take on many shades of meaning and drift over time into contradictory paths. Like all purposeful action, improvements produced some surprising results, unanticipated consequences yielding conflicts of interest that sometimes suggested negative intentions or abusive designs. Innocent striving in a sea of opportunities was not *supposed* to be a dangerous thing, and so powerful was the positive value implied in the word "improvement" that for most of the nineteenth century Americans refused to suspect it. As a result, when they encountered consequences at odds with benevolent intentions, they looked for agents of corruption. These they "found" where experience had taught them to look: in unfaithful governors, powerful institutions, wealthy or privileged individuals. For two generations and more, liberty fostered "improvement" without having to answer for hardships and injuries that were blamed instead on ghosts of a former age. In the meantime, liberal*ism*—that is, liberal capitalist claims about the immutability of market forces—sank deep roots into America's culture of exploitation.[1]

Conquering Space and Time

The first and most pervasive application of the concept of improvement in the early republic was found in campaigns for "internal improvement," which meant mostly roads, canals, and turnpikes—things designed to improve communication in the sprawling American landscape. Unimproved nature presented rivers, harbors, swamps, forests, and mountains that either fostered or impeded interaction across space. Since time immemorial civilization had prospered where nature provided good harbors, navigable rivers, and easy communication with neighbors. From the beginning New World colonizers had scrambled to claim such favored places for cities, towns, and private plantations, but soon enough people had to settle for less desirable sites. Thus arose the impulse to improve the natural landscape by clearing rivers of rocks and debris, dredging harbors, building hard-surfaced roads, bridging streams, and even cutting canals to connect waterways left separate by some oversight of nature. On the smallest local scale internal improvements rarely sparked any controversy: most people benefited from a local road, bridge, or waterway. But as visions expanded to regional and even national scales, the expense of major roads and canals required investment from large communities of people who could not, by the very nature of geography, equally profit from the installations. Individuals, towns, or regions not sharing in such advantages understandably perceived their misfortune as a *disadvantage* imposed upon them not by nature but by promoters of internal improvements, men whose names readily were known. When such projects enjoyed public support in terms of money, rights-of-way, or franchise, suddenly the state found itself accused of *favoring* the few at the expense of the many—and that was one meaning of "corruption"![2]

Consider for example, the Potomac River and George Washington's desire to open a grand thoroughfare to the national interior. Any map of the day showed the upper Potomac approaching the Monongahela, which flowed north to join the Ohio at Pittsburgh. From there the waters flowed south and west, more or less uninterrupted, all the way to New Orleans. To Washington's continental eye, this natural convergence marked a great central artery of trade capable of cementing the West to the Union with the "indissolvable [*sic*] band" of commerce.[3] That this national artery washed the banks of his own farm, Mount Vernon, was just a happy coincidence in Washington's mind; but viewed from Baltimore, near the mouth of the Susquehanna River, Washington's canal threatened to make that city a permanent backwater. Meanwhile Philadelphia's merchants schemed to divert traffic away from Baltimore by prohibiting improvements in the lower Susquehanna River. Finally, New York boosters set their sights on improving the best natural route to the West—the Hudson-Mohawk corridor—which rose barely six hundred feet (compared with two thousand to three thousand elsewhere) on its way to the "western waters." As a result of this interstate rivalry, Congress refused its patronage to any one project, effectively throwing the nation's commercial geography into the hands of state and local forces or private investors.[4]

Even inside Virginia, potential investors close to the James River balked at advantaging Washington's Northern Neck. More shamefully, Henry Lee stopped paying his installments to the Potomac Company so he could invest his capital in lands near the Great Falls, the value of which would be boosted by the canal he would not help build. Such behavior exposed the conflict between private interest and common good. Without a network of roads and waterways binding frontier communities to the older Atlantic economy, the greater Union—already including Kentucky (1792) and Tennessee (1796) and expecting five to seven more interior states—seemed unlikely to cohere as an economic or political unit. Everyone understood what was at stake, yet charges of favoritism and corruption subverted the most popular public works. Ohio, Indiana, and Illinois, for example, bought support for expensive programs by scattering benefits widely in omnibus schemes that soon collapsed in bankruptcy. Elsewhere, promoters turned to private investment through chartered corporations. This privatization insulated the state from charges of corruption, but it also ignored demands of the "commons" for fair and equal treatment. Even Adam Smith acknowledged the importance of the hand of the sovereign in designing and building a national transportation infrastructure.[5]

Aside from the national "Cumberland" road, linking the new state of Ohio with the capital in Washington, and some post roads mostly through unsettled Indian territory, the federal government took a secondary role in early internal improvement. Interregional canals promised a more profound impact on transportation, especially for heavy goods. But canals were *very* expensive and funding them remained an obstacle. In 1817 the state of New York took unprecedented risks by investing over $7 million in the Erie Canal. Armed with little more than a spirit level and surveyors' chains, men like Benjamin Wright, James Geddes, Charles Broadhead, Canvass White, John Jervis, and Nathan Roberts taught themselves canal engineering on the fly, inventing in the process hydraulic cement, and inadvertently creating what amounted to a "school" of civil engineering. ("Diplomas" simply read "He worked on the Erie Canal.") Completed in 1825, this 360-mile waterway poured lumber, wheat, meat, and cheese into New York City while ferrying immigrants, housewares, tools, and capital into the Great Lakes basin. New York port became by the early 1830s the most important place to do business in the United States, a momentary advantage its business people parleyed into permanent hegemony through ancillary investments.[6]

Behind the drive for internal improvement lay the widespread conviction that markets alone gave value to undeveloped natural resources. New York congressman Peter B. Porter pleaded for assistance to lift a "great evil" under which frontier farmers labored. They found no local buyers for their crops and could not afford to ship them to Atlantic ports. "The single circumstance of the want of a market" threatened disaster in the Great Lakes and Ohio Valley regions, in the southern backcountry, into the cotton frontier, and "down east" in Maine. Wherever people saw lands that were capable of rich productions lying vacant for want of a "vent" for produce, the cry went up for improvements. Successful responses simply amplified the demand from the next neighboring places. New York's Erie Canal set off "canal fever" in Pennsylvania, Ohio, Maryland, Indiana, Illinois, and

Virginia, producing by 1840 over three thousand miles of artificial water-ways. (Even Congress was moved to support two national projects: the Chesapeake and Delaware Canal and the Chesapeake and Ohio Canal.) Cities without water connections west, such as Baltimore and Boston, toyed with experimental railroad technology to see if they could counteract from scratch the "natural" advantages enjoyed by their rivals.[7]

Every breakthrough ramped up demand—and created collateral damage to interests that once had been favored. Hudson River farmers and New Jersey dairies complained bitterly when produce poured in from upstate New York, flooding what once were "their" markets. Bridges displaced traditional ferries; turnpikes bypassed village inns; canals at river obstructions —such as one projected at the falls of the Ohio in Louisville—pitted steamboat interests against the teamsters and warehousemen who handled the portage around the obstruction. Thus did Americans discover a concept both central to capitalist enterprise and yet so contrary to earlier notions of fair play and common rights: "creative destruction." One man's improvement invariably resulted in somebody else's injury and sparked a new round of investment to recover the loss.[8]

Additional gains in transportation and communication resulted from the development of steamboats. By 1807 the efforts of several passionate inventors produced the first viable prototype—Robert Fulton's *Clermont*. Essentially coasting vessels with engines mounted amidships driving paddle wheels on either side, these early steamboats made possible the *upstream* navigation of rivers too swift or too narrow for tacking conveniently by sail. This profoundly extended the area of service for shipments heading into the interior. Even more dramatic gains were realized on the shallow, winding rivers of the trans-Appalachian frontier. Over time a new design emerged in western riverboats, featuring very shallow drafts, wide beams, huge wheels at the stern, and towering twin stacks. By the late 1850s these behemoths, tricked out with bric-a-brac staterooms and piled high on the decks with bales of cotton, became the symbols of Old South opulence memorialized forever in the lithographs of Currier and Ives. What mattered more, however, were the hundreds of unglamorous boats that plied the treacherous rivers, moving people, goods, and information at astonishingly low prices. Cheap to build (about $30,000 in 1840), often independently operated, largely unregulated and uncoordinated, steamers perfectly suited the small capital and independent ambitions of antebellum entrepreneurs who balked at the huge expense and management apparatus required by canal or later railroad projects.[9]

By 1840 the internal improvement movement dramatically had altered the spatial landscape of a country that now stretched beyond the Mississippi River. In 1800, for example, a trip from New York to New Orleans, Louisville, or Detroit took about four weeks; by 1840 less than two. Information distributed through the postal system moved even quicker. Geographer Allan Pred has estimated that in the pre-telegraphic United States news in the neighborhood of New York City circulated five times faster in 1840 than it had fifty years before. All of Pennsylvania and the Chesapeake as well as major western centers such as Cincinnati, Louisville, and New Orleans, got the news at least twice as fast. Transport costs for produce and manufactures, while difficult to state precisely, fell by orders of magnitude. Historian Ronald Shaw cited antebellum wagon rates between fifteen and twenty-five cents per ton-mile; canal rates came in at two cents or less.[10]

By 1840 roughly six hundred steamboats prowled American waterways, half of them on western rivers. Consuming an average of about forty cords of wood per day, steamboats accounted for dramatic deforestation along interior rivers. They slashed upriver transportation costs by a factor of ten. Nothing moved very quickly. On even the best roads vehicles moved at the pace of animals walking (express mail coaches excepted). To prevent damaging wakes canal boats never exceeded three or four miles per hour, and river steamers only exceeded five or ten miles per hour when racing (often with explosive results). Vagaries of weather still interrupted communications regularly, and nobody expected it to be otherwise. The first "conquest" of space and time seems unremarkable today, but in the 1830s and '40s these phenomenal gains exceeded all expectations. It remained for the modern steam railroad to introduce a second revolution far more dramatic, adding speed as well as convenience to the demands of commercial geography.[11]

Railroads grew out of demand for improved land transportation where waterways did not exist. First conceived as a dry and durable roadway (parallel wooden beams, perhaps fitted with straps of iron, laid on a well-drained bed of stone), the goal was simply to keep heavy trucks from churning up the road. When England's pioneer Liverpool and Manchester Railway (opened 1830) adopted steam traction in place of cable-winding engines, inventors began to dream of grander long-distance lines, laid out wherever the grade could be managed, and powered with engines capable of hauling tons of freight at a time. The next twenty years of experimentation in Europe and America eventually produced a combination of roadway, vehicles, and motive power so successful that the next generation completely forgot such a thing ever was unimaginable. But in the 1830s public confidence (and public investment) still favored canals, forcing railroad promoters to seek corporate charters, private investment, and indirect public assistance. Both the Baltimore and Ohio and Boston's Western Railway, America's first two long lines, served as laboratories working out dozens of technical problems including track and rail design, motive power, financing, governance, traffic control, freight handling, maintenance, pricing, and operations. Originally imagined as endpoint carriers, early railroads discovered that their customers wanted service from any two points on the line, or from one line onto the next, suggesting more of a web or network. Several short lines through upstate New York—running parallel to the Erie Canal—developed through-tickets and way-bills to facilitate this complex business. (They eventually would merge into a single firm.) To avoid collisions on single-track roads, companies adopted fixed schedules and assigned to conductors with excellent watches the task of keeping everyone safe.[12]

Railroads truly fascinated antebellum Americans and more than any other development fixed in their minds the idea of boundless improvement. In 1839 one celebrant, toasting the opening of the Harlem Railroad, claimed that railways "have leveled old prejudices—created new affinities—and given new impetus to the great cause of civilization. May their extent be unlimited." Time itself was restructured by steam locomotion; space "conquered," and distance "annihilated." At the opening of the Washington Branch of the Baltimore and Ohio, journalist Hezekiah Niles proclaimed a "victory of science over time and space." By the eve of the Civil War trunk lines connected New York with Chicago and St. Louis and pioneer roads already were pushing through Missouri and Iowa. Visionaries dreamed of transcontinental links to the Pacific Coast, and from there the trade of the Orient would flow seamlessly into American markets. In a fit of rhetorical exuberance, Missouri senator Thomas Hart Benton called the transcontinental route an "American road to India" on which the world's merchants would "fly across our continent on a straight line to China," bringing America "wealth and dominion" for "thousands of years to come." Natural opportunities exploited by ambitious and clever internal improvements could not fail to reward the American people. Viewed through the lens of the culture of exploitation, these interventions, no matter how powerful or dramatic, were seen overwhelmingly as benevolent endeavors.[13]

Crafting the Rules of Law

Early American improvers found themselves wanting certain fundamental changes in the cultural and legal framework that had governed business activity in the eighteenth-century English tradition. First, the old genteel tradition of discriminating among one's creditors had to be stopped. Second, chartered corporations must be refashioned into engines of private enterprise. Third, ancient rights, which in the past had prevailed over disruptive innovation, must be quashed in behalf of "progress" for the "greater good." Finally, risk-takers needed protection, such as bankruptcy procedures and limited shareholder liability, for the kinds of setbacks that often accompanied promising improvements or technical innovations. In short, the modern system of capitalist enterprise that soon would be fueling the culture of exploitation required new rules that minimized downside risks of "desirable" innovations. In the rapidly democratizing political culture of the new United States, such changes triggered popular suspicion making appropriate legislation hard to adopt. Judicial interpretation in many cases provided key adjustments in the rules governing enterprise, setting up an instrumentalist dialog for most of the nineteenth century between democratic legislation and liberal jurisprudence.[14]

Begin at the intersection of class and contract obligations. In the stratified world of Georgian England (and America), honor sometimes prevented genteel creditors from hounding delinquents of the same social class. Imprisonment—the common punishment—implied an unwillingness to pay that could be cured by the loss of one's liberty; but gentlemen did not throw their equals in jail. Nevertheless, when delinquents endangered important corporate undertakings (such as Washington's Potomac Canal) the gloves began to come off. The revolutionary hero "Light-Horse Harry" Lee found himself imprisoned by his fellow Virginia planters who no longer honored his pleas for accommodation because he made no adjustments in the use of his own resources. From a different quarter, as middling interests came to dominate state legislatures there developed a temptation to pass "stay laws" to protect large numbers of citizens (voters) who found themselves embarrassed by a turn of markets. The general Panic of 1819 brought these issues to a head as thousands of "innocent" parties found their assets dissolving through no apparent fault of their own. This moral distinction between licentious debt and innocent embarrassment still appealed to many: even as late as 1837 New York merchant Philip Hone lamented his inability to pay his most "deserving" creditors first. But cold facts and commitments better served the emerging market economy.[15]

Before the nineteenth century, in the English legal tradition nonbank corporations had been chartered primarily to manage charitable endowments for schools, hospitals, and other institutions of community benefit. In the capital-poor states of the early American republic, lawmakers quickly adapted the device to encourage entrepreneurial projects of public utility, such as turnpike roads and bridges. Both objectives—roads and bridges—had belonged for centuries among the duties of the sovereign, but tax-averse Americans desperately wanted public works at someone else's expense. Early turnpike and bridge charters traded monopoly rights to collect tolls for the use of investors' money, for a term of years (often 60) or until their capital had been repaid, and under strict guidelines protecting access and the public interest. Charters specified in great detail the nature of the roadway to be created, the responsibilities of the operators, and legal obligations of the incorporators. Before 1810 nearly all such charters fixed for the life of the contract a specified schedule of tolls—six cents for a score of sheep or hogs, twelve cents for a score of cattle, six cents for a two-wheeled sulky or chaise with one horse (nine cents for two). Intended to prevent abuse of monopolistic privileges, such schedules document a widespread confidence that the terms of business could be known two or three generations into the future. People thought that both goods and their value would remain unchanged for decades—as they had (theoretically) for generations before.[16]

In a world of freedom, growth, and improvement such static notions quickly proved unworkable. Changes in the volume and nature of traffic rendered detailed regulations unenforceable. Often parties saw these charters not just as business investments but as valuable franchises—more akin to annuities—that guaranteed an income for shareholders. For example, in 1785 the Massachusetts General Court chartered the Charles River Bridge Company, allowing it to collect tolls into the 1850s. By the early 1820s traffic had completely overwhelmed the bridge's capacity. Massachusetts authorized a new bridge nearby, and Charles River Bridge owners sued for damages despite having made back fifteen times the original investment.

Supreme Court precedents, such as the Dartmouth College Case (1819), seemed to bar one legislature from abrogating contracts made by an earlier one; but after years of litigation Chief Justice Taney ruled in 1837 that the public interest no longer could be sacrificed to the obligations made by generations past.[17]

For marshalling private resources to do what the sovereign authorities could not (or would not) do, chartered corporations proved enormously useful to early Americans. At the same time private law, special privileges, and the granting of franchises so inflamed the suspicions of voters that lawmakers approved them at their peril. Banks remained the special objects of popular suspicion, but turnpikes, bridges, wharves, warehouses, water-works, and manufacturers also fell under careful scrutiny for evidence of aristocratic privilege. To shield themselves from the charge of favoritism, New York lawmakers pioneered general incorporation systems that bureau-cratized the process such that corporate "privilege" became available to any group of incorporators who met specified generic conditions. Removed in this way from special acts of legislation, the American corporation stood ready by the third decade of the nineteenth century to evolve into a com-mon instrument of business and shed its clothing of public interest. Here too was a major step in the direction of the Smithian ideal of laissez-faire: after creating the corporate entity, the state was expected to keep hands off its pursuit of private interests.[18]

Innovation itself often produced legal frictions that would be resolved in new ways in nineteenth-century America. Going back generations in the English common law, prior rights to flowing water, access to footpaths, even sunlight on your windows had been guaranteed against encroachment by neighbors. In the well-developed world of early modern England, this protected the rights of existing millers, allowed common people to travel through the parish, and prevented urban builders from casting nearby housing into permanent shadows. In the United States, where so many resources had yet to be developed, newly liberated entrepreneurs took to damning up streams, fencing off land, and building big houses with new enthusiasm after the Revolution. Inevitably some neighbors objected, and often enough traditional rights prevailed; but gradually courts responded to the pleas of innovative entrepreneurs and started ruling on behalf of enterprise over private rights. Legal historian Morton Horwitz identified the New York case of *Palmer v. Mulligan* (1805) as an early example of a ruling curbing common law protections in favor of entrepreneurial activity.

As a new standard slowly took hold—favoring innovation and progress—jurists steadily expanded a preference at law for entrepreneurs who promised utilitarian benefits.[19]

As if the presumption of state favor was not enough to encourage innovation, antebellum improvers sought two additional legal advantages that often put them at odds with the republican culture of the founding era: bankruptcy protection and limited corporate liability. Great risks accompanied grand visions, and novel technologies could swallow fortunes in false starts and failed experiments. The first canal investors, for example, lost most of their capital, as did many steamboat inventors and private investors in the public-works systems of Pennsylvania, Indiana, and other jurisdictions. Prudent investors hung back; yet, the example of Erie and the rise of New York port also proved that the cautious might forever inherit the lesser kingdom. In a dynamic capitalist marketplace, entrepreneurs sought ways to differentiate failure caused by sloth or misbehavior from failures resulting from the risks inherent in reaching toward the unknown. If a man went broke developing a railroad he was worthy of rehabilitation; if he went broke in wild speculations or from buying yet another cotton farm in the overheated Mississippi Delta, the judgment of the market must stand. In a special extension of the same idea, if a corporation—say a railroad—borrowed millions for expansion, the original stockholders wanted to limit their own liability to the amount of their initial investment. To common debtors, however, both bankruptcy and limited liability looked like crooked deals resembling the special immunities that once kept gentlemen out of prisons—a species of preferment completely at odds with equality before the law.[20]

A legal culture that encouraged improvers and favored capitalist social relations did not come together quickly. With two dozen states making laws and all sorts of judges and magistrates passing judgments, ancient customs and local peculiarities survived long into the nineteenth century. As late as 1841 the Supreme Court of Alabama upheld the centuries-old municipal practice of licensing bakers and fixing the "assize of bread" to best provide subsistence to the urban poor. That said, the federal commitment to comity among the states and the sanctity of contracts, coupled with rising geographical mobility, longer lines of commercial interaction, and the promiscuous blending of personal expectations in new interior communities, tipped the scales steadily in favor of a single common standard governing economic life. As that standard took shape it clearly favored enterprise over tradition, activity over inertia, equality over special privilege, and freedom over community restraint. The consequence of this evolution in legal culture was what historian J. Willard Hurst once called a tremendous "release of energy."[21]

Fostering Useful Knowledge

Energy alone did not produce revolutionary improvements or displace the traditions and customs that had served for generations to restrain the spread of innovation. But the sudden gift of liberty and equality did foster among the impatient and restless Americans a hunger for literacy and education as well as access to the specialized knowledge that earlier had been locked away in the "secrets" that masters of every trade guarded for generations. For centuries artisan traditions maintained technical knowledge in the heads and hands of the masters who trained the next generation, imparting to their charges both ancient techniques and whatever innovations had crept into workshop practice. Three developments growing out of Enlightenment intellectual ambitions gradually set the stage for a radical transformation in the creation and dissemination of useful knowledge, a transformation that institutionalized technological information and made possible the industrial revolution of the nineteenth century. First, clever artisans labored to improve the tools and machines of their trade, embedding ever more information in the hardware of production rather than relying only on the art and memory of skilled practitioners. Second, other clever artisans, working with printers and engravers, produced "how-to" books, manuals, and encyclopedias filled with instructions for everything from compounding medicines to constructing window frames. Finally, both gentlemen and common persons stirred themselves to institutionalize science, invention, and progress in the useful arts. In postrevolutionary America, the pursuit of improvement through technology became a nationwide obsession, the negative impact of which often went unnoticed outside the ranks those immediately affected.

Consider first the hardware: the creation of tools and machines that contained within their operations information and skills once lodged in the persons of the workers themselves. Textile machinery stands as the best example of this trend, which began in England in the eighteenth century. In 1733 John Kay rigged a simple sling on his handloom that made it possible to throw the shuttle back and forth across a wider beam. Thanks to this "flying shuttle" productivity soared, creating pressure on the supply of yarn that was made by women, one thread at a time, as it had been for a thousand years. In 1764 Richard Hargreaves devised an ungainly-looking hand-cranked "spinning jenny" on which a single operative could spin eight yarns at once. Next Richard Arkwright perfected a "water frame," driven by machine power, that produced a stronger thread but again only one at a time. Samuel Crompton crossbred the two ideas, and "Crompton's mule" quickly revolutionized the production of cotton cloth in what became Britain's "dark satanic mills." This cluster of "smart machines" was joined in 1804 by a French invention, the Jacquard loom, that used a primitive punch card computer to produce beautiful complex coverlets while tended by operatives who knew little about the design. These machines, endowed with skill and information, quickly found their way to the new Untied States, where they were copied and improved by relentless tinkering by dozens of workers and entrepreneurs. In time they would so transform the means of production that "manufactured" came to mean, not made by hand, but made by machine in factories.[22]

The second strand of improvement fed off the proliferation of published materials that laid before a large, anonymous audience, the technical "mysteries," recipes, and processes of skilled trades. Rarely seen before 1780, imprints with the phrase "useful arts" in the title appeared in England and America in rapidly increasing numbers toward the end of the century. For example, *One Thousand Valuable Secrets, in the Elegant and Useful Arts, Collected from the Practice of the best Artists* appeared in Philadelphia in 1795, cataloging the best methods for engraving, making glass, paint, dyes, pigments, casting in molds, distilling liquors, fishing, bird catching, and on and on. In 1807 Jacob Johnson republished in Pennsylvania a three-volume *Book of Trades, or Library of the Useful Arts* which first had appeared in London three years before. In Liverpool in 1816 James Smith published *The Mechanic, or, Compendium of Practical Inventions*, collecting 213 articles. In the next decade George G. Carey's collection, *The Artisan; or, Mechanic's Instructor; Containing a Popular, Comprehensive, and Systematic view of the most Useful Sciences*, appeared in London. Weavers, carpenters, millwrights, engravers, even physicians and surgeons, found the secrets of their trade available in books by the early 1800s. As historian W. J. Rorabaugh observed, these publications "devalued apprenticeship" and "subverted the master's authority"—often because apprentices now could learn that their masters knew less than they presumed about their own trades.[23]

Campaigns to encourage and promote manufactures and technology sprang from the effort of genteel intellectuals and the working classes themselves. In 1785 an Association of Tradesmen and Manufacturers of the Town of Boston protested postwar economic conditions and lobbied on behalf of protection for domestic manufactures. (It is worth noticing the interchangeable nature of the terms "artisan" and "manufacturer" at this early date.) Similar organizations sprang up in Providence, New York, Philadelphia, New Haven, and Baltimore—all places where populations of skilled workers considered it their right and civic duty to advocate the interests of American producers and consumers. Elite members of Philadelphia's American Philosophical Society established a variety of prize competitions to encourage invention and practical problem-solving. In Philadelphia Tench Coxe, assistant secretary to Hamilton, organized a society for promoting "Manufactures and Useful Arts," and he lectured up and down the seaboard encouraging others to do likewise.[24]

The interests of elite and leather-apron activists began to diverge in many places as the new century dawned. Mechanics groups added mutual aid benefits, self-help programs, libraries and reading rooms all designed to prevent their loss of independence as capitalist markets evolved. In 1812, a group of middling tradesmen who felt unwelcome at the Philosophical Society, organized an "Academy of Natural Sciences of Philadelphia" dedicated to "SCIENCE UNCONNECTED with RELIGION or POLITICS." Dedicated to radical inquiry, "free thought," and popular science education, the new academy sponsored a variety of public lectures on useful things such as chemistry, botany "for ladies," and entomology. Within a few years the editor of the academy's journal, William Maclure, published a treatise on geology that flatly contradicted the Genesis story. In 1824 the Franklin Institute (also Philadelphia) launched similar ambitious programs of research, promotion, technological improvement. Proclaimed a speaker there in 1825: "The present is, pre-eminently, an age of inquiry, and of enterprise, of discovery, of invention, and of universal improvement. It is an age, full of destiny; and if we are just to ourselves, of most auspicious augury to our country."[25]

Useful knowledge and technical education even penetrated the ivy halls of Harvard College. At his death in 1814, a British physicist named Benjamin Thompson, Count Rumford, endowed a Harvard professorship to give regular courses and public lectures in the practical sciences. Jacob Bigelow, a medical doctor already on the staff at Harvard Medical School, took on the new charge. In 1816 he delivered an inaugural address that canonized the excitement coming into focus on the role of practical science and innovation for the world to come. In the "history of philosophy," Bigelow began, everything was "permanent and progressive." The practical triumphs of science showed a "uniform tendency" to "promote the happiness of mankind." Extending their trajectory forward promised "an unlimited prospect for the future." Gone in Bigelow's assessment were the organic cycles of rise and decline, birth and death, that had defined the human condition since the Creation. Bigelow is credited with coining the word "technology," and in 1829 he published an important encyclopedia called *Elements of Technology; Taken Chiefly from a Course of Lectures Delivered at Cambridge, on the Application of the Sciences to the Useful Arts.* Enthusiasm for bridging the practical and theoretical in higher education spread slowly among American universities, as most real inventions still sprang from workshops and teams of technicians working on canals, railroads, or in machine shops such as Brown and Sharpe in Providence, Rhode Island. Nevertheless, institutional foundations were being poured that soon would bring higher education into service to the culture of exploitation through the Cooper Union in New York (1859), Massachusetts Institute of Technology in Cambridge (1861), and a national system of technical universities created by Congress under the Morrill Act (1863).[26]

Perfecting Technique

Improvements, of course, did not wait for the establishment of the cultural infrastructure that would sustain industrialization throughout the nineteenth century. Much of the impetus for change came from simple commonsense responses to increasing demand that resulted from improved transportation and the emergence of larger long-distance markets for goods and services. Upward pressure on aggregate demand came from simple population growth: 31.5 million in 1860, up from 3.9 at the 1790 census. American families in the early republic grew about as fast as was possible— adding four or five children per decade and losing fewer of them to early death. Add to this voluntary immigration of 5.3 million and uncounted enslaved Africans imported (illegally after 1808) for the booming southern cotton culture. Between 1800 and 1860 these free individuals purchased from the federal government nearly 160 million acres of undeveloped land, cut off its forest cover, plowed up its grasses, and planted it with cotton, wheat, and corn (an enormous environmental transformation by itself).[27]

Domestic consumer demand grew also because of increased specialization and the steady rise in market involvement especially among rural households. Where links with an urban market improved, farmers focused more energy on meat, produce, or dairy production, shifting away from the diversified "safety-first" strategies that characterized husbandry in the eighteenth-century countryside. Specialization increased marketable output while it narrowed a household's economic footprint. With the resulting cash income people purchased from their neighbors (or the neighborhood store) more of the things they once made at home, stimulating further specialization by rural carpenters and cabinetmakers, weavers, blacksmiths, cobblers, tinkers, and harness makers. Expanding markets rewarded new players with wider consumer choices and rising levels of material prosperity that masked any risk of dependency. Evidence of prosperity in one place stirred up desires elsewhere, resulting in new demands for internal improvements for better access to markets to "vent" the surplus piled up by newly focused specialized producers. The upward spiral was dramatic and infectious.[28]

Consider an extraordinary example of the complex linkages between improved access to markets and local growth in the wake of the Erie Canal. Rochester, New York, in 1817 was a wilderness village of about 700 souls; by 1840 it had exploded into a city of nearly 20,000. Sitting at the falls of the Genesee River, in the heart of a vast landscape perfect for agriculture, Rochester reeked of potential if only a market could be found for the wheat that could be grown on the tens of thousands of acres in its hinterland. Shortly after the Erie Canal gained legislative approval, confident Rochester boosters erected mills at the great falls and began making flour. Once the canal arrived (1823), nearby wheat cultivation quickly tripled. Pre-canal flour exports stood at 26,000 barrels; output topped 200,000 five years later and half a million by 1840. The secondary impact proved just as dramatic. Coopers struggled to produce a staggering number of barrels, and wheat farmers spent winter months cutting blanks for barrel staves. Other tradesmen flocked into town to make or peddle all the goods and services needed by the burgeoning population. Blacksmiths pounded out tools, nails, horseshoes, wagon tires, and other hardware fittings. House carpenters threw up new dwellings as quickly as possible—adopting the new "balloon frame" construction technique. Growing at roughly a thousand people per year, the resident population created extraordinary demand for every sort of manufactures—from shoes and hats to carpets, cookstoves, and pianos, which Rochester firms sprang up to provide.[29]

The pressure of these sudden demands revolutionized manufacturing itself. Traditionally, products had been made in small shops of master craftsmen who owned the capital equipment *and* the "secrets" of their craft. They took on apprentices, bound to work for a term of years in exchange for a technical education. Each shop employed one or two journeymen— "graduate student" assistants in this trade-school system—working for minimal wages while perfecting their skills and saving money to start their own establishments. Goods were "bespoke," that is, custom ordered in advance by the purchaser, and everyone in the shop learned the whole business from start to finish. Rising demand was met by the replication of shops, not by increased output per hour by workmen already engaged. But when demand rose very quickly, as it did in the boom town of Rochester, some enterprising masters turned to innovations inside the shop.[30]

Dramatic productivity gains resulted from surprisingly modest changes in workshop protocols. By subdividing complex tasks, masters routinized low-skill activities and reserved to themselves and their best journeymen the finishing touches requiring true "mastery" of the craft. Skilled shoe-makers cut up expensive leather and performed complex final assembly steps, but journeymen could wield the awl and anyone who sewed (even women) might stitch together uppers. Coopers' assistants assembled flour barrels from mass-produced blanks. Specialty shops mass-produced standardized windows and doors that could be installed by rough carpenters without the services of skilled joiners. Clever workmen developed jigs and frames for standardizing tasks, each time embedding in equipment (capital) the information that once came through the hand from the human mind. Traditional shops became protofactories. Resident masters evolved into merchant-managers who often moved out of the shop to a quiet town-house. Journeymen developed truncated skills and earned too little ever to establish an independent household. Throughout urban America, the stealth advance of such "bastard workshops" ramped up production to meet booming markets, but the workers would see no improvement in their condition. In New York City, by the 1820s, historian Sean Wilentz found that nearly half of workmen in manufacturing suffered career stagnation as "journeymen-for-life."[31]

One case of "improved" technique made a special impression on manufacturing trades for generations to come: the construction of complex assemblies from interchangeable parts. Pioneered at the Springfield and

Harper's Ferry Armories and perfected at the Connecticut handgun factories of Samuel Colt, this breakthrough became known as the "American System" of manufacturing. Once again, the idea transferred precious information from the craftsman's hands into the tools, molds, and dies designed to produce nearly identical pieces. And like the "bastard workshop" in other trades, the change crept up on a generation of artisans because the first iterations still required fine fitting. At first gunsmiths enjoyed relief from the tedium of fabricating every part from raw stock; however, as machine tools grew more precise, tolerances improved and assembly required less filing and fitting—until eventually, none at all. On that day the gunsmith became an assembler, nothing more.[32]

Another impressive (but not more important) harbinger of a new industrial order was the interlocking system of big machines found in textile factories. British-style water-powered spinning machines first appeared in Pawtucket, Rhode Island, early in the 1790s, reproduced by an English immigrant named Samuel Slater. These early spinning mills proliferated all over southern New England, producing a glut of yarn and a boon for cottage weavers who suddenly could earn more at the loom than at the plow. Drawn to any technical bottleneck, inventors gradually perfected the equipment required to mechanize weaving as well, so that by the 1830s the whole operation of textile production moved into vast new factory complexes. At Lowell, Massachusetts, enormous waterworks harnessed the mighty Merrimack River to power a tangle of shafts, pulleys, and belts driving dozens of machines tended by hundreds of "operatives"—mostly young women and children working ten- or twelve-hour shifts six days per week. In the early stages of industrialization these giant factories produced only the coarsest and cheapest products, but smaller specialty manufacturers scrambled to acquire mechanical advantages as quickly as possible. The proliferation of steam engines in the 1830s enabled producers to leave the rural mill-seats and better exploit urban markets and labor pools.[33]

The transition to industrial employment for white artisans, unmarried girls, women, and children posed a delicate set of issues, especially after the Revolution promised a universal right to independence and happiness. The "benevolent" developers of Lowell crafted a paternalistic boardinghouse system to swaddle New England farm girls entering factory jobs so that their "virtue" and future marriageability might be preserved. Forced to locate where the power source was best, smaller rural textile mills often built new villages from scratch to attract a workforce. Samuel Slater hired whole families, giving the husbands farm work nearby so he could employ their wives and children for wages in the factory. Both the boardinghouse and the mill village likely appeared advantageous in prospect, making the first steps into industrial employment both attractive and more or less voluntary. Only when market forces—competition, overproduction, further mechanization, or commercial and financial disruptions—caused manufacturers to lay off workers and redeploy their capital for more "improved" equipment did the dangers of dependency clearly appear. After the Panic of 1837, for example, both the Lowell girls and the families that worked in Slater-style mill towns found themselves out of work, out of money, and bound in debt to their employers for unpaid room and board. Improved "labor saving" devices had ushered in a level of dependency completely unexpected by employees—and perhaps their employers as well. Here was an early sign that the *system* of industrial development might entrap its beneficiaries in ways not imagined in a universe of small private firms, face-to-face relations, and limited economies of scale. Textile workers had no difficulty recognizing their own loss of freedom under the new regime; what they found hard to believe, however, were the complaints of their employers that they too felt powerless in the culture of exploitation.[34]

While northern industrialists learned how to rationalize manufacturing and exploit white labor with greater efficiency, southern farmers reinvented plantation slavery. In a way slavery itself was a "labor-saving device" that allowed the master to claim all the gain from the work of black hands without the nuisance of paying wages. While the tobacco culture languished after the Revolution, planters from Georgia westward turned to growing cotton for British industry. Once again technology opened the door to this revolutionary development: in 1793 inventors fashioned the first effective engine for cleaning the pesky seeds out of short-staple cotton. Using earlier tools a worker might clean five pounds of cotton per day, but with the new hand-cranked gin he or she could process fifty. Nothing deserves more credit for the transition of southern agriculture to short-staple cotton than the invention of this simple machine. And of course the cotton culture reinvigorated African slavery as an American labor system and perpetuated the bondage of millions for three more generations.[35]

As cotton plantations spread across the lower South (and into the nineteenth century) slavery itself evolved into a more modern, more efficient, more flexible, and more demanding institution. Antebellum critics faulted slavery for being inefficient and irrational, charges that long were repeated by historians who took comfort in seeing the persistence of slavery as a great historical anomaly. In the last generation, scholars have described as a "second slavery" the vast industrial deployment of enslaved Africans in the era of the cotton culture, portraying a more nimble, self-conscious, and businesslike system of labor management. Compared to the old tobacco culture of the Chesapeake, this new slavery adapted to technology, industrial settings, artisanal deployments, urban markets, leasing and rental arrangements, and rigorous tracking by masters of farm inputs and outputs, worker productivity, reproductive legacies, and time management experiments worthy of any northern factory at mid-century. Historian Walter Johnson portrays Mississippi Valley planters as hard-driving entrepreneurs fully committed to advancing dreams of wealth and glory on a world stage right up to the fall of Fort Sumter. Other detailed studies reveal a wide variety of personalities among the master class but little evidence of the clueless indifference to market forces or shrewd business that marked interpretations long ago. Perhaps most important, recently scholars have shown beyond a doubt that the emerging capitalist systems in the United States were integrated fully with and heavily dependent upon slavery in the South and elsewhere in the world. On the eve of the Civil War, American prosperity owed much to enslaved African Americans, the slaveholding master class, and the entrepreneurial actors in the North whose business intersected every day with the slave-based economy. The culture of exploitation in its most visceral and brutal form—slavery—lay at the root of the nation's cotton economy.[36]

Controlling Risk and Information

Sometimes improvements came in completely intangible form as new ideas, or new ways to manage and exchange information, facilitate transactions, or control risk. The circulation of information captured the attention of the revolutionary founders literally from the beginning. In behalf of informing the electorate in this new self-governing republic, nobody questioned the virtue of spreading "intelligence" as broadly and cheaply as possible. Even under the Articles of Confederation the post office enjoyed pride of place among the duties of the government, and under the Constitution its importance increased. Far and away the largest component of the federal establishment, the postal service adopted an unusually generous policy regarding newspapers in the mail. After a lively debate, in 1792 Congress settled on a plan to distribute newspapers for a nominal fee (a penny for a hundred miles) and codified a customary practice of allowing editors to exchange with each other for free. Thereafter, whether by mail stage or saddle bag, news in the mail became the information lifeblood of public life in America. The impact proved dramatic. By the 1820s, writes historian Richard John, newspapers made up a third to a half of the total weight of the mail. By 1840 every paper printed in the United States received free of charge an average of 4,300 exchange papers every year. That year thirty-nine million newspapers passed through the system. The circulation of information in the American interior astonished the French aristocrat Alexis de Tocqueville, who proclaimed in 1831, "I do not think that in the most enlightened rural districts of France there is intellectual movement either so rapid or on such a scale as in this wilderness."[37]

As markets grew larger and more complicated, specialized information relating to business gained in importance. Colonial newspapers long had printed shipping news and prices current while retailers' ads contained nothing more than lists of goods newly available in town. In 1812 Baltimore publisher Hezekiah Niles introduced a *Weekly Register* that emphasized business and commercial news. In 1827 in New York Samuel Morse and Arthur Tappan introduced a *Journal of Commerce*, still mostly detailing import/export and coastal trade. As domestic commerce increased, newspapers at interior towns provided similar information to assist local buyers and sellers. Out of New York in 1839 came *The Merchant's Magazine and Commercial Review*, containing business news and all kinds of statistics giving entrepreneurs everywhere something like equal access to the information required to throttle cheats and scammers. In 1846 J. D. B. DeBow started a southern monthly, *DeBow's Review*, in part to correct the Yankee bias some thought had crept into the public prints. With little coinage and no central banking system, merchants conducted business with a bewildering variety of currencies issued by hundreds of banking corporations. Banknote reporters began publishing, for their subscribers, weekly lists of discount rates, bank closures, and counterfeit notices. In larger business markets banks created clearance systems, such as the Boston area Suffolk System, to facilitate the exchange of notes and stabilize discounts. At greater distances merchants took unmeasurable chances. Another subscription service, the Mercantile Agency (1841), created by New York merchants Arthur and Lewis Tappan, collected for subscribing lenders personal information on individuals all over the country, establishing the first credit reporting agency.[38]

Since the advent of long-distance trade, the value of commodities always was tied to their actual supply in the market. In the eighteenth century, when a shipload of tea from China arrived in Boston or Baltimore, the price of tea was affected immediately by the fact of its being for sale. Merchants understandably craved advance information that would allow them to know about market demands before the fact of supply was widely known. They sent letters ahead in sealed pouches hoping to advantage their distant correspondents; they bribed ship captains, pilots, and supercargoes to secure information on the contents of the hold while the ship made its way to the docks; at New York harbor's Sandy Hook, men lit bonfires and released pigeons to signal the arrival of vessels (whose contents they only surmised). Every merchant understood the agony of landing in Barbados with a shipload of butter (or worse, ice) only to find the market glutted. If only they could separate the knowledge of supply from the thing itself!

One early and effective step in that direction came on January 5, 1818, when New York's Black Ball line of sailing ships adopted a regular schedule of transatlantic crossings. Before that day saltwater vessels had sailed when the hold was full and the operators ready. Passengers might idle away days, even weeks, in port waiting for the signal, or their trip might be prolonged by an opportunistic detour ordered at the last minute. In such a world, time was *not* money. But in 1818 the volume of traffic to and from Liverpool warranted the risk of announcing regular service, twice a month, every month, with the promise to embark, empty or full, in pursuit of a new virtue: timeliness. Soon scoffers warmed to the idea of scheduled service as the Black Ball gathered up the business of travelers, high-value goods, money, news, letters, and other documents with time-related importance. Coastal packets copied the scheme, as did some steamboats, express freight carriers, and early canal packets. When later railroads embraced tight scheduling (as a convenience for their own operations), their customers already expected as much and delighted in the greater speed and efficiency of railway travel.[39]

Another "software" innovation developed by New York merchants streamlined the transport of southern cotton from America to Liverpool. Armed with regular service and thus the best price information from England, New York middlemen gathered the English buyers to bid on the cotton trade that "rightly" belonged to Charleston, Savannah, or New

Orleans. At the same time, shipping whole bales of cotton to New York only to reship them to Liverpool seemed a waste of time. New York brokers developed a system of selling cotton in New York from samples of bales which then shipped direct to Liverpool from southern ports, saving hundreds of miles of transport for the bulky commodity itself. Southern traders howled in protest, but their Yankee colleagues provided the package of credits, assurances, and services that English importers of cotton demanded.[40]

What finally gratified the utopian dreams of nineteenth-century merchants was the successful launch in 1844 of Samuel Morse's telegraph. Under technical development in Europe and America for years, a workable electromagnetic telegraph was patented more or less simultaneously in 1837 by an English team and the American Morse. Finally granted congressional funding of $30,000, Morse strung his demonstration wires between Baltimore and Washington (forty-four miles) just in time for the 1844 presidential nominating conventions, both of which took place in Baltimore in May. After the first dramatic message—"What Hath God Wrought," transmitted May 24—politicians trapped in Washington reportedly did nothing but watch for Morse's news from the Baltimore convention site. Instantaneous communication proved useful to political operatives, and telegraphic intelligence from the 1846 Mexican-American War did more than anything to familiarize Americans with this new communications landscape. But it was business that felt the most dramatic impact from telegraphic messaging. Finally data and prices flashed instantly across space while goods and people made their patient way from one place to another. In time (about twenty-five years) undersea cables would collapse the information float worldwide and create a global "present-tense" market unimaginable in earlier times. Railroads seized on it immediately for accurate train control and troubleshooting. Tighter schedules, faster trains, more accurate tracking of shipments on the move all were made possible by the telegraph that ran, by 1860, along virtually every railroad line.[41]

As reported two generations ago by historian Robert G. Albion, the rise of New York port resulted from a masterful convergence of innovations at the hands of Manhattan merchants and state politicians. The Erie Canal, of course, played a central role, as did the Black Ball line of packets, and the creative efforts of the city's cotton brokers. In addition, New York insurance underwriters perfected forms of marine, fire, and life insurance that mitigated various risks in markets floating on credit, trust, and good intentions.

New York warehousemen, the city's system of dockside auctions, flexible bankers, commercial publishers, news-gatherers, and credit snoops—all together they made doing business in New York more efficient than it could be anywhere else in the early United States. Eagerness of the city to host the business of the new nation gave New York an "open for business" feeling unmatched in other ports. This combination of factors proved so effective that, when railroads superseded canals as primary commercial conveyance, New York merchants forced the railroad to come to them in order to gain from the advances made in the generation of "internal improvement."[42]

Improving Character Itself

No meditation on the idea of improvement in early America would be complete without considering the widespread interest in cultivating personal virtue and character as Americans took up their experiment with liberation. The miracle of "self-creation" by which they constituted themselves a new nation marched in lockstep with concerns for self-cultivation, moral, spiritual, intellectual improvement, and that civic virtue without which republicanism surely must falter. Boundless opportunities for personal improvement, mobility, and self-fashioning captured the imagination of postrevolutionary Americans. Ironically, the impulse that first manifested itself in community associations for charity, benevolence, and collective uplift devolved over time into a cult of the "self-made man." Liberal individualism took root, leaving autonomous individuals obsessed with "self-control" in a heartless world of market forces, temptations, and moral failure.

We already have seen how communities of artisans organized themselves into mechanics' societies for mutual improvement and protection. The same urge produced other kinds of young men's associations, library societies, lyceums, and the like, dedicated to fostering benevolence and helping maintain civic virtue in a new social order where freedom displaced tradition and disorder threatened conventional expectations. The problems and their solutions were spelled out neatly on July 4, 1833, by Amasa Walker in a speech to the "Young Men of Boston Associated for Moral and Intellectual Improvement." Before an audience comprising members of twelve different self-help organizations, Walker challenged his own generation to resist self-gratification and help complete the "splendid temple of American liberty."[43]

Young men, Walker observed, recently drawn to the city by economic opportunities, found themselves swept "down the current of sensuality, constantly inclined to mere animalism." These new organizations made it "honorable to be exemplary," while membership provided a "certificate of good character." Temperance, of course, was one virtuous objective. Public education was another. Wholesome entertainments must be generated for young men and women, and Walker went out of his way to stress that women, who had "*heads*, as well as *hearts*," should be enlisted in the cause of "virtue and knowledge." "Undisciplined" avarice corroded "every social, benevolent, and humane sensibility." Reading, science, and inquiry naturally helped a young man moderate his desires, "enjoy his competency, and use it for the good of others." Standing at precisely the temporal divide between romantic republicanism of the revolutionary era and the competitive liberalism to come, Walker imagined a day when the purpose of wealth was to "use it for the general good." True equality would come when "the free institutions of our happy land" firmly rested "on the imperishable foundation of universal intelligence, and public virtue."[44]

Alas, the universal happiness Walker imagined never quite materialized. Voluntary associations *did* proliferate, especially among the middle ranks, but controversy swirled around reform objectives such as temperance and common schools. Thomas Jefferson famously lobbied for public common schools in Virginia to facilitate a broadly literate electorate. Benjamin Rush proposed a similar idea for Pennsylvania, and the Land Ordinance of 1785 set aside Section 16 of public lands for the support of schools in the West. Nevertheless, basic schooling faltered in most places in the early republic. Taxpayers rebuffed all nonessential burdens. Country people—especially in the slave-heavy South—saw little urgency in "book learning" for commoners while elites hired private tutors for their own children. Frontier states such as Indiana "borrowed" the value of school lands to build jails and courthouses. In the 1830s Massachusetts named Horace Mann the first secretary of their new State Board of Education, and Mann campaigned tirelessly for public, nonsectarian schools both as a civil right and a necessary safeguard against social chaos. But because schools taught moral and ethical values, some Protestants and nearly all Catholics resisted curricula designed to alienate their children from the ideas taught at home. Because many school reformers also pushed temperance and antislavery, German and

Irish ethnics as well as most slaveholders eyed them suspiciously. Finally, romantic celebrations of equality, such as Walker's cited above, generated fears among a new class of capitalist employers that schools would foment restlessness among the working classes just as employers tried to impose factory discipline.[45]

In 1845 Catherine Beecher, founder of a Female Seminary and staunch advocate of public education, pleaded for American women to "save their country" by stepping up and demanding schools for the children. By then census data showed that *"one million adults"* could not read or write and that twice that many children had no schools to attend. In Indiana, Illinois, Iowa, and Missouri less than half the children had access to schools; throughout the South the proportion of white children in school was even lower. Bad as that was, education was "losing ground every day." A famous New England evangelical reformer—daughter of Lyman Beecher, sister of Henry Ward Beecher—Catherine Beecher no doubt stirred the hearts of sympathetic readers, but no Beecher would win to the common school cause persons suspicious of New England's cultural pretensions, religious intolerance, and flagrant antipathy to slavery.[46]

If school reform caught on slowly, self-cultivation through lyceums and public lectures thrived after 1830. Talks on political economy, chemistry, horticulture, astronomy, and natural history drew ready audiences in small towns as well as major cities. Temperance campaigners spread out across the country as did home missionaries, prison reformers, advocates of institutions for the care of the insane, for the "rescue" of fallen women, and the "protection" of seamen on shore leave. Audiences found it impossible to judge the quality of what they were told by traveling experts in phrenology, magnetism, and homeopathic or Thomsonian medicine. Stage presence, rhetorical skill, popularity, and reputation kept speakers on the circuit. In the 1830s Ralph Waldo Emerson became one of the most successful lecturers in the country, but one wonders if people understood his transcendental musings or simply enjoyed the celebrity of hearing the great man in person. Communitarians peddled visions of utopia in radical phalansteries, free-love enclaves, interracial settlements, millenarian congregations, and celibate Shaker communities. Derision turned violent whenever such speakers strayed too far into unorthodox sexual, racial, or economic arrangements, something Shakers, Fourierists, Rappites, and Mormons learned the hard way. After 1831, as Garrisonian abolitionists gained momentum in the North and upper Midwest, their speakers were pelted with eggs and tomatoes. In 1837 abolitionist printer

Elijah Lovejoy was murdered by an Illinois mob, and a decade later African American lecturer Frederick Douglass was beaten and left for dead outside Pendleton, Indiana. The fabric of American values, once thought to be universal and benevolent, began to tear as one person's edification struck others as dangerous madness.[47]

To navigate this complex world of contradictory messages, young people and their parents studied advice that was published in religious periodicals, medical tracts, and advice books specifically designed for youths going out into a market-driven world where parents and neighbors no longer watched over their affairs. The temptations of alcohol, tobacco, gambling, and lewd entertainments naturally stood condemned as likely to destroy the hopes of youth, but sexuality itself also came in for a new degree of disapprobation. Where society once focused on containing sex within marriage, a new sexual ethic after 1830 elevated self-restraint and self-denial to an absolute virtue. The mating impulse itself came to be seen as pathological, a brute relic that, if not mastered completely, was bound to destroy the indulgent youth. Advice on how to suppress sexuality turned up everywhere, while other "experts" labored to prevent any discussion (in print or in person) of basic facts about sex, conception, and especially contraception. Masturbation came in for especially heavy condemnation: experts warned parents not to allow adolescents any privacy and to investigate fully signs of happiness or giggling as evidence of brain-rotting habits. Even in marriage, gratification and pleasure were proscribed. Coitus more than monthly, or indulged for any purpose other than procreation, was said to threaten the health of adult bodies. Children, once an unavoidable "gift" from God, now stood as evidence of moral weakness if not criminal intent. South Carolina political economist Thomas Cooper wrote in 1833, that those who "marry and beget children" without the "probable means" of supporting them commit "a crime" by "plundering their neighbor's earnings."[48]

Self-control, self-denial, self-restraint, self-cultivation, self-creation—the responsibility for any and all outcomes seemed to pile onto the liberal individual by the latter years of the antebellum period. Historian Brian Luskey has exposed the ambivalent matrix of demands and temptations confronting youths who entered urban business communities seeking the fortune which theory promised to hardworking men of good character. Especially as northerners grew more impatient with the persistence of chattel slavery, so-called free labor became the defining touchstone of the capitalist North. Free state critics of emerging "wage slavery"—Orestes Brownson for example—failed to carry the argument against free-labor ideologues, in part because proslavery fanatics, such as Virginia's George Fitzhugh, used the same arguments to defend slavery as an organic, benevolent system that bound masters and servants harmoniously. Enjoying lawful freedoms denied chattel slaves, white men and women in the late antebellum economy found it literally impossible to protest their increasing powerlessness in the marketplace. As a result, negative outcomes and disappointments readily were blamed on the failure of individuals to make the most of their time and opportunities. In a free country everyone can be rich. Why on earth are you not?[49]

No word captured the promise of the age quite like "improvement." Who could fault a person for wanting to improve the conditions of life on earth—especially life among a free people blessed by God and history with continental resources, utopian institutions, intelligence and industry enough to remove any barrier, solve any problem, and unlock the secrets of the natural world for the benefit of mankind? Science, theology, philosophy, political economy, all the disciplines of human wisdom seemed to support an optimistic reading of the progress of the American people in the first half of their new century. Boundlessness defined the universe of possibilities. Horizontally, Americans faced a continental landscape that to them appeared to be empty and destined for development by the agents of civilization. Vertically, American ingenuity promised to intensify the fruits of labor and innovation such that no shortages need occur, no consequences need impinge, no discouraging words need dampen their enthusiasm. "Young America" strutted onto the world stage, strong, brash, confident, and charmingly innocent of guile or greed. The culture of exploitation had begun to take its mature form, and the cult of improvement cast a positive light on the consequences—good, bad, or indifferent—of Americans' ambitions. One might almost conclude that a people so blessed and so situated were not acting on their own behalf but merely fulfilling something like a destiny that was written in the book of time before they came of age.

CHAPTER 7

Destiny

A PATRIOTIC FABLE: *Once upon a time a large population of free Americans, responding to an invitation from the government of Mexico, exercised their "natural right" to leave one country and settle in another for the purpose of improving their lives. Once established in the Texas wilderness, these intrepid pioneers found themselves "enslaved" by a Mexican government that revoked the "guarantees" they had been offered. Because of this abrogation of the original terms of settlement [ran the argument], Texans were "rightfully and absolutely released" from all "allegiance" or "duty" to the Mexican state. Had they staged a revolution to secure their independence, nothing could have been more legitimate; but they did something even more noble by mounting a "resistance to revolution," rejecting new restrictions laid down in contradiction to the emigrants' original compact. Once wholly independent, those same Texans freely sought—and received—incorporation into the United States. The Mexican state cried foul, claiming an aggressive assault upon its territory and its honor. What could be "more preposterous" [concluded our narrator] than the hue and clamor raised by Mexico, that the annexation of Texas amounted to a seizure of her territory?*[1]

Such a narrative was published in 1845 in an expansionist journal, *The United States Magazine and Democratic Review*. A few months later a war broke out with Mexico, by the end of which the United States owned (counting Texas) over half of Mexico's territory. According to this story, the "self-evident" truths enshrined in the Declaration of Independence guaranteed free people an "unalienable" right to throw off a tyrannical regime and establish another better suited to their desires. Like the colonists in British North America about a century before, the Texas pioneers suffered an abridgment of "rights" they claimed but never had been granted, and they feared "enslavement" by laws not of their own making. They had imagined (were encouraged to do so) that despite laws on the books to the contrary, they did not need to worship in the Catholic Church or give up their African slaves. Mexico specifically outlawed slavery (although infractions had gone unpunished), and when Mexico moved to enforce these laws, Americans rebelled, claiming a "natural" right to dismember the Mexican federation in defense of their (illegal) institutions. Now they begged for admission to the Union, supported by American enthusiasts in both parties and both sections who thought the United States ought to encompass the whole continent of North America.

Keep your eye on the shape of this argument. The friends of Texas annexation embraced this narrative and celebrated Texas independence (as well as its admission to the Union) as perfect expressions of the rights of free people everywhere. Those who dared to label annexation "unrighteous," "spoliation," or "territorial aggrandizement," stood condemned for "checking the fulfillment of our manifest destiny to overspread the continent allotted by Providence for the free development of our yearly multiplying millions."[2] Thus was coined a phrase—"manifest destiny"—a sentiment with deep roots in the colonizing process, now inscribed on triumphal banners celebrating the culture of exploitation and America's unique—exceptional—claim to carry that flag. Any resemblance of the Texas argument to claims made in the 1760s by their colonial ancestors was hardly coincidental. Several threads from the Stamp Act crisis could be seen running through the Texas story: innocent victims oppressed and enslaved by corrupt and arbitrary rulers bent (for no reason) on destroying a free and prosperous people. If Providence had destined the United States to "overspread the continent," who could fault the innocent agents of that world-historical outcome?

Destiny transcends ambition or desire, whether individual or collective. Destiny implies a purpose external to the living generation, a calling from a higher authority. Destiny ennobles purposeful actions and lends an aura of virtue to the consequences, whether great gains or tragic sacrifices. Most importantly, destiny is not to be ignored or impeded; to stand against it is to court disaster. Unfortunately destiny is not always manifest, or not so clearly manifest as to be self-evident. Americans arrived at the middle of the nineteenth century exhilarated by the astonishing results of a liberated people spreading freely across a rich store of natural resources. But their celebration of progress masked deep unresolved issues. The patriotic Texas narrative serves as an example of how one could spin events on the ground to fit the patterns required by "destiny." But modern readers familiar with the coming of the Civil War will notice that the argument not only echoes the revolutionary movement but eerily foreshadows a secessionist posture struck in 1861 by Texas and ten other states. *That* dismembering of empire would *not* be celebrated. The idea of destiny simultaneously empowered and endangered the American experiment in republican government. On its face the impending crisis appears to have been about slavery and freedom (a house divided), and so it was. But also at stake was lingering confusion about the gift of liberation itself: did freedom reside in the people as a whole (the commonwealth) or in emancipated persons who only incidentally shared the same landscape, markets, and social space? Did liberation empower "We the people," or all persons individually?

Base Desires, Grand Explanations

By the middle of the nineteenth century an American sense of destiny had taken root in the national consciousness. Not that it went uncontested. Every claim for a national destiny generated discord, often because of the dissonance produced when rhetorical ideals clashed so blatantly with the base desires that seemed to motivate people's actions. From the beginning of colonization, transparently self-serving narratives had misrepresented the Indians as savages, British officials as tyrants, and a monarch's demand for obedience as the enslavement of American slaveholders. To rally support for the Revolution elite leaders had promised a kind of popular government most of them distrusted, and when the first constitutions enshrined too much of that democratic spirit they rushed to create a stronger national framework and called it a "federal" constitution. Finessing the problem of slavery in their new republic of liberty, the framers cynically counted their chattel for representation as "three-fifths of all other Persons." When the rise of cotton rekindled demand for slaves across the frontier, Thomas Jefferson comforted himself and others by declaring such dispersal a prelude to slavery's extinction. From the beginning American statesmen craved empire as well as local political autonomy. Such a pattern of delicate phrasing and self-delusion continued apace into the raucous nineteenth century, creating a positive voice-over narrative to cover scenes of wasteful "improvement," trespass, conquest, displacement, and dissimulation.[3]

This habit of seeing base private desires as part of a world-historical mission sustained a chorus of higher purposes that became known as "manifest destiny." Had the great powers of the world not been utterly distracted for fifty years by wars and revolutions, or had the resident Natives not been so beaten down by disease and dependency, American dreams about "manifest destiny" might have foundered early on; but such was not the case. The idea of destiny blossomed on two levels: in the collective awareness of emerging nationalism, and in the absolute confidence with which individual frontiersmen seized the objects of their private ambitions with or without any formal approval by governing authorities. Time and again interested parties invoked the "right" of self-creation to gratify immediate desires. They did so in frontier Ohio, forcing the Congress to set up the territorial system. They did so in Kentucky and Tennessee, bringing those new states into the Union in less than a decade of national existence. They did so all over Spanish Florida in the 1810s until the Transcontinental Treaty (1819) finally legitimized what settler transgressions already had done. They did so in Texas, where better than anywhere else, we can see the ambivalent forces at work in American expansion.[4]

In 1820, on the eve of Mexico's own independence, an American named Moses Austin secured a huge grant of Texas land on which to seat three hundred families from the United States. At the time powerful Comanche Indians dominated Mexico's northern wilderness. Louisiana planters gazed hungrily across the Sabine River into Comanche country, and Mexico hoped that Austin's emigrants would help anchor the region and deflect the kind of mischievous squatters that plagued West Florida. Moses died before he led anyone into this promised land, but his son Stephen clung to the grant through years of chaos in Mexican governments. By 1823 he was offering settlers spreads of over four thousand acres. Existing laws discouraged slavery (the offspring of slaves were born free) and mandated Catholic worship; but American emigrants assumed they enjoyed some exemption and, at first, nobody tried to enforce these expectations. With the cotton culture in full bloom, American planters poured into East Texas even as one Mexican government after another tried to discourage Americanization and stamp out African slavery. Austin and his followers in Texas struggled to preserve what they saw as their rights (that is, free land, Protestantism, and slavery), resulting by 1836 in a Texas revolution to liberate these holders of slaves. (At the Alamo, folk heroes Jim Bowie and Davy Crocket both died fighting for "freedom.") Now wedged between antislavery Mexico and proslavery Louisiana, the Lone Star Republic quickly requested admission to the Union.[5]

The annexation of Texas triggered bitter debates that both nourished and poisoned the idea of "manifest destiny." For one thing, Mexico promised war if the United States took in Texas, and American leaders showed little interest in such a military adventure. Slavery, of course, played a part in the arguments. At the time of the Revolution most people outside Georgia and South Carolina thought slavery was dying in the United States. Then came cotton. Watching in horror as planters spread their slave-based system across the Southwest, in 1819 free blacks and antislavery whites in the North mounted protests against Missouri statehood. The resulting "Mason-Dixon Line" divided the empire of liberty into "free soil" and "slave country." Around each label there developed a working ideology—a coded narrative about the promise of freedom and the meaning of progress. Both sides suspected the other of subverting their future prospects, but Congress and the political parties agreed for the sake of peace to eschew all sectional politics and suppress open discussion of the slavery question.[6]

Beneath this artificial comity resentments festered over tariffs, banking, roads, and canals. Both political parties—Whigs and Democrats—struggled to prevent their platforms from aligning with the slave-based sectional framework. Intensely afraid of becoming a helpless minority within the Union, planters guarded states' rights and resisted all federal actions they chose to construe as favoring free-soil interests (such as tariffs, banking, roads, and canals). After Missouri, new states were added in pairs, one slave, one free, to balance sectional power in the Senate. By 1836 Louisiana Territory north of the Mason-Dixon line still beckoned to free-soil pioneers, but the South had no frontier. Texas might give them a future. At the same time radical northern voices began calling for the abolition of slavery, everywhere, immediately. Even a small number of such firebrands now made it hard to keep sectional interests from poisoning national politics. When the Texas petition arrived in Congress (December 1836), tempers were frayed, partisan anxieties high, and sectional goodwill in short supply. Faced with a tinderbox, President Andrew Jackson postponed the Texas question, at least until his successor, Martin Van Buren, could be inaugurated.[7]

The Panic of 1837 and the long depression that followed preoccupied Congress and kept annexation at bay for another four years. Whigs won the election of 1840, but their candidate, William Henry Harrison, immediately died, thrusting Virginia's John Tyler into the presidency. A Whig in name only, Tyler's "hobby" was Texas annexation, and he pushed it as a way to quiet the sectional issues. Proslavery southern leaders such as John C. Calhoun seized annexation as an absolute birthright. Sympathetic northern expansionists saw Texas as a useful step (hardly the last) toward a shared developmental future because a new southwestern frontier made possible sectional balance as settlers flowed into Kansas, Nebraska, and Minnesota territories. Artful spokesmen in Congress tried to deflect antislavery objections with outlandish claims that Texas held the key to eventual emancipation. Blacks, they said (as if they were free to do so), inexorably migrated toward the equator, their natural habitat. Texas provided the only "drain" through which they could exit the United States. Many voters in the northern West warmed to this racist argument, if only to postpone the day of reckoning and register their hatred of blacks as well as slavery.[8]

Antiannexationists—especially in the Whig party—structured their objections around a profoundly different vision of American destiny. Democrats, they said, believed that progress involved nothing more than seizing new land on which farmers and planters carried out their timeless labors. Territorial expansion, said the Whigs, served no larger purpose than to harvest agrarian votes for a party that worked to obstruct any semblance of modernization. For Whigs, progress depended on industry, commerce, technology, and the constant encouragement of innovation—in a word, modernization. Frustrated for decades by Jacksonian Democrats who torpedoed his American System of developmental policies (national banking, tariff protection, and aid to roads and canals), Whig senator and presidential hopeful Henry Clay resisted Texas in hopes of exacting more cooperation on economic policy. At stake was the question of whether mere liberation was all that was needed to fulfill the American destiny, or whether a free people required coordination and guidance to accomplish great things. Democrats clearly said no; Clay's Whigs thought guidance was essential to achieve *collective* progress and realize the nation's potential. Confident that slavery itself would expire in time, Clay yearned for the day when his planter-colleagues gave up their fight against national economic policy and recognized their common destiny inside the culture of exploitation.[9]

Tyler's treaty of annexation in 1844 failed to gain Senate approval. Meanwhile James K. Polk won the Democratic nomination for president and launched the most aggressive expansionist campaign in American history. Polk's nomination terminated any hopes Tyler had for a second term. As one journal put it, Polk won the election riding Tyler's hobby (Texas) "all saddled and bridled and ready"—not the first man to go "to Texas on a stolen horse."[10] Convinced it was both good political strategy and cosmic national destiny, Polk made it his mission to finish the continental nation of his dreams. Polk planted one foot squarely on Jacksonian rejections of Clay's American System and the other on the "re-occupation" of Oregon territory and the "re-annexation" of Texas. In February 1845, after Polk's election and before his inauguration, Tyler managed to drive annexation through Congress, all but guaranteeing war with Mexico. After settling the Oregon question with a line at the forty-ninth parallel, in 1846 Polk sent his army across the Rio Grande, sparking hostilities with which to justify his war of aggression.[11]

Fracturing the Vision

The sordid story of the Mexican-American War has been told a dozen different ways, but it usually comes out the same: having "crushed" the Mexican "aggressors" and occupied the capital in Mexico City, the United States *paid* the vanquished nation millions to secure clear title to everything south of Oregon and west of Louisiana, namely California, New Mexico, and greater Texas. Disingenuous narratives, so convoluted as to defy simple logic, decorated both official explanations and the rhetoric found in the press. To cover his nakedness, Polk called the cession an "indemnity" from Mexico for starting an unjust war. The president stood ready to accept territory in lieu of cash, and he asked for $3 million to "enable" negotiations. Some congressmen blanched, but most people were not offended. The genius of Polk's appeal lay in recognizing that American destiny was tied, not to slavery or free soil per se, but to an acquisitive urge that was served by both. The emerging culture of exploitation could draw upon three competing technologies: slavery and the cotton culture, free-soil family farming, and free-labor capitalist industry. New systems of commerce, transportation, law, and financial services could be made to serve all three. All that new land in the West (so Polk's argument ran) afforded a neutral opportunity for further development: ambitious American settlers could be trusted to adopt—as they had done since the 1790s—whatever system they believed best fit the landscape before them.[12]

In such a narrative, the rich green valleys of Oregon and central California welcomed farmers of every description. The drier short-grass plains sustained ranchers, as they had for generations in Spanish California. The most arid regions—the so-called Great American Desert—likely marked the natural edge of the southern Cotton Kingdom, while the incredible ranges of mountains no doubt gleamed with undiscovered mineral wealth. As had been the case on the trans-Appalachian frontier, private settlers poured into these lands before Uncle Sam gained title. Even before the Oregon Treaty of 1846 well over five thousand settlers had traversed the fabled Overland Trail to plow up the lush Willamette Valley. By the end of 1847 some two thousand Mormons, driven by hostile neighbors from Missouri and Illinois, had trekked to the edge of the Great Salt Lake, where they hoped nobody would care how they prospered. Real estate hucksters such as Lansford Hastings sold golden dreams of life in the Central Valley of California, along with travel advice that gave at least one group—the Donner Party—a most gruesome experience. Then in 1848 the cry of "Gold!" went up from Sutter's Mill, and Polk's benign point of view acquired what should have been a new lease on life. Instead it set the table for the final bifurcation of manifest destiny into fiercely competing doctrines that would tear the Union apart.[13]

Polk's land grab could not be digested in the Congress of the United States because his permissive embrace of all three strands of modernization —slavery, free soil, and industrialization—could not be sustained. Back in 1846, firmly believing his party's claim that expansion was not about slavery, Pennsylvania Democrat David Wilmot threw down a simple proviso that ruined the political game. If slavery had nothing to do with extending the area of freedom, he said, let the friends of "manifest destiny" bar it in advance from any newly acquired lands. Horrible cries rose up from both ends of the political spectrum: from planters caught in their own webs of disinformation, and from the old custodians of compromise politics who saw this would destroy the middle ground. The Wilmot Proviso became a weapon with which a small clutch of antislavery members paralyzed the workings of Congress. By the spring of 1850 almost nothing had been accomplished on a long agenda of difficult matters including statehood for California, now teeming with free-soil residents. In January Henry Clay introduced an "Omnibus Bill" that balanced California statehood with a stronger national fugitive slave act (criminalizing any *failure* of northern parties to return runaway slaves), organized new territory on the principle of "popular sovereignty" (allowing settlers to decide about slavery when they wrote a constitution), and abolished slave trading but not slavery itself in the District of Columbia. For Clay procedures, not destinies, defined the American political system; through such horse-trading Congress had managed for thirty years to navigate questions of federal authority, constitutional construction, slavery and freedom. Staring into the abyss, statesmen now must do the right thing.[14]

What indeed was the "right thing" to do? In the Senate John C. Calhoun, South Carolina's senior proslavery statesman, delivered a blistering explanation of what it was that "endangered the Union." The South no longer felt safe because the rapid growth of the North now gave a "preponderance" of votes in the House, the Senate, and the Electoral College, to states that did not support slavery. Had this resulted, he said, from "the operation of time, without the interference of government, the South would have had no reason to complain; but such was not the fact." Calhoun then let fly a work of revisionist history asserting that federal laws from the very beginning had served (on purpose) to limit, exploit, and punish the slaveholding states. To northern ears this sounded bizarre: starting with the Constitution's three-fifths clause and ending with recent vetoes of banks and internal improvements, it seemed that southern interests had their own way in the national government almost without exception. But now Calhoun was turning it all inside out, fabricating a tale of free-state aggression that left the South hopelessly disadvantaged and threatened with emancipation that could only end in race war. For him, national destiny depended on sectional balance (which protected slavery). Unless Congress did something to restore equilibrium and silence antislavery agitators, the outcome *must* be disunion.[15]

The dying Calhoun (he would not live out the month) lay gasping on a litter in the aisle while Virginia's James Mason read these incendiary words. Although he tortured the facts to prove a pattern of northern hostility, Calhoun was not wrong about the precipice before them. California and Oregon Territory soon would add three free states to the Union, while Minnesota Territory and the remains of the Louisiana Purchase promised several more in time. Even subdividing Texas would not rebalance the Senate if slavery was excluded from the Mexican cession. The balanced Senate

alone protected southern slavery: without it a northern majority *could* man-
date emancipation in the South, prohibit migration into free states, and
create for the cotton kingdom a kind of Haitian nightmare. Before now
there had been no such desire. Northern politicians did not take advantage
of their clear majority in the House but rather suppressed attacks on slavery
itself and defended the right of the southern states to protect their institutions. But Calhoun's accusatory narrative inflamed the tempers of members
grown weary of catering to what now looked like a ravenous aristocracy
bent on thwarting the vigorous enterprising North.

Daniel Webster of Massachusetts, Calhoun's equal in service and reputation, rose to recover "the harmony" that once made "the blessings of this
Union so rich and so dear." Approaching Calhoun with a delicate touch,
Webster blamed the immediate crisis on "impatient men," fanatical persons
(he meant free-soil Democrats) unable to live with the flaws that inevitably
stained the collective affairs of a people. Shame on them: they voted to
annex Texas and half of Mexico then voted to exclude slavery, creating this
perilous impasse. At the time of the Constitution, Webster reminded the
chamber, the South had acquiesced in—even agreed with—the widespread
belief that slavery was "evil," a "blight," a "scourge," and a "curse." But
after 1800, due to the "sudden, surprising, and rapid growth of the cotton
planting interest," the South had reembraced slavery, grown "warm in its
favor" and hungry for new lands. All this was natural, and Webster imputed
no dishonor on the South. Faced with this dramatic reversal of expectations, northern statesmen (and voters) had gratified each new southern
demand and embraced both Texas and the Mexican cession as important
to the "destiny of this empire."

All this balance and accommodation, said Webster, came despite the
North possessing what Calhoun called a stranglehold on federal power.
Far from inhibiting southern progress, northern interests had endured the
resurgence of slavery—and would continue to do so as long as they were
not pressed to revere it as a "positive good" or admit it into regions where
all agreed it was banned. Throttle the free-soil rebels and the old harmony
could return. Then, in a final step toward reconciliation, Webster abandoned Wilmot's statutory ban on slavery. California and New Mexico, he
said, were "destined to be free," because the climate and soil would not
support cotton planting: "I would not take pains to re-affirm an ordinance
of nature; nor to re-enact the will of God. I would put in no Wilmot Proviso . . . to wound the pride of the gentlemen who belong to the Southern

States." Intended as a peace initiative, Webster's gesture infuriated antislavery men in his own party and section, but it failed to mollify Calhoun. The old cadaver gathered his dwindling strength and rose to repudiate all of Webster's claims—political, historical, and environmental.[16]

Webster's speech represented the best of the compromise tradition, but that template was far more damaged than anybody yet understood. National integration, both cultural and economic, was poorly served by the live-and-let-live liberalism that sustained the compromise vision. Additionally, moral critics of slavery brandished claims about right and wrong that made compromise seem cynical and venal. William H. Seward, a younger senator from New York, denounced the concept directly. Legislative bargains, he said, were "radically wrong and essentially vicious." They canonized past mistakes and tied the hands of statesmen confronting new situations. The Constitution ordained no such balance of slave and free states as Calhoun imagined. At the founding twelve of thirteen states allowed slavery, but the exercise of liberty had abolished it in many and barred it from other regions not yet developed. Seward freely mixed unimpeachable truths with inflammatory opinions. The Constitution obligated Congress to "secure the blessings of liberty," but nowhere did it grant a power to *create* the institution of slavery. (True.) Slavery was "temporary, accidental, partial, and incongruous" while freedom was "perpetual, organic, universal" and "in harmony" with the Constitution. (Inflammatory.) The kind of federative compact of states that Calhoun cherished (the Articles of Confederation) had been superseded by the Constitution now in force. (True.) As a result, the Union had become a "national democracy," and further compromise only sacrificed freedom for the many to protect the rights of a few to enslave their work force indefinitely. (Inflammatory.)

Seward sandwiched his brief against compromise between claims for national destiny that assumed the extinction of slavery and the worldwide triumph of freedom. American principles of government already were "renovating" Europe and Africa; now California and Oregon promised to extend that example to the Pacific. The "ripening civilization of the West" in its "circuit of the world," would "meet again and mingle with the declining civilization of the East, on our own free soil," resulting in a new "more perfect civilization . . . under the sway of our own cherished and beneficent institutions." Wrapping himself in world-historical claims reaching back a hundred years, Seward saw a "higher law" than the Constitution, charging American "stewards" to manage the public domain for the happiness of all mankind. No Christian nation "free to choose" would now establish slavery; therefore Seward opposed its extension. Freedom placed the North on the path to the future; slavery placed the South at odds with unfolding history. For Seward, no Union as it was—half slave and half free—should be revered.[17]

For months the stalemate ground on. The sudden death of President Zachary Taylor shifted the partisan lines just a bit, and Illinois senator Stephen A. Douglas stepped in to guide Clay's proposals through as separate bills, each with a different combination of supporters. His success caused a nationwide celebration of the Compromise of 1850. Proclaimed as a final solution to agitation of the slavery question, the agreement offered "popular sovereignty" as the key to the genius of American government. Talk of extending *or* restricting slavery by act of Congress (lawmakers now explained) usurped the right of the people to govern themselves. Popular sovereignty looked so appealing because it claimed to be automatic and incorruptible. Nothing could be simpler than to let the settlers come, call their own convention, and draft a constitution to suit their desires on the pressing question of slavery. This procedural garment (as old as the republic itself) sustained the illusion of a solution and allowed everyone time to walk back from a dangerous ledge. Let destiny be destiny.

The Harmony of Interests

The reverence for Union that motivated compromise politics reflected convictions in the founding generation that Independence—and therefore liberty itself—could not prevail outside a viable national framework capable of holding its own in a world of clashing empires. That said, consensus proved elusive on the shape and reach of the national government. Among the leading nationalists of 1787, James Madison fell into opposition almost immediately because of Hamilton's aggressive economic program. The opposition movement he and Jefferson launched promised minimal governance and maximum local autonomy as a counter to the Federalists' centralizing overreach. But by the end of the second war with Britain (1815) it was clear that the interests of the nation once again required more coordination. In 1816 Congress passed three pillars of economic policy (a new national bank, some protective tariffs, and aid to internal improvements), aimed at harmonizing regional interests by fostering growth and development. Madison vetoed internal improvements for technical reasons, but a high degree of confidence and goodwill welcomed his successor, James Monroe, so the idea of mutually satisfying destinies briefly flourished in the public mind. In the House, young Henry Clay of Kentucky took the lead in advocating economic nationalism; at the War Department, John C. Calhoun of South Carolina (not yet a sectional fanatic) pushed as firmly for roads, canals, and national defense; while at the State Department, John Quincy Adams (son of the Federalist president, now reinvented as a National Republican) secured all of Florida and claimed diplomatic hegemony over the whole Western Hemisphere. The old Federalist party disintegrated, leaving only varieties of Republicans on the political playing field. For a moment the founders' ideal of politics without parties appeared to be in reach.[18]

This rhetoric of harmonizing interests rested on a platform of economic theory sketched out by Philadelphia economist Mathew Carey and brought to full systematic perfection a generation later by Henry C. Carey, his son. The elder Carey insisted that the nations prospered in "exact proportion to the encouragement of their domestic industry." Free markets tempted individuals to chase accidental windfalls, but protectionist policy focused everyone's ambition on *collective* national growth and welfare. Free markets turned citizens into competitors, while protection freed them from savage foreign exploitation. Free-trading farmers and planters sometimes wallowed in fat markets that doubled and tripled prices for cotton, tobacco, and corn; but when the bubbles burst, as in the Panic of 1819, markets turned with a vengeance on urban artisans who were the countrymen and natural customers of agricultural producers. In the wake of that panic Carey published broadsides extolling balanced home markets where agriculture fed manufacturing, artisans supplied farmers, and no sector sacrificed others for short-term gain. The United States enjoyed extraordinary natural and political advantages (Carey listed a dozen of them), and it ought to enjoy "a higher degree of prosperity and happiness" than any other nation.[19]

At the center of the "harmony of interests" argument lay the idea of *national* (collective) prosperity. Balancing home production with home consumption, proper economic policies should guarantee good wages, comfortable livings, and steady (not speculative) growth. When they exported raw cotton and imported iron and cloth, America farmers merely enriched English merchants while depriving their countrymen of wages and profits they might earn from making these things at home. In hundreds of data-filled pages, the younger Carey tried to show that wages and prices rose during years of higher protection and collapsed whenever the tariff walls went down. Throughout the discussion he wove a critique of naturalized greed. Competition, said Carey, fostered discord, while protection encouraged men "to combine their efforts" to improve "their common condition." Competition dispersed population all over the western wilderness; protection fostered concentration and efficient urban development. Competition engendered the constant overproduction of raw commodities; protection encouraged more modest developmental goals. Free trade might yield limited short-run gains for the exporters of cotton, but it sacrificed long-term holistic economic development. Ignoring the strident objections of abolitionists, Carey embraced slave labor as a necessary feature of the American economy. As a result he could easily bid for the interests of southern planters by stressing not their peculiar institution but their shared interest in material prosperity. If planters embraced the big picture rather than their narrow, reflexive defense of slavery, surely northern interests would see the futility of making war on slavery. The United States was large, free, independent, richly endowed, and blessed with popular republican governments: why on earth would it sacrifice national prosperity in future for the sake of emancipation—or an extra penny-a-pound on cotton wool today?[20]

Summing up his analysis in light of the Compromise of 1850 and the future of the Union, Carey took on the rhetoric of mission and national destiny. With Pacific shores in sight, some Americans now dreamed of "monopolizing the commerce of the world," but this would be a tragic mistake. Two systems confronted the world at mid-century, and the contrast between them was stunning. One looked "to the centralization of wealth and power"; the other to the rise of home markets "for the products of the land." One promised "pauperism, ignorance, depopulation, and barbarism"; the other "increasing wealth, comfort, intelligence . . . and civilization." One produced "universal war"; the other fostered "universal peace." Carey's system was the only one that tended toward "ELEVATING while EQUALIZING the condition of man throughout the world." Here was the true mission of the Americans: cultivate the harmony of interests in home markets and, by doing so, raise worldwide the value of land, the level of wages, intelligence, morality, freedom, and happiness. Show that the "happiness of individuals, as well as the grandeur of nations," could be promoted not by war and competition but by the biblical rule: "Do unto others as ye would that others should do unto you."[21]

Of course such stirring appeals to a higher mission and harmony of interest worked best when citizens believed they were serving a shared destiny. Alas, the political goodwill that first gave voice to this vision did not survive Monroe's administration. By the presidential campaign of 1824, partisans of Andrew Jackson were teaming up with the southern extremists to attack the bank, tariff, and internal improvements. Denouncing any nationalist tilt as old-fashioned Federalist corruption (dressed up in a new suit of clothes), party strategist Martin Van Buren built a political coalition of southern planters and northern "plain republicans" designed to protect economic liberty for common (white) people against the fancy corporate schemes of economic nationalists. In Jackson's democracy all a man required to succeed was access to land, security in property (including his enslaved workers), and protection from the predatory schemes of the "monied aristocracy." In such a yeoman's commonwealth, competition naturally protected independent actors and would block agents of corruption. Jacksonian Democrats portrayed the program of the economic nationalists—the American System—as serving class and sectional interests, designed to pauperize the working man, build up the urban North, and coddle slavery agitators who always threatened political peace. The appeal was so successful that by the 1840s many working men in the North, farmers in the West, and planters all over the South believed that the Jackson creed alone preserved their personal freedom.[22]

Why did Jackson's liberal rhetoric displace so readily the harmony of interests? First, automatic self-acting systems generally appealed to nineteenth-century Americans. Liberty itself was thought to be a natural condition requiring only the lifting of arbitrary barriers, and many people hoped that republican governments would require no more guidance than a watchman to ferret out corruption. Since the publication of *Wealth of Nations* people also had dreamed of automatic economic principles that likewise would allocate wealth and opportunity without the interference of corruptible, passionate interests. Adam Smith's "invisible hand" of competition offered just the ticket. In the wake of the Revolution many Americans, suspicious of their governors, had moved, one by one, toward

embracing Smith's doctrine of laissez-faire—that is "leave it alone." In
practice, people often suffered when entrepreneurs introduced new ways of
doing things, or when powerful new players broke into once-isolated markets. If the state was behind these changes people knew at once who to
blame; but the invisible hand was *invisible*, and the architects of hardships
(if known) dismissed any suffering as the inevitable price of "progress."
Taking advantage of this simple truth, Jacksonians blamed their voters' discomforts on the policies of their enemies while praising markets as perfect
alternatives to influence peddling.[23]

Second, the high-minded arguments of the Careys notwithstanding, the
beneficiaries of tariff protection appeared to be just as venal as their enemies said. Tariff debates in Congress exhibited little of the restraint and
mutuality for which "harmony" theories argued. Carey insisted that subsidies helped to sustain good wages, but over the decades since 1819 skilled
workers had suffered big losses—especially in the textile trades where protection likely did more to encourage investment in new machines. Vast new
capital requirements, cutthroat competition, and economies of scale that
flooded markets with low-end goods—these were features of emerging
industrialization that contradicted the mutual flow of resources between
producers and consumers. Both Careys advocated small-scale, local enterprises where worker-consumers and farmer-producers literally traded with
each other. But market competition and productivity revolutions (whether
mechanized or not) forced the managers of factories to sacrifice labor in
favor of capital formation. The disastrous experience of factory workers
during the Panic of 1837 and the years of depression that followed left the
new class of "operatives" persuaded that there was no mutuality and very
little harmony connecting their interests with those of their employers.[24]

Third, the marketplace as arbiter of interests never took a stand on
moral or ethical questions—especially slavery. Policy objectives that came
back frequently to Congress for balance and adjustment (which tariffs and
internal improvements unavoidably did) repeatedly stumbled on hot-
button issues touching slavery and abolition. Committed to releasing the
energy of free white economic actors, Democratic liberalism treated slavery
as a matter of personal and local preference—exactly as did the Constitution of 1787. Individual states were free to emancipate or not, and individual
persons freely could move to a state whose policies proved most congenial.
Unfortunately, the sense of entitlement that flowed from liberty gradually
undermined this live-and-let-live solution. Freedom to enslave blacks

clashed with freedom from sharing the workplace or the public sphere with African Americans. This factor helped energize the free-soil crisis of the late 1840s.

The Devil in the Details

Except for the slavery question, world-historical forces had spread before ambitious Americans the greatest example yet of opportunity and mission as promised by the culture of exploitation. Aggressive sexual metaphors stirred up the patriots: "The American people," crowed *DeBow's Review*, "while yet scarce 'hardened into manhood,' swept across the 'impassable' mountains, overspread the great valleys, and penetrated in immense numbers . . . to the very shores of the Pacific Ocean." After 1850, with the compromise in place, Oregon rapidly filling with settlers, and prospectors rushing to the gold fields of California, Americans turned their attention to practical problems of how to get *through* this rugged wilderness and secure the extravagant pleasures it promised. Intrepid pioneers had worked out primitive access with wagon trails to Oregon and California, but this overland journey took five months of very hard traveling. Emigrants frantic for gold sometimes sailed to Central America, crossed the isthmus, then continued by ship to San Francisco, consuming perhaps three months in the process. Before the arrival of a telegraph line (1861) simple communications took two or three weeks (ten days by pony express from St. Joseph, Missouri). Finally, much of the distance was dry plains and rugged mountains, choked with snow in the winter, home to grizzly bears and angry mounted Indians who sought revenge on vulnerable trespassers. The fabled "Asiatic commerce," object of western nations "from the Phoenicians down to the present day," was about to fall in their lap (this was Thomas Hart Benton's outsized rhetoric). But no such destiny could be realized until Americans found some way to close a gap of two thousand miles between St. Louis and the Pacific—and the devil lay in the details.[25]

Fortunately, Polk's territorial gamble coincided with the emergence in the 1840s of viable railroad technology that offered the only compelling solution to these huge spatial demands. Free to abandon the dictates of "natural" streams and waterways, iron rails could open a durable highway through all kinds of physical terrain, while steam locomotion contributed speed and power never before imagined. A train could carry its own fuel and water through deserts and mountain passes and speed across the home-lands of aggrieved resident Natives, delivering goods and people to Pacific shores in a matter of days, not weeks or months. As early as 1844, one vision-ary, Asa Whitney of New York, laid out a plan for building a link from Milwaukee to the Pacific. Reprising George Washington's earlier argument, Whitney feared that the "enterprising people" of the Far West would declare independence and capture the commerce of Asia as their own. Alas, his pro-posal (and others) quickly brought into view the tangled objections that had crippled internal improvement since the founding of the republic.[26]

Early infrastructure debates had foundered on one of three critical issues. First, if built by private investors, "monopolists" gained control of essential public thoroughfares, threatening common rights and equal access. This objection had attached quickly to private bridge and turnpike companies in the Atlantic states. State-funded public works solved this problem but they concentrated taxpayer dollars in specific places, unavoid-ably privileging one location to the disadvantage of others (the second objection). The resulting jealousies corrupted the legislative process. Finally, long-distance projects required interstate agreements or federal reg-ulation that triggered endless debates about centralized power and states' rights. In the 1820s state borrowing backed up with federal land grants had launched a canal boom; but by the 1840s Jacksonian hostility coupled with several state bankruptcies left everyone leery of public works. Private rail-road corporations began filling the void, chartered by the states and sup-posedly "clothed" with enough public interest to minimize the danger. But private capitalists balked at transcontinental projects because the Far West presented vast stretches of unproductive land through which a railroad had to be built in order to claim the glistening prizes on the opposite coast.[27]

Whitney's scheme was crafted carefully to slip past Jacksonian objec-tions to both national public works and powerful corporations. He wanted Congress to sell to him personally (no stockjobbing corporation) a sixty-mile strip of land along the most eligible route to Oregon (via South Pass now in western Wyoming). He would develop the better lands to finance construction of the railroad. At the end of twenty-five years Congress could assume control of the railroad or Whitney and his heirs would run it as a business. Objections poured in from everywhere. A "covetous speculation," cried some; a dangerous monopoly. Congress must not abdicate control of this national highway. Congress had no right or power to make such a highway either. Whitney's far-northern route (passing only through federal territory) offended friends of Chicago, St. Louis, and all southern routes, especially after Americans acquired the Mexican cession. Compromise rhetoric notwithstanding, suspicions darkened even the most technical assessments of climate, topography, and snowfall as if each had been corrupted in behalf of slavery or free soil.

Missouri's senator Thomas Hart Benton, one of the Democrats struggling to maintain sectional balance and sidestep the free-soil death trap, offered an alternate scheme for modernization without consolidation or privileged corporate power. Lay out a "national road" from St. Louis to San Francisco along a central route using one of three passes recently discovered through the Colorado Rockies. Set aside a corridor one mile wide through which to run a railroad track, a road for wagons or sleighs, a plank road, macadam road, or "track by magnetic power"—whatever systems of conveyance might be developed in future. Do it now while the whole territory fell under Congress's jurisdiction (neither slave nor free) and reserve it to national purposes "for all time to come." No private resources were "equal to the opening" of such a road. No stockjobbing schemers or European bondholders should be allowed to threaten the sovereign interests of the people. A central national road at public expense accommodated everyone and privileged none.[28]

Neither Whitney nor Benton prevailed in his transcontinental scheme. Taking the lead instead was Illinois senator Stephen A. Douglas, the man who floor-managed the Compromise of 1850 and now led the northern wing of the Democratic party. Trusting (too much) his own success, Douglas hoped the way was clear for organizing Kansas and Nebraska and launching a corporate railroad to San Francisco, backed with enormous grants of free public lands. The choice of a route promised real and symbolic benefits to the friends—or enemies—of slavery, a conflict Douglas tried to finesse by lifting the ban on slavery in Nebraska and Kansas territories. But lifting the ban, free-soilers argued, invited slavery into Kansas. As had been amply demonstrated throughout the South, plantation slavery marginalized small family farmers. Furthermore, free white labor would not work alongside enslaved Africans. Popular sovereignty effectively meant *closing* the public domain to the sons and daughters of freedom whose own dreams of prosperity lay in a free-soil West. The backlash against the Kansas-Nebraska Act realigned local politics in frankly sectional terms, and in 1856 a sectional candidate, the swashbuckling explorer John C. Fremont, polled shockingly well in the presidential canvass.[29]

Having abandoned all pretense of neutrality, a brand-new Republican party set about claiming the whole of national destiny for "free soil, free labor, and free men." Desperate Democrats turned on each other and the compromise tradition disintegrated as violence erupted in "Bleeding Kansas." New England abolitionists nurtured, funded (and armed) a free-soil colony at Lawrence, Kansas. Proslavery forces (mostly settlers from nearby Missouri) burned it to the ground. Antislavery terrorist John Brown butchered five slaveholding settlers at Pottawatomi Creek, after which Brown went into hiding, sheltered by leading Boston Republicans, to plot his insurrection at Harper's Ferry. Civility collapsed, and not just on the frontier. Preston Brooks beat Massachusetts senator Charles Sumner half to death with a cane on the floor of the Senate in Washington. In 1860, when Abraham Lincoln captured the presidency without *any* southern electoral votes, political discourse died and John C. Calhoun's worst nightmare suddenly came to pass. Douglas's Kansas-Nebraska gamble built no railroad to the Pacific, but it did destroy forever the compromise game that had sustained the American Union.[30]

Nature, Artifice, and Freedom

At stake in the 1850s were the building blocks of destiny, the key elements of the culture of exploitation. What was the meaning of geographic space? (A barrier? A challenge?) Must the "natural" laws of trade abolish the "natural advantages" of location by fostering "artificial" means of high-speed transportation? Where did liberty reside? (In the commonwealth or in the competitive individual?) How did people and institutions acquire dominion over other free agents in the marketplace? Was slavery a natural tool of human progress or shameful aberration? Could people of different races share a common space, opportunity, and mission? Was this culture of exploitation a mere consequence of history—or its purpose? Did freedom entitle people to any particular outcome, or did it merely license aggressive individuals to compete? Was there a national destiny? Or was the experimental American republic a grand self-serving illusion?

First, the question of space. Before steam transportation, economic geography stood pretty much as a fact of nature. Nearby places enjoyed advantages over distant markets; and while the burden of transportation might be reduced overall by technical improvements, the spatial order of things rarely was altered disproportionately. Railroad systems, however, quickly displayed a capacity to overturn the natural advantages of, say, river towns or port cities, by redirecting traffic and manipulating rates to neutralize the impact of space and time on individual transactions. Not only was this distortion possible, it was the primary reason for building a railroad system. Farmers near Chicago could stand on an equal footing with farmers from upstate New York only if the rate structure to New York City positively *favored* more distant competitors. Such discrimination violated centuries of law and custom among common carriers, never to collect different fees for substantially similar services. By the time of the Civil War, however, trunk-line railroads argued that "natural laws of trade" gave them no choice but to use such pricing practices. Modern "artificial" systems had been naturalized within the economic landscape. Thus was common sense apparently repealed by large corporate enterprises, chartered by the people's government, but governed by the profit motive.

Ironically competition—the very force that ought to protect consumers from harm—lay at the heart of the railroad rate dilemma. When railroads met at competing points, the carriers cut their rates to secure a larger volume of traffic, and shippers reaped a windfall. Captive shippers at noncompeting points paid compensatory premiums that kept the railroad from losing money. Differentials between long- and short-haul services, carload discounts for large customers, rebates, drawbacks, and the bewildering complexity of official tariff schedules convinced the common shipper that he was powerless in the grip of railroad officials who grew exceedingly rich while insisting that their industry was barely surviving. After decades fighting discriminatory rates, one Iowan frustrated by the new economic landscape declared "if rates were a guide, Omaha was situated between Chicago and Iowa, Denver was on the Mississippi, and San Francisco on the Missouri, while the interior towns of Iowa and Nebraska were located on Behring Strait." Something was terribly wrong in a liberty-loving republic when a railroad corporation was allowed to redraw the map so profoundly.[31]

As markets grew large and complex all kinds of other service providers appeared to acquire the freedom to dictate terms and conditions to independent citizens. Commodities brokers quoted take-it-or-leave-it prices for cotton, wheat, tobacco, and livestock. Banks and insurance underwriters refused to negotiate with ordinary customers (although very large buyers sometimes gained an advantage). Large-scale employers—especially in textile factories—set wages, hired, and fired "free labor" hands without regard for what was once called a "living wage." Where did such power come from? Market forces, they replied. In the name of the common man, Jacksonian vigilance prevented the state from granting anyone this kind of power over others, and yet here it was. Where was the leak? And where was liberty for workers and small producers who found themselves mired in complex systems that stripped them of that independence their grandparents once believed was the whole point of securing freedom?[32]

What was the role of slavery in producing the impasse that ruined the 1850s? The party of Lincoln whipped up a generalized fear that the "slave power" wished to install their labor system all over the North. If slavery itself did not threaten the freedom of northern citizens, the prospect of its expansion clearly did. Free-soil Democrats claimed that the spread of slavery further degraded conditions for free white men. Antislavery racists raised such a cry against integration, social equality, and sexual "amalgamation" that moderate Republican politicians, such as Abraham Lincoln, frankly denounced all such intentions. In a famous 1858 exchange with Stephen A. Douglas, Lincoln assured an Illinois audience that freedom for blacks meant the right to get wages—nothing more. Such racist positions up north convinced the South that emancipation, when it came, would lock down in their midst an angry, degraded, and vengeful mob of freed persons. At the same time more and more northern observers felt, however vaguely, that their "character," "prosperity," and "destiny" were tied to the eventual "extinction of slavery." Lincoln promised in every possible way that he had no intention of ending slavery in the states, but who in the South could believe him? His oft-quoted claim that a "house divided" could not stand—that the nation must finally embrace one system or the other—invited the worst interpretation. And other leaders in his party made no secret about their ambitions.[33]

In Virginia, one fanatical proslavery advocate finally found the logical bottom of the arguments he and his kind had been polishing for several years. "Liberty and equality are new things under the sun," wrote George Fitzhugh in 1850, launching a critique of free-trade liberalism that mirrored (in horrible burlesque) the arguments of Henry C. Carey. "France and the Northern States of our Union" alone had tried to live under "universal liberty and equality of rights." The experiment was a disaster. Liberty made enemies of capital and labor, while the ethic of brutal competition empowered the strong to destroy the weak. Over the next six years Fitzhugh developed his theories into a full-blown attack on the liberal capitalist system, but instead of commonwealth and consensus, Fitzhugh offered slavery as the necessary antidote to social disintegration. "A Southern farm," he argued, was the "beau ideal of Communism," a "joint concern," in which the enslaved consumed more than the master and were "far happier" because they always were "sure of a support." In slavery, structured inequality, unquestioned authority, and obligations of ownership kept masters from hurting their "people." No such barriers stayed the exploitative hand of free-labor employers. Fitzhugh did not recommend enslaving other whites, but the implication was unmistakable: "half of mankind are but grown-up children, and liberty is as fatal to them as it would be to children." Resurrecting an ancient, organic social ideal, Fitzhugh reached back to the reciprocal, unequal, paternalistic forms of the early modern English village, then he gave them a demonic twist. Equals could only be rivals, he reasoned, and government existed to limit that private competitive urge. Slavery provided a reliable framework for social peace and harmony. Freedom produced only "cannibals" who devoured one another for profit.[34]

Fitzhugh may be dismissed as a nut, but such proslavery advocates gathered momentum during the 1850s. Gone were the apologies of the founding era, and in their place emerged full-throated defenses of slavery as essential to freedom and the progress of the white race. Southern eyes cast around once more for new frontiers in Cuba and Central America. Campaigns began to reopen the slave trade (banned since 1808) and replenish the labor force with fresh captives taken from Africa. Such aggressive expansionist sentiment coming from the "slave power" further convinced wary northerners that future accommodations could not stand. The Supreme Court decision in *Dred Scott v. Sandford* (1857), stripping blacks of all rights under the Constitution, seemed a step toward nationalizing slavery itself. Meanwhile, the critique of free labor as "wage slavery," which appealed to many critics of factory employment, became hopelessly tainted with proslavery lunacy. Portraying the cotton plantation as the ideal example of "harmony of interests," George Fitzhugh effectively spiked Henry Carey's dream of mutual progress through republican governance and social consensus. Offered up as the only alternative to totalitarian slavery, wage labor in the liberal capitalist marketplace seemed to be all that working people could cling to if they wished to remain "free."[35]

Finally, what of destiny? And what of the culture of exploitation? The American sense of destiny derived from two distinct eighteenth-century parents: the rise of British imperialism and the revival of political republicanism. Colonial Americans owed their very existence to British mercantile outreach, the aggressive deployment of capital through trade, slavery, and colonization that historian Sven Beckert has called "war capitalism." Dependent on state power to seize territory, control subject people, force open markets, and service the long-distance slave trade, war capitalism set the stage for industrialization.[36] Reimagined through Adam Smith's lens of free competitive markets, division of labor, and specialization, British imperialism morphed into classical free-trade liberalism during the nineteenth century. Economists obscured the legacy of violence and state sponsorship with exaggerated claims about natural advantages, entrepreneurial genius, and immutable market forces. As the social costs of industrialization mounted, theorists insisted nothing could be done: global laws of supply and demand controlled every aspect of the system. Still, liberal theory promised that with more growth and specialization prosperity would spread. When antebellum Americans dreamed of securing control over "Asiatic commerce," they were tapping their inheritance from this economic parent.

Just as important, beginning in the 1760s, a utopian strain of classical republicanism had energized Americans' attacks on British corruption and imperial authority. Everything "grand" about the rebellion derived from a sense of a higher purpose than crass self-interest and home rule. As custodians of liberty, revolutionary Americans imagined a world-historical mission to forge a new kind of polity—at once a popular commonwealth and an empire for liberty—where freedom and equality, independence and prosperity ushered in a new world order. Science, the arts, and useful knowledge all sought refuge in this new seat of civilization, governed by reason and consent, committed to the good of the whole. Corrupt institutions (whether church or state) were banished, along with hereditary privileges and class prerogatives. The energies of people were released. Republican constitutions shaped vehicles for governance, supposedly responsive to the needs and demands of the sovereign people. Great hope lay in the belief that a free people with abundant resources could enjoy economic liberty without triggering the negative effects so clearly displayed in Manchester or London. When antebellum Americans talked about the blessings of self-government and their unique opportunities for progress, they were referencing this side of the family legacy.

One might expect genetic analysis would explain how the third generation of Americans came to such an intractable impasse by 1861, but nothing was that simple. Out of suspicion more than conviction, southerners clung to the liberal strain and left themselves open to colonization by British cotton merchants. In defense of states' rights (mostly to protect slavery), they made war against the exercise of power by federal authorities, forcing developmental initiatives out of public and into private hands over which they had no political control whatsoever. To protect a culture of exploitation based on cotton and enslaved Africans they conflated modernization with antislavery and struggled against both. Meanwhile privatization undermined the commonwealth ideal and slowly disabled the substantive claims of artisans, tradesmen, farmers, and local merchants, by right, to a decent living. Schooled by history, tradition, and now by liberal political economists, Americans could not imagine that freedom had turned on itself; if their destiny was clouded there had to be an enemy at work. For the North, the slave power fit the bill. In turn the planters thought that the real threat of strangulation came not from worldwide cotton markets but from antislavery fanatics who thirsted for their destruction. For northern farmers and workers, the eclipse of freedom came from encroaching African laborers, whether slave or free, whose presence they believed degraded work and threatened white supremacy. For radical abolitionists, the judgment of God Almighty promised to stop the republic in its tracks unless they purged the national sin of African slavery. Finally, for the emerging captains of industry, the political stalemate itself threatened the integrated market economy on which all future growth and prosperity depended.

Each perspective owed something to the complex blend of liberal and republican traditions; by 1861 each had arrived at its threshold of tolerance. Reaching back to the right of revolution enshrined in the Declaration of Independence, South Carolina and ten other states launched a new independence movement, consciously modeled on the first, and charging the northern states with exactly the crimes once laid at the feet of King George: centralization of authority, economic consolidation, discriminatory treatment, corruption, and the threat of enslavement to unchecked arbitrary power.[37] The Lincoln government countered that the Union, once made, could not be dissolved; that the destiny of the republic could not be sacrificed by its constituent parts. The states were not free to renounce the blessings of Union (nor, it seemed, were the people free to protect themselves from the new culture of exploitation); but the Union was free to preserve its collective mission through the use of devastating force. Destiny would be clarified, and this time the empire would not be dismembered.

CHAPTER 8

Mastery

PHILADELPHIA, 1876. PEOPLE GAPED in awe and wonder. Rising forty-five feet above the floor, generating more than 1400 horsepower, the mighty Corliss engine mesmerized crowds at the Centennial Exposition. Steam from a boiler, decorously hidden off-site, silently moved twin pistons (forty-four inches by ten feet) that actuated giant walking beams (nine feet wide, twenty-seven long) attached to a thirty-foot flywheel that turned nearly a mile of shafts and pulleys linked to every piece of equipment on display in Machinery Hall. Journalists gave it the lead in column after column. Dignitaries spluttered in amazement. In its shadow working men reverently ate their lunch. The poet Walt Whitman reportedly sat half an hour just watching the colossus at work. Proof, wrote the *New York Times* on May 15, 1876, that American industry now dominated the field: England's engine builders had "absolutely nothing to show against the great Corliss engine." The American's heart thrilled with pride, wrote another poet, Joachim Miller, when he saw "the vast exhibition of art and prowess" on display. But great as it was, Miller called it only "the acorn from which shall grow the wide-spreading oak of a century's growth."[1]

The Centennial Exhibition itself was a gamble for the American republic, only partly reconstructed from its devastating Civil War, desperately hoping to live up to the extraordinary standard set by Queen Victoria's Great Exhibition (1851), and still in the throes of a financial panic whose roots could be found in wartime debts, greenback dollars, and the return to the gold standard. Inviting the muse of human genius to America to celebrate the great centennial, Walt Whitman cried out "Away with themes of war! Away with War itself! . . . and in its stead speed Industry's campaigns." Exalting "practical, manual work" as the newest form of poetry, Whitman gloried in the great works ahead and laid before the muse the artifacts of recent progress: the Atlantic cable, the Pacific railroad, the Hoosac Tunnel, and the Brooklyn Bridge, the "triumphs of our time." The "earth all spann'd with iron Rails—with lines of Steam-ships threading every sea," with "Victory on thy left, and at thy right hand Law," the American Union now would be the seat of "one common indivisible destiny, for All."[2]

Indeed the stain of slavery had been expunged by emancipation, but over four million African Americans still suffered in a racial caste system and a program of labor dependency that hardened into debt peonage. More clearly gone was the so-called slave power—that obstructionist block of southern congressmen who had defended slavery by crippling the prewar government so that little could be done in behalf of the market economy, industrial development, or internal improvements. After 1865 victorious Republicans in Washington drove a stake through the heart those neo-anti-federalist sentiments, declaring once for all the triumph of the *national* Union. Even loyal states in the North and West found their pleas for local autonomy and states' rights silenced in the postwar era by the nationalistic voices now crediting themselves with suppressing rebellion, freeing the enslaved, and saving the republic from oblivion. In politics, the "bloody shirt" of Civil War memory kept Republican voters in line, freeing congressmen to tend to the needs of big money and corporate interests. The industrial working class, increasingly composed of immigrants from southern and eastern Europe, was mastered by corporate employers whose control of the party system deflected worker grievances. As northern commitments to Reconstruction relaxed, southern "redeemer" governments dissolved the voting power of nominally free blacks. Triumphant white America stood purified and ready to explode across the world stage. "Progress is the law of life," proclaimed a historian of the Centennial, casting as uncontested fact a sentiment hazarded sixty years before by Harvard's Jacob Bigelow.[3]

When the great fair opened May 10, 1876, rhetoricians rose to the occasion. First up, a Methodist bishop, the Reverend Matthew Simpson, thanked God for giving "our fathers . . . Thy chosen people" the vast land of the New World, "long veiled from the ages" and marked by "untold treasures." Liberty, virtue, free schools, discoveries, and "multiplied inventions" had fostered "national prosperity and progress." With the Union affirmed as "indissoluble," Simpson hoped the century to come would be even better than the last: "more radiant with the light of true philosophy, warmer with the emanations of a world-wide sympathy." Centennial Commission head Joseph R. Hawley voiced a similar appeal for reconciliation and future "glories," before yielding the rostrum to President Grant. "One hundred years ago," began the president, "our country was new and but partly settled." Necessity "compelled us" to spend our time "felling forests, subduing prairies, building dwellings, factories, ships, docks, roads, canals, machinery, etc. etc." Proud of these achievements, Grant regretted "we have not done more" and invited fairgoers to study the achievements of all the nations that lay displayed before them. There followed a hundred-gun salute after which the parade of dignitaries made its way to the exhibition buildings to see what America had done and what remained to be perfected. Nobody worried about how cotton was grown in the New South. Few questioned the right of capital to dictate terms to industrial workers. Mastery produced unheard-of wealth and distributed it somewhat more widely than ever before. The culture of exploitation had come of age and infused the United States with an astonishing momentum. What could possibly be better?[4]

Transport and the Laws of Trade

Job one for the postwar Union was the functional integration of the sprawling national marketplace. In 1869 two corporations generously subsidized with federal government land grants—the Union Pacific and Central Pacific railway companies—completed the first transcontinental railroad line. A leading irritant in the sectional crisis in the 1850s, this railroad stood as a centerpiece of *one* vision of a modern United States, a vision that now laid claim to the Union victory and the national identity as if there had been no doubts. The work of reckless financiers, swashbuckling engineers, and thousands of common laborers (Irish navvies and Chinese contract workers held in virtual slavery to the construction companies), the railroad spanned a thousand miles of undeveloped prairie and short-grass plains and then another thousand miles of shockingly rugged mountain terrain. When finished it linked Chicago with the coast at San Francisco. Soon enough three additional lines bridged the vast expanse of the great West, while total railroad mileage by 1890 more than tripled to nearly two hundred thousand miles. In 1883 Congress adopted standard time zones, imposing in every village in the country, by legislative fiat, a uniform definition of "high noon" that no antebellum government would have dared. Three years later, in an act of reconciliation both practical and symbolic, broad-gauge southern railroads moved one rail on their entire network three inches inward to accommodate the standard gauge (4 feet 8½ inches) that prevailed in the North. Standardization, uniformity, interchangeability—these were the virtues without which commerce and contracts could not thrive across the vast spaces composing the United States.[5]

More important than even the size of the railroad network was the integration of operations that knit dozens of discrete firms into large regional systems. Beginning in the 1850s pioneer railroads in the East worked out systems for coordinating schedules, transferring passengers and freight, sharing rolling stock, pricing, billing, ticketing, and parsing out complicated revenue streams. Transportation itself—the commodity for sale—was an ephemeral thing the value of which depended as much on the needs of the buyer as it did on the cost involved in providing the service. Unless regulated by law, the price of such services (like tavern and innkeepers' charges) tended to settle on "what the market would bear." Private profit-seeking companies built the American railroads; their goal was to compete in the market. But once in place, railroads appeared to shippers to be part of the market itself, an essential infrastructure without which other entrepreneurs found no market at all.

Within this complex network one might find two or three—or maybe a dozen—different ways to get from here to there. Perfect markets would distribute traffic over direct, efficient routes, but shippers in no hurry often found rival carriers selling inefficient, roundabout services for less money than direct connections. As a result, individual railroads had no choice but to manipulate prices based on cost, demand, efficiency, and the competitive strategies of rivals. The root cause of what often looked like irrational pricing lay in the enormously high fixed costs that motivated railroads to generate revenue whether it yielded much profit or not. Expensive locomotives, miles of railroad spiked to the ground, stations, coal yards, water tanks, and hundreds of cars only paid back the interest on borrowed money when trains were *moving* filled with freight.[6]

These peculiarities of railway economics—an ephemeral product, high fixed costs, inflexible capital investment, arbitrary pricing—created powerful incentives to merge, consolidate, coordinate operations so as to minimize points of friction. Systems grew through outright purchase, lease, or interchange agreements, and managers acquired more control over costs *and competition*, manipulating rates to maximize traffic volume and therefore gross corporate revenues. Several rate-making "evils" quickly developed. Simple price competition operated fiercely in places where two or more lines offered nearly identical services (say, from Chicago to New York). This "cutthroat competition" drove prices to the margin and often below, and it fostered the practice of poaching business by pricing roundabout routes at a loss in order to service fixed costs. To cover these losses railroads sought compensation wherever they could justify higher rates. Consider long- and short-haul rates. All service required handling of passengers and freight, but short trips recouped those expenses over fewer miles, producing much higher costs per mile. Carload lots garnered discounts for shippers because the carrier did not have to scramble to fill the conveyance. Fair enough, but in the absence of clear cost accounting such justifiable reasons for rate discrimination invited further arbitrary distortions; secret rebates, drawbacks, and special deals squeezed profits from some consumers to offset discounts for others. The most egregious differentials occurred at so-called way points—minor stations served by a single railroad that intersected with other lines at major competing centers. Agents in such places charged many times the long-haul rate per mile, even when identical products were carried for less on the same train in the same direction to the same destination. Desperate shippers at way points encouraged branch line construction to get up competition, forcing the dominant firm to defend itself by purchasing the new, unneeded mileage. This further drove up the fixed costs that caused such compensatory pricing in the first place.

Rate discrimination lay at the heart of what the postwar generation called "the railroad question." Alas, it also defined the original promise of rail transportation, which was to overcome space and time and create an artificial geography in which distant parties could compete as if they were neighbors. No level field would do: hundreds of miles always would separate Ohio from New York City, Chicago from Ohio, Omaha from Chicago, and so on. Pro rata pricing—charging the same per mile for similar services—did nothing to alter natural geography, and this was the whole reason for building roads, canals, and railroads. Yet the power to redraw the map in favor of distant western communities equally empowered the railroads to discriminate against way points, small shippers, and residents in noncompeting cities and towns.[7] The new railroad network made it possible to master time and space but could not answer the central questions: Who should wield such power? In whose behalf? To what end?

One obvious solution to the cutthroat competition that drove rate discrimination could be found in consolidation. Local short lines merged into interregional trunk lines—the Pennsylvania, the New York Central, the New Haven, the Burlington, the Santa Fe—resulting in streamlined operations, reduced transaction costs, uniformity, efficiency, and economies of scale. Long trunk lines in turn built, leased, or forged alliances within a network of branches creating a service territory in which they could (theoretically) relax their competitive guard and focus on cost control. In some cases, rival firms set up pooling agreements by which they distributed traffic and revenues according to predetermined ratios, eliminating all reason for poaching. Unfortunately, popular economic culture, celebrating competition as an absolute virtue, condemned all such efforts to suppress competition as hurtful *by definition*, whether they were in fact or not. Consolidation and collusion might well have generated savings to be shared by lowering prices, but nobody knew how to analyze the true costs of transportation, nobody trusted monopoly power (in the hands of business or government), and nobody imagined that the flamboyant rogues and tycoons who filled the board rooms of Gilded Age corporations could possibly have the general welfare in their sights.[8]

Guided by Smithian economic theory as well as their visceral distrust of giant corporations, American shippers and voters forced their states to adopt schemes of rate regulation, always seeking a ceiling but never requesting a rate floor that might have stopped cutthroat competition. Struggling under a patchwork of regulatory regimes, interstate railroad managers bribed and bullied local authorities, plotted in secret to evade state controls, and flooded the courts with objections, citing the "equal protection" clause of the new Fourteenth Amendment to invalidate local police powers. In a series of "Granger Cases" in the 1870s, the US Supreme Court upheld the rights of the states to protect their citizens from "foreign" corporations; but both Congress and the Court soon tilted the other way, moving steadily toward a rigid embrace of the Smithian principle of laissez-faire. By the 1880s railroad leaders such as Charles E. Perkins explained (often and at length) that regulatory interference in the use of private property—no matter how benevolent, moral, or Christian the intent—always produced "exactly the opposite effect." Americans wanted cheap transportation, Perkins said, and the existing system delivered it like no other on earth. (In

the aggregate this was true, but it utterly ignored the matter of rate discrimination, something Perkins dismissed as illusory.) Liberal formalists like
Perkins insisted that private interest *never* failed to yield the best economic
outcomes. It was "inexpedient" *in every case* to interfere with business.[9]

Despite the triumph of laissez-faire theory, the railroad question consumed much of the political energy of the age. By the 1880s three clear
positions had emerged: nationalize the system and run it (as in Europe) as
a public utility; erect a national regulatory framework to impose order,
prevent monopoly, and foster competition; or do nothing and let the natural laws of trade work their magic. It was an axiom of American political
culture, left over from the Revolution, that corruption and patronage naturally accompanied large-scale government initiatives. Scandalous bribery in
the Grant administration (1869–77) reinvigorated antebellum doubts about
the capability of government to handle large and complicated business. As
a result, calls for nationalization failed to mobilize farmers and shippers
who thought of themselves as entrepreneurs and believed absolutely in the
virtues of uncorrupted markets. At the same time, distortions in the transportation markets persisted, proving to critics (and even some business-
men) that railroads might represent a special case. For free competition to
work among the *users* of railroads, students of the problem concluded,
federal regulation was required to eliminate corruption, combination, and
collusion—the perceived root causes of monopolistic tendencies. Accordingly the Interstate Commerce Act (1887) enshrined competition as the
centerpiece of national economic policy, charging a relatively weak bureau-
cratic commission and the much stronger federal courts with protecting
the ideal of Smithian markets regardless of real-time experiences. On a
continental scale time and space stood defeated: enterprise and innovation
had delivered them into the hands of a wealthy, ambitious, and ideologi-
cally rigid business elite.[10]

The Rise of Big Business

Much to everyone's surprise, the conquest of time and space ushered in,
not the happy interaction of a million small actors, but the astonishing rise
of a small number of giant firms that gained unprecedented control of their
own lines of business. Technology and markets proved to be the key to
success in the new economy: invest in new technology and dominate the

market through economies of scale made possible by technical advantages. The steel magnate Andrew Carnegie stands as the premier example of a "self-made" man securing fabulous riches and legendary mastery through hard-driving entrepreneurship. Like nearly all self-made men, Carnegie was handed his initial stake in the game of capitalism by wealthy, well-placed friends; nevertheless, this plucky son of an immigrant handloom weaver fixed his eye on the main chance with uncanny resolve and singular determination. Through the sponsorship of Tom Scott of the Pennsylvania Railroad, Carnegie leaped from messenger boy to division manager and learned industrial investing, following hot tips on sleeping cars, iron bridges, and railroad securities. In 1873 he set his sights on the Bessemer process for making steel railroad rails. (They were hellishly expensive but worth it in the long run.) His business plan—elegant and novel—focused on arranging the best technology in the most efficient plant, producing the highest quality product, watching the cost of inputs, and selling the largest volume for lower prices than his competitors. He held back enormous profits for reinvestment whenever the business-cycle slumped, taking advantage of bargain prices for expansion and retooling while piling up inventory for flush times ahead.[11]

Carnegie's methods contradicted conventional wisdom in much of the business community. Industrial investors, for example, expected to collect fat dividends twice a year and did not appreciate his insistence on retaining company earnings. As quickly as possible Andrew gathered up controlling shares in his partnerships to silence contrary views. He ran his plants as hard and fast as possible (boosting output by whole orders of magnitude), gladly rebuilding furnaces and fixtures every three or four years and incorporating technical refinements each time. He paid his managers modest salaries (except for technical wizard Bill Jones) and forced them to accept profit sharing instead; then he shared little of the profits. His customers were railroad owners, and he spared no effort to meet their expectations. He cut no corners except on the wage bill, human labor being easier to find and replace than alternative buyers. Over time, as business grew, he seized control of coal lands, iron mines, coking plants, puddling furnaces, steamship and railroad connections, so that no transactions (or surprises) threatened his promise to deliver steel rails on time at bargain prices. Called vertical integration, such a strategy marked the efforts of many Gilded Age industrialists who, confronted with high capital investments and cutthroat competition, found that freedom for suppliers compromised control for

the dominant enterprise. Over time the human and environmental consequences made Pittsburgh literally unlivable, but Carnegie moved away from
the smoke and grime, took coaching trips in Scotland, and sang the praises
of the business system that rewarded him and other top-level predators
with wealth and power never seen before.[12]

John D. Rockefeller, another titan of the Gilded Age, learned slightly
different lessons in the oil business that took him to the same destination:
nearly total control of his industry. Compared to Bessemer rail manufacturing, oil refining required fairly simple equipment but close attention to
process, volume, speed, chemistry, and transaction costs. In the 1870s oil
meant lighting oil—kerosene. Like everything else in their retail market,
consumers bought lamp oil without reference to brand or producer; all
they knew was what it cost and whether it smoked or exploded when
burned. Crude oil, marketed in rising quantities by dozens of small producers, passed through refineries that turned it into kerosene and various lubri-
cants at steadily falling prices. The industry was threatened constantly by
oversupply of crude and excess refining capacity. In 1872, Rockefeller
launched an audacious scheme, through a shell called the South Improvement Company, to secure large rebates on railroad charges and drawbacks
on shipments from anyone not a party to his conspiracy. Public exposure
discredited the South Improvement contract but not before Rockefeller
used it to bully his competitors in Cleveland into selling him their plants.
Thus began a relentless campaign to mop up competition and restrain oil
production in order to stop downward pressures on prices.[13]

Rockefeller's Standard Oil Company routinely paid fabulous dividends
ranging from 40 to 100 percent, but like Carnegie Rockefeller also spent
huge sums (either borrowed or retained from earnings) to modernize plant
and capture economies of scale. His methods—including secret deals, bribery, and something close to blackmail—while not technically illegal at the
time, struck everyone as brutal and unfair. Skillfully he bullied the railroads,
themselves plagued with high fixed costs and cutthroat competition, to
assist his campaign of domination. Having made himself their largest oil
shipper, he dictated terms then shared the benefits with allies while punishing independents. When long-distance pipelines undermined his sweet-
heart deal with the railroads, Rockefeller moved to construct his own
network of pipes. His strategy was simple: maximize volume, minimize
costs, and crush (as needed) competitors who dared to encroach on his
turf. In 1882 he developed the corporate trust to consolidate control over

multiple firms. The Standard Oil Trust then concentrated manufacturing by closing two-thirds of existing refineries and focusing capital investments on large new plants strategically located near the marketing centers of Cleveland (for the interior trade) and New York (for exports). With refining under control, Rockefeller's companies moved to capture both crude oil supply (backward integration) and wholesale marketing (forward), eventually controlling even the cans in which consumers purchased Standard kerosene. Such extraordinary mastery gave Rockefeller classic monopolistic powers which he used to crush upstart producers, refiners, and distributors. Consumers reaped the benefit of quality and service at reasonable retail prices. Competition might be excellent in theory, but managerial control produced a new two-headed monster never imagined by Adam Smith: monopoly profits coupled with consumer benefits. The only big loser was the less-than-giant, less-than-ruthless independent rival businessman, whose plight Ida Tarbell tried to champion in her muckraking *History of Standard Oil* (1904).[14]

The problem, which even Tarbell recognized, was that these new industrial titans abused their rival producers far more than consumers of their products. Common sense asserted that no one would charge less than the cost of production; therefore, the lowest price set by cutthroat competitors *must*, by definition, be sufficient. Large producers tried to explain that their anticompetitive efforts aimed at curbing ruinous price wars rather than gouging the consumer, but nobody believed them. Success always proved fleeting. New technology and market control, wherever they yielded significant economies of scale, delivered to savvy entrepreneurs immediate windfall profits; but productivity gains quickly glutted markets and drove down prices again. In 1885, for example, James B. Duke adopted two new Bonsack cigarette machines that each produced over 100,000 "tailor made" cigarettes per day. To protect this enormous advantage Duke frantically reached backward to purchase raw tobacco and coordinate curing and drying while also investing heavily in advertising and his downstream sales organization. By 1889 Duke produced 834 million cigarettes which he sold at record low prices while still collecting very high profits. Of course Duke's rivals copied his strategy, forcing the leader to organize a horizontal combination—the American Tobacco Company—to suppress cutthroat competition. Soon the makers of matches followed suit, and busy Americans finally had a vice they could enjoy on the job and during very short breaks.[15]

Certain technological innovations required a whole new business model before they could break into the mass consumer market. Isaac Singer's sewing machines, for example, were small and cheap enough to be purchased for use in the home, but expensive enough to benefit from a program of installment credit and complicated enough to need demonstration by skilled drummers and support in the form of parts and service. Typewriters followed a similar path into the mass market. Parts for McCormick's reaper more likely could be made by a local smith or machine shop, but the sales-and-service network developed in the late 1870s made it far less risky for ordinary farmers to adopt a whole system of complex machines. Mass production techniques yielding economies of scale kept the retail price of new equipment within reach of thousands of consumers, while the mass distribution networks made possible by the railroads quickened the flow of products, parts, and services from urban centers of commerce and industry into the farthest reaches of the countryside.[16]

Economies of scale worked their magic in wholesale and retail distribution as well. As the railroad network matured all kinds of manufacturers clamored for a piece of the burgeoning household consumer market. Retailers such as Marshall Field in Chicago invented the department store, a one-stop shopping center offering clothing, soft goods, hardware, furniture, watches, clocks, and household machines, on display, in stock, cash-and-carry, and even offering a money-back guarantee to unhappy customers—something no small town vendor could possibly afford. With data from the sales floor in hand, retailers contracted with manufacturers to mass-produce specialty items and store brands, often at discounted prices, allowing the vendor to tighten his grip on the satisfied consumer. Sears and Roebuck put the same concept into a catalog delivered by the railroad-enabled postal service to every outhouse in the Midwest. Suddenly men, women, and children in the most remote rural communities could flip through the pages of this wish book, make their selections, mail off the order, and in two weeks their coveted objects arrived at the mailbox. Eventually Sears sold socks and underwear, flatware and china, tables and chairs, patented cook stoves and bathtubs, even whole houses in which to use the aforementioned products.[17]

No single formula guaranteed the rise of big business or success for the would-be tycoon, but two common elements marked the emergence of very large firms in the industrial marketplace. First, economies of scale boosted productivity by whole orders of magnitude, creating excess capacity and rewarding giant innovative companies with the potential to dominate the market. Second, cutthroat competition among huge capital-intensive firms with excess productive capacity forced down prices, benefiting consumers but focusing producers' attention on mastering costs and driving into bankruptcy smaller, less competitive firms. These cutthroat conditions taught successful entrepreneurs to neutralize competition wherever possible, whether by integrating backward through their supply chains, consolidating horizontally with their immediate rivals, or manipulating wholesale and retail markets for their products. Wages paid for what Walt Whitman called "healthy toil and sweat"—potentially a positive feature of the free labor system—now appeared as a wasteful drag on the balance sheet, to be reduced wherever possible by crushing worker demands or replacing human hands with new capital equipment. Progress seemed less interested in sharing the fruits of modernization with the "common man" than in advancing the extravagant rewards to a few big winners in the new industrial game. Only in the next century would American capitalists such as Henry Ford discover the role of disposable income in workers' hands as a critical element in the circulation of wealth.[18]

Not every line of products enjoyed the benefits of mass production or economies of scale. In an exhaustive study of business and industry in the late nineteenth century Alfred D. Chandler Jr. and his students found that heat-using industries, fluid processes, and products for which mechanization proved successful generally profited from the rise of big business. Other lines—rope, for example, and furniture—could not be transformed by a magical machine or a heat-using process that facilitated higher volumes or faster "through-put." Of course at the time nobody understood why; consequently many trusts, pools, and combinations were mounted in restraint of trade where no particular advantage ensued and classical consumer injury more likely resulted. Absent a thorough understanding of cutthroat competition and economies of scale, legislators, courts, and critics of the business system railed against *all* restraint of trade as violations of the sacred principle of competition in a free economy. In 1890 Congress finally responded with the Sherman Antitrust Act prohibiting all such combinations and assigning to the federal courts the job of policing and ensuring a competitive marketplace. With the judiciary firmly wedded to the Smithian doctrine of laissez-faire, robust state intervention developed very slowly. Ironically, the more immediate effect of the Sherman Act was to outlaw cartels and informal associations, setting off a wave of outright mergers in the closing years of the nineteenth century. What the state *would* not do and collusion *could* not do the visible hands of management did. Investment bankers such as J. P. Morgan seized the moment to impose order and damp down the ravages of cutthroat competition.[19]

Continuing Innovations

Technology drove most of the forces that fostered the rise of big business in post–Civil War America. Since the middle of the 1700s a virtual explosion of new machines and devices in England, Europe, and North America had powered an "industrial revolution" that was reaching maturity in the final decades of the nineteenth century. Beginning with steam engines, textile machinery, steamboats, steam railways, and all kinds of mechanization, the combination of fossil fuels and mechanical gadgets in the hands of capitalist entrepreneurs profoundly reorganized economic and material life in what was then called the "modernizing" world. In the early United States, the extension of personal freedom and agency in the era of "improvement" had stimulated hundreds of clever individuals, who typically worked alone or in small workshops, with little or no theoretical or scientific training. Most inventors hoped to realize a fortune by solving a well-known problem and securing monopoly rights to the profits. Along with the famous few—Eli Whitney, Samuel Colt, Laomi Baldwin, Cyrus McCormick, Samuel F. B. Morse, and Isaac Singer—a legion of similar American tinkerers had piled up, by mid-century, nearly eighteen thousand patents for novel tools, machines, techniques, and processes. Breakthroughs were not limited by nationality; both the American paper industry and Carnegie's steel revolution, for example, depended on imported equipment and techniques. Upon this sea of innovations floated the entire apparatus of industrialization, rapid transportation, mass production, and mass distribution. Early inventors often spent as much time in the courts defending their claim to exclusive rewards as they spent in their actual workshops. The process was wasteful, chaotic, and unpredictable, sometimes rewarding not the most creative individual but the one with the best business plan or access to law and capital. Nevertheless, in the aggregate, the free market in innovation accelerated the rate of change dramatically. In the Civil War era the number of patents granted annually jumped from 5,000 to 10,000; after 1875 it topped 20,000 per year. Starting with the Great Exhibition in London in

1851, the nations of the western world acquired a habit of coming together every few years to brag of their technical prowess and show off their latest accomplishments.[20]

As firms and industries grew large, representing enormous capital investments in technical hardware and physical plant, the need for a regular flow of innovations became more acute. With their rapidly evolving technology, railroad companies were among the first to generate engineering departments to work out "fixes" for problems and perfect design innovations. Because private lines had to interchange traffic with each other on a daily basis, innovations spread quickly throughout the networks. At the same time, with thousands of miles of roadway and thousands of pieces of complex machinery, path dependency—the tendency of technical systems to limit subsequent refinements to fixes compatible with existing equipment—favored convergences within a common universe of technical possibilities. Hence the universal embrace of the "T" rail, the flanged wheel, signaling systems, telegraphy, and generally compatible designs for locomotives and rolling stock. Really great new ideas—such as the Westinghouse automatic air brake and the Janney automatic coupler—swept the industry: a combination of business self-interest and public safety legislation (the "carrot-and-stick") encouraged the adoption of these improvements despite the considerable short-term expense.[21]

Thomas Edison famously invented automatic telegraph systems, phonograph recording, and the electric light bulb, but his most important contribution was to the process of invention itself. A skilled telegrapher by occupation, the urge to invent drove Edison to devise all kinds of improvements to equipment for sending, receiving, and recording telegraph messages. These efforts forced him to study electricity itself, slowly mastering the science behind his technology in order to perfect, for example, the "multiplex" technique of sending several messages in both directions along a single telegraph wire. His mastery of electromagnetic phenomena allowed him to make the conceptual leap from recording dots and dashes to recording sound vibrations, leading to microphones and phonograph recordings. Intent on perfecting his inventions and making them commercially profitable, Edison pursued innovation and commercialization simultaneously, using profits from one new device or process to finance further development. He hired teams of machinists and technicians and installed them at his Menlo Park facility (1876), often cited as the first purpose-built "invention factory" and the germ of what became the modern industrial "R & D" lab. In 1878, Edison turned his attention to electric lighting. Once he had a filament in hand that produced a warm and pleasant glow inside a sealed bulb and lasted long enough to serve in general applications, he set about developing the whole system for generating and distributing power without which light bulbs themselves were useless.[22]

The Menlo Park model inspired Edison's friends and rivals alike. Alexander Graham Bell set up his own lab in 1881 and Bell Telephone Company followed suit in 1883. George Eastman established a Kodak laboratory to conduct basic research on photography for the purpose of stimulating further technological evolution. Chemical and pharmaceutical firms created proprietary research centers as a way of building product lines and protecting profitable innovations. The links between research science and product development grew much tighter in part because cutthroat competition among consolidated corporate giants placed large capital investments at risk should alternative inventions pop up in rival hands. At some point "path dependencies" forged a commitment to technical solutions not easily abandoned for the "next big thing." For example, Thomas Edison's equipment used the direct current with which he long had been familiar, but direct current decayed badly over long distances, forcing Edison to locate generating plants relatively close to his subscribers. Nicola Tesla invented a system using "alternating current" that was adopted by George Westinghouse, that allowed transmission over far greater distances. This set the stage for a great battle between rival systems. Run by men of business as much as science, both Edison Electric (DC) and Westinghouse (AC) campaigned ruthlessly to discredit each other's equipment as dangerous and unreliable.[23]

Institutionalization of innovation also proceeded in educational institutions, in part thanks to federal patronage under the Morrill Act (1862). Originally passed in 1857 but vetoed by a president tangled up in the sectional crisis, the Morrill Act bestowed grants of unsold federal land on collegiate institutions "to promote the liberal and practical education of the industrial classes." The newly opened Massachusetts Institute of Technology (1861) seized the opportunity along with Cornell University, the University of Delaware, and Pennsylvania State University. Iowa State (1862) was the first new school created specifically because of the Morrill Act, followed quickly by Michigan State, Kansas State, Purdue, and Texas A and M. Agriculture, mining, science, engineering, technology, and design edged out philosophy, the classics, and rhetoric in these new programs of practical education. The last generation to come of age in the nineteenth century moved into business and industry firmly convinced that scientific understanding (not just curiosity or good luck) provided the generative force behind innovation and progress.[24]

As we saw in the antebellum period, some innovations revolutionized not hardware but process and procedure. Emancipation, for example, stripped away from the cotton plantation the foundation of its labor system. Hoping to empower the freedmen, some abolitionists called for land reform and redistribution—forty acres and a mule to each African American family. But land reform violated property rights (which many Americans held dear) while the prospect of a million independent black rural households threatened the social structure of the South in ways too "horrible" to imagine. As a result, southern landowners—with tacit support from northern economic interests—invented a crop lien system by which they reenslaved the freedmen and returned them to the cotton fields. Stripped of their voting rights by terror and legislation, black sharecroppers signed contracts with their landlords and furnishing merchants, binding them to grow the staple crop and extending credits for expenses to be paid from the proceeds of the harvest. Vagrancy laws forced able-bodied men to enter such contracts or face incarceration (where they would join forced labor gangs for the state or county government). Men then deployed their own wives and children in the cotton fields, driven not by the master's whip but by their mounting debt at the store. Dictating prices for goods advanced and cotton sold, at year's end furnishing merchants and landlords always presented croppers with an unpaid balance, generously taking a promissory note and rolling it forward in perpetual dependency. Thus was the system of plantation agriculture "updated" and "improved" in the New South with little or no real change in racial liberties or social relations.[25]

Industrial labor, already routinized and notorious in New England textile mills, experienced similar (if less creative) innovations with the postwar rise of big business. Often the dominant or only employer in a community, giant firms such as Carnegie Steel and Standard Oil hired hundreds of individual workmen. While legal fictions pretended that each employee bargained for his daily wage, these firms dictated terms, freely cut wages as markets demanded, and fired protesting workers. Women and children filled more shop floors and mining tunnels, where exploitation went unchecked by health or safety standards. Collective action to improve wages or working conditions met with legal rejection (as illegal restraints of trade) or with blacklists, lockouts, and violence. Railroad workers caught agitating for cause found themselves dismissed by their current employer—and unemployable on any other line. In 1892 at Carnegie's Homestead plant near Pittsburgh, an army of Pinkerton guards brought a violent end to the ironworkers' strike. Carnegie pretended in public to tolerate unions, so his right-hand man, Henry Clay Frick, carried out the massacre while Andrew enjoyed a vacation in Scotland. Two years later in the model industrial town of Pullman, Illinois, the Palace Car company locked out striking sleeping car workers. To protect the federal mail (carried by railroads with sleeping car service), President Grover Cleveland sent in the US Army to "keep the peace" with violence. Exactly the kind of collectivist impulse that yielded trusts and pools in corporate boardrooms, brought down on the working classes the iron fists of capital and the state.[26]

By the end of the nineteenth century, Americans had mastered an astonishing number of technological problems, invented undreamed-of tools, products, and processes, and even mastered the business of innovation itself. Courts sustained the rights and privileges of organized capital almost without exception. New academic institutions encouraged technological improvements and fostered wholly new discoveries through basic research in science and technology. What had been a leap of faith at the start of the nineteenth century—the confidence that science and the useful arts would generate answers to all our questions—became a solid "fact." Jacob Bigelow's wild-eyed claims of 1816 stood thoroughly vindicated by century's end. The supernatural hand of Providence, so prevalent in the rhetoric of the founding era, had taken on more natural imagery. Less benevolent than the God of the ancestors, this modern Providence owed more to the "contriving brain and the skillful hand" (James C. Malin's evocative phrase) than to its biblical counterpart. Guided more by the laws of trade than the law of Moses, this "spirit of the times" celebrated progress and possibilities. As Americans (at least among the comfortable classes) turned their faces toward the twentieth century, a triumphal sense of adequacy and competence in the face of all challenges took flight.[27]

The Arid Regions

Since the arrival of Englishmen in Jamestown, the found environment—for the most part dense, well-watered forests—had set the agenda for development. Tree removal had been the prime objective of American pioneers for

250 years, and practically everything people made they made from wood. The grand prairies of Illinois and Iowa presented something of a problem: a tangled, impenetrable mat of roots bound the rich, friable soil while head-high grasses deprived settlers of their primary building material. Soon enough, however, John Deere and James Oliver developed sharp steel plows with which to break the prairies, and rail transportation brought in lumber from Wisconsin and Michigan. West of the Missouri River the challenges grew more severe. Early American explorers such as Stephen Long and Zebulon Pike had denounced as desert great swaths of country just east of the Rocky Mountains, in part because of startling landforms such as the sand dunes in southeastern Colorado. Much of what we now call the Great Plains was covered in short perennial grasses on which grazed enormous herds of bison and wild horses. Thomas Jefferson imagined these lands as permanent reserves for the Native Americans displaced from eastern forests, and actual pioneers at mid-century clamored for a quick way *across* the dry plains and the mountains to settle lush valleys in Oregon and California. As late as the Civil War the arid West seemed more like a barrier than a resource to the tens of thousands of individuals who gave force to the westward movement.[28]

After the Civil War, however, people began to imagine the arid and mountain West as belonging to "Manifest Destiny" after all. Irrepressible boosters such as Colorado territorial governor William Gilpin saw the West as a storehouse of riches needing only a bit of correction to unlock its potential. Space itself—distance—could be neutralized by rail transportation; lumber and hardware could be purchased with cattle grazed (for free) on the open range; and the universal shortage of rainfall easily was rectified with irrigation and water management. The federal Homestead Law (1862, giving 160 acres to actual settlers) drew farmers steadily farther into the dry plains. Wind-powered water pumps (Halladay's windmill on sale after 1854) made it possible to water stock, locomotives, and kitchen gardens. In the 1870s barbed wire revolutionized fencing in a treeless environment. By then climate scientists such as Cyrus Thomas and Samuel Aughey were pushing a theory that "rain follows the plow" to explain an up-tick in precipitation west of the hundredth meridian. Others credited railroad lines or magnetic telegraph wires with altering the environment. Whatever the cause, experts quickly proclaimed the improvement permanent. Wherever wheat matured without irrigation, hopes soared.[29]

What had changed, of course, was not environmental reality or even technological prowess; what had changed were the desires of people who now saw the West as a place in which to pursue their ambitions. Four important vectors converged by the 1870s. First, overland travel to the Pacific coast required the pacification of Native Americans who were being pressed into smaller and more marginal spaces. The postwar Union Army took up the challenge with vigor, waging war on both the Indians and the bison on which they depended. Second, transcontinental railroads needed, at the very least, station stops with fuel and water. To be viable such outposts must grow into towns with permanent residents, sources of food, and some kind of exports sustaining a local economy. Third, federal land grants to overland railroads left those companies with millions of acres of land that must be sold to retire construction debts. Talk of barren plains and deserts hardly encouraged colonization along these important thoroughfares. Finally, mineral strikes together with surveys of the vast stocks of timber ripe for harvest transformed the mountains themselves into valuable sites for development.[30]

One scientific explorer who studied the arid regions on behalf of the federal government was Major John Wesley Powell, a one-armed Civil War veteran who spent several postwar years exploring the canyons of the Colorado River. Charged by Interior Secretary Carl Schurz with surveying public lands in the Rocky Mountain region, Powell started with a comprehensive rainfall map that displayed graphically the signature problem of western lands. Rainfall alone would not sustain agriculture beyond the hundredth meridian, where less than twenty inches fell per year. American land law and water rights traditions both reflected the humid environments where rains fell freely on everyone, where 160 acres made a plausible farm, and where riparian doctrine (running water goes to the adjacent landlord) had served English-speaking farmers for hundreds of years.

Keenly aware of the difference in this arid environment, Powell concluded that traditional agriculture was not possible in most of the arid West. Less than 3 percent, he believed, could be "redeemed" by irrigation; the rest might best remain in grasslands grazed by cattle, carefully managed to prevent permanent damage in the hot summer months. Neither the Homestead Law nor its companion Timber Culture Act (1873, granting 160 acres to planters of trees) and Desert Land Act (1877, giving land to those who would irrigate it) dealt realistically with the water problem. To make the best use of available water Powell urged the creation of irrigation districts with land surveyed in watersheds, not the rectangles of the prevailing survey system. Homesteading farmers needed up to 2,500 acres—far more than individuals could afford at traditional prices—and settlement should top out at densities well below those seen on earlier frontiers. For land to have agricultural value, rights to available water must inhere in the land to be irrigated, and water must be *used* to secure one's right to it. For democracy to survive men of small capital must be guaranteed access to water, and laws should be devised to prevent monopolists from buying it up and turning landholders into powerless dependents.[31]

Citing the example of Mormons in Utah, who carefully parceled out land and water with one eye constantly fixed on the good of the whole community, Powell called for profound revisions of the standard American notions of freedom, enterprise, and property rights. Individual initiative and private capital, left to their own devices, likely would scoop up the best arable land, mining claims, timber lands, and water sources, leaving vast stretches of range undeveloped and unusable. Time was of the essence: every passing year saw thousands more settlers putting down roots, becoming stakeholders who in time would prevent the kind of planning and regulation that made the Mormons so successful. Unfortunately, Powell's bills to revise both water and land law systems died in Congress. No one in the age of mastery was inclined to welcome the idea of limits or modify patterns that had made the United States such a rising force in the late nineteenth-century world.[32]

Rather than accept Powell's advice to accommodate the environment, most people chose to see western lands as temporarily "deficient" in rainfall and subject to improvement by hardworking, innovative settlers. Railroads, desperate to colonize their land grants, whipped up dreams of independence and prosperity for beleaguered eastern families. The Atchison, Topeka, and Santa Fe (ATSF) pushed western Kansas as the perfect place for wheat, corn, and fruit; the Northern Pacific sang praises of Dakota and Montana plains; the Burlington advertised millions of acres in Iowa and Nebraska, ignoring the difference in rainfall; the Great Northern urged pioneers to quit "working for others" and invest in "five or ten acres of Washington fruit land." Wealthy speculators launched huge "bonanza farms" in North Dakota—until a devastating drought returned in 1888. As dry-farming dwindled, enthusiasm for irrigation soared. The notion of "deficiency" gave rise to convictions that technology could rectify what nature had failed to provide. By the 1890s a cult of irrigation was conjuring fantastic visions of the western cornucopia.[33]

In the first instances irrigation systems simply diverted surface water through man-made ditches crisscrossing crop land and pastures. Precipitation stored in the mountain snowpack slowly melted and ran downhill to service the settlers' needs. Impounds and reservoirs extended such systems, but large-scale facilities called for cooperative or corporate intervention—in short, internal improvements. Westerners reprised old debates from the era of Jackson and Clay, about public or private control, corporate monopolies, and the role of the state in economic development. Informed by desire as much as science, a new generation of boosters proclaimed that aridity itself was not a curse but a blessing. Irrigation bestowed upon the husbandman a level of control unimagined in the humid East, where natural rainfall came too soon, too late, too much, or too little. By mastering the inputs of moisture, farmers could wring from a few acres of western land more valuable produce than the output of whole farms in Ohio. William E. Smythe, editor of *Irrigation Age*, declared the arid West the "better half of the United States."[34]

Upon this claim Smythe built his radical vision of a modern agrarian democracy in which the western states replaced their eastern sisters as the font of "liberty and equality." They boasted "more water-power than New England; more coal, iron, and oil than Pennsylvania; larger and better forests than Maine and Michigan"; and better "wheat and corn than Illinois and Indiana." In the arid West democracy would flourish even as it dwindled in the urban, industrial, monopolistic East. Large holdings worked by sharecropping tenants must utterly fail in arid country while small parcels of five to twenty acres, properly supplied with water, supplied the family farmer with everything he wanted. With eight or more families living on a quarter section, rural isolation would disappear. Farmers could live in villages (like English peasants of old) and enjoy schools, churches, and each other's company. Properly managed by community associations and popular governments, irrigation facilities guaranteed democracy by ensuring the success of independent husbandmen and bankrupting would-be monopolists. In a flight of counterfactual fancy Smythe concluded that the Pilgrims, had they landed at San Diego first, surely would have dismissed the forested East as "comparatively worthless."[35]

In the 1890s Smythe led a national campaign for major programs of irrigation to develop "forty million forty-acre farms" in the arid regions. At first advocates asked to have public lands ceded to the states which, in turn, might fashion laws to facilitate development. Other voices urged private capitalists—perhaps the railroad corporations—to take the lead in shaping the western landscape. Critics warned that western state governments had shown little evidence of dealing wisely with land and water, while private capital could not be relied on to serve the greater public interest. The private investor, Smythe warned, might "change his mind, or lose his fortune, or death may arrest him and wreck a thousand hopes." Only the "public capitalist" (that is, the federal government) was "dependable." As the century drew to a close, advocates for national intervention gained significant momentum. By 1900 both Republicans and Democrats endorsed some form of national irrigation program. In language reminiscent of the early internal improvement movement, President Theodore Roosevelt proclaimed the projects "too vast" for private or state-level management. "The Government should construct and maintain these reservoirs as it does other public works." There followed in 1902 the Newland Reclamation Act and the start of huge public water projects in the West. With enormous government support, technology and enterprise set out to transform the Great American Desert into the Garden of Eden. In his popular book, *The Conquest of Arid America* (1899), Smythe put it thus: "When Uncle Sam . . . waves his hand toward the desert and says, '*Let there be water!*' we know that the stream will obey his command."[36]

Celebrating the Triumph

By the end of the nineteenth century Americans had taken to congratulating themselves on the astonishing progress of their new nation—their growth and prosperity, their preference for peace, their democratic institutions, technological inventiveness, personal freedoms, public education, rates of literacy, social equality, and boundless opportunity. No less a player in this age of mastery than Andrew Carnegie wrote one classic benediction for the process by which Americans achieved a central place in the modernizing world. Himself the leading example of the rags-to-riches, self-made business tycoon (a life he shrewdly misremembered in important particulars), Carnegie penned his most famous book, *Triumphant Democracy* (1886), to show Great Britain how and why his adopted land (their former colony) had in just a century "reached the foremost rank among nations." First in agriculture, first in manufacturing, leading the race for practical inventions, the United States stood poised to "out-distance all others" in the century ahead. Why? Carnegie credited three factors: the native genius of ethnically British people; the "topographical and climatic" advantages of

North America; and the influence of political institutions "founded upon the equality of the citizen."[37]

A penchant for schematic and formulaic reasoning characterized Carnegie's logic in *Triumphant Democracy*—a penchant shared by most contemporary analysts. Carnegie spent nearly six months each year living in his native Scotland, and he nursed deep grievances against aristocratic influence that propped up the monarchy, the House of Lords, and leisured aristocrats vis-à-vis the entrepreneurs. Stripped of hereditary titles and organized on principles of political equality, Americans (he liked to believe) rewarded work, intelligence, and ambition without regard for class standing or ancient prerogatives. There was "not one shred of privilege to be met with anywhere in all the laws." Only two things threatened the American experiment: slavery and the rise of non-British immigration. The first had been expunged. Every slave now "was a citizen, with equal voice in the State." The second threat was neutralized by offering public schools and citizenship, "Democracy's 'gift of welcome' to the newcomer," who then "could not help but grow fond of his new home." There followed five hundred pages of statistical gazetteer describing cities and towns, occupations, education, religion, pauperism, crime, agriculture, manufacturing, mining, commerce, art, literature, and government. Apparently clueless as to why the atmosphere in Pittsburgh destroyed all plant life and why the steelworkers lived in such squalor, Carnegie saw nothing in need of repair in the land that had made him so rich and happy.[38]

Another popular spokesman giving voice to America's triumph was Russell Conwell, a Baptist clergyman and founder of Philadelphia's Temple University. Shortly before Carnegie's book appeared Conwell began reading to enchanted audiences a Chautauqua essay called "Acres of Diamonds." Prolix and rambling, this fifteen-thousand-word lecture (delivered more than six thousand times over forty-five years) celebrated economic opportunity for any honest person willing to strive for his own advancement. Built loosely on an Arab fable pointing out the folly of seeking riches abroad (when acres of diamonds lay buried in one's own garden), Conwell's lecture praised wealth as a blessing, a virtue, an obligation to be pursued by all men. Opportunities for "great wealth" lay "within the reach of almost every man and woman" in America (he did not elaborate on how). Never "in the history of the world did a poor man without capital have such an opportunity to get rich quickly and honestly. In America the poor were made poor "by their own shortcomings." Do not pine for a stake or inheritance.

Inherited wealth only cripples the rich man's son and deprives him of the thrill to be had when a young man works and saves, buys a little house, and carries his bride through the door saying "I have earned this home myself. It is all mine, and I divide it with thee." This cult of the "self-made man" Conwell further illustrated with examples from business titans such as John Jacob Astor, Cornelius Vanderbilt, Elias Howe, and Cyrus McCormick. To the claim that the rich were crooks, Conwell answered emphatically, No! "Ninety-eight out of one hundred rich men in America are honest. That is why they are rich."[39]

Nearly tautological in its structure, this kind of proof by assertion sustained a generation's outsized confidence in freedom, democracy, and enterprise even as evidence to the contrary accumulated everywhere. Carnegie himself, for example, got his stake in the business world through the generous sponsorship of his mentor, Tom Scott. Later he remembered his mother mortgaging the house to enable his purchase of the Adams Express shares with which he launched his capitalist career—but biographer Joseph Frazier Wall could find no evidence to support that claim. To be sure there were extraordinary tales of striking it rich in the middle decades of the nineteenth century, but the cult of the self-made man took root just as the structure of giant corporate enterprises narrowed the range of opportunity in one field after another. What historian Alfred D. Chandler Jr. called the "visible hand of management" labored ardently to smother the bumptious market forces that rewarded maverick entrepreneurs. John D. Rockefeller's entire business plan focused on crushing reckless wildcat oil producers. As part of his campaign for total control, Andrew Carnegie (through his surrogate, Henry Clay Frick) had massacred striking workers at the Homestead plant. Finance capitalists such as J. P. Morgan sought stability and order, not the endless chaos that sprang from wildly competitive markets. The most successful "self-made" men seemed determined to pull up the ladder of opportunity behind themselves.[40]

Irrigation guru William E. Smythe composed his own explanation for the "economic greatness of the United States," this time giving appropriate recognition to the "resources of a virgin continent." Smythe faulted the colonial generations for "looking backward" to England rather than "forward to the conquest and subjugation" of the land before them. The American career as "empire builders" only started, he wrote, with the War for Independence, after which the world began to realize "that the American was to be the master of the new continent," moving westward "as naturally and inevitably as the sun in its course." Ignoring the violent displacement of the Native Americans (he called it a "peaceful conquest"), Smythe oddly employed martial language to describe the war waged "on the forest, the plain, the desert, and the mountain" to create "a better civilization than the world had seen." Acknowledging the arguments made by Carnegie and many others on behalf of triumphant democracy, Smythe countered that if republican institutions alone were enough to explain America's prosperity no monarchy still would be standing. America flourished, he concluded, precisely because freedom and equality energized a people *turned out on* "the continental expanse of marvelous resources awaiting the labor and genius of man."[41]

This widespread urge to celebrate sparked another campaign to hold an exhibition in 1892, this time to mark the four hundredth anniversary of Columbus's voyage. Chicago won the honors. Just sixty years past its own infancy, and only twenty years after a devastating fire, the rude upstart city deep in the American interior beat out New York and other rivals with a brash proposal backed up by $10,000,000 in cash, to construct a fairground on the grandest scale yet. "Other world's fairs," gushed a correspondent in the *Century Illustrated Magazine*, "have celebrated the civilization of a race, but the Columbian Exposition will glorify the world's transcendent migration," the "human energy that handed the torch of civilization across an ocean."[42]

So often dismissed as nothing more than a world-class stockyard, Chicago aspired to top the recent Paris Exposition of 1889 in scale and scope and number of visitors. Daniel Burnham, the Chicago architect who managed the whole affair, envisioned a purpose-built city of outstanding architectural beauty housing exhibits from around the world and boasting something—anything—more spectacular than Eiffel's tower. Hobbled by a slow start, frustrating delays, and enormous technical challenges presented by the saturated soils along Chicago's southern lakeshore, Burnham finally mobilized five leading architects along with landscape designer Frederick Law Olmstead behind a stunning plan to be executed in an even more stunning time frame of roughly sixteen months! With no time to build in brick and stone, Burnham expediently finished his fairgrounds with "staff," a semidurable mixture of plaster of paris and jute that could be cast in panels, columns, or any other shape. Lightweight and easily attached to frameworks with common nails, staff made it possible to finish the buildings in less than half the usual time. According to one enthusiastic reporter, a workman "may walk to his job with a square yard of the side of a marble palace under each arm and a Corinthian capital in each hand." Rough joints were no problem "since a little wet plaster serves to weld the pieces into a finished surface." All smoothed out and spray-painted with white lead and linseed oil, the gleaming famed "White City" opened in May 1893.[43]

The White City captivated visitors with its grand exhibit halls, beautiful grounds, stately lagoons, and the stunning backdrop of Lake Michigan itself. Burnham never found his Eiffel Tower but the Chicago fair picked up an equally impressive and entertaining landmark: the Ferris Wheel. Located on the Midway Plaisance, connecting the main grounds in Jackson Park with satellite installations to the west, this enormous attraction rose 250 feet above the ground and afforded riders a bird's-eye view of the whole extraordinary landscape. Additional thrills were promised by a "Spiral Railway Tower" of 560 feet and a hydraulic "Sliding Railway" racing from one end of the Midway to the other at top speeds of one hundred miles per hour. Electric lighting on a scale never seen before anywhere (using the Westinghouse alternating current system) dazzled visitors inside the cavernous exhibit halls and all over the grounds. Capitalizing on the public's fascination with exotic "primitive" races, the Midway offered living villages and (racist) ethnographic displays of Native American, African, and Pacific peoples along with scandalously clad entertainers. One could find there "camel drivers and donkey-boys, dancing girls from Cairo and Algiers, from Samoa and Brazil, with men and women of all nationalities, some lounging in oriental indifference, some shrieking in unison or striving to outshriek each other." Dressed up as anthropology, the Midway doubled as a freak show reminding middle-class white Americans how lucky they were and how far they had progressed.[44]

In conjunction with the fair the American Historical Association held its annual meeting in Chicago that summer. At the Art Institute downtown, a young Wisconsin academic, Frederick Jackson Turner, delivered his now-famous paper, "The Significance of the Frontier in American History." The recent United States census had reported it could no longer identify a coherent "frontier" line in the American West. Claiming that the "existence of an area of free land, its continuous recession, and the advance of American settlement westward" *explained* American development, Turner suggested those original conditions no longer obtained for the future. He was not especially alarmed, but it remained unclear, in Turner's view, just how the United States would prosper and grow without the aid of this frontier process.[45]

The 1893 fair proved remarkably successful by almost any measure. It covered six hundred acres—more than any world's fair to date, and it boasted exhibits from forty-six different countries. Some twenty-seven million visitors toured the fairgrounds, basking in science and technology, art, music, ethnographic kitsch, and vulgar displays of oriental sensuality and African "savagery." Reviews and commentaries filled the pages of the popular prints that summer; revenues at the gate retired the enormous investments put up to mount the show. Chicago glowed with pride. The fair grounds at Jackson Park reverted to municipal control, a lasting monument to the great celebration; but nothing could preserve the actual structures that had made such an impression. Everyone knew that in the harsh climate of northern Illinois staff would disintegrate in maybe six years or less. Chicago's White City was a theater set, a Potemkin village, an edifice that only *looked like* the thing it stood for. Perhaps Mark Twain was right—the age of mastery was, not a golden age, but a gilded one.[46]

Americans celebrated fin de siècle with boisterous claims of mastery, but in so many ways the scene on the ground offered only the appearance of mastery. The final decade of the century also was racked by violence and conflict. The year of the fair marked the start of another punishing business depression that threw tens of thousands out of work, bankrupted one railroad after another, and drove all kinds of struggling firms into mergers and consolidations. For the first time investment bankers gained the upper hand in the business community, ushering in a system of finance capitalism that would dominate the twentieth century. Organized labor tried (and mostly failed) to gain a foothold from which to rescue some bargaining power in the changing American economy. They were met with violent repression. Ethnic conflict and hostility reached new levels as industry attracted (or actively recruited) refugees from even grimmer markets in eastern and southern Europe. With unparalleled cynicism Congress passed the Dawes Act (1887) that stripped land away from the remnants of Native American nations, leaving individual Indians with small allotments and throwing the rest on the market for hungry white settlers. The "Jim Crow" system of racial segregation grew more thorough, more codified, and more pervasive throughout the South and was emulated informally in the North as well. In politics, angry third-party movements and different reform initiatives tried to break down the two-party game that sustained unaccountable congressmen and urban machines. Presidential assassinations in 1865 and 1901 bookend the age of mastery (with one more in between), and even Chicago's spectacular fair was marred by the shooting death of the mayor two days before it closed. The culture of exploitation might seem triumphant at the White City, but its costs and consequences lay scattered, unaccounted for, in every direction.[47]

CHAPTER 9

Prophecy

BY THE END OF the nineteenth century many people noticed that environmental degradation was threatening many aspects of American greatness. The most "advanced" industrialized cities boasted unbreathable air, rank, crowded, filthy housing, streets piled high with garbage and animal waste, foul water, and open privies. In places such as Pittsburgh, shrouded in acid-laden coal smoke, foliage ceased to thrive; in working-class districts the ground was covered with mud, rock, gravel, trash, sewage, and occasional boardwalks, but nothing green. Food supplies, even if plentiful, were wholly unregulated and plagued with adulterations. Industrial workplaces had become outrageously dangerous; workers risked life and limb, ingested poisonous pollutants, and under prevailing "fellow servant" rulings incurred personal liability for accidents and losses in the mines, at machinery, or on shop floors. The blowback from progress had begun reaching into the middle and upper classes, resulting in scattered smoke-abatement campaigns, driven by garden club women (whose flowers died) and housewives who could not scrub away the smoke and soot. Finally—and not by any means of least importance—industrialists themselves began to imagine running short of the natural resources Americans had taken for granted for three hundred years.[1]

This gradual awakening of people to the consequences of modernization set the stage for a conservation movement that drew its energy from separate impulses but eventually converged into a critical perspective. Spectacular natural features, such as the geysers of Yellowstone, the granite cliffs of Yosemite, and giant Sequoias on the northwest coast, kindled an urge to preserve such wonders for the amazement and edification of future generations. Deforestation in New England and the upper Midwest slowly impressed upon local boosters what James Madison tried to explain back in 1818: it takes longer to grow a tree than a field of corn. The death of waterways, long burdened with urban sewage and industrial waste, now poisoned as well with mine tailings and new synthetic dyes, pigments, and chemicals, threatened the survival of everyone who depended on them as sources of—wait for it—water. Finally, middle-class Americans with newfound leisure time to spend camping, hunting, fishing, or riding their new bicycles, found to their dismay that the forests were gone, the fish were dead, there was nowhere to ride a bicycle, and such spectacular destinations as Niagara Falls were overrun with cheesy vendors hawking food and souvenirs.[2]

Of course there had been critics of the culture of exploitation since before the Revolution, but such countervailing voices seldom got a hearing in the face of boosters and believers in America's extraordinary mission. Critics almost always drew on one of two vocabularies (sometimes both at once): the language of restraint, moderation, and stewardship, or the language of beauty and reverence that motivated poets, painters, and sometimes preachers but rarely turned the heads of political economists. Articulate critiques in either register encountered all sorts of countervailing voices. For much of the antebellum period, for example, the pace of growth and progress masked the importance of negative consequences, especially when relocation to "greener pastures" so readily solved any problems. "Scientific" experts in political economy generated confidence in data-driven claims that more progress would alleviate the hardships which accompanied the early market revolution. An exponential explosion of technological innovations seemed to verify that claim. The popular celebration of hard-boiled, masculine materialism in the business and political cultures drove to the "feminine" margins criticisms framed in aesthetic, sentimental, or spiritual language. Finally, preoccupations with social reforms that focused on immediate symptoms of wealth inequality or community disintegration appeared to be more urgent and important than matters of resource depletion in some long-distant future.

Philosophical Stirrings

There is for sale today in the bookshop at Walden Pond a little volume that reprints together two of the earliest foundation texts in the canon of

American nature writing: Ralph Waldo Emerson's "Nature," and Henry David Thoreau's "Walking." This writing, boasts the back cover, "defines our distinctly American relationship to nature." Annie Dillard credits Emerson's 1836 essay with launching John Muir's career as a wilderness wanderer: "Emerson's wild metaphysic still underlies American nature writing and still caps American thinking about nature." Such claims seem fair enough looking back from the twenty-first century, but these first philosophical stirrings made no such dramatic impact on nineteenth-century Americans caught up in the dreams of improvement, destiny, and mastery. More like cautionary whispers, these early works of prophecy at best created a platform on which later, more boisterous critics could stand and proclaim dissenting views.[3]

While these writers shared something with the older advocates of husbandry and resource conservation, those eighteenth-century voices stood squarely on a utilitarian platform of "man-in-nature" that belonged to an agrarian world in which one scarcely could imagine human enterprise except in the context of natural resources. But as the triumphalist ethic of modernization became dominant in the nineteenth century, human ingenuity promised to overcome all material limitations. One needed a new place to stand if one were to lever the course of history into a different trajectory. Emerson surely offered such a new platform with his transcendentalist unification of metaphysical and physical nature. Keenly aware of the commodification by which mankind possessed the natural world, Emerson pushed back with the claim that there was also "a property in the horizon" which no man owned but "the poet." This was, Emerson argued, "the best part of these men's farms, yet to this their warranty-deeds give no title." Emerson went on to celebrate a childlike purity found in communion with the natural world: "Standing on the bare ground,—my head bathed by the blithe air, and uplifted into infinite space,—all mean egotism vanishes. I become a transparent eye-ball; I am nothing; I see all; the currents of the Universal Being circulate through me; I am part or particle of God."[4]

A transparent eye-ball? Emerson's poetics captured a following in part because his writing first was received as public lectures, where his oratorical performance garnered universal praise. But the meaning of his mystical ramblings utterly bewildered many of his listeners. That which seemed comprehensible also seemed blasphemous, atheistic, at war with even the most liberal Unitarian precepts of religion; the rest of his ideas struck early reviewers as disgusting, "illogical," "inconsistent," "gorgeous in style and wild in theory," "amazing nonsense" buried "beneath verbal rubbish" so that nobody could see the ideas. Historian Mary Kupiec Cayton quite rightly locates a major source of Emerson's unease in the emerging culture of self-interest that replaced human love with "appropriation." And yet, despite his paean in *Nature* to woods and bare ground, Emerson actually did not like the raw countryside and once cited Cambridge as a "better place to study than the woodlands." Indifferent to the apparent contradictions, Emerson alternated harsh critiques of commercial America with celebrations of human ingenuity, progress, and the westward march of civilization. In one flash of insight (one he might well have turned upon his own "transparent eye-ball") Emerson said that one could tell what people thought about abstract truths by looking at the clergy, who were disdained by "practical men" because they "could do nothing." Typically, they were "addressed as women."[5]

To be dismissed as women was a stinging rebuke in the masculine, aggressive world of ruthless enterprise and cutthroat competition. Emerson's famous acolyte, Henry David Thoreau, fared little better as he tried to break into print with his own, more accessible brand of nature appreciation. Unlike Emerson, whose "nature" was strictly philosophical, Thoreau truly did love the natural world—the country around Concord, Massachusetts, the neighborhood rivers, the Maine woods. As his observations of landscapes grew keener he began to break down the boundary between human and nonhuman life. While most of his friends by 1845 warmly embraced the cause of liberation for enslaved African men and women, Thoreau found himself extending a similar cry in behalf of fish prevented by a dam at Billerica from returning to their birthplace to spawn. "Still patiently, almost pathetically" trying to fulfill their destiny, "with instinct not to be discouraged, not to be *reasoned* with," the shad struggled only to be "met by the Corporation with its dam." Had "Nature" given them "heart to bear their fate?" He thought not: they were "armed only with innocence and a just cause." "Poor shad!," came the lament, "where is thy redress?" Biographer Laura Dassow Walls declared this extension of his ethical community to nonhuman life forms "novel, shocking, ridiculous." But Thoreau gave "the rest of his life to this revolutionary insight."[6]

Harvard graduate, brooding neophyte, practical handyman, sometime employee in his family's pencil factory, young Henry Thoreau wanted more than anything to become a writer and join the rarified literary cadre that had formed around Emerson in Concord. He wrote a few pieces for Emerson's magazine, *The Dial*, and spent some time in New York trying to break into print there; but he had not yet impressed his mentor except as a carpenter. While in New York he composed a scathing review of a utopian manifesto by J. A. Etzler that promised paradise in this world, in ten years, if men would associate and pledge themselves to develop new energy converters. Such technological optimism appealed broadly: even Emerson, in "The Young American," had celebrated railroad iron as "a magician's rod" capable of stirring the "sleeping energies of land and water." Cooperative—or associational—experiments, designed to blunt the acquisitive ethic of commercial capitalism, intrigued many of the Concord intellectuals. Bronson Alcott and Nathaniel Hawthorn each spent a season pitching manure at Brook Farm. But Thoreau found utopians such as Etzler wanting in rigor or consistency.[7]

Etzler's argument and Thoreau's critique of it warrant attention as a prelude to the perspective that blossomed at Walden Pond. Based on preposterous calculations of the energy available in wind, waves, tides, falling water, and sunlight, Etzler promised a system of new machines that would deliver "everything desirable for human life . . . in superabundance, without labor, and without pay." The "whole face of nature" would be "changed into the most beautiful forms": mountains leveled, valleys filled, lakes drained—or created—to suit, canals and roads built so that thousands of tons might be moved "one thousand miles in twenty-four hours." By harnessing nature's powers, any "wilderness, even the most hideous and sterile," could be converted into "fertile and delightful gardens." This was the doctrine of "improvement" squared or cubed, and Thoreau skewered it with sarcasm: "Who knows but by accumulating the power until the end of the present century . . . reserving all that blows, all that shines, all that ebbs and flows, all that dashes, we may have got such a reserved accumulated power as to run the earth off its track into a new orbit. . . . Or, perchance, coming generations . . . availing themselves of future inventions in aerial locomotion . . . may migrate from earth, to settle some vacant and more western planet." Etzler's vision ramped up a thousand times mankind's habits of abusing nature on the cheap and dirty. Rather than "succumb" to nature, people would completely remake it: disembowel volcanos, grub up earthquakes, improve the colors of flowers and the songs of birds. Such a dreamland evaporated, however, when touched by the greed of unreformed humans. In a startling move at the end of his review, Thoreau identified "love" as the "wind, the tide, the waves, the sunshine," the only power that could bring about true paradise. Not technology, industry, ambition, or enterprise, but love. Sadly, despite the efforts of the wisest men "in all ages," love had been little "applied to social ends."[8]

In the spring of 1845, Thoreau struck out to find the inner source of a reformed human nature on which he placed his hope for the world. He borrowed an axe and set to work building a writer's retreat, a tiny house on a scruffy piece of land in Walden Woods recently purchased by Waldo Emerson. Moving into his cabin July 4, he set to work furiously transforming his notes from an earlier trip into *A Week on the Concord and Merrimack Rivers*. At the same time he started filling notebooks with observations and musings about the solitary life, human nature, spiritual truths, animal habits, the changing seasons, justice, inequality, greed, ambition, and the place of mankind in the firmament of nature. For over two years he kept up this experiment in spiritual focus and material simplicity. He calculated to the penny just how little it cost to keep body and soul together (conveniently ignoring occasional lunches and dinners in town and picnic baskets left by visitors). He surveyed all dimensions of the lake before him, proving (contrary to local folklore) that Walden Pond *had* a solid bottom (102 feet down), and proposing that truth itself also rested on a solid rock of reality. As a result, this transcendentalist with feet of stone brought his readers closer—if only a little—to an accessible critique of the culture of exploitation.[9]

The text Thoreau finally published as *Walden, or Life in the Woods*, contained meditations on practically everything, organized thematically, not formally argued but offered up in a meandering, first-person monologue. His long first chapter, "Economy" contained the boldest statements of his intentions along with a stinging rebuke of mankind's preoccupation with work, with making a living, with getting ahead. He dared to call "frivolous" the fixation on "Negro Slavery" when so-called free men endured bondage as well: "It is hard to have a southern overseer; it is worse to have a northern one; but worst of all when you are the slave-driver of yourself." So pervasive were the claims of the culture of exploitation that people honestly thought there was "no choice left." Not true, he declared: there were as many alternative ways "as there can be drawn radii from one centre." The dazzling improvements of the age were illusionary, "pretty toys," "improved means to an unimproved end." Railroad promoters said that everyone soon could "ride somewhere, in next to no time, for nothing." Skeptical Henry suspected that when that new locomotive pulled away and the smoke cleared, the people would see "that a few are riding, but the rest are run over." In a move sure to offend the better classes, Thoreau denounced philanthropy as a hypocritical ruse. There was "no odor so bad" as that which arose from "goodness tainted." If he knew a man was coming to his house to do him good, Henry wrote, "I should run for my life." Do-gooders everywhere hacked at the branches of evil but never struck at the root—often because the root was the source of their wealth and power.[10]

Looking back we can see in Thoreau a keen and coherent dissent from the enthusiastic values of his time. Contemporaries did not see it the same way. For one thing, like Emerson Thoreau rejected the "truth" of Christian traditions in favor of a more generic, universal spiritualism that was seen as heretical, atheistic. Reviewers of *Week on the Concord and Merrimack Rivers* pounced angrily on offhand remarks about the ugliness of churches. Disguised as a travel narrative, *Week* was littered with "ridiculous speculations, moon-struck reveries and flat nonsense" guaranteed to offend good Christian readers of any persuasion. *Walden* was better received because it was read merely as "the autobiography of a hermit . . . containing many shrewd and sensible suggestions, with a fair share of nonsense." Most reviewers identified the author as an Emersonian and a nut: "strange, fantastical, a humorist," a "way-ward genius," something like "a clown who for a moment" might distract them. More serious critics pointed out the obvious fact that, if everybody followed his lead, "squatting upon solitary duck-ponds, eschewing matri-mony, casting off all ties of family," society would soon collapse. An especially arch reviewer from Boston found in Thoreau's pages "pithy sarcasm, stern judgment, cold condemnation" but not "one sign of liberality, charitableness, kind feeling." The civilization Thoreau so disdained, this reviewer concluded, was the product of centuries of human progress, the "culminating point" of mankind's natural "desire to live in company." Finally, Thoreau's distrust of superficial reform must have irritated the swelling army of antislavery activists just then entering the final act of their showdown with the "Slave Power." While they hacked away at the branches of African slavery nobody seemed bold enough to strike at the root of the problem, the culture of exploitation that made slavery essential to American freedom.[11]

Man and Nature Reimagined

To understand man's relationship with nature Henry David Thoreau retired to a small plot of land on the banks of Walden Pond; to the same end George Perkins Marsh looked outward to the history of the world over the last two thousand years. Born into a sturdy Vermont family (his father served in Congress) the young George Marsh spent his youth studying languages so intensively that he nearly ruined his eyesight. Educated at Philips Academy and Dartmouth College, Marsh then studied law and started adult life as an attorney, banker, and businessman. Nothing in those callings stirred his passions; instead he immersed himself in Scandinavian studies and linguistics. Business failures plus the tragic deaths of his first wife and first-born son kept him off balance into his thirties. Elected to Congress in 1843, Marsh finally found his stride in government service. Appointed minister to Turkey in 1849, he spent most of the rest of his life in diplomatic postings, where he combined official responsibilities with scholarly investigations that informed major publications on *The Camel* (1856) and *The English Language* (1860). Social evolution and the environmental impact of human progress occupied the center of his intellectual restlessness, and it was in this area his most memorable contributions lay.[12]

Marsh's central environmental insight, the one that anchored his book *Man and Nature*, grew out of his close observation of the landscape in his native Vermont. On a carriage ride in the mountains as a boy, his father had explained to him the concept of a watershed—the geographical place where rainfall naturally flows to different destinations. In time Marsh expanded his understanding of a watershed to comprise the entire landscape drained by a river system and subject to the hydrological cycles of the seasons. The circulation of moisture through these systems is what sustained life, and Marsh observed that deforestation disrupted this cycle, permanently destroying the productivity of the landscape. In an address to the Rutland Agricultural Society in 1848 he detailed the "inconveniences" already apparent in Vermont from a "want of foresight in the economy of the forest." Trees anchored the thin soils found on steep hillsides while they accumulated "vegetable mould," which gently washed down to enrich fertile bottomlands. Woods encouraged the retention of rainfall, slowed runoff and minimized spring freshets, equalized humidity, reduced evaporation, moderated the impact of scorching sun and wind, and fostered the sustained renewal of farmland. But in a "single generation" of excessive cutting Vermont displayed such "tokens of improvident waste," as "bald and barren hills," dry streambeds, "ravines furrowed out by the torrents of spring," and the eroding banks of ever-widening rivers. Entire watersheds collapsed when stripped of their natural forest cover. In much of Europe,

Marsh reported, disasters had been averted because forest economy was regulated strictly by government authorities; but in America, where public opinion "in practice constitutes law," one could only appeal to "enlightened self-interest" to introduce reforms and "check the abuses."[13]

Over the next decade Marsh expanded his studies to include the hard-used Mediterranean basin and other parts of the world where deforestation caused "desertification," irretrievably destroying viable landscapes. An astonishing linguist, Marsh ransacked sources in some twenty languages and studied in person the degraded Mediterranean countryside while serving as American minister to Turkey and later Italy. The resulting book was *Man and Nature; or, Physical Geography as Modified by Human Action* (1864). In the very first sentence Marsh stated his objective: to show that nature's complex order, however elegant and durable it appeared to students in the eighteenth century, indeed was changed by human action. Human impact disrupted "the spontaneous arrangements of the organic and inorganic world," generally to its detriment. What this proved, Marsh concluded, was that nature was vulnerable and human beings enjoyed "a power of a higher order than any of the other forms of animated life." Supporting evidence littered human history. The rise and fall of ancient civilizations followed the pattern Marsh had observed first on the hillsides of Vermont: wasteful exploitation triggered environmental collapse that in turn undermined the civilization which depended on the landscape. Nature, "left undisturbed," generally established a state of equilibrium, a "permanence of form, outline, and proportion," but everywhere man planted his foot "the harmonies of nature" were turned "to discords." Against this "essentially destructive" power wielded by human beings, nature stood "wholly impotent." Knowing that his claim contradicted the central assumptions of his generation, Marsh sounded an urgent alarm. The earth was "fast becoming an unfit home for its noblest inhabitants."[14]

Marsh leveled special criticism at business corporations: they had "no souls," their managers "no consciences." Corrupt state governments and fossilized jurists did their bidding while convincing the people that "pecuniary" interest was the highest principle and government inaction the key to liberty. Here was a broadside attack on the reigning ideology of progress through unchecked private enterprise which sustained Gilded Age American business and law. With clarity and calm Marsh set the table for many an argument to come in the various campaigns of "progressive" reformers. With confidence he predicted that another "era of equal human crime and human improvidence" would so undermine "productiveness" or trigger "climatic excess, as to threaten depravation, barbarism, and perhaps even the extinction of the species." The magnitude of the crisis could not readily be proved, but Marsh was certain the world could not "afford to wait till the slow and sure progress of exact science has taught it a better economy."[15]

The scientific perspective displayed in *Man and Nature* clearly anticipated the complex systems approach at the center of modern ecological studies. (It also rather stunningly presaged the painful debates around twenty-first-century warnings of climate change.) But lest we rush to assign too "green" a sensibility, consider the exceptional place Marsh claimed for mankind in the scheme of the Creation. Humans descended, he believed, from "more exalted parentage" than all other things; consequently people were not "submissive" to the dictates of nature. In an 1860 essay for the *Christian Examiner*, Marsh spelled out a theory of human exceptionalism that owed as much to the distant past as it prophesied a greener century ahead. Mankind was locked in a "perpetual struggle with external Nature." "Untamed and unresisted," nature impeded humans' "development," "growth," "enjoyments," and "highest aspirations." Only by "rebellion against her commands and the final subjugation of her forces" could "man achieve the nobler ends of his creation." By "controlling nature" humans could "vindicate their claim" to be a "special creation living indeed *in* Nature, but not . . . wholly subject to her inflexible laws." Here was the Adamite commission restated in triumphal nineteenth-century language. Marsh celebrated advancements in science and technology—what he called the "mechanic arts"—as central to the progress of civilization. His criticism focused only on the heedless shortsighted ambition to "extract" a larger gain out of nature's resources. Modern humans had "forgotten that the earth was given" for "usufruct alone, not for consumption, still less for profligate waste." Clearly Marsh represented a step along the way from eighteenth-century "husbandry" toward the "wise use" conservation ethic of the early twentieth century; but he showed little desire to subject the human community to limitations or restrictions arising from raw nature. His ultimate hope was to "emancipate" people from the power of the "external world" and so facilitate the "conquest of the yet more formidable and not less hostile world that lies within."[16]

Appearing in the midst of the American Civil War, *Man and Nature* did not have the immediate impact later enthusiasts might imply. A critic writing in the *North American Review* praised the erudite sweep of Marsh's scholarship ("his mind drains a vast surface of knowledge") as well as his eclectic collection of sources ("side by side with Humboldt . . . we find a neighbor from Vermont with his thermometer"). This generally positive reviewer noticed the apocalyptic burden of Marsh's findings yet managed to conclude that, on the whole, the volume was "consoling" because the same intelligence that caused human mischief might be "equally potent for remedy and the restoring of equilibrium." Another reviewer acknowledged the tendency among Americans to "waste rather than thrift," since nature here was "so prodigal" and resources "so imperfectly developed." A third expressed hope that, in a republic, "personal interests" might yield "without stubbornness to the public welfare" and went on to urge the book on "every farmer's club and every village library." In 1874 a second edition, retitled *The Earth as Modified by Human Action*, received wider notice and a more positive assessment in part because by then the costs of reckless progress and unrestricted enterprise clearly could be seen in so much of the United States. An essay in the *International Review*, for example, explained that a decade before, Marsh's arguments were "only of curious interest" to Americans, whose woods still seemed "exhaustless" and whose fifteen hundred million acres of unsurveyed public lands were assumed to have the same "exuberant fertility" as the "prairies of Illinois and Iowa." But the rapid extension of railways to the West had stripped the eastern region of its tree-covering while recent settlers in the Far West reported "barren plains," "lava-overflows," "sterile and forbidding" regions "swept by tornadoes," and landscapes "wilder" than the Scottish Highlands. Already people attributed "unwelcome changes of temperature and humidity to our reckless disturbance of the equilibrium of nature." Marsh's warning, "so able and so learned," could not fail "to command a wide attention." Yet fail it did outside a rather narrow community of persons already doubting the character and trajectory of progress in the postwar United States.[17]

Modern biographer David Lowenthal credits Marsh as being the first American to "conjoin all human agency in a somber global picture." Linking "culture with nature, science with history," *Man and Nature* was, Lowenthal writes, "the most influential text of its time next to Darwin's *On the Origin of Species* [1859]." Published at the "peak of Western resource optimism," it "refuted the myth of limitless plenty and spelled out the needs for conservation." But its impact proved incremental and far from revolutionary. Marsh's work played a major role in the work of New York state commissioners who set aside the Adirondacks Park using his arguments on watersheds to lift their preservation campaign from one of mere scenery and recreational preference to one of lasting environmental importance. His focus on the beneficent role of woodlands buoyed the earliest efforts to establish a national program of forest management, and it intersected positively with parallel efforts to preserve special places—natural wonders—for aesthetic and recreational purposes. By the end of the century conservationists, worried about future stocks of timber, lifted up Marsh's call for "wise-use" management; chief United States forester Gifford Pinchot called the book "epoch-making." Teddy Roosevelt had it reprinted in 1906 for a White House conservation conference. Later environmental defenders from Lewis Mumford to Wallace Stegner and Stuart Udall cited Marsh with reverence, and in the latest edition of Lowenthal's biography (2003) historian William Cronon canonized Marsh as the parent of modern environmental sensibilities. But most of this celebration lay thirty, fifty, even a hundred years in the future. Neither Marsh's wisdom nor his passion deflected in any meaningful way the culture of exploitation ascendant in the last third of the nineteenth century. Several more pieces of the critical mosaic would have to come into focus before a picture took shape in the minds of some early twentieth-century advocates of conservation and environmental protection.[18]

Wilderness Wonders

The "wise-use" managerial regimes that characterized late nineteenth-century conservation efforts focused on trying to perpetuate resource exploitation and gratify the growing demands of human populations. Many environmental advocates, especially after 1960, lost patience with such objectives and turned instead toward a rigorous protection of wilderness for its own sake. This wilderness ethic had roots in the Gilded Age as well. Drawing on the sense of the sublime that marked the early Romantic poets and antebellum landscape painters, friends of extraordinary "natural wonders" and pristine "wild places" came together in postwar America to articulate another thread of prophecy that grew up alongside the conservationists. Chief among these voices was a Scottish immigrant mechanic, inventor, millwright, plant collector, sheep herder, self-taught geologist, and inveterate mountain wanderer named John Muir.

Henry David Thoreau wrote eloquently about the virtues of walking in nature, but John Muir did more actual walking than perhaps any other person in nineteenth-century America. Newly arrived in frontier Wisconsin, the eleven-year-old boy started hiking all around his local "wilderness," studying plants and noting with distaste the destructive impulse that urged his neighbors to cut down and plow up everything they found. Coming of age just before the Civil War, Muir longed to emulate the famous naturalist, Alexander von Humboldt, and walk through South America or Africa. Instead, he enrolled at the university in Madison, where he met a natural history professor, Ezra Carr. Carr and his wife, Jeanne, would mentor Muir for decades and link him to major players in the exciting world of academic scientists. But still unfocused about his ambition (and worried about the Civil War draft), in 1863 Muir left Madison and started walking southward. A devastating eye injury in Indianapolis left him temporarily blind; when his eyesight recovered he struck out on a thousand-mile hike to the Florida Gulf coast. On page one of a brand new journal he wrote "John Muir, Earth-planet, Universe," then proceeded to fill page after page with descriptions of what he saw and meditations about its meaning. A bout with malaria convinced him that the South was bad for his health. He gave up plans to continue on through South America; instead he took a steamer to New York and then booked passage to the golden shores of California.[19]

Muir arrived in San Francisco in early 1868. That gold rush community held no appeal for him, so he struck off across the Central Valley toward the High Sierra mountains, arriving in May at the spectacular Yosemite Valley. Declaring it paradise found, Muir fell in love with this splendid natural park surrounded by stark granite walls lofting more than three thousand feet above the valley floor. He took a job watching eighteen hundred sheep for "Smokey Jack," and spent the winter getting acquainted with what was destined to be his spiritual headquarters for the rest of his life. The sheep disgusted him ("hoofed locusts" he called them), but the mountains stirred his soul. Armed with a blanket, two loaves of bread, and a few scoops of coffee, he would climb and hike for days, exploring in close detail the stunning landscape marked by crumbling rocks, talus fields, sheer escarpments, winding drainages, and spectacular waterfalls. Popularized after 1862 by Albert Bierstadt's extraordinary paintings, Yosemite became a "must-see" stop for travelers taking advantage of the new transcontinental rail line to explore the rugged wonders of the West. Easily approached along the Merced River, Yosemite Valley attracted summer tourists who flocked to see El Capitan and Yosemite Falls, and spend a night or two in a "wilderness" hotel. Muir thought the tourists shallow and disappointing: "the blank fleshly apathy" with which they approached "the rock and water spirits of the place" he found "amazing." For most of three years Muir lived in and hiked around the valley. By 1871 he had concluded that his "main work" in life would be the study of these mountains.[20]

For John Muir, science and poetry served the same fundamental purpose: to know the Creation and mankind's place in it. He started writing travel essays for local magazines and soon was identified as a field expert on regional geography. The Smithsonian asked for reports as he climbed and studied the highest peaks in California. Having previously mastered botany and taxonomy, he now studied mountain geology in order to answer the central question: how was this canyon created? Prevailing opinion insisted that only a sudden, violent subsidence could account for the size and depth of Yosemite, but Muir became convinced that a new "ice age" theory put forth by Harvard's Louis Agassiz better explained what he saw on the face of the rocks themselves. According to Agassiz, much of the continent once had been covered with glacial ice that carved and shaped the land, after which meltwater slowly eroded the beds of creeks and rivers. In 1871 Muir spotted a living glacier near the headwaters of the Merced and concluded that ice indeed was the author of this landscape. Of course such excavations could only have occurred on a time scale infinitely longer than the four thousand years prescribed by Christian dogma, but the evidence was carved into the rock face—the "great open book of Yosemite glaciers." Late that year, in a short piece for the New York *Tribune*, Muir sketched out—in his trademark spirit-filled language—his claim for the ancient work of ice in sculpting the earth. Water worked "openly," noisily, in plain sight, but glaciers exerted their "tremendous energies in silence and darkness," "outspread, spirit-like, brooding above predestined rocks unknown to light, unborn, working on unwearied through unmeasured times, unhalting as the stars, until at length, their creations complete, their mountains brought forth, homes made for the meadows and the lakes, and fields for waiting forests, earnest, calm as when they came as crystals from the sky, they depart." There followed in 1874–75 a series of seven much longer essays detailing the process of glacial formations, soil- and mountain-building, and the specific configuration of ice sheets responsible for Yosemite.[21]

Muir the walker had turned into Muir the nature writer, spending winters in San Francisco and saving the summer months for exploration and discovery. His mentors, the Carrs, now lived in Oakland, and leading thinkers passed through pollenating John's homegrown understanding of plants and animals, rocks, and glacial ice. Louis Agassiz visited, as did Ralph Waldo Emerson and Asa Gray. The leading American advocate of Darwin's evolutionary theories, Gray came back in 1877 with English naturalist, Joseph Hooker; both men joined Muir in a climb up the fourteen-thousand-foot peak of Mount Shasta. A series of expeditions to the wilds of Alaska further stoked Muir's fascination with glaciers, reinforced his theories about the mountain-sculpting properties of ice, and sharpened anew his disdain for frontiersmen. Returning to California in 1880, Muir settled into a new role as a husband, father, and manager of his in-laws' expansive fruit farm.[22]

From all his reading, exploring, field work, and conversation with experts of all descriptions, Muir perfected an aesthetic and spiritual sense of a natural world on which human beings depended but which did not depend on them. Robert Underwood Johnson, editor of the *Century Magazine*, pressed him into service in behalf of campaigns to create an extensive national park around the existing (and grossly mismanaged) state park on the Yosemite Valley floor. For Johnson's magazine in 1890 Muir produced his finest descriptions of Yosemite, weaving together botanical, geological, and topographical details with lyrical flashes of light and drama. Time and again he courted disaster on wet slippery rocks, behind thunderous cascades, in relentless pursuit of the perfect view, the most sublime experience —usually adding the disclaimer: do not try this yourselves! Noting the extraordinary stands of giant sequoia trees—destined to live five thousand years if not destroyed by man—Muir paused his poetic portrait to advocate protection of the "fountain region above Yosemite" before big timber and "sheepmen" managed to destroy it all. A few years later, addressing the new Sierra Club (of which he was founder and president), he happily reported that four years of federal protection had restored much of the region's beauty. Armed soldiers drove out illegal shepherds and their flocks, while native plants returned as if by magic: "in the work of beauty Nature never stops." He spoke with scorn of how California's earlier proclamations of protection for Yosemite had resulted only in protecting privileged despoilers whose sheep and pigs and tourists benefited from the exclusion of rivals. Federal troops now patrolled the Sierra forests of "big trees" (*Sequoiadendron giganteum*), but most of the set-aside park land remained vulnerable to poaching and trespass, while none of the equally amazing coastal redwoods (*Sequoia sempervirens*) enjoyed protection of any kind. Vigilance alone would save the forests from greedy and interested parties.[23]

Muir spent the presidential campaign year 1896 traveling with a blue-ribbon panel of experts tasked with assessing the health of America's forests. Their official report echoed much of what George Perkins Marsh had written thirty years before and called for more vigorous protections and management for designated forest reserves. (Gifford Pinchot, a commission member, eagerly awaited creation of just such an office.) State politicians and timber barons howled in protest as scientists and bureaucrats moved toward institutional oversight of critical national resources. Not officially a part of the commission (and so not bound to the language of its report), Muir published his own summary view in the *Atlantic* in 1897, pronouncing the original forests of America the best "ever planted" by God: "rich beyond thought, immortal, immeasurable, enough and to spare for every feeding, sheltering beast and bird, insect and son of Adam; and nobody need have cared had there been no pines in Norway, no cedars and deodars in Lebanon and the Himalayas, no vine-clad selvas in the basin of the Amazon. With such variety, harmony, and triumphant exuberance, even nature, it would seem, might have rested content with the forests of North America, and planted no more." The stone axes and fires of the Indians did no more harm to these forests than "gnawing beavers and browsing moose," but the "steel axe of the white man" sealed their doom. Early settlers, Muir wrote, "claiming Heaven as their guide," regarded trees as "pernicious weeds." "Chips flew thick and fast; trees in their beauty fell crashing by millions, smashed to confusion, and the smoke of their burning has been rising to heaven [for] more than two hundred years." Across the country they marched until at last the settlers reached "the wild side of the continent," and entered "the last of the great aboriginal forests on the shores of the Pacific."

Warming to his anger, Muir cataloged a variety of shortsighted exploitations by which hunters, settlers, and lumbermen skimmed off easy fortunes, leaving piles of waste behind. Often as not the resources were stolen from the public domain. He mocked the railroad companies who touted their "scenic routes" through the great West: "Come, travel our way. Ours is the blackest. . . . No other route on this continent so fully illustrates the abomination of desolation." Under the "Timber Culture Act" (1873) less than fifty thousand acres had been planted with "stunted, woebegone, almost hopeless sprouts of trees" at the same time that millions of acres of "the grandest forest trees" were stolen, destroyed, or sold for nothing. All sorts of regulations had failed; only the powerful hand of the federal government now could save the remnant of America's forests. "Any fool can destroy trees," Muir concluded; they cannot run away or fight back. Since Christ's time on earth God had saved the California redwoods from "drought, disease, avalanches, and a thousand straining, leveling tempests and floods," but he could not "save them from fools,—only Uncle Sam can do that."[24]

John Muir perfected a style and voice that blended Henry David Thoreau's sensibilities with common words and images that ordinary readers of late-century magazines could take to heart. Nobody needed a transcendentalist's handbook to understand the dramatic exploits or flights of visual fancy with which Muir carried his readers into the High Sierra or across the ice-choked Alaskan wilderness. And packaged this way in pleasing nuggets of travel-and-description, Muir's wilderness ethic found an easy way into the consciousness of readers who might otherwise have been put off by a strident attack on America's history of progress and exploitation. Many of these readers—perhaps most of them—hoped somehow to square their rising expectations for progress and prosperity with the moral high ground claimed by commentators such as Muir. Their perspective was not revolutionary. But by the closing decades of the nineteenth century, Muir's warnings, combined with those of Marsh, Thoreau, Emerson, and many others, had managed at least to establish a platform on which conservation and preservation finally could get a hearing.

Conservation, Preservation, Resource Management

If God could not save the redwoods, as John Muir so boldly claimed, what could "Uncle Sam" do for them? America's republican governments at every level—local, state, and federal—had been complicit for a century in fostering a liberal, capitalist economy, aggressively expanding across the continent, privatizing natural resources and depleting those resources for short-term gain. At least since the third decade of the nineteenth century, most candidates for office and the voters who elected them expected the government to foster growth, facilitate access to undeveloped land, displace and pacify Native Americans, encourage innovation and capital formation, improve transportation, enforce private contracts, protect entrepreneurial freedom, and gratify the people's "pursuit of happiness" in every way possible. Under the systems of comity and equal protection made possible by the Constitution (and the new Fourteenth Amendment), private capital enjoyed unprecedented freedom to operate across jurisdictions; nonresident investors could transform the conditions of life in places far from where they lived, making mockery at times of local sovereignty or political control. Badgered by threats from aggressive entrepreneurs (mining and logging companies, cattle barons, railroad corporations), local and state governments routinely sacrificed long-term prudence for short-term gains that promised a quick burst of local profits as well as reelection votes. Bribes, pay-offs, and favoritism corrupted governments from city hall to the United States Senate. Reformers of every stripe learned to seek relief from higher authorities capable of rising above the bosses and local "fixers" whose hands held the levers of power. This, of course, is why John Muir looked to "Uncle Sam" to protect his Sequoias: charged with promoting the "general welfare" of the nation as a whole, Congress might find the courage to contradict interested parties who saw in the redwoods only millions of board feet of lumber.[25]

The turn of the twentieth century stands as a pivotal moment in the conservation movement, but preservation sentiments had been developing for a generation and more. Clear back in the age of Jackson the western painter George Catlin proposed creating a wilderness sanctuary on the Great Plains where Indians and buffalo together might be preserved "in their pristine beauty and wildness." Others mourning the cheesy commercialization of Niagara Falls worried that Americans would save none of their natural endowments. It was Yellowstone, in far-western Wyoming, that moved a party of eastern developers in 1870 to campaign for public protection before this dazzling collection of geysers, mud pots, and hot springs, smelling faintly of brimstone, fell into the hands of mere sharpsters. In 1872 President Grant signed the authorization reserving a million acres—but making no appropriation of money—as a "pleasuring ground" for the people. However admirable, this impulse rested more on commercial than spiritual or environmental foundations. Protectors of Yellowstone blocked mining and "spoliation" to preserve the site for future tourists who would enjoy tasteful amenities, just not a quick-and-dirty carnival like Niagara. Western railroads embraced the same kind of protection for scenic places along their hard-won routes through the Rocky Mountains. Back in 1864, goaded by New York *Tribune* publisher Horace Greeley, the Civil War Congress had ceded two parcels in Yosemite to California to make a state park—which trust Muir insisted had been abused shamelessly. In 1890

Congress designated fifteen hundred square miles as Yosemite National Park (the old state park persisted at the center until 1906). The same Congress created two redwood forest reserves and, in the Forest Reserve Act of 1891, authorized the president to set aside other tracts for protection as seemed appropriate. William McKinley brought these preserves to a total of about fifty million acres, but he proved unwilling to block mining, grazing, or wildlife destruction at the hands of local exploiters. There things remained until 1901, when an assassin's bullet landed Theodore Roosevelt in the Oval Office.[26]

Plagued since childhood with debilitating asthma, Teddy Roosevelt overcame his physical challenges with a combination of obsessive activity and brutal will. Fascinated first by birds and later mammals, and following the customs among naturalists of his generation, Roosevelt killed and stuffed hundreds of specimens for study and classification. In adulthood this collector's urge matured into a passion for hunting large mammals—deer, bison, cougars, moose, bears, and eventually African megafauna. Contrary to John Muir's universal sense of animal rights, Roosevelt promoted both naturalist collecting and "respectful" trophy hunting—but not the wasteful mass slaughter carried on by commercial bison hunters who claimed only the tongues and hides of these magnificent beasts. With a passion for the American West, for outdoor recreation, and for preserving both the wilderness and its game animals for future seekers of the "strenuous life," Roosevelt forged a synthesis of conservation and preservation that bewildered many but suited quite well the window for moderate criticism that was just then opening on America's culture of exploitation. Special places—such as Yellowstone or Yosemite—deserved preservation as examples of natural splendor, but protections did not preclude "wise use" in the form of timber harvest or outdoor recreation. Guided closely by Gifford Pinchot, the university-trained expert in charge of the Bureau of Forestry, Roosevelt would introduce science, planning, and management into all questions about natural resources. Perpetual exploitation—"sustainability" in modern terminology—was his goal. Happy enough to stay the hands of small-minded property owners and heartless corporations, Roosevelt did so only to guarantee freedom of enterprise, development, and economic growth for the multitude of citizens into the future.[27]

Thrust unexpectedly into the role of chief executive, Roosevelt belabored the Fifty-Seventh Congress in 1901 with an overlong and detailed message outlining his agenda. He staked out a claim that *some* regulation of business corporations was perfectly compatible with property rights, called for a new Secretary of Commerce and Industry to harmonize employers and working people, praised the Department of Agriculture for its worldwide plant explorations, then turned to resource conservation. Forest protection, he explained, was but "a means to increase and sustain the resources of our country and the industries which depend upon them." Whatever "destroys the forest" he insisted, "threatens our well-being." Citing "widespread demand by the people of the West" for the extension of forest preserves, the president asked for power to transfer public lands to the Agriculture Department and consolidate authority over them in a new Bureau of Forestry. Although he did not say so Roosevelt knew that existing authorities (the General Land Office and Interior Department) had done little to curb spoliation at the hands of state agents and private interests. Following the logic of George Perkins Marsh and John Wesley Powell, Roosevelt added water resources to his list of essential national objectives: the "reclamation" of arid lands would require reservoir projects too large to be mounted by states alone. Finally—icing on the conservationists' cake—forest preserves protected wild creatures so that big game hunters might still enjoy the thrill of bagging a trophy specimen. Sensible development, permanent wise-use husbandry, popular recreation, and the seating of genuine homesteaders on public lands topped the president's policy objectives. Privatization by corporate interests looking for short-term gain stood condemned in Roosevelt's view.[28]

With boundless temerity not seen in recent presidents, Roosevelt demanded the enlargement and redirection of the role of the federal government in American resource policy. With massive river improvements for agricultural commerce, vast forest preserves managed by powerful government experts, and large-scale reclamation of the arid West, Uncle Sam would seize the initiative and set the agenda for future development in the western half of the country. Roosevelt believed that energy in government, like energy in private life, could stave off weakness and correct for the infirmities that one found scattered about in nature. As he had rescued his own body from the limitations of childhood disease, he intended to rescue the profligate nation from its self-destructive habits before the consequences became irreversible. Before he left office Roosevelt had gotten his reorganized Forest Service with Pinchot at the helm. He had steered through Congress the 1902 Newlands Reclamation Act for western water projects and the 1906 Antiquities Act allowing him to set aside national monuments of cultural significance. He created 150 new national forests (mostly by executive order), five national parks, eighteen national monuments, and fifty-five bird or wildlife preserves. During a long trip to the West he personally surveyed the elk herds in Yellowstone, concluding (against his hunter's instincts) that cougars should not be killed but allowed to prey on the thriving ungulates. He visited the Grand Canyon and came away determined to add it to the list of sacred places. On to California, where he spent three nights camping with John Muir in the High Sierra above Yosemite Valley (where Roosevelt promised to save the Mariposa Sequoia and take back into federal hands the Yosemite Valley itself). Holed up against a snowstorm, the two of them spent one night ranting about crooked land agents, miners, and lumbermen, and dancing wildly around a dead pine that Muir set on fire to the absolute delight of his president.[29]

The various threads of prophecy laid down in the nineteenth century seemed to be converging during the Roosevelt presidency. By 1909 the institutional and ideological footings of the twentieth-century American conservation movement had been poured. Parks, forests, and wildlife preserves found permanent homes in the American popular mind, as long as they did not inconvenience *too much* the ordinary business of getting and spending, building up, and tearing down. Chicanery continued to plague matters of resource allocation, but the worst kinds of bribery, corruption, and theft at least had been called out and condemned. Thus began a long and complicated dance among activists and interest groups all seeking to maximize the "public good" from their perspectives. To see how complicated we need look no further than the battle over Hetch Hetchy Valley, which began in Roosevelt's administration and ended with the inundation of one of John Muir's favorite places on earth.

Of Cathedrals and Water Tanks

The Hetch Hetchy Valley carries the Tuolumne River out of the High Sierra and into the Central Valley of California. Like the more famous and iconic Yosemite Valley a few miles to the south, Hetch Hetchy boasted a lush flat plain bounded by vertical granite walls nearly two thousand feet high. John Muir described it in 1873 as being so like Yosemite Valley that few visitors could tell them apart. The river enters through a long narrow canyon stretching east and south toward the summit; at the outlet granite walls come nearly together forming a narrow defile and creating, in flood times, a vast natural lake on the valley floor. Dam builders marveled at the fact that glaciers had done most of the work for them: plug the outlet with a high dam and the resulting reservoir could produce up to four hundred million gallons of water per day not to mention electric power. If Hetch Hetchy struck John Muir as a sacred place, the same formations impressed hydraulic engineers as having been designed by God specifically for impounding water.[30]

Roughly 160 miles west of Hetch Hetchy, the city of San Francisco had grown like Topsy since the mid-century California gold rush. As in so many Gilded Age cities, political corruption saddled San Francisco with bad government and irresponsible utility franchises. In the 1890s reform mayor James Phelan drove a band of notorious thieves from city hall and secured a new municipal charter (1900). He then turned his attention to public utilities—especially the much-reviled Spring Valley Water Company. Told by technical consultants that projects at Lake Eleanor and Hetch Hetchy would secure water and electric power for the city for a century to come, Phelan set wheels in motion that delivered in Washington a request to dam up the valley in Yosemite Park. Chief US Forester Gifford Pinchot supported the plan, insisting that a reservoir at Hetch Hetchy met his standard test: the greatest good for the greatest number. President Roosevelt wavered, worried about alienating too many interested local parties. Feeling bound to protect the integrity of Yosemite Park, Interior Secretary Ethan Hitchcock denied the permits requested. Then in April 1906, a devastating earthquake and fire destroyed San Francisco, and a cry went up—probably greatly exaggerated—that only Hetch Hetchy could preserve the city from such fiery destruction in future.[31]

Fifty years ago historian Roderick Nash told the Hetch Hetchy story as a simple clash of warring perspectives. One privileged human need and economic development; the other clung to the sublime integrity of nature-as-found. Exploitation versus preservation; civilization against wilderness. The heated rhetoric stoking the controversy begged for such a Manichean interpretation. Muir repeatedly called the friends of the project "thieves and robbers" and labeled the enterprise "dark damn dam damnation." In his most often quoted flourish, Muir proclaimed about Hetch Hetchy that one might "as well dam for water-tanks the people's cathedrals and churches, for no holier temple has ever been consecrated by the heart of man." In response, San Francisco city engineer Marsden Manson belittled Muir and the "so-called nature loving societies" as witless dupes being used "as cats-paws" by corrupt "grasping interests." In 2005 historian Robert Righter published a more satisfying narrative in which good and evil get lost in a swirl of interested parties in Washington, in Congress, in San Francisco and Yosemite, all bent on flooding Hetch Hetchy—or saving it for widespread tourist development.[32]

In March 1907 James R. Garfield replaced Hitchcock at Interior and Gifford Pinchot invited Phelan and his friends to take another run at Hetch Hetchy. Garfield approved permits to explore developments at Lake Elea-nor and Hetch Hetchy. John Muir appealed directly to Roosevelt but received a lukewarm reply: "If, as you say, nine-tenths of the citizens took ground against the Hetch Hetchy project," Roosevelt likely would oppose it; but so far everyone seemed "for it," and the president would not stifle local development in behalf of a valley "hardly anyone wanted . . . under national control." Muir and his friends at the Sierra Club mobilized to raise up a public outcry and change the president's mind. Yosemite National Park and (by inference, they suggested, all national parks, reserves, and monuments) stood defenseless before predatory interests that would profit from their "spoliation." In November Muir let fly a broadside in the *Out-look* magazine condemning any and all "gain-seekers trying to despoil" nature's "sublime wonderlands." Unable to deny that Hetch Hetchy seemed like a perfect place to impound water, Muir instead impugned the motives of San Franciscans, lumping them in with all kinds of "mischief-makers and robbers" determined to plunder the nation's resources for selfish gain. A few weeks later, in the *Sierra Club Bulletin*, he further assaulted the "tem-ple destroyers, devotees of ravaging commercialism" who showed "perfect contempt" for Nature and worshiped instead "the Almighty Dollar." Spe-cial scorn was heaped on schemers who "disguised" themselves in "smug-smiling philanthropy . . . shamelessly crying, 'Conservation, conservation, panutilization,' that man and beast may be fed and the dear Nation made great." As Jesus drove the money changers from the temple, Muir exposed such hypocrites and joined the "universal battle between right and wrong."[33]

For the next few years Muir, with the help of Robert Underwood John-son and other well-known preservationists, hammered away at the friends of the Hetch Hetchy dam, alluding darkly to their hidden agenda, their suppression of evidence, their abuse of powerful connections in Washing-ton (such as Pinchot, who they caught colluding with Marsden Manson a full year before anyone in Washington held public hearings). Editorials warned that this invasion of Yosemite set dangerous precedents: "If Hetch Hetchy Valley is destroyed we may look after a while to see power houses built in the Grand Canyon of the Yellowstone and the falls used to run factories in the National Park." Sanitary considerations, wrote Johnson, would force San Francisco to lock people out of the Tuolumne watershed, closing more than half of Yosemite National Park. Pro-dam rhetoric proved no less hyperbolic. City engineer Manson repeatedly slandered the "nature lovers" as "nature fakers." Such "short-haired women and long-haired men" reminded him of feminized dreamers such as Henry David Thoreau. James Phelan dismissed them as "sentimentalists," strangers who knew nothing of the place and depended on "hearsay," heartless idealists who would sacrifice a million people forced to "live in sweltering cities" to preserve the beauties of a meadow. The *San Francisco Call* ran a cartoon depicting Muir as a plump housewife in a flowered hat sweeping back the flood from Hetch Hetchy as if it were progress itself. Muir fired back that Phelan and Manson were agents of Satan, "cunning drivers" working "in darkness like moles," "monopolizing capitalists" seeking to make "private gain" out of "universal public loss."[34]

For reasons not entirely clear Phelan and Manson stuck tenaciously with the Hetch Hetchy dam even after engineering surveys showed that adequate water could be had at other sites. Offered a compromise deal—to develop Lake Eleanor first and postpone Hetch Hetchy until the city absolutely required it (perhaps fifty years hence)—engineer Manson replied that he would work at Lake Eleanor *only* if permitted simultaneously to dam Hetch Hetchy for electric power. Behind the scenes, rival water companies jockeyed for position. Meanwhile Muir and friends joined ranks with the promoters of roads, hotels, and tourism who sought to preserve the valley not as wilderness but for recreational development. Shifting interests ironically left Muir in league with the corrupt old San Francisco water monopoly as well as the private utility giant Pacific Gas and Electric, giving credence to Manson's charges that the nature lovers were being used by dishonest brokers. For about six years the battle over Hetch Hetchy plagued bureaucrats in Washington. Congressmen, friends of industrial development, advocates of water and power projects, city politicians, nature writers, journalists, outdoor recreation enthusiasts, and tourism promoters all jockeyed for preferment. Teddy Roosevelt left office to hunt big game in Africa. Gifford Pinchot fell out of favor with President William Howard Taft. Richard

Ballinger came and went at the Interior Department. Finally, in 1913, Congress passed the Raker Act authorizing San Francisco to dam up Hetch Hetchy—but on their own dime. President Woodrow Wilson signed it, observing that the project "seemed to serve the pressing public needs of the region." The objections of its opponents he thought "were not well founded."[35]

It took another twenty years to complete the Hetch Hetchy Project. Designed by John Freeman on a grand scale that far exceeded the needs (and resources) of San Francisco, the combination water and power system first required a dam at Lake Eleanor to generate electricity for use at the Hetch Hetchy site. Roads into the canyon, a fifty-eight-mile railroad, and a small city housing five hundred workers had to be built before the dam itself could be started. Chief engineer Michael O'Shaunessy removed over one hundred feet of silt and rubble from the riverbed just to reach the bedrock on which to plant his concrete colossus. World War I drove up the cost of labor and materials, causing frustration and delays. Political conflicts between private and public utility promoters complicated many details. In 1923 the dam itself was finished, rising 430 feet above the riverbanks. O'Shaunessy described the placid lake that resulted as a "man-made mirror," a "magnet to all real nature lovers," and a refutation of Muir's hysterical campaign. The electric powerhouse followed that summer, but the waterworks so desperately called for in 1907 took another decade to complete. Meanwhile the rehabilitated Spring Valley Water Company managed to provide San Francisco with plentiful water, allowing East Bay cities such as Oakland to shy away from sharing the expense of the Hetch Hetchy system. Terms of the Raker Act required San Francisco to furnish roads and amenities for recreation at the new reservoir long before any water reached the city. Not until 1934—fully twenty years after authorization—was the project finished. Clearly a pivot in the narrative arc of conservation and preservation in the late Progressive era, the battle for Hetch Hetchy ended in a kind of a draw. The valley itself was lost, of course, but recreation as a virtue gained traction, "nature" gained a credibility it never had seen in the nineteenth century, and developmental boosters may have learned something of the dangers of overselling the promise of big interventions intended to control the environment.[36]

Much about the conservation legacy started by men such as Roosevelt and Muir would be bitterly contested throughout the twentieth century, especially the reservation of public lands and the assertion of a national "common interest" at the expense of local private development. Three centuries in the making, the culture of exploitation calmly asserted that private use of public resources lay at the heart of the American way of life. Consequently, "seizure" of public lands by the people's government contradicted private rights and local expectations; such government "overreach" was challenged time and again—and is being challenged still. But countervailing voices on behalf of "nature," born of such fragments of prophecy as we have seen in this quick review, persisted in the public discourse, giving rise to expanding awareness, scientific investigations, and (from time to time) efforts to restrain the destructive impulses at the heart of industrial capitalism. Gradually regulations chipped away at workplace hazards, air and water pollution, reckless waste disposal, and wasteful resource depletion, but such battles did not become easier. In a free self-governing republic rational discourse might have enabled an intelligent process of compromise and accommodation in addressing such concerns, but time and again rhetorical polarization, such as that seen in the Hetch Hetchy contest, dissolved the middle ground of reason, corrupting claims for "private rights" or the "general welfare" into disingenuous masks behind which bad actors sought to hijack the policy agenda. Muir's Sierra Club flourished as a champion of preservation and the "wilderness" wing of environmental activism. However, significant conservation accomplishments generally owed more to practical voices who brought together advocates of wise-use management, hunting, fishing, and outdoor recreation, "roughing it" woodcraft, and genteel tourism (by rail car, horseback, bicycle, and automobile). Nevertheless, such mixed-use regimens in parks and preserves repeatedly pitted developers, conservationists, preservationists, environmentalists, and advocates of the sublime against each other in a continuing struggle with the enduring culture of exploitation.

Looking back over the centuries one can see the roots of the modern American culture of exploitation, but one also can see that this exploitative construct only gradually eroded our social or economic values until, sometime in the nineteenth century, it had been naturalized fully in our minds. Buried in our authentic past we find concepts such as "just price," "living wage," "husbandry," "stewardship," and rights to a share of the wealth of the community—that is, the "commonwealth." This is not to say the "good old days" were all that good. Inequality defined the social and economic systems before the rise of liberal capitalism; but individual freedom and the pursuit of private happiness prevailed, not by servicing the commonwealth ideal but by turning individuals away from the common good. Privatized religion, political freedom, Ricardian economics, scientific progress, technological innovations, divergent material interests, and a paranoid fear of political corruption gradually convinced individuals that prosperity and salvation would be found, not in community or public policy, but in competitive striving in a marketplace where everyone was suspect and everything was up for the taking. Insisting that such markets derived from natural laws—as fixed as gravity itself—the advocates of modern exploitation disqualified critical voices as agents of superstition, sentiment, envy, or sloth. A brief look at some of these voices of prophecy, however, reminds us that the liberal triumph never was complete, its claims not true outside the system of axioms that defined them. Having mapped the triumph of the culture of exploitation we can see better the turning points where incremental choices, brick by brick, produced the edifice of modernization, advanced its claims of inevitability, and erased the evidence of people ever having seen another way.[37]

Epilogue

On January 30, 2018, in addressing the State of the Union after the first year of his presidency, Donald J. Trump announced that "we have ended the war on beautiful clean coal." Throughout the 2016 campaign Trump had promised to bring back "clean coal," endlessly citing mine owners' claims that coal is cheap, safe, and clean, and that coal mining is an honorable calling on which huge numbers of Americans depend. Latest figures show that barely 50,000 people make their living mining coal (140,000 work at Kohl's department stores). Mine safety records have slipped since Trump proudly rolled back regulations; wages for West Virginia miners start at about the average for a full-time gig at Wal-Mart. Robert Murray and a handful of coal magnates have harvested most of the fruits of Trump's efforts, but the rhetoric pours forth unabated. Clean coal will help make America great again, reckless mining and mountain-top removal will shower prosperity throughout Appalachia, and fossil fuels will propel the American economy back into the driver's seat of the global capitalist juggernaut.[1]

Unfortunately, "clean coal," like harmless tobacco, is a fantasy, a dream lake on which the addicted sail their hopes in service of an industry about to lose its place of honor in the story of American progress and modernization. In real market terms, scrubbing coal smoke to reasonable levels of carbon dioxide emissions costs more than the market will bear. Taking the long view, "progress" driven by the burning of fossil fuels cannot possibly deliver a rising standard of living to the world's people in the twenty-first century. Simple math suggests that expanding consumption for seven or eight billion persons to the level of an average American would deplete the resources of three—possibly five—planets like Earth. Also, increased atmospheric concentrations of carbon dioxide from burning fossil fuels threaten to raise global temperatures with catastrophic impact on agriculture, weather patterns, coastal communities (where the vast majority of people live), and the economy. If there were no other reason to question the trajectory of "progress" or the modern culture of exploitation, the challenge of climate change alone justifies urgent reconsideration of our assumptions and behaviors.[2] Let it stand proxy for why we need to question what we "know" about where we have been.

Gathering Clouds

For over thirty years, climate scientists have been churning out research establishing a very broad consensus that the Earth is getting warmer. Starting in the 1980s they began releasing warnings that a rise in surface temperature of two degrees Celsius or more might bring us to a "tipping point" after which cascading feedback would unleash irreversible consequences. Rising ocean temperatures might hyperenergize tropical storms and disrupt weather patterns, producing wild swings of drought and flood, extraordinary heat waves, and record-breaking cold. Horticultural zones would creep toward the poles, and with them communities of flora and fauna. Glaciers and polar ice would melt, raising sea levels worldwide. What makes this scarier is the possibility that once begun, these changes might reinforce themselves in ways that would prevent remediation. In 2009 the chair of the United Nation's Intergovernmental Panel on Climate Change (IPCC) told the G8 leaders that in order to limit global warming to the recommended two-degree target the world would have to "peak global emissions no later than 2015." That did not happen, and subsequent calculations now suggest that even a 1.5 degree increase (likely by 2040) will produce catastrophic coastal flooding, drought, and poverty. All of a sudden the scientists are telling us that changes which once took millennia could happen in a single lifetime. Not surprisingly, social scientists, politicians, and the general public found these warnings so startling that at first they could not credit them as real.[3]

Back in 1972 the United Nations sponsored the first world conference on the human environment in Stockholm, Sweden, just as the United States was embracing environmental protection as a fit subject for federal legislation. Tepid resolutions followed, but little else. In 1987 a UN commission, chaired by Norway's Gro Harlem Bruntland, called for a sustainable alternative to old-fashioned economic growth—one that met "the needs of the present without compromising the ability of future generations to meet their own needs." The next year the UN created the IPCC to create an objective and transparent record of what the world's best scientists believed was happening and what mitigation made sense as the evidence mounted. Seeing that the impact of climate change would fall unevenly on different nations, the UN structured the IPCC to be a forum for rational analysis, outside of the competitive state systems that characterized most international relations. Guided by science, the IPCC hoped to rise above local and short-term questions about who suffers most and who ought to pay.[4]

Out of the 1987 Bruntland Report grew the movement for a huge "Earth Summit" in June of 1992 to be held in Rio de Janeiro. The organizers promised to help governments "rethink economic development and find ways to halt the destruction of irreplaceable natural resources and pollution of the planet." One hundred seventy-two nations (108 heads of state, including George H. W. Bush) gathered and adopted unprecedented statements in support of environmental stewardship as well as "binding" conventions to prevent climate change and the loss of biological diversity. Among the important claims embraced by the signatories were these:

- that human beings are "entitled to a healthy and productive life in harmony with nature,"
- that "scientific uncertainty" ought not be used to delay efforts to prevent degradation,
- that sovereign nations may exploit their own resources but not "cause damage" to the environment of others,
- that "eradicating poverty and reducing disparities in worldwide standards of living are 'indispensable' to sustainability,"
- that "the full participation of women is essential" for the same,
- that developed countries should "acknowledge" responsibility for the "pressure" they place on global resources as well as the financial and technological resources "they command."

At face value the agreements coming out of Rio seemed impressive and quite hopeful. The United Nations Framework Convention on Climate Change (UNFCCC) committed everyone (including the US) to "attempt" to reduce greenhouse gas emissions. It specifically challenged rich nations to lead the way because poorer countries had to focus on alleviating poverty. However, as the *Wall Street Journal* noted in reporting ratification by the Senate (without dissent), the treaty, at US insistence, did not compel specific reductions.[5]

Within a year the UNFCCC determined that only mandatory targets would motivate the world's leading economies to curtail greenhouse gasses. Negotiations began in 1995 and resulted in a complex and creative set of goals and mechanisms—the Kyoto Protocol—by which rich countries could moderate the "sting" of binding targets. Adopted in December 1997, the agreement was scheduled for implementation in 2005. President Bill Clinton signed the Kyoto Protocol in 1998, but he did not submit it to the Senate for ratification because the Byrd-Hagel Resolution already had disapproved (95 to 0) any international agreement that did not impose restrictions on developing countries. The next president, George W. Bush, refused to reconsider. Bush did not openly dispute the science of climate change, but he prioritized the demands of the American people for short-term benefits and economic growth. Without help by the United States, global emissions would not come down enough; further, if the Americans thought that Kyoto gave a free pass to China and India, the rest of the world saw America's noncompliance as an even bigger deal-breaker. Eventually Canada, Russia, and Japan backed away as well. A drift away from cooperative internationalism could be seen among politicians and voters throughout the developed world, made worse in 2008 by the worldwide financial meltdown, which spiked unemployment, threatened banking systems, and wrecked many real estate markets.[6]

A funny thing happened on the way to the next major summit on global warming: Americans lost their confidence in the scientific evidence of climate change. Starting with the Reagan administration in the 1980s, various interests sharpened their critique by stressing the costs of regulation and the likely decline in standards of living if anything threatened existing systems. Lifting up property rights, individual freedom, and fear of government intrusion—central elements in the American experience of modernization—interested parties (such as fossil fuel producers) teamed up with conservative advocates of economic liberty to portray environmentalists as fanatics determined, not to save the natural environment, but to disable the systems of modern prosperity. Climate science in particular proved ripe for such assaults because it depends fundamentally on model-built projections of what *might* happen decades into the future. Such projections are based on minute changes in the present, the importance of which seem counterintuitive to lay interpreters.

A powerful pushback appeared in 2001 when Cambridge University Press (publisher of first-rate environmental books) came out with *The Skeptical Environmentalist* by Bjorn Lomborg. In 540 pages of dense statistical analysis, Lomborg offered a contrarian reading of an enormous body of evidence and came to the conclusion that things were getting better, not worse. Juxtaposing his optimistic take on the numbers with the most reckless claims of environmental activists, Lomborg "proved" that the dangers were mythical and that technological prowess doubtless could meet climate challenges. With obvious relief such mainstream prints as the *Economist*, the *Wall Street Journal*, and the *New York Times* labeled Lomborg's book a "triumph," written not by "a steely-eyed economist at a conservative Washington think tank but a vegetarian, backpack-toting academic who was a member of Greenpeace for four years." Profoundly encouraged, climate skeptics redoubled their efforts. In 2006 former vice president Al Gore seized the public stage with a documentary film, *An Inconvenient Truth*, which won two Oscars and got millions of people talking for the first time about the dangers of climate change. Opponents quickly joined the debate, including Lomborg with a countervideo called *Cool It: Are We Saving the World or Just Burning Money?* (2010). By highlighting the speculative nature of the methodologies, the fact that probabilities always show a margin of error, and the historical success of modern ingenuity at meeting challenges for over two centuries, technological optimists kept the focus on the "possible" rather than the "probable" import of accumulating science. Friends of the "business-as-usual" culture of exploitation relaxed; less cautious climate deniers dismissed global warming as hysteria whipped up by scientists eager for fame and liberal politicians hungry for power.[7]

In 2008 the election of Barack Obama, a progressive intellectual and America's first African American president, created an illusion of momentum for environmental advocates and students of global warming. But even center-left Democrats like Obama bowed to Wall Street banks, corporate interests, energy companies, and liberal economists. Inheriting the worst financial crisis since the Great Depression of the 1930s, Obama understandably prioritized short-term recovery over deep structural change or expensive regulations aimed at solving problems that might not be visible for half a century. Resource development fared well in the Obama years (especially hydraulic fracking), but so too did wind and solar energy, hybrid cars, and tough auto-emission standards. Only the most problematic old-school energy sources—coal, offshore oil, and nuclear power—lost ground after 2008. The National Academy of Sciences set about preparing an exhaustive report on *America's Climate Choices* (2011) that recommended positive action by setting a "nationally uniform price on carbon dioxide emissions"—loosely referred to as "cap-and-trade."[8] But partisan opponents of the Democratic president worked to stir up class and racial hostilities against a mixed-race American with one Kenyan parent and a Harvard law degree. In October 2010 Senator Mitch McConnell (minority leader soon to become majority leader) vowed to make Obama a one-term president. Failing that, McConnell helped make his second term the least productive of legislation since the election of James Buchanan.

In 2012 the debate about climate change seemed to run off the rails into fantasy. Among nine Republican candidates for president, not one would acknowledge global warming as an issue. Blaming the Obama administration for phantom offenses, one after another the candidates pushed each other toward the libertarian free-market end of the political spectrum, promising to reinvigorate the systems of the past that (supposedly) were being suppressed by Obama's creeping socialism. Newt Gingrich even promised to colonize the moon for mining.[9] While the presidential canvass heated up, Senator James Inhofe (R-OK) published *The Greatest Hoax: How the Global Warming Conspiracy Threatens Your Future*. Chair of the Senate committee responsible for environmental protection, Inhofe denounced the whole issue of climate change as an elaborate conspiracy against American prosperity and "common sense values." Dismissing Al Gore as a sore loser (over the 2000 presidential election), his movie as a cynical money-making scam, and the UN's IPCC as a tool of America's jealous foreign enemies, Senator Inhofe opened his book by simply asserting his major premise: "Why . . . when man-made global warming is totally debunked . . . is this book necessary?" His answer: environmental "extremists" were committed (perversely) to imposing a cap-and-trade system of carbon limitations—"the largest tax increase in American history." Fame-seeking, liberal, one-world, domineering, pop-culture elites (he named Gore, George Soros, Michael Moore, Leonardo DiCaprio, and Barbara Streisand) would falsify anything to preserve the legislative "crown jewel" with which they hoped to end prosperity and progress for most of the American people. Why would they wish to do this? Because "if you control carbon, you control life," and total control is a "goal irresistible to the power-hungry left."

There followed two hundred pages of stories, testimonials, snide dismissals, and comic interludes (including an igloo on Capitol Hill built by his grandchildren one February, proving the planet was cold as ever). Like any full-throated conspiracy exposé, Inhofe's message was so distorted as to be effectively irrefutable.[10]

All this barrage of negative assertions yielded the desired results. Polls began showing a decline in the number of Americans who believed in climate change. One indicated that 13 percent fewer people thought that *scientists* believed global warming was occurring while another 7 percent said that scientists *knew* it was not (but lied anyway). A recent Pew report determined that ideological conviction more than any other variable determined people's attitudes toward climate science. After dicing their sample for many different characteristics—education level, gender, class, race, general scientific knowledge, and level of personal interest in the problem of climate change—researchers found that conservative Republicans (self-identified) overwhelmingly disbelieved climate scientists. Seventy percent of "liberal Democrats" trusted the climate scientists compared with only 15 percent of "conservative Republicans." Most Americans (more than 80 percent) favored more wind and solar energy, but most Republicans (about 70 percent) also want to see expansion of fossil fuels. To a degree not found on any other scientific topic, control of the narrative was passing to people who wished to portray climate change as a mythical threat cooked up by liberal, international, wing nut, tree-hugging extremists conspiring to destroy American freedom and prosperity.[11]

In such a moment of gridlocked perspectives in the United States, world leaders gathered, this time in Paris, to negotiate another round of agreements aimed at slowing global warming and reducing greenhouse-gas emissions. In December 2015 delegates pledged to keep global temperatures in the twenty-first century from rising more than two degrees Celsius above preindustrial levels. Unlike Kyoto, the Paris Agreement imposed no targets and relied on "nationally determined contributions" to accomplish its ambitious goals. No enforcement mechanism existed beyond the public reporting of countries failing to meet their self-imposed targets. Nevertheless, parties around the world optimistically embraced the agreement: 195 countries signed and 174 have formally ratified. In September 2016 the United States and China both formally joined the agreement, marking a commitment to "lead by example" by the producers of 40 percent of the world's greenhouse gasses. Speaking in China, President Obama said he hoped this step would "give the rest of the world confidence—whether developed or developing countries—that a low-carbon future is where the world is heading."[12]

America's role in promoting that low-carbon future came to a screeching halt two months later. The 2016 presidential election unfolded in ways so bizarre that pundits and historians will puzzle about it for decades to come. From a field of seventeen candidates, only three made it past the Ides of March: Ohio governor John Kasich, Texas senator Ted Cruz, and New York real estate developer Donald J. Trump. At first dismissed as a comic spoiler, Trump shocked the Republican establishment by marching through one primary after another. Not even coordinated "Stop Trump" efforts managed to derail his implausible progress; by May he emerged as the presumptive nominee. After entertaining a wild grass-roots challenge from Vermont senator (and self-proclaimed socialist) Bernie Sanders, Democrats settled on Hillary Clinton and more or less basked in the presumption she easily would become the first female American president. Trump's outrageous style, his penchant for verbal missteps, and an extraordinary piece of video tape that showed him bragging about vulgar sexist behavior while making his TV show did nothing to prepare observers for an election-day upset.[13]

Trump's campaign was like nothing Americans had seen in recent politics. Under the banner theme "Make America Great Again," he denounced nearly every aspect of the world commercial and diplomatic order that had taken shape in the previous decades. He announced his intention to run with the startling claim that the United States "used to have victories," but not any more. China beats us. Japan beats us. Islamic terrorists were "eating large portions of the Middle East," growing rich on oil we "should have taken." Mexico laughs at our border patrols, sending over drugs, criminals, and rapists by the thousands. Our military has eroded, and our nuclear arsenal "doesn't work." Obama's nuclear deal with Iran threatened to wipe out the state of Israel. The American economy was dead in the water. Gross domestic product stood "below zero." (How is this possible?) Real unemployment he said approached 20 percent. Americans could not get jobs because China had our jobs, Mexico had our jobs. That "big lie" called Obamacare—the Affordable Care Act—produced such outrageously high deductibles "you'd have to be hit by a tractor" to use it. Good Americans suffered because our leaders were "stupid," weak, corrupt, puppets of lobbyists in Washington, and dupes on the world stage. On and on he rambled, painting a dystopian picture of a nation on the eve of destruction that required one thing to bring it around: "our country needs a truly great leader. . . . We need a leader that wrote 'The Art of the Deal.'"[14]

Seasoned observers must have stood gape-mouthed. Not since Huey Long in the 1930s had anyone heard such wild demagoguery. Reporters and columnists pointed out that nearly everything Trump said was untrue, which opened one of the biggest fronts of his war on reality: relentless attacks on "fake news" in the media. Reckless and unrestrained by facts and figures, Trump rang the changes on this shotgun populist appeal for the next sixteen months, promising imminent destruction to America's enemies, repatriation of American jobs, stratospheric economic growth, a crackdown on deficits, terrorists, job-stealing immigrants, welfare cheats, and fancy academics with their regulatory agencies. Savagely he slandered his opponents—especially "crooked Hillary"—letting it be known (or inferred) that once elected he would "lock her up." Over time Trump's message grew more racist, sexist, and xenophobic. He promised to drain the swamp in Washington, where "losers" were "selling this country down the drain." He would build a wall to stop Mexican immigration, and make Mexico pay for it. He would restore the old manufacturing economy, and create energy independence by restoring "clean coal" to its rightful place on the throne of industrial power. A man of no known religious traditions, he promised to put Christians back in charge of American life (for which purpose he chose as his running mate Indiana governor Mike Pence).[15]

American liberals chuckled through most of the campaign. Conservative pundits such as *New York Times* columnist David Brooks and Bill Kristol of the *Weekly Standard* cringed at the flagrant dishonesty, narcissism, ignorance of political and constitutional norms, race-baiting, class-baiting, and grandiosity that grew worse as election day neared. But Americans who felt forgotten, disrespected, and endangered by global capitalists and the multicultural fixations of identity politics turned out in droves to put this astonishing character over the top and into the Oval Office. Cabinet appointments soon revealed where the "real" Donald Trump was heading: for Education Secretary Betsy DeVos, a fierce critic of public schools; for Health and Human Services Tom Price, an equally fierce critic of Obamacare with a history of trading in pharmaceutical shares; for Energy Secretary Rick Perry, a major friend of Texas oil and gas, who as a candidate had promised to eliminate the Energy Department; for Interior Ryan Zinke, a "conservative conservationist" who immediately reintroduced lead shot for hunters (which had been banned for the sake of scavenger birds); for State Department Rex Tillerson, former CEO of Exxon with friendly ties to Russian president Vladimir Putin. Great wealth, minimal government service, and hostility to the mission of their designated agency characterized most of Trump's nominees. His EPA Director, Scott Pruitt, spent several years as Oklahoma's attorney general suing to block all environmental regulations coming out of Washington. Flatly denying the existence of a scientific consensus, Pruitt insisted global warming was at best a theory and suggested it might be a blessing because humans "flourished" during warming trends. To head his Council on Environmental Quality, Trump nominated Kathleen Hartnett-White, an outspoken critic of climate science who called carbon dioxide "the gas of life on this planet," dismissing Obama-era efforts to reduce emissions as "deluded and illegitimate."[16]

Almost immediately after his inauguration Trump pulled the US out of a multilateral trade deal, the Trans-Pacific Partnership, insisting that signatories played Americans for fools. Soon a blizzard of executive orders began rolling back regulations, cancelling subsidies, and lifting restrictions all in service of a surprisingly belligerent reassertion of American ambitions with deep roots in the culture of exploitation. Green lights met oil and gas developers in the lower forty-eight, Alaska, and offshore. Public lands protected as national monuments were reopened to local control and development. In July 2017 Trump formally withdrew from the Paris Agreement on climate change. Other signatories promised to press on regardless, but leadership on that front shifted toward Europeans such as French president Emmanuel Macron. In September, at the United Nations General Assembly, Trump renounced the implicit internationalism of previous administrations and promised always to put American interests first—inviting other leaders to do the same for their own citizens. In January 2018 he told the World Economic Forum at Davos, Switzerland, that "unelected bureaucrats" no longer could crush American business (by enforcing regulations passed by Congress?). Having sounded like a closed-door protectionist, now Trump insisted that "America first" did not mean "America alone," and invited other nations to open their economies to unfettered exploitation. In his mind free markets only exist when private interests enjoyed unrestricted access to resources, money, and consumers without interference from "predatory behaviors" including "industrial subsidies" and "pervasive state-led economic planning." Fearing the fast-rising leadership role played by the Chinese economic powerhouse, Trump sought to delegitimize their intentional nationalistic strategies and restore *private* business competition as the only true path to freedom and prosperity.[17] As the 2018 midterm elections loomed, Trump publicly endorsed "nationalism" as a far better point of view than any multilateral concern for health of the planet and its people. It would be hard to imagine a more thorough endorsement of twentieth-century "business as usual," or a more impassioned rejection of the ethos of cooperation and economic reorientation for which environmentalists so desperately hoped.

The Road Ahead

Where does this leave us now? When I began this book a dozen years ago I intended to stop it at 1900 because great environmental histories of the twentieth century are numerous and compelling. Environmental consciousness had gained significant traction both in academic circles and in the public discourse, especially after 1970. I saw a more pressing need to connect the precolonial world of early modern England to the start of the "American Century" than to review all the excellent studies of public lands and water rights, industrial pollution, workplace hazards, public health, species loss, and habitat destruction that recently have filled library shelves. I thought the "greening" of America was well advanced and that the cultural pillars of nineteenth-century capitalism were destined to bow before alternative points of view. The "progress" of "enlightenment," which had been eclipsed in the nineteenth century by self-serving blinders made of destiny and hubris, seemed to be on track again in service to such issues as resource depletion, population control, human rights, and climate change. I wanted to lend historical aid and comfort to what sometimes looked like new and crazy ideas by showing their deep roots in past culture and the choices by which they had been left behind.

Recent setbacks to the contrary notwithstanding, an awakening may still be in the offing. Ham-fisted modernization of the 1960s variety seems harder to sell worldwide. Underdeveloped countries are finding the courage to ask tough questions about the demands of outside capitalists and the cultural price of the "great transformation" they offer. Global actors—mostly nongovernmental organizations concerned with clean water, clean air, poverty, food supply, public health, agricultural viability, and habitat destruction—carry out important work despite the incredible barriers thrown up by civil wars and refugees, droughts and famines, terrorist infiltrations, shortsighted resource developers, and the cynical interference of competing nation states still seeking hegemony in the coming world order. And, however flawed it may be, the Paris Agreement continues to enjoy the support of most leading economies, including China, India, Brazil, and the European Union. One recent study of NGOs and sustainable initiatives traces this hopeful trajectory even while acknowledging the limits of nongovernmental action in a world of competing nation states.[18]

In the past generation environmental analysts and historians have produced a corpus of reasoned exposition and explanation that ought to make it possible—if we have the will—to arrive at sensible conclusions about the state of our world and the steps most likely to perpetuate it into another century. Alfred Crosby, *Ecological Imperialism* (1986); David Landes, *Wealth and Poverty of Nations* (1998); Kenneth Pomeranz, *The Great Divergence* (2000); Jared Diamond, *Collapse: How Societies Choose to Fail or Succeed* (2004); Clive Ponting, *A New Green History of the World* (2007); Ian Morris, *Why the West Rules—For Now* (2010); and countless others have given us credible portraits of the context and consequences of progress over time. In 2004 the publisher Chelsea Green issued a thirty-year update to the classic (and much maligned) MIT/Club of Rome study, *Limits to Growth*, in which the authors reiterate their warning about resource "overshoot." Both Oxford and Routledge have published weighty handbooks on climate science and law. Cambridge lists a dozen new books on climate change since 2015. Internet websites by the hundreds pop up for any search related to climate, environment, or sustainability.[19]

Economists, often mere acolytes of the culture of exploitation, are beginning to admit the limitations of the liberal—or neoliberal—model that since Ricardo has guided our understanding of "natural laws" in the marketplace. For example, Wolfgang Streeck recently published *How Will Capitalism End: Essays on a Failing System* (2016). In February 2018 the *New York Times Sunday Magazine* carried an essay by Pankaj Mishra showing how China's ascendancy contradicts orthodox neoliberal claims that state interference always ruins prosperity. In fact, in the second half of the twentieth century, postcolonial state-guided economies restored war-torn Europe and Japan and breathed incredible life into India and China. If textbooks tend still to reaffirm the free-market axioms of Milton Friedman and F. A. Hayek, some scholars are challenging the classical paradigm with new theoretical and statistical approaches. Thomas Picketty, *Capital in the*

Twenty-First Century (2014), levels a serious critique at the economics establishment. His study, "Brahmin Left vs. Merchant Right," traces how political leadership in western democracies has come to represent dueling groups of elites at the expense of citizen voters. Joel Moykyr's *A Culture of Growth* (2017), explores the Enlightenment origins of the modern economy. Elinor Ostrom won the Nobel Prize in economics (2009) for her work on collective action and "governing the commons." In *Undoing the Demos: Neo-Liberalism's Stealth Revolution* (2015), political theorist Wendy Brown mounts a savage critique of the "commodification" of all values by the most extreme advocates of economic rationality. Labor economist Robert Reich has come out with a plea for resurrecting the commonwealth tradition and rediscovering the *social* purpose of human striving.[20]

Historians of energy have given us much to consider going back over fifty years. In 1955 Fred Cottrell published *Energy and Society*, exposing the important relationship between social order, economic development, and dominant use of energy converters. Since then Lewis Mumford, Donald Carr, Barry Commoner, Howard T. Odum, Daniel Yergin, J. R. McNeill, Alfred Crosby, Richard Rhodes, and many others have analyzed that important connection as it changes over time. In a remarkable book, *The Entropy Law and the Economic Process* (1971), Nicolas Georgescu-Roegen tried to universalize economic calculations by converting everything from price (transactional and relative) to energy converted (inherent and irrecoverable), exposing the failure of classical economics to account for the Second Law of Thermodynamics. Most recently Vaclav Smil produced a revised version of his most authoritative survey, *Energy in World History* (original 1994). On the critical issue of greenhouse gases and climate change, Smil reproduces the latest data and draws unequivocal conclusions. Carbon dioxide (from burning fuels) and fugitive methane (from natural gas production) are causing anthropogenic climate change. The consequences for plant productivity and human habitation will be significant. The latest UN IPCC report included far more startling estimates for the rate of global warming and the time left (virtually none) to make effective corrections. Disappointing data from late 2018 show the globe on track to produce a record 37.1 billion tons of carbon dioxide, a *rate of increase* up 40 percent over 2017. There "is no easy technological fix," writes Smil, and the "only potentially successful approach" is through "unprecedented international cooperation." On the positive side, "this worrisome challenge also offers a fundamental motivation for a new departure in managing human affairs."[21]

The Monty Python crew urges us to "always look on the bright side of life," and that is just what Harvard psychologist Steven Pinker has done in a new book, *Enlightenment Now* (2018). Reviewing mountains of data confirming improvements in the human condition, Pinker concludes that progress is real and more progress is essential. Pinker's argument differs completely from the climate deniers, however, because he promotes, not the mindless pursuit of existing ways, but the rigorous application of reason and science in clear-eyed responses to the problems at hand. Pinker's thesis brings us back to what I am calling the culture of exploitation: it clearly grew out of the Enlightenment projects of the eighteenth century, but it has become a kind of secular theology that now must be interrogated just as fiercely as the Roman church in the days of Voltaire. Privileging human life as a singular good (a point that may distress ecologically minded critics), Pinker sees our natural capacity for "sympathy" as the key to universalizing the benefits of material gain while working to remedy the consequences of past mistakes such as global warming. In short, he would direct progress toward enhancing the common good rather than increasing the "take" of the powerful few. Eschewing the negativity of so many critics of our current condition, Pinker manages to rescue an optimistic outlook from disingenuous ideologues like Inhofe while furthering the call for serious engagement with the real world as it is. Bill Gates called Pinker's tome "my new favorite book of all time."[22]

Pinker's optimism seems at once refreshing and naive. Refreshing because it offers relief from the dystopian drumbeats of environmental "Cassandras." At the same time, he pins his hope on the capacity for human reason and "sympathy" to disable all forms of religious, ethnic, racial, national, and mythical superstition, clearing the way for science and universal humanism. But such a wholesale revision of human cultures seems unlikely. It is my hope that the reinterpretation of historical constructs outlined here will prove more achievable and more palatable than dislodging religious, ethnic, and tribal identities. By confining myself to American constructs I hope to suggest that our *particular* edition of the culture of exploitation is rooted in a past we share and cherish—and could repudiate—regardless of what other tribes and nations find it in their power to do. We cannot save the world or compel others to mend their ways, but we can do our own useful work in more virtuous ways and see what emerges in time.[23]

In the end, the point of this book has not been to point us toward a certain solution but to expose the *historical* nature of things we are *told* are true and immutable, but which in fact are contingent and subject to revision. Most of the central tenets of what I have called here the culture of exploitation emerged in the past four hundred years. They were embraced as new "truths" and discoveries on which men and women pinned their hopes for a better future. Over time their origins faded into "accepted wisdom." For example, three hundred years of African slavery energized the "rise of the West"—a phrase that itself suggests auto-levitation and masks heavy lifting by millions of enslaved human beings. Organized campaigns of exclusion, dispossession, and extermination erased the indigenous populations in the United States (and elsewhere), clearing the way for mythic assertions of continental emptiness and heroic narratives about conquering a "howling wilderness." In the eighteenth century, new Enlightenment ideas fed the confidence of intellectuals such that they could let go of religious foundations and embark on scientific inquiries into the nature of the world, the cosmos, and life itself. The result was modern science, and its handmaid, technology, by which human beings came to see themselves as capable of rising above the beasts and controlling our environment like no other species. A new science of popular politics inflamed the assertiveness of ordinary men and women, who, in the wake of democratic revolutions, assured each other that nobody knew better than "we the people" what needed to be improved. There is nothing inherently evil about science, technology, or democratic liberation, but each is susceptible of being corrupted or misconstrued in the service of objectives that are less than reasonable.

Intoxicated with the thrill of staging a world-historical experiment in liberty, nineteenth-century Americans sized up their continental inheritance and seized every opportunity to "improve" it at will. At first embrace, the mutually liberating frameworks of capitalism and democracy appeared to disestablish corrupt institutions and usher in an age of equality. The resulting transition to a market-based economy produced enormous gains but also the beginnings of new kinds of inequality and dependency. Anxieties mounted in the antebellum period, but further expansion and full-throated cries of "destiny" kept Americans' attention focused on conquest and growth until the problem of slavery forced a reckoning in the Civil War. Having jettisoned slavery (which many now thought of as a tragic error), postwar Americans doubled down on the claims of economists celebrating free labor, industrial progress, and property rights. The number of citizens without property to defend rose steadily during the industrial expansions of the Gilded Age, but falling prices for all kinds of goods helped mask the stagnant or declining wages earned by more vulnerable Americans. Waves of "swarthy" immigrants from southern and eastern Europe suffered the worst indignities; this erected a buffer of ethnic "otherness" between the most miserable newcomers and "birth-right" native-born citizens. While much of the original substance of American liberty and equality leached out along the way, by the end of the century Americans took pride in their rise to wealth and power on the world stage, mastery in the modern sense.

Despite our best efforts to sanitize the past and anoint the present as the only path history might have taken, choices *were made* in the construction of the modern American culture of exploitation. For example, the Christian traditions coming out of the late Middle Ages celebrated stewardship and charity as well as dominion and entitlement. Good Christian colonizers might have chosen to curb their acquisitive impulse (as they often were told to do). They might have recognized the Natives as children of God instead of savage children of Satan; they might have recognized at once that chattel slavery contradicted everything found in the Gospels. Received culture nourished by self-interest lured them to the choices they made—choices they often were not aware of having made in any active or positive sense. But where critical voices were raised, effective consensus pushed them quickly to the margins of public discourse. As the colonies grew and prospered, Americans might have recognized the windfall of abundance as the author of their achievements rather than simply crediting themselves with genius and industry. But they did not. Our revolutionary founders might have lifted up the commonwealth tradition when they crafted constitutions (indeed, some of them tried) rather than encouraging an atomistic impulse toward the sort of freedom that Thomas Hobbes had foretold darkly. Freedom from want, freedom for community advancement, freedom for collective prosperity and safety—these variations were not unknown to 1780s Americans, but they were let go in the rush to embrace competitive individualism and economic liberty. Some economists now recognize two major sources of "market failure"—imperfect information and limited benevolence.[24] Confident that freedom would cure the first while moral sense supplied the second, Adam Smith entrusted self-interest to do what neither church nor state in his day was doing: police the common good.

After the Revolution, when they turned and faced the interior of the continent, these new Americans had another chance to recognize the presence (and rights) of the Natives, the impact of their own wasteful practices on the costal landscape, and the moral dilemma presented by slave labor in a free society. Instead, with stars in their eyes, they saw boundless forests, prairies, plains, and mountains, empty, begging to be used for the benefit of these new carriers of rights and "right" in behalf of civilization. Mobilizing energy, intellect, science, and practical ingenuity, as well as the money made by stripping and selling their continent's resources, Americans turned their backs on stewardship, husbandry, commonwealth, and benevolence, preferring to race forward instead and remedy any consequences with technological fixes. The beguiling concept of "improvement," itself potentially benevolent, became, in the hands of parties whose self-interest became their only guide, an excuse to justify innovation regardless of its impact on friends and neighbors or the environment. If improvement allowed self-deception, the idea of destiny magnified the fault, setting up collective delusions that positively immunized Americans from any feedback loop. Oddly enough, even the moment of confession and absolution implicit in the Civil War was hijacked by advocates of destiny who offered up the Union victory as the triumph of the modern culture over antique, illiberal values that never had contributed to freedom or progress.[25]

Pride verging on hubris accompanied the arrival of Americans to mastery and power at the dawn of the twentieth century. Despite vigorous movements for social justice and reform, many of them aimed at improving the lives of those most dependent and vulnerable, Americans as a whole rolled into the new century with confidence bolstered by hearty economic growth. After "saving Europe" in two world wars, surviving the Great Depression, and launching the Marshall Plan, we shouldered the challenge of defending the "free world" against aggressive totalitarianism. Pouring this new wine into the old skins of "destiny," we learned to see everything that was in our "vital interest" as virtuous and everyone who differed as vicious. Thus the Manichean perspective that drove our conquest of North America spread across the globe. When in 2001 Osama bin Laden's terrorist network struck three iconic American targets, a bewildered President George W. Bush declared that they must "resent our freedom." Few could imagine a legitimate grievance against the patronage of the United States. At the United Nations President Trump recently asserted (because no one else would say it for him) that America "has been among the greatest forces for good in the history of the world."[26] A case can be made for this claim, but such naive self-righteousness grates on the ears of other nations who see reality through different lenses. When Trump sings out "In God We

Trust," it sounds more like Bob Dylan's haunting lament, "With God on Our Side." Then the self-proclaimed Islamic Caliphate responds with "Allahu Akbar," and the fighting begins.

A colleague who generously read the manuscript of this book called it "a classic jeremiad," after a scolding sermon delivered by seventeenth-century Puritan divines. We "knew what was right," said the preacher, "but were free to do wrong, and we did." Now the promised destruction looms, but there may still be time. "As we were free to err, so we are free to repent and reform, if only we will."[27] It may seem pretentious to suggest a prophetic calling, but consider how often the voice of the past calls us to see who we are and what we have done. It would be unfair simply to denounce the choices of our ancestors, even though the consequences of their actions sometimes proved reprehensible. At the same time, to learn from the sins of the fathers might suggest a path to reconciliation and understanding on which a profoundly different world order could be built.

For at least two centuries under global capitalism, the culture of exploitation has promised the less prosperous people of the world that they would enjoy a wealthy future as soon as they put their shoulders to the wheel. Do like us and catch up, and we can all enjoy the benevolent results. Indeed, global poverty has declined—at least as measured by modern economic indicators; but environmental limits now threaten this fundamental assumption of modernization. Furthermore, much of the world's workforce labors in slave-like conditions to turn the wheels that generate riches for the wealthiest few. They cannot "do like us" unless they are free to do so. Sometimes wealthy nations solve their most serious health and waste dilemmas by exporting filth and dangerous jobs to countries too poor to turn down opportunities. Industrial polluters dream of high-tech solutions that allow them to continue business as usual, but high-tech solutions often drive up the total footprint of productive systems. (Think stack scrubbers for coal smoke.) Resource depletion can be met with clever alternatives, but once again the cost-benefit analysis sometimes proves disappointing. (Motor fuels made from Iowa corn yield precious little real gain when all the costs are considered.) The rich cannot continue to grow richer and expect the poor to get rich as well. If the rich insist on pursuing their own advantages, the poor must suffer disastrously. Can it really be true that the wealthiest people on Earth cannot afford to share with the victims of the exploitation that has generated all these riches? If the poor, at home and abroad, are to inherit a future at all, the rich will have to change their ways *for the benefit of others, not just themselves.*

Thus we return to acquisitive self-interest, economic nationalism, and problem of the common good. Self-centered, self-righteous, self-created, self-governed, self-obsessed individuals simply cannot foster community. The natural result of atomistic individualism is a Hobbesian dystopia marked by suspicion, competition, and anger. In the past, families, clans, tribes, ethnicities, religious groups, and nationalities set boundaries inside of which empathy and love was supposed to blunt the impulse to scratch and bite. In many ways these smaller units still perform this function, but modernization has created such vast global specialization and interdependency that fostering empathy only at the tribal level simply will not do. In the shrinking global village of the twenty-first century people who are "not like me and mine" regularly must interact. But the culture of exploitation keeps insisting that competitive self-interest is the law of nature and we dare not lower our guard for fear of being cheated, conquered, or destroyed. This is precisely the argument that propelled Donald Trump into the White House and explains the rise of xenophobic, populist regimes in Europe and South America. As long as individuals, families, clans, tribes, or nations must come out *the winner*, there never can be peace or community. And as long as private opulence is never adequate, national incomes never satisfactory, standards of living never sufficient, even among the richest of people, there will only be some winners—and many many losers.

The utopian side of the American experience contained a commonwealth ideal and support for terms like "sufficient," "adequate," and "satisfactory." Even if honored in the breach, restrictions on the sin of "avarice" were commonplace in the cultures of our ancestors, and they survive in ethical creeds from secular humanism to Jesus's "Sermon on the Mount." In the culture of exploitation, backed up by classical economic claims about the virtue of greed as a human motivation, these words are dismissed as childish sentiments without a place in the "real world."[28] But we *can* embrace that commonwealth tradition without abandoning our history or our heritage. Information *can* be exchanged freely so that market transactions register genuine consumer desires and not the fruits of fraud and deception. Benevolence *can* be encouraged as a virtue linked to the general welfare. American freedom has been, and can be, enjoyed within notions of sufficiency and the common good. Reason and science can be tools for

solving problems and distributing wealth, not just acquiring wealth ourselves.

In *The Lorax*, the greedy "Once-ler" cut down the "Truffula Trees" to
knit "Thneeds," a thing so useless and attractive that the market for it grew
exponentially. Speaking for the trees and the living things that loved them,
the Lorax begged him to stop. But only when the last tree was felled did the
factory shut down, leaving a barren landscape with bad air, foul water, and
no living things. In sorrow and disgust, the Lorax ascended into heaven,
"heisted himself . . . without a trace." Years later a boy sought out the story,
and the thoroughly shamed Once-ler confessed that the word of the Lorax
now seemed perfectly clear: "Unless someone like you cares a whole awful
lot, nothing is going to get better. It's not." Then he handed the boy the
last Truffula Seed:

> Plant a new Truffula. Treat it with care.
> Give it clean water. And feed it fresh air.
> Grow a forest. Protect it from axes that hack.
> Then the Lorax and all of his friends may come back.[29]

It is a redemption story, the point of which our children recognize without
effort. Whether we adults have a new Truffula seed or not, we can learn to
be comfortable *and* to share. With luck, cooperation, and real ingenuity we
can address the climate and environmental crises of the coming century.
We can reimagine the gift of liberty and the meaning of American freedom.
We can try once more (in the words of Tom Paine) to make the world
anew. Go and read again *The Lorax* of Dr. Seuss.

A WORK OF THIS scope necessarily floats on a sea of other people's scholarship reaching back two generations or more. The notes in each chapter carry specific citations as well as reference notes back into the supporting literature. To avoid piling on, in most cases I have chosen to limit reference notes to fairly recent works through which interested readers easily can find their way back to earlier scholarship. The last fifty years have seen the most creative, insightful, and challenging outpouring of scholarly work the profession ever has seen. This is not to say certain earlier classics no longer matter, but the bar keeps rising higher and higher as the profession grows in size, breadth, and depth.

The internet, of course, has produced a literal storm surge of information, much of it free, all of it acquired with a few quick keystrokes. However, this embarrassment of riches comes to us raw, undifferentiated, often unchecked by curators of any sort, and sometimes willfully distorted. For readers who might be less familiar with the kinds of resources available in modern research libraries, I want to mention at this point a number of encyclopedias and professionally curated reference collections that can be helpful when trying to navigate the more lawless discussions one finds in modern media. Reliable statistical information can be found at "Our World in Data," https://ourworldindata.org/ or in old-fashioned print forms such as Ben Wattenberg, ed., *A Statistical History of the United States* (New York, 1976). More specialized scholarly conversations can be engaged in fine reference works such as: Stanley L. Engerman and Robert E. Gallman, eds., *The Cambridge Economic History of the United States*, 3 vols. (Cambridge, UK, 1996–2000); Howard Lamar, ed., *The New Encyclopedia of the West* (New Haven, CT, 1998); *Blackwell Companions to American History*, 33 vols. to date, twenty-two of which bear on the periods covered here; the *Oxford*

Handbooks to History, 64 vols. to date, at least twelve of which bear on these periods; the *Oxford History of the United States*, 12 vols. to date, seven of which deal with our periods; the *Oxford History of the British Empire*, 5 vols. to date, three of which are pertinent. Scribners have published two excellent reference works, Mary Kupiec Cayton and Peter Williams, eds., *Encyclopedia of American Cultural and Intellectual History*, 3 vols. (New York, 2001) and Mary Kupiec Cayton, Elliot J. Gorn, and Peter W. Williams, eds., *Encyclopedia of American Social History*, 3 vols. (New York, 1993).

Even more specialized guides and finding aids exist for most subfields of modern historical scholarship as well. A quick search for guides to environmental history, women's history, Native Americans, African Americans, slavery, the African slave trade, empire, colonization, and industrialization will turn up aids useful for exploring details. The Library of Congress and the National Archives maintain enormous online libraries of government documents, publications, images, and some manuscripts. Huge subscription databases comprising imprints from special collections worldwide offer full-text access to Early English Books, Early American Imprints, American Periodicals, historical newspapers, and many other sources, most of which can be used through major libraries or private subscription. The letters and papers of many leading actors (especially so-called Founding Fathers) have been collected, curated, and published in multivolume letterpress editions as well as in online portals that give general readers quick access to primary source material once seen only by the top scholars in the field. Niche topics such as the ratification of the United States Constitution boast comprehensive documentary collections; the same can be said for the First Federal Congress and the Black Abolitionists Papers. The editors, publishers, and sponsors of these ambitious projects—including private foundations and several government agencies—are to be commended for diligence and perseverance. Modern scholars and casual researchers alike are richly blessed by these projects.

Unavoidably there will be omissions from this comment and from the chapter notes as well. Apologies in advance if I have slighted any members of the extraordinary community of scholars with whom it has been my privilege to engage. As this tide of public discourse continues to rise—like the levels of the sea in the coming century—it will become all the more difficult to acquire anything like mastery of the conversations. But mastery (as I have argued above) probably is illusory, and if insight is like fresh air, water, and sunlight then there can never be too much of these.

Introduction

1. I am using the term in its most generic and descriptive sense and not in reference to the theoretical constructs employed by social scientists in the last generation. A formal "modernization theory" reigned in historical sociology and development studies beginning in the 1960s and served for many years as a model for studying the process in various parts of the world. Fierce critics denounced it as imperialistic and deterministic. Alternative "dependency theory" and "world-systems theory" then entered the conversation. For an introduction to this literature see Ronald Inglehart and Christian Welzel, *Modernization, Cultural Change, and Democracy* (Cambridge, UK, 2005); and Alvin Y. So, *Social Change and Development: Modernization, Dependency, and World-System Theories* (Newbury Park, CA, 1990).

2. An extraordinary resource can be found at Our World in Data, accessed Feb. 20, 2018, https://ourworldindata.org/. UN sources count 1.8 billion "moderately or severely food insecure" in 2015, accessed Feb. 20, 2018, https://ourworldindata.org/hunger-and-under nourishment. See also Global Footprint Network, "Country Overshoot" graphic, accessed Feb. 20, 2018, https://www.footprintnetwork.org.

3. See, for example, Walt W. Rostow, *Stages of Economic Growth*, 2nd ed. (Cambridge, UK, 1971), 17–31; also Ian Morris, *Why the West Rules—For Now* (New York, 2010).

4. See Sven Beckert, *Empire of Cotton* (New York, 2014), chaps. 2–3; Clive Ponting, *A New Green History of the World* (New York, 2007); David Brion Davis, *Inhuman Bondage: The Rise and Fall of Slavery in the New World* (New York, 2006); Thomas Kuhn, *The Structure of Scientific Revolutions*, 2nd ed. (Chicago, 1970). For a unique perspective see Immanuel Wallerstein, *The Modern World-System*, 4 vols. (orig. 1974–2011; repr. Berkeley, 2011).

5. See Karl Polanyi, *The Great Transformation* (orig. 1944; repr. Boston, 1957).

6. Alan Taylor, *American Colonies* (New York, 2001).

7. See Carolyn Merchant, *The Columbia Guide to American Environmental History* (New York, 2002); Richard N. L. Andrews, *Managing the Environment, Managing Ourselves* (New Haven, CT, 1999); also handy is Hal K. Rothman, *The Greening of a Nation? Environmentalism in the United States Since 1945* (Belmont, CA, 1998).

Chapter 1

1. David Underdown, *Fire from Heaven: Life in an English Town in the Seventeenth Century* (New Haven, CT, 1992), 12. Social historians deploy this language for early modern

England and much of Europe well into the seventeenth century. The classic study of this worldview is Arthur O. Lovejoy, *The Great Chain of Being: A Study of the History of an Idea* (Cambridge, MA, 1936). Much of my portrait here draws on Robert Bucholz and Newton Key, *Early Modern England, 1485–1714: A Narrative History*, 2nd ed. (London, 2009); Keith Wrightson, *Earthly Necessities: Economic Lives in Early Modern Britain* (New Haven, CT, 2000); Henry Kamen, *Early Modern European Society* (London, 2000); and James R. Farr, *The Work of France: Labor and Culture in Early Modern Times* (New York, 2008).

2. Bucholz and Key, *Early Modern England*, 26–29.

3. Wrightson, *Earthly Necessities*, 99–102. On the plague and its impact see for example Norman F. Cantor, *In the Wake of the Plague: The Black Death and the World It Made* (New York, 2001); and L. R. Poos, *A Rural Society After the Black Death: Essex, 1350–1525* (Cambridge, UK, 1991).

4. John Locke, *Second Treatise of Government* (orig. 1690; repr., ed. Thomas P. Person, Indianapolis, IN, 1952), 29. For all reprinted sources, the page number(s) are from the reprinted edition.

5. See D. W. Meinig, *The Shaping of America*, vol. 1, *Atlantic America, 1492–1800* (New Haven, CT, 1986), parts 1–2; Alan Taylor, *American Colonies* (New York, 2001), chaps. 2–3; Alfred Crosby, *Ecological Imperialism: The Biological Expansion of Europe, 900–1900*, new ed. (Cambridge, UK, 2004), chaps. 5–6; J. H. Elliott, *Empires of the Atlantic World: Britain and Spain in America, 1492–1830* (New Haven, CT, 2006), part 1.

6. Edmund Dudley, *The Tree of Commonwealth* (orig. 1509; repr., ed. D. M. Brodie, Cambridge, UK, 1948), 31.

7. Ibid., 31–89, quotation 31.

8. Ibid., 34–48, quotations 36, 44–48.

9. Ibid., 90–91.

10. Wrightson, *Earthly Necessities*, 34; Bucholz and Key, *Early Modern England*, 24–27, 161–62; J. P. Cooper, "The Social Distribution of Land and Men in England, 1436–1700," *Economic History Review*, 2nd ser., 20 (1967): 419–40; Lawrence Stone, "Social Mobility in England, 1500–1700," *Past and Present* 33 (1966): 16–55. For contemporary accounts see William Harrison, *The Description of England*, 2nd ed. (orig. 1587; repr. Ithaca, NY, 1968), chap. 5.

11. Wrightson, *Earthly Necessities*, 34; Bucholz and Key, *Early Modern England*, 161–62.

12. The classic study is Joan Thirsk, *Agricultural Regions and Agrarian History in England, 1500–1750* (Basingstoke, UK, 1987); see also W. G. Hoskins, *The Making of the English Landscape* (orig. 1955; repr. London, 1985), chaps. 4–5.

13. On shopping patterns see Christopher Dyer, "The Consumer and the Market in the Later Middle Ages," *Economic History Review*, 2nd ser., 42 (1989): 305–27.

14. Wrightson, *Earthly Necessities*, 30, 55, 95; compare with Europe in Kamen, *Early Modern European Society*, 20–21.

15. See Robert O. Bucholz and Joseph P. Ward, *London: A Social and Cultural History, 1550–1750* (Cambridge, UK, 2012), chaps. 1, 2, 6; Steve Rappaport, *Worlds Within Worlds: Structures of Life in Sixteenth-Century London* (Cambridge, UK, 2002).

16. Wrightson, *Earthly Necessities*, 52–53; Dyer, "The Consumer and the Market," 305–27.

17. See Winifred Rothenberger, *From Market Places to Market Economies: The Transformation of Rural Massachusetts, 1750–1850* (Chicago, 1992), chaps. 1–2, for theoretical issues;

also E. P. Thompson, "The Moral Economy of the English Crowd in the Eighteenth Century," *Past and Present* 50 (1971): 76–136.

18. Thompson, "Moral Economy," 83; see also Alan S. C. Ross, "The Assize of Bread," *Economic History Review*, 2nd ser., 9 (1956): 332–42.

19. Joel Kaye, *Economy and Nature in the Fourteenth Century: Money, Market Exchange, and the Emergence of Scientific Thought* (Cambridge, UK, 1998), chaps. 3–5.

20. Ibid., 62–101, quotations 73, 70.

21. Wrightson summarizes the several explanations for the inflationary crisis in *Earthly Necessities*, 115–20. The crises of the sixteenth-century rural economy sparked two generations of debate starting with R. H. Tawney, *The Agrarian Problem in the Sixteenth Century* (orig. 1912; repr. New York, 1967); R. H. Tawney, "The Rise of the Gentry, 1558–1640," *Economic History Review* 11 (1941): 1–38; Lawrence Stone, *The Crisis of the Aristocracy, 1558–1641* (Oxford, UK, 1965); Cooper, "Social Distribution of Land and Men"; and T. H. Aston and C. H. E. Philpin, eds., *The Brenner Debate: Agrarian Class Structure and Economic Development in Pre-Industrial Europe* (Cambridge, UK, 1985).

22. See Bucholz and Key, *Early Modern England*, 65–115.

23. Stone, "Social Mobility in England," 16–29, quotation at 24; Wrightson, *Earthly Necessities*, quotation 143.

24. Thomas More, *Utopia*, trans. Ralph Robinson (orig. 1556), in Susan Bruce, ed., *Three Early Modern Utopias* (Oxford, UK, 1999), 22. See John Walter and Keith Wrightson, "Dearth and the Social Order in Early Modern England," *Past and Present* 71 (1976): 22–42.

25. R. H. Tawney and Eileen Power, eds., *Tudor Economic Documents*, 3 vols. (orig. 1924; repr. New York, 1961), 1:42–43; John Hales's charge to the juries (1548), reprinted in *A Discourse of the Common Weal of this Realm of England* (orig. 1581; ed. Elizabeth Lamond, 1893; repr. Cambridge, UK, 1954), xlv–xlvii. On rural unrest see Wrightson, *Earthly Necessities*, 149–58. Documentation on Hales was included in Lamond's 1893 edition of *Discourses of the Common Weal*, xxxviv–lxxii, quotations lxvi–xvii. Lamond argued that Hales was the author of *Discourses*, but Mary Dewar has since built a stronger case for Thomas Smith. See Mary Dewar, ed., *A Discourse of the Commonweal of this Realm of England, Attributed to Sir Thomas Smith* (Charlottesville, VA, 1969), xx–xxv, 38; Mary Dewar, "The Authorship of the 'Discourse of the Commonweal,'" *Economic History Review*, 2nd ser., 19 (1966): 388–400. Wrightson reproduces a good price table in *Earthly Necessities*, 118.

26. Poor laws, 1597, in Tawney and Power, *Tudor Economic Documents*, 2:346–54, quotation 347; 43 Elizabeth, c. 2, 1601, "Act for the Relief of the Poor," accessed Mar. 23, 2019, http://statutes.org.uk/site/the-statutes/seventeenth-century/1601-43-elizabeth-c-2-act-for-the-relief-of-the-poor; Elizabethan "Statute of Artificers" (1563) in Tawney and Power, *Tudor Economic Documents*, 1:338–51, quotation 339; see also "An Act for the Maintenance of Husbandry and Tillage (1597), ibid., 1:84–86; William Lambarde's charge to the grand jury of Kent, 1583, quoted in Wrightson, *Earthly Necessities*, 214; "An Act for the Maintenance of Husbandry & Tillage," in Tawney and Power, *Tudor Economic Documents*, 1:84.

27. On the link between empire and state formation see David Armitage, *The Ideological Origins of the British Empire* (Cambridge, UK, 2000), 13–23. See also R. R. Davies, "The English State and the 'Celtic' Peoples 1100–1400," *Journal of Historical Sociology* 6 (1993): 1–14.

28. Nicholas Canny, *Kingdom and Colony* (Baltimore, 1988), chap. 1; also Nicholas Canny, "The Ideology of English Colonization: From Ireland to America," *William and Mary Quarterly*, 3rd ser., 30 (1973): 575–98.

29. Quotation from the title of Humphrey Gilbert, *A Discourse How Her Majesty May Annoy the King of Spain* (1577). See Kenneth R. Andrews, *Trade, Plunder, and Settlement: Maritime Enterprise and the Genesis of the British Empire, 1480–1630* (Cambridge, UK, 1984), 63, 77–79, 97–100, 256–79, 304–40. See also Robert Brenner, *Merchants and Revolution: Commercial Change, Political Conflict, and London's Overseas Traders, 1550–1653* (Princeton, 1993), chaps. 1–3; and the first seven essays in *The Oxford History of the British Empire*, vol. 1, *The Origins of Empire*, ed. Nicholas Canny (Oxford, UK, 1998), 1–169.

30. For a good summary portrait see "Merrie Olde England, ca. 1603," in Bucholz and Key, *Early Modern England*, 158–211.

Chapter 2

1. Thomas More, *Utopia*, trans. Ralph Robinson (orig. 1556), in Susan Bruce, ed., *Three Early Modern Utopias* (Oxford, UK, 1999), 42–48, 122. For recent assessments of the enormous literature on the European encounter with the New World see Stephen Foster, *British North America in the Seventeenth and Eighteenth Centuries* (Oxford, UK, 2014); Jack P. Greene and Philip D. Morgan, eds., *Atlantic History: A Critical Appraisal* (New York, 2009); J. H. Elliott, *Empires of the Atlantic World: Britain and Spain in America, 1492–1830* (New Haven, CT, 2006); Stephen Greenblatt, *Marvelous Possessions: The Wonder of the New World* (Chicago, 1991); Karen Ordahl Kupperman, ed., *America in European Consciousness, 1492–1750* (Chapel Hill, NC, 1995); and J. H. Elliott, *The Old World and the New, 1492–1650* (Cambridge, UK, 1970). For economic development see John J. McCusker and Kenneth Morgan, *The Early Modern Atlantic Economy* (Cambridge, UK, 2009).

2. See Jack P. Greene, *The Intellectual Construction of America: Exceptionalism and Identity from 1492 to 1800* (Chapel Hill, NC, 1993), 11–17; Howard Mumford Jones, *O Strange New World; American Culture: The Formative Years* (orig. 1952; repr. New York, 1964), 40–50.

3. "John Hawkins' voyage to new Hispania 1564," in Richard Hakluyt, *Hakluyt's Voyages*, selected and edited by Irwin R. Blacker (New York, 1965), 155; Philip Amadas and M. Arthur Barlow, "Voyage to Virginia, 1584," ibid., 292–93; Thomas Hariot, *A Briefe and True Report of the New Found Land of Virginia* (orig. 1588; repr. New York, 1951); John Smith, *Complete Works of Captain John Smith*, ed. Philip L. Barbour, 3 vols. (Chapel Hill, NC, 1986), 2:102. See James Horn, *A Kingdom Strange: The Brief and Tragic History of the Lost Colony of Roanoke* (New York, 2010). Because of widely differing treatments of early English spellings, I have modernized most words in these early texts.

4. "George Percy's Account of the Voyage to Virginia and the Colony's First Days," quoted in Warren M. Billings, ed., *The Old Dominion in the Seventeenth Century: A Documentary History of Virginia, 1606–1700*, rev. ed. (Chapel Hill, NC, 2007), 30; Smith, *Complete Works*, 2:186, 225, 206–7; William Simmonds, "The Proceedings of the English Colonie in Virginia since Their First Beginning from England in the Year of Our Lord, 1606, till The Present 1612, with All Their Accidents That Befell Them in the Journies and Discoveries," quoted in Billings, *Old Dominion*, 32. See also Kathleen Donegan, *Seasons of Misery: Catastrophe and Colonial Settlement in Early America* (Philadelphia, 2014); James Horn, *A Land as God Made It: Jamestown and the Birth of America* (New York, 2005); and Timothy Sweet, *American Georgics: Economy and Environment in Early American Literature* (Philadelphia, 2002), chap. 1.

5. Smith, *Complete Works*, 2:154, 156, 159, 202, 160. See Edmund S. Morgan, *American Slavery, American Freedom: The Ordeal of Colonial Virginia* (New York, 1975), chap. 4; James H. Merrell, *The Indians' New World: Catawbas and Their Neighbors from European Contact*

Through the Era of Removal (Chapel Hill, NC, 1989), chaps. 1–2. More generally see Michael Guasco, *Slaves and Englishmen: Human Bondage in the Early Modern Atlantic World* (Philadelphia, 2014); Anthony S. Parent Jr., *Foul Means: The Formation of a Slave Society in Virginia, 1660–1740* (Chapel Hill, NC, 2003); Philip D. Morgan, *Slave Counterpoint: Black Culture in the Eighteenth-Century Chesapeake and Lowcountry* (Chapel Hill, NC, 1998); James Horn, *Adapting to a New World: English Society in the Seventeenth-Century Chesapeake* (Chapel Hill, NC, 1994); and Alan Kulikoff, *Tobacco and Slaves: Development of Southern Cultures in the Chesapeake, 1680–1800* (Chapel Hill, NC, 1986).

6. Smith, *Complete Works*, 2:157, 3:276–77, 2:420–21.

7. Ibid., 2:113, 233, 420–23, 3:288.

8. Ibid., 2:436–37; [Council of Virginia], *A True Declaration of the Estate of the Colonie of Virginia* (London, 1610) quoted in Sweet, *American Georgics*, 32.

9. See Morgan, *American Slavery, American Freedom*, chaps. 6–16.

10. Hakluyt, *Voyages*, 19–20; Daniel Vickers, *Farmers and Fishermen: Two Centuries of Work in Essex County, Massachusetts, 1630–1830* (Chapel Hill, NC, 1994), 85–88; Smith, *Complete Works*, 1:419–41, 2:420, 427, 423–24. For context see Allan Greer, *Property and Dispossession: Natives, Empires, and Land in Early Modern North America* (Cambridge, UK, 2018); Margaret Ellen Newell, *Brethren by Nature: New England Indians, Colonists, and the Origins of American Slavery* (Ithaca, NY, 2015); Daniel K. Richter, *Trade, Land, Power* (Philadelphia, 2013); Alan Gallay, *The Indian Slave Trade* (New Haven, CT, 2002); Daniel K. Richter, *Facing East from Indian Country* (Cambridge, MA, 2001). For environmental impact of fisheries see John F. Richards, *The Unending Frontier: An Environmental History of the Early Modern World* (Berkeley, CA, 2003), 547–59; Virginia DeJohn Anderson, *Creatures of Empire: How Domesticated Animals Transformed Early America* (New York, 2004); and William Cronon, *Changes in the Land: Indians, Colonists, and the Ecology of New England* (New York, 1983).

11. William Bradford, *Of Plymouth Plantation, 1620–1647*, ed. Francis Murphy (New York, 1981), 69–70. See Gloria L. Main, *Peoples of a Spacious Land: Families and Cultures in Colonial New England* (Cambridge, MA, 2001).

12. "Governor Bradford's History," Dec. 18–19, 1620, and Mar. 7, 1621, in Alexander Young, ed., *Chronicles of the Pilgrim Fathers of the Colony of Plymouth from 1602 to 1625* (Boston, 1841), 167, 183, 132–33, 206; Bradford, *Of Plymouth Plantation*, 74–75.

13. Robert Cushman, "Of the State of the Colony, and the Need of Public Spirit in the Colonists," Dec. 12, 1621, in Young, *Chronicles of the Pilgrim Fathers*, 255–68, quotations 256–57, 263, 265, 268.

14. Bradford, *Of Plymouth Plantation*, 227, 228, 233, 266. See Thomas Morton, *New English Canaan, or New Canaan, Containing an Abstract of New England* (Amsterdam, 1637) for a remarkable and sarcastic critique of the self-righteous sensibilities of the Plymouth Calvinists.

15. Robert Cushman, "Reasons and Considerations Touching the Lawfulness of Removing out of England into the Parts of America," 1621, in Young, *Chronicles of the Pilgrim Fathers*, 239–49, quotations 243–46 (emphasis original).

16. Edward Winslow, "To all well-willers and furthers of Plantations in New England," 1624, in Young, *Chronicles of the Pilgrim Fathers*, 270–75, quotation 272; Bradford, *Of Plymouth Plantation*, 197–98.

17. Bradford, *Of Plymouth Plantation*, 227, 228, 233, 266.

18. Bradford, *Of Plymouth Plantation*, 356; Main, *Peoples of a Spacious Land*, 24, makes the very important point that by the beginning of the Puritan Great Migration, so-called Pilgrims constituted perhaps no more than one-fourth of the "Old Colony."

19. John Winthrop, "A Modell of Christian Charity," (1630), accessed May 3, 2005, http://history.hanover.edu/texts/winthmod.html. See Virginia DeJohn Anderson, *New England's Generation: The Great Migration and the Formation of Society and Culture in the Seventeenth Century* (Cambridge, UK, 1991).

20. Bradford, *Of Plymouth Plantation*, 75; "Winthrop's Conclusions for the Plantation in New England," *Old South Leaflets* 2, no. 50 (n.d.): 5–6; John Winthrop to Simonds D'ewes, July 21, 1634, in *Winthrop Papers*, 6 vols. (Boston, 1929–47), 3:171–72; Winthrop to John Endecott, Jan. 3, 1633/34, ibid., 3:149. The reiteration of the Adamite commission reads: "And the fear of you and the dread of you shall be upon every beast of the earth, and upon every fowl of the air, upon all that moveth upon the earth, and upon all the fishes of the sea: into your hand are they delivered" (Gen. 9:2 RSV. All biblical quotations from Revised Standard Version).

21. See Kenneth A. Lockridge, *A New England Town, the First Hundred Years: Dedham, Massachusetts, 1636–1736* (New York, 1970); and John Demos, *A Little Commonwealth: Family Life in Plymouth Colony* (New York, 1970). Many such community studies followed. For a more recent approach see Michael Winship, *Godly Republicanism: Puritans, Pilgrims, and a City on a Hill* (Cambridge, MA, 2012).

22. John Winthrop, "Essay on the Ordering of Townes" (n.d., c. 1635), in *Winthrop Papers*, 3:181–85, quotation 184. Winthrop recorded on December 11, 1634, that he and other elites were *not* elected to Boston's commission to divide town lands because voters feared that "the richer men would give the poorer sort no great proportions . . . and leave a great part at liberty for new comers and for commons." John Winthrop, *The History of New England from 1630 to 1649*, ed. James Savage, 2 vols. (Boston, 1953), 1:181.

23. Winthrop, "Ordering of Townes," in *Winthrop Papers*, 3:184.

24. Darrett B. Rutman, *Winthrop's Boston: A Portrait of a Puritan Town, 1630–1649* (Chapel Hill, NC, 1965), 23–40.

25. Rutman, *Winthrop's Boston*, 35; Martha O. Howes and Sidney Perley, eds., *Town Records of Salem Massachusetts, 1634–1691*, 3 vols. (Salem, MA, 1868–1943), 1:7, 27–28, 30–31, 76, 107, 196; *Town Records of Manchester*, 2 vols. (Salem, MA, 1889–91), 1:8; Nathaniel Bradstreet Shurtleff, ed., *Records of the Governor and Company of the Massachusetts Bay in New England*, 5 vols. (Boston, 1853–54), 1:84, 89–91, 101–14; John Winthrop to John Winthrop Jr., Jan. 15 and 31, 1637/38, in *Winthrop Papers*, 4:9–10. For economy see Stephen Innes, *Creating the Commonwealth: The Economic Culture of Puritan New England* (New York, 1995); and Bernard Bailyn, *The New England Merchants in the Seventeenth Century* (Cambridge, MA, 1955). On town promotions see John Frederick Martin, *Profits in the Wilderness: Entrepreneurship and the Founding of New England Towns in the Seventeenth Century* (Chapel Hill, NC, 1991), esp. chaps. 6 and 8.

26. Shurtleff, *Records of [. . .] Massachusetts Bay*, 1:84, 91, 104, 109, 111, 126; on Robert Keayne see Bailyn, *New England Merchants*, 41–44.

27. William Wood, *New England's Prospect*, 3rd ed. (orig. 1639; repr. Boston, 1764), 57; Edward Johnson, *Johnson's Wonder-Working Providence* (orig. 1654; repr., ed. J. Franklin Jameson, New York, 1967), 246–48. Bernard Bailyn calculates that up to a third of the elite of

Massachusetts returned to England after Parliament's revolution, depriving the rising American generation of the fervent leadership that had founded the colony originally. See Bailyn, *The Barbarous Years* (New York, 2012) 471–73.

28. [Council for Virginia], *Declaration of the State of the Colonie*, (London, 1620), 4.

29. Morton, *New English Canaan*, 60.

30. Winthrop, *History*, 1:138; Johnson, *Wonder-Working Providence*, 68, 253–54; Thomas Shepard, *The Works of Thomas Shepard*, 3 vols. (Boston, 1853), 1:350–51.

31. Quoted in Karen Ordahl Kupperman, *Providence Island 1630–1641: The Other Puritan Colony* (Cambridge, UK, 1993), 31; see generally chap. 2. My summary relies heavily on Kupperman.

32. Ibid., 35–49, quotation 45.

33. Ibid., chap. 6.

34. Ibid., 321; see chap. 11 generally.

35. Gary A. Puckrein, *Little England: Plantation Society and Anglo-Barbadian Politics, 1627–1700* (New York, 1984), 3–7; Richard Ligon, *A True and Exact History of the Island of Barbados* (orig. 1657; edited, with an introduction, by Karen Ordahl Kupperman, Indianapolis, IN, 2011), 10, 68–70; Simon P. Newman, *A New World of Labor: The Development of Plantation Slavery in the British Atlantic* (Philadelphia, 2013), 4–7; also Richard S. Dunn, *Sugar and Slaves: The Rise of the Planter Class in the English West Indies, 1624–1713* (Chapel Hill, NC, 1972); and Russell R. Menard, *Sweet Negotiations: Sugar, Slavery, and Plantation Agriculture in Early Barbados* (Charlottesville, VA, 2014).

36. Quoted in Puckrein, *Little England*, 56, 11, see 56–71. See also Henry Winthrop to Emmanuel Downing, Aug. 22, 1627, and Henry Winthrop to John Winthrop, Oct. 15, 1627, in *Winthrop Papers*, 1:356, 361.

37. Quoted in Puckrein, *Little England*, 12–13; see the Kupperman edition of Ligon, *True and Exact History*, 66–90, 108, 183. For an earlier first-person account see "The Voyage of Sir Henry Colt," 1631, in V. T. Harlow, ed., *Colonizing Expeditions to the West Indies and Guiana, 1623–1667* (London, 1925), 54–102.

38. For an insightful comparative treatment of property and colonization in New Spain, New France, and New England, see Greer, *Property and Dispossession*; also Colin G. Calloway, *The Scratch of a Pen: 1763 and the Transformation of North America* (New York, 2007); and Kathleen Duval, *The Native Ground: Indians and Colonists in the Heart of the Continent* (Philadelphia, 2006).

39. In recent postcolonial scholarship these stories are lifted entirely out of the traditional narratives of European discovery or "progress" and linked instead to the imperialist process. See Lorenzo Veracini, *Settler Colonialism: A Theoretical Overview* (New York, 2012).

40. J. Hector St. John de Crevecoeur, *Letters from an American Farmer, and Sketches of Eighteenth-Century America* (orig. 1782; repr., ed. Albert E. Stone, New York, 1986), 69. For the abundance trope see, for example, Robert Burton, *The English Empire in America, or, a View of the Dominions of the Crown of England in the West-Indies* (orig. 1685; 5th ed., London, 1711), 59.

41. David Armitage, "The New World and British Historical Thought: From Richard Hakluyt to William Robertson," in Kupperman, *America in European Consciousness*, 55–75; see in the same volume essays by Luca Codignola, John M. Headley, Karen Kupperman, and J. H. Elliott.

Chapter 3

1. John Locke, *Second Treatise of Government* (orig. 1690; repr. ed. Thomas P. Person, Indianapolis, IN, 1952), i.e., chap. 5, para. 49. See Henry F. May, *The Enlightenment in America* (New York, 1976).

2. On the Enlightenment more generally see May, *Enlightenment in America*; Jose R. Torre, *The Enlightenment in America, 1720–1825* (London, 2008); Caroline Winterer, *American Enlightenments: Pursuing Happiness in the Age of Reason* (New Haven, CT, 2018); Keith Thomas, *Man and the Natural World: Changing Attitudes in England, 1500–1800* (London, 1983).

3. William Byrd II to Charles Boyle, July 5, 1726, in Marion Tinling, ed., *Correspondence of Three William Byrds of Westover, Virginia*, 2 vols. (Charlottesville, VA, 1977), 1:355. For a good introduction to Byrd see Kevin Joel Berland, *The Dividing Line Histories of William Byrd II of Westover* (Chapel Hill, NC, 2013), 3–41.

4. William Byrd II to Charles Boyle, Feb. 2, 1726/27, in Tinling, *Correspondence*, 1:357–58.

5. See Norman Fiering, "The First American Enlightenment: Tillotson, Leverett, and Philosophical Anglicanism," *New England Quarterly* 54 (1981): 307–44; and Sidney E. Ahlstrom, *A Religious History of the American People*, 2nd ed. (New Haven, CT, 2004), part 2.

6. John Tillotson, *The Works of the Most Reverend Dr. John Tillotson*, 12 vols. (London, 1748), 1:94.

7. John Tillotson, *Fifteen Sermons on Several Subjects*, ed. Ralph Barker, 2nd ed. (London, 1704), 235–69, quotations 249, 253–55; Tillotson, *Works*, 1:99–128, quotation 128.

8. William Wollaston, *Religion of Nature Delineated* (orig. 1722; 5th ed., London, 1731), 128.

9. William Byrd II, *The Commonplace Book of William Byrd II of Westover*, ed. Kevin Berland, Jan Kirsten Gilliam, and Kenneth Lockridge (Chapel Hill, NC, 2001), 149; see editors' introduction, 59–60.

10. William Byrd II, *Prose Works of William Byrd of Westover*, ed. Louis B. Wright (Cambridge, MA, 1966), 312.

11. William Byrd II to Jane Pratt Taylor, Apr. 3, 1729, in Tinling, *Correspondence*, 1:392; Byrd, *Prose Works*, 290; Pierre Marambaud, *William Byrd of Westover, 1674–1744* (Charlottesville, VA, 1977), 49.

12. See Ahlstrom, *Religious History*, chaps. 24–26; David D. Hall, *Worlds of Wonder, Days of Judgement* (Cambridge, MA, 1990); David D. Hall, *A Reforming People* (New York, 2011).

13. See Robert Middlekauff, *The Mathers: Three Generations of Puritan Intellectuals* (New York, 1971); Kenneth Silverman, *The Life and Times of Cotton Mather* (New York, 1984); and Charles Cohen, "In Retrospect: Robert Middlekauff's 'The Mathers,'" *Reviews in American History* 29 (2001): 635–46.

14. See Perry Miller, *The New England Mind: The Seventeenth Century* (Cambridge, MA, 1939); Perry Miller, *The New England Mind: From Colony to Province* (Cambridge, MA, 1953), 195–201. On the witch trials see Richard Francis, *Judge Sewall's Apology: The Salem Witch Trials and the Forming of an American Conscience* (New York, 2005), esp. 179–204.

15. [Benjamin Colman], *Gospel Order Revived, being an answer to a book lately set forth by [. . .] Increase Mather [. . .] entitled The Gospel Order* (New York, 1700); Increase Mather, *The order of the gospel, professed and practised* [sic] *by the churches of Christ in New England, justified by the Scripture, and by the writings of many learned men, both ancient and modern*

divines; in answer to several questions relating to church discipline (Boston, 1700). On the fracturing of theological harmony see Middlekauff, *The Mathers*, chap. 12; and Silverman, *Cotton Mather*, chap. 5.

16. Benjamin Colman, *God deals with us as rational Creatures: And if Sinners would but hearken to Reason they would repent* (Boston, 1723), quotations 8, 10.

17. See Jon Butler, *Awash in a Sea of Faith: Christianizing the American People* (Cambridge, MA, 1990), chap. 2; and Patricia Bonomi, *Under the Cope of Heaven: Religion, Society, and Politics in Colonial America* (New York, 1986), chap. 2.

18. Quoted in Daniel Walker Howe, *Making the American Self: Jonathan Edwards to Abraham Lincoln* (orig. 1997; repr. New York, 2009), 34; Jonathan Edwards, *Puritan Sage: Collected Works of Jonathan Edwards*, ed. Virgilius Ferm (New York, 1953), 62–92, 164–68, 599.

19. See Frank Lambert, *Inventing the "Great Awakening"* (Princeton, 1999), 116–24; and Frank Lambert, *Pedlar in Divinity: George Whitefield and the Transatlantic Revivals, 1737–1770* (Princeton, 1994), chap. 2.

20. Romans 1:18–26. See Thomas, *Man and the Natural World*, esp. chaps. 1–2; Julie Robin Solomon, *Objectivity in the Making: Francis Bacon and the Politics of Inquiry* (Baltimore, 1998), chap. 1; and Carolyn Merchant, *Death of Nature: Women, Ecology, and the Scientific Revolution* (New York, 1980).

21. Susan Scott Parrish, *American Curiosity: Cultures of Natural History in the Colonial British Atlantic World* (Chapel Hill, NC, 2006), esp. chaps. 1–3; N. Jardine, J. A. Secord, and E. C. Spary, eds., *Cultures of Natural History* (Cambridge, UK, 1996).

22. Thomas Sprat, *History of the Royal-Society of London*, 1667, quoted in Parrish, *American Curiosity*, 15, 66. See Raymond Phineas Stearns, *Science in the British Colonies of America* (Urbana, IL, 1970); and Frederick E. Brasch, "The Royal Society of London and Its Influence upon Scientific Thought in the American Colonies," *Scientific Monthly* 33 (1931): 336–55, 448–69.

23. Maude Woodfin, "William Byrd and the Royal Society," *Virginia Magazine of History and Biography* 40 (1932): 23–40, 111–23, quotation 121.

24. For sketches of American fellows see Stearns, *Science in the British Colonies*, chaps. 10–11; Silvio Bedini, *Tinkers and Thinkers, Early American Men of Science* (New York, 1975), 73–79.

25. Cotton Mather, *The Christian Philosopher* (1721), ed. Winton U. Solberg (Urbana, IL, 1994), lvii–lxix; on gravity, 89; on progress, 303; on man, 236–318. See Winton U. Solberg, "Science and Religion in Early America: Cotton Mather's 'Christian Philosopher,'" *Church History* 56 (1987): 73–92.

26. Cadwallader Colden to William Douglass, Dec. 1728, in *The Letters and Papers of Cadwallader Colden*, 9 vols. (New York, 1918–37), 1:272. See Alfred R. Hoermann, *Cadwallader Colden: A Figure of the American Enlightenment* (Westport, CT, 2002).

27. Hoermann, *Cadwallader Colden*, 93–98; Bedini, *Tinkers and Thinkers*, 118–21; Cadwallader Colden, *An Explication of the First Causes of Matter and of the Cause of Gravitation* (New York, 1745); and Cadwallader Colden, *The Principles of Action in Matter, the Gravitation of Bodies, and the Motion of the Planets, explained from those Principles* (London, 1751); Thomas Slaughter, *The Natures of John and William Bartram* (New York, 1996).

28. Parrish, *American Curiosity*, 40–45, 190, chaps. 5, 6, 7. On credibility and distortions see Mary Louise Pratt, *Imperial Eyes: Travel Writing and Transculturation* (New York, 1992).

29. See Joyce E. Chaplin, *Benjamin Franklin: First Scientific American* (New York, 2006), chap. 3.

30. Chaplin, *Franklin*, 84–159.

31. Howe, *Making the American Self*, 41. On the popular impact of scientific thinking see Sara Gronim, *Everyday Science: Knowledge of the Natural World in Colonial New York* (New Brunswick, NJ, 2009).

32. William Penn quoted in Richard Blome, *Present State of His Majesties Isles and Territories in America* (London, 1687), 91; Robert Beverly, *History and Present State of Virginia* (orig. 1705; ed. Louis B. Wright, Chapel Hill, NC, 1947), 275–78.

33. John Oldmixon, *The British Empire in America, Containing the History of the Discovery, Settlement, Progress and State of All the British Colonies on the Continent and Islands of America*, 2 vols. (London, 1708), 1:iii–xxxviii; see John Brewer, *The Sinews of Power: War, Money, and the English State* (New York, 1989).

34. Hugh Jones, *Present State of Virginia, from Whence is Inferred a Short View of Maryland and North Carolina* (orig. 1724; ed. Richard L. Morton, Chapel Hill, NC, 1956), 131–35; Alexander Hamilton, *A Gentleman's Itinerarium* (1744), quoted in Alan Taylor, *American Colonies* (New York, 2001), 313; Peter Kalm, *Travels into North America*, 2nd ed., 2 vols. (London, 1772), 1, 26–27, 48–55, 97–98, 194–95, 211–12, 307–8; Andrew Burnaby, *Travels through the Middle Settlements of North-America in the years 1759 and 1760, with Observations Upon the State of the Colonies* (orig. 1775; 2nd ed. repr. Ithaca, NY, 1960), 53–54, 73, 81, 89, 100–104.

35. Oldmixon, *British Empire*, 1:161; Beverly, *History*, 233; Cadwallader Colden, *History of the Five Indian Nations Depending on the Province of New York in America* (orig. 1717; repr. Ithaca, NY, 1964), quoted in Hoermann, *Cadwallader Colden*, 167. On walking purchase see Erik Hinderaker, *Elusive Empires: Constructing Colonialism in the Ohio Valley* (Cambridge, UK, 1997), chaps. 3–4; Daniel K. Richter, *Trade, Land, Power* (Philadelphia, 2013), chap. 8.

36. See Alan Kulikoff, *Tobacco and Slaves: Development of Southern Cultures in the Chesapeake, 1680–1800* (Chapel Hill, NC, 1986); T. H. Breen, *Tobacco Culture: The Mentality of the Great Tidewater Planters on the Eve of Revolution* (Princeton, 1985). Population statistics from John J. McCusker and Russell Menard, *The Economy of British North America*, 2nd ed. (Chapel Hill, NC, 1991), 153, 136.

37. Burnaby, *Travels*, 14, 22–24, 27; Jones, *State of Virginia*, 129–45.

38. Taylor, *American Colonies*, 307; McCusker and Menard, *Economy of British North America*, 54. Turner's original formula can be seen in Frederick Jackson Turner, "The Significance of the Frontier in American History," *Report of the American Historical Association*, 1893, 199–227.

39. For an introduction to this literature see Drew R. McCoy, *Elusive Republic* (Chapel Hill, NC, 1981), chap. 1; for a detailed analysis see Ronald Meek, *Social Science and the Ignoble Savage* (Cambridge, UK, 1976).

40. See J. E. Crowley, *This Sheba Self: The Conceptualization of Economic Life in Eighteenth-Century America* (Baltimore, 1974); Albert O. Hirschman, *Passions and the Interests: Political Arguments for Capitalism Before Its Triumph* (Princeton, 1977); J. G. A. Pocock, *The Machiavellian Moment: Florentine Political Thought and the Atlantic Republican Tradition* (Princeton, 1975); Isaac Kramnick, *Bolingbroke and His Circle* (Cambridge, MA, 1968).

41. See T. H. Breen, *The Marketplace of Revolution: How Consumer Politics Shaped American Independence* (New York, 2005); Marc Egnal, *A Mighty Empire: The Roots of the American Revolution* (Ithaca, NY, 1988); John Brewer, *The Pleasures of the Imagination* (New York, 1997).

42. Benjamin Franklin, "Observations Concerning the Increase of Mankind," in Benjamin Franklin, *Papers of Benjamin Franklin*, ed. Leonard Woods Labaree, William B. Willcox, and Barbara Oberg, 42 vols. to date (New Haven, CT, 1959–2017), 4:225–34.

43. William Smith, *Some Thoughts on Education with Reason for Erecting a College in This Province and fixing the same at the City of New York* (New York, 1752), v–vii, 18–19, 23–24.

44. Burnaby, *Travels*, 110–14; Kalm, *Travels*, 1:149.

Chapter 4

1. See Richard Beeman, *The Variety of Political Experience in Eighteenth-Century America* (Philadelphia, 2004); John M. Murrin, "The Great Inversion," (orig. 1980), repr. in Andrew Shankman, ed., *Rethinking America: From Empire to Republic* (New York, 2018), 31–98; and T. H. Breen, *The Marketplace of Revolution: How Consumer Politics Shaped American Independence* (New York, 2004).

2. Bernard Bailyn, *Origins of American Politics* (New York, 1968), 11; Bernard Bailyn, *The Ideological Origins of the American Revolution* (Cambridge, MA, 1967), 26. Originally prepared as the introduction to the (never completed) six-volume *Pamphlets of the American Revolution, 1750–1776*, ed. Bernard Bailyn and Jane N. Garrett (Cambridge, MA, 1965), comprising seventy-two annotated documents, Bailyn's essay alone redirected scholarship for the next forty years.

3. See C. Bradley Thompson, *John Adams and the Spirit of Liberty* (Lawrence, KS, 1998), esp. the bibliography, 327–31; and Gordon S. Wood, *The Creation of the American Republic, 1776–1787* (Chapel Hill, NC, 1969), chap. 14. For Adams's biography see David McCullough, *John Adams* (New York, 2002).

4. John Adams, "Dissertations on the Canon and the Feudal Law," (1765), in Gordon S. Wood, ed., *John Adams, Revolutionary Writings, 1755–1775* (New York, 2011), 114–23, 130–36, quotations 115, 117.

5. For context see Edmund S. Morgan and Helen M. Morgan, *The Stamp Act Crisis: Prologue to Revolution* (Chapel Hill, NC, 1953).

6. *The Charters of the following Provinces of North America [. . .] to which is prefixed A Faithful Narrative of the Proceedings of the North American Colonies in Consequence of the late Stamp-Act* (London, 1766), 2, (hereafter cited as *Faithful Narrative of the Stamp Act*).

7. Quoted in Wood, *Creation*, 52; John Adams, "Draft of an Essay on Power," Aug. 29, 1763, in Wood, *Revolutionary Writings*, 88–90. See also Robert A. Smith, *Eighteenth-Century English Politics: Patrons and Place-Hunters* (New York, 1972).

8. John Adams to Abigail Adams, July 3, 1776, in Lyman H. Butterfield et al., *Adams Family Correspondence*, 13 vols. to date (Cambridge, MA, 1963–2017), 2:27–31.

9. For the general story work backward from Alan Taylor, *American Revolutions: A Continental History, 1750–1804* (New York, 2016); Jack N. Rakove, *Revolutionaries: A New History of the Invention of America* (Boston, 2010); Robert Middlekauff, *The Glorious Cause: The American Revolution, 1763–1789*, rev. ed. (New York, 2005); Gary B. Nash, *The Unknown American Revolution: The Unruly Birth of Democracy and the Struggle to Create America* (New York, 2006); and Gordon S. Wood, *Radicalism of the American Revolution: How a Revolution Transformed a Monarchical Society into a Democratic One Unlike Any That Had Ever Existed* (New York, 1992).

10. *Faithful Narrative of the Stamp Act*, 1; Virginia, Pennsylvania, Maryland, and Connecticut responses reprinted in Edmund S. Morgan, ed., *Prologue to Revolution: Sources and*

Documents on the Stamp Act Crisis, 1764–1766 (Chapel Hill, NC, 1959), 47, 51, 52–56; John Adams, "Braintree Instructions," Oct. 10, 1765, in Wood, *Revolutionary Writings*, 125–28.

11. *Faithful Narrative of the Stamp Act*, 1–18, quotations 3, 6, 10.

12. Ibid., 18.

13. See Dirk Hoerder, "Boston Leaders and Boston Crowds, 1765–1776," in Alfred F. Young, ed., *The American Revolution: Explorations in the History of American Radicalism* (DeKalb, IL, 1976), 233–71; Alfred F. Young, *The Shoemaker and the Teaparty: Memory and the American Revolution* (Boston, 1999), 33–34, 93–96, 102; Alfred F. Young, "Ebenezer Mackintosh: Boston's Captain General of the Liberty Tree," in Alfred F. Young, Gary B. Nash, and Ray Raphael, eds., *Revolutionary Founders: Rebels, Radicals, and Reformers in the Making of the Nation* (New York, 2011), 15–33. See also Alfred F. Young and Gregory H. Nobles, *Whose American Revolution Was It? Historians Interpret the Founding* (New York, 2011).

14. See Robert A. Gross, *The Minutemen and Their World* (New York, 1976); Woody Holton, *Forced Founders: Indians, Debtors, Slaves, and the Making of the American Revolution in Virginia* (Chapel Hill, NC, 1999), esp. chap. 3; Terry Bouton, *Taming Democracy: "The People," the Founders, and the Troubled Ending of the American Revolution* (New York, 2007); Edward Countryman, *A People in Revolution: The American Revolution and Political Society in New York, 1760–1790* (Baltimore, 1981), chaps. 2–3; Jesse Lemisch, *Jack Tar and John Bull: The Role of New York's Seamen in Precipitating the Revolution* (New York, 1997); Paul A. Gilje, *Liberty on the Waterfront: American Maritime Culture in the Age of Revolution* (Philadelphia, 2004), chap. 4; Richard Alan Ryerson, *The Revolution Is Now Begun: The Radical Committees of Philadelphia, 1765–1776* (Philadelphia, 1978), chap. 2; A. Roger Ekirch, *Poor Carolina: Politics and Society in Colonial North Carolina, 1729–1776* (Chapel Hill, NC, 1981), esp. chaps. 5–6.

15. Two letters signed "Rusticus," one in the *Pennsylvania Journal*, Nov. 3, 1773, and the second published as a broadside (surviving copy reprinted in New York, Dec. 4, 1773), in Paul Leicester Ford, ed., *The Writings of John Dickinson*, vol. 1, *Political Writings, 1764–1774* (Philadelphia, 1895), distributed as vol. 14 of *Historical Society of Pennsylvania Memoirs*, 457–64.

16. See Countryman, *A People in Revolution*, 39–41; Young, *Shoemaker and the Teaparty*, 99–107.

17. [Thomas Jefferson], *Summary View of the Rights of British America. Set forth in some Resolutions intended for the Inspection of the Present Delegates of the People of Virginia Now in Convention* (Philadelphia, 1774), 5–7, 12–14, 20, 22–23. On radical committees see also Willi Paul Adams, *The First American Constitutions: Republican Ideology and the Making of the State Constitutions in the Revolutionary Era*, trans. Rita Kimber and Robert Kimber, expanded ed. (Lanham, MD, 2001), chap. 1; and Richard D. Brown, *Revolutionary Politics in Massachusetts: The Boston Committee of Correspondence and the Towns, 1772–1774* (Cambridge, MA, 1970).

18. On republicanism see Bailyn, *Ideological Origins*, chaps. 3–4; Wood, *Radicalism*, part 2; J. G. A. Pocock, *The Machiavellian Moment: Florentine Political Thought and the Atlantic Republican Tradition* (Princeton, 1975); and Daniel Rodgers, "Republicanism: The Career of a Concept," *Journal of American History* 79 (1992): 11–38. For the complex understanding of the concept of liberty in eighteenth-century British America, see Michal Jan Rozbicki, *Culture and Liberty in the Age of the American Revolution* (Charlottesville, VA, 2011). On slavery as a metaphor see Eric Foner, *The Story of American Freedom* (New York, 1998), 29–37.

19. "Suffolk Resolves," *Journals of the Continental Congress, 1774–1789*, 34 vols. (Washington, DC, 1904–37), 1:32–37, quotation 32–33.

20. See T. H. Breen, *American Insurgents, American Patriots: The Revolution of the People* (New York, 2010), chap. 6; Gross, *Minutemen*, chap. 5.

21. "Declaration [. . .] Setting Forth the Causes and Necessity of their taking up Arms" (drafted by Thomas Jefferson and John Dickinson), *Journals of the Continental Congress*, 2:140–57, quotation 154.

22. [Thomas Paine], *Common Sense* (1776), in Philip S. Foner, ed., *The Complete Writings of Thomas Paine*, 2 vols. (New York, 1945), 1:4–39, quotations 25, 30.

23. *Declaration of Independence*, July 4, 1776. For a fine-grained history of the independence decision see Pauline Maier, *American Scripture: Making the Declaration of Independence* (New York, 1997); for another interpretation see Danielle Allen, *Our Declaration: A Reading of the Declaration of Independence in Defense of Equality* (New York, 2014).

24. Quoted in David Hackett Fischer, *Liberty and Freedom: A Visual History of America's Founding Ideas* (New York, 2005), 1–2.

25. T. H. Breen, "Samuel Thompson's War: The Career of an American Insurgent," in Young, Nash, and Raphael, *Revolutionary Founders*, 53–66; see also Breen, *American Insurgents*, chaps. 7–8.

26. Gary B. Nash, "Philadelphia's Radical Caucus That Propelled Pennsylvania to Independence and Democracy," in Young, Nash, and Raphael, *Revolutionary Founders*, 67–85.

27. See Robert McDonnell, *The Politics of War: Race, Class, and Conflict in Revolutionary Virginia* (Chapel Hill, 2007); Holton, *Forced Founders*; and Rhys Isaac, *The Transformation of Virginia, 1740–1790* (Chapel Hill, 1982), esp. chaps. 8–11.

28. Ekirch, *Poor Carolina*, 210–11, see chaps. 5–7; also Roger Ekirch, "Whig Authority and Public Order in Backcountry North Carolina, 1776–1783," in Ronald Hoffman, Thad W. Tate, and Peter J. Albert, eds., *An Uncivil War: The Southern Backcountry During the American Revolution* (Charlottesville, VA, 1985), 99–124; and Jeffrey J. Crow, "Liberty Men and Loyalists: Disorder and Disaffection in the North Carolina Backcountry," in Hoffman, Tate, and Albert, *Uncivil War*, 125–78.

29. Ray Raphael, *A People's History of the American Revolution: How Common People Shaped the Fight for Independence* (New York, 2001), 246, see chap. 6; also see Gary B. Nash, "The African Americans' Revolution," in Edward C. Gray and Jane Kamenski, eds., *Oxford Handbook of the American Revolution* (New York, 2012), 250–70; and Alan Taylor, *The Internal Enemy: Slavery and War in Virginia, 1772–1832* (New York, 2013), 28–29. On the hopes of African Americans see James Oliver Horton and Lois E. Horton, *In Hope of Liberty: Culture, Community, and Protest Among Northern Free Blacks, 1700–1860* (New York, 1997); and Douglas Egerton, *Gabriel's Rebellion* (Chapel Hill, NC, 1993). The number of black loyalists is from Maya Jasanoff, *Liberty's Exiles: American Loyalists in the Revolutionary World* (New York, 2011), 351–52; see also Jerry Bannister and Liam Riordan, eds., *The Loyal Atlantic: Remaking the British Atlantic in the Revolutionary Era* (Toronto, 2012), 21.

30. See Teresa Anne Murphy, *Citizenship and the Origins of Women's History in the United States* (Philadelphia, 2013); Rosemarie Zagarri, *Revolutionary Backlash: Women and Politics in the Early American Republic* (Philadelphia, 2007); and Carol Berkin, *Revolutionary Mothers: Women in the Struggle for America's Independence* (New York, 2005).

31. See Robert M. Calhoon, "Loyalism and Neutrality," in Jack P. Greene and J. R. Pole, eds., *Blackwell's Companion to the American Revolution* (Oxford, UK, 2000), 235–47; Jerry Bannister and Liam Riordan, "Loyalists and the British Atlantic, 1660–1840," in Bannister and

Riordan, *The Loyal Atlantic*, 3–36; Paul H. Smith, "The American Loyalists: Notes on Their Organization and Numerical Strength," *William and Mary Quarterly*, 3rd ser., 25 (Apr. 1968): 259–77; Trenton Cole Jones, "'The Rage of Tory-Hunting': Loyalist Prisoners, Civil War, and the Violence of American Independence," *Journal of Military History* 81 (July 2017): 719–46.

32. John Adams, "Thoughts on Government" (1776), in John Adams, *The Papers of John Adams*, ed. Robert J. Taylor et al., 17 vols. to date (Cambridge, MA, 1977–2014), 4:85–93, and see various private letter versions, 73–84; John Adams to Richard Henry Lee, Nov. 15, 1775, ibid., 3:307–8.

33. John Adams to Mercy Otis Warren, Apr. 16, 1776, in Adams, *Papers*, 4:124–25; see Countryman, *American Revolution* (New York, 1985), 138. On class, character, and representation see Wood, *Creation*, chap. 5; and Wood, "Interests and Disinterestedness in the Making of the Constitution," in Richard Beeman, Stephen Botein, and Edward C. Carter II, eds., *Beyond Confederation: Origins of the Constitution and American National Identity* (Chapel Hill, NC, 1987), 69–109.

34. Quoted in Woody Holton, *Unruly Americans and the Origins of the Constitution* (New York, 2007), 109. State constitutions can be found on the website of the Avalon Project, Yale Law School at http://avalon.law.yale.edu/subject_menus/18th.asp; W. Adams, *First American Constitutions*, usefully analyzes these stories in a number of different registers.

35. W. Adams, *First American Constitutions*, 198–99; property qualifications for each state are collected in an appendix, 315–27.

36. William Thompson quoted in Wood, *Creation*, 482–83; see Gross, *Minutemen*, 163–64; Maryland Constitution of 1776, art. 2, accessed Mar. 28, 2019, http://avalon.law .yale.edu/17th_century/ma02.asp; Pennsylvania Constitution of 1776, sec. 7, accessed Mar. 28, 2019, http://avalon.law.yale.edu/18th_century/pa08.asp.

37. Edmund Morgan, *Inventing the People: The Rise of Popular Sovereignty in England and America* (New York, 1988), esp. part 3.

38. See Peter S. Onuf, *The Origins of the Federal Republic: Jurisdictional Controversies in the United States, 1775–1787* (Philadelphia, 1983).

39. See *Articles of Confederation*, accessed Mar. 28, 2019, http://avalon.law.yale.edu/ 18th_century/artconf.aspquotation, Articles 2 and 10.

40. For an excellent judicious summary of the economic struggles during and after the War for Independence see Cathy Matson, "The Revolution, Constitution, and New Nation," in Stanley L. Engerman and Robert E. Gallman, eds., *Cambridge Economic History of the United States*, 3 vols. (Cambridge, UK, 1996–2000), 3:363–401; see also John J. McCusker and Russell R. Menard, *The Economy of British America, 1607–1789*, 2nd ed. (Chapel Hill, NC, 1991), esp. chap. 17.

41. See Robert A. Becker, "Currency, Taxation, and Finance, 1775–1787," in Greene and Pole, *Blackwell's Companion to the American Revolution*, 388–97. On the history of taxes see Robin L. Einhorn, *American Taxation, American Slavery* (Chicago, 2006), chaps. 1–3.

42. See Holton, *Unruly Americans*, 131–32.

43. See Matson, "Revolution," 367–68. Numbers are offered only as orders of magnitude; precise accounting is misleading, and economists disagree wildly about the scope and value of these debt obligations and currencies, making it difficult to cite "objective" statistics. See John J. McCusker, *How Much Is That in Real Money?* (Worcester, MA, 1992); John L. Smith, "How Was the Revolutionary War Paid For?" accessed Nov. 13, 2015, http://allthings

liberty.com/2015/02/how-was-the-revolutionary-war-paid-for/. McCusker, *Real Money*, 333, lists dollar-sterling rates at roughly three-to-one. See Holton, *Unruly Americans*, 37–38 for distribution of bondholders by 1790.

44. Holton, *Unruly Americans*, 55–64. See Pauline Maier, *Ratification: The People Debate the Constitution, 1787–1788* (New York, 2010), 1–26; Richard Beeman, *Plain, Honest Men: The Making of the American Constitution* (New York, 2009); Joseph Ellis, *The Quartet: Orchestrating the Second American Revolution, 1783–1789* (New York, 2015); and Edward J. Larson, *The Return of George Washington* (New York, 2014).

45. See Countryman, *American Revolution*, 184–86.

46. Thomas Jefferson to James Madison, Jan. 30, 1787, in J. C. A. Stagg, ed., *The Papers of James Madison, Digital Edition* (Charlottesville, VA, 2010); George Washington to Henry Lee Jr., Oct. 31, 1786, in Theodore J. Crackel, ed., *Washington Papers, Digital Edition* (Charlottesville, VA, 2008); David P. Szatmary, *Shays' Rebellion: The Making of an Agrarian Insurrection* (Amherst, MA, 1980); and John K. Alexander, *Samuel Adams: America's Revolutionary Politician* (Lanham, MD, 2002), 202–3.

47. One of the most evocative versions of this story is in Wood, *Creation*, chap. 12 entitled "The Worthy Against the Licentious." Compare Beeman, *Plain, Honest Men*; and Jack N. Rakove, *Revolutionaries: A New History of the Invention of America* (Boston, 2010), chap. 8.

48. James Madison, "Vices of the Political System of the United States (Apr. 1787)," in Stagg, *The Papers of James Madison, Digital Edition*.

49. George Washington to President of Congress, Sept. 17, 1787, in Crackel, *The Papers of George Washington, Digital Edition*; Samuel Adams to Richard Henry Lee, quoted in Alexander, *Samuel Adams*, 203; for Wilson see Morgan, *Inventing the People*, 281.

50. James Madison to Thomas Jefferson, Feb. 19, 1788, in Stagg, *The Papers of James Madison, Digital Edition*. Maier, *Ratification*, charts the process in grass-roots detail, an achievement made possible by the heroic efforts of John Kaminski, Gaspar Saladino, and their assistants at the Wisconsin Ratification Project that produced Merrill Jensen, John P. Kaminski, and Gaspar J. Saladino, eds., *Documentary History of the Ratification of the Constitution*, 26 vols. to date (Madison, WI, 1976–2015).

51. Richard Price, *Importance of the American Revolution* (Boston, 1784), 1–9, 57–70, quotations 7, 4, 5, 8, 64, 63, 57, 59.

52. See Rosemarie Zagarri, "Suffrage and Representation," in Greene and Pole, *Blackwell's Companion to the American Revolution*, 661–67.

53. Robert Morris quoted in W. Adams, *First American Constitutions*, 158.

54. Quoted in W. Adams, *First American Constitutions*, 190.

55. Thomas Jefferson to James Madison, Oct. 28, 1785, in Stagg, *The Papers of James Madison, Digital Edition*. See Seth Cotlar, " 'Every Man Should Have Property': Robert Coram and the American Revolution's Legacy of Economic Populism," in Young, Nash, and Raphael, *Revolutionary Founders*, 337–54.

56. Drew R. McCoy, *Elusive Republic* (Chapel Hill, NC, 1981), 136–45, quotations 140.

57. Ibid., 146–65; also Jonathan Gienapp, *The Second Creation: Fixing the American Constitution in the Founding Era* (Cambridge, MA, 2018); Thomas K. McCraw, *The Founders and Finance: How Hamilton, Gallatin, and Other Immigrants Forged a New Economy* (Cambridge, MA, 2014); John R. Nelson Jr., *Liberty and Property: Political Economy and Policymaking in the New Nation, 1789–1812* (Baltimore, 1987), chap. 2; Cathy D. Matson and Peter S. Onuf, *A*

Union of Interests: Political and Economic Thought in Revolutionary America (Lawrence, KS, 1990), chap. 8.

58. Thomas Jefferson, "Memorandum of Conversations with the President," Mar. 1, 1792, Mar. 11–Apr. 9, 1792, July 10, 1792, in *The Papers of Thomas Jefferson*, ed. Julian Boyd et al., 43 vols. to date (Princeton, 1950–2017), 23:184–90, 258–65, 24:210–11; Thomas Jefferson to George Washington, May 23, 1792, ibid., 23:535–40.

59. McCoy, *Elusive Republic*, 150, 159; Nelson, *Liberty and Property*, chaps. 2–4.

60. Alfred F. Young, *The Democratic Republicans of New York, the Origins, 1763–1797* (Chapel Hill, NC, 1967); Stanley Elkins and Eric McKitrick, *The Age of Federalism* (New York, 1993), chap. 11.

61. See Paul A. Gilje, *The Road to Mobocracy: Popular Disorder in New York City, 1763–1834* (Chapel Hill, NC, 1987).

Chapter 5

1. Quotations from Hugh Henry Breckinridge and Philip Morin Freneau, *A Poem on the Rising Glory of America: Being an Exercise Delivered at the Public Commencement at Nassau-Hall, September 25, 1771*, Literature Online, accessed Feb. 2, 2016, http://literature.proquest .com., quotation lines 717–20; Philip Morin Freneau, *Poems of Philip Freneau, Written Chiefly During the Late War* (Philadelphia, 1786), 42–58, quotations 57–58; [Timothy Dwight], *America: or A Poem on the Settlement of the British Colonies addressed to the Friends of Freedom and their Country* (New Haven, CT, 1780), 9–11; Aaron Hall, *An Oration Delivered at the Request of the Inhabitants of Keene, June 30, 1788; to Celebrate the Ratification of the Federal Constitution by the State of New Hampshire* (Keene, NH, 1788), quotations 6–7, 11. See Eric Wertheimer, "Commencement Ceremonies: History and Identity in 'The Rising Glory of America,' 1771 and 1786," *Early American Literature* 29 (1994): 35–58; and Stephen Adams, "Philip Freneau's Summa of American Exceptionalism: 'The Rising Glory of America' Without Breckenridge," *Texas Studies in Literature and Language* 55 (2013): 390–405. For the big picture see David Waldstreicher, *In the Midst of Perpetual Fetes: The Making of American Nationalism, 1776–1820* (Chapel Hill, NC, 1997).

2. See James D. Drake, *The Nation's Nature: How Continental Presumptions Gave Rise to the United States of America* (Charlottesville, VA, 2011).

3. Jedediah Morse, *The American Geography*, 2nd ed. (London, 1792), iii, ix–xvi, 34–62, 364. For a critical introduction to maps and geography in this period see Martin Bruckner, *The Geographical Revolution in Early America: Maps, Literacy, and National Identity* (Chapel Hill, NC, 2006).

4. Morse, *American Geography*, 193, 161, 168, 202, 212, 240.

5. Ibid., 251, 261. On farming see Richard Lyman Bushman, *The American Farmer in the Eighteenth Century* (New Haven, CT, 2018).

6. Morse, *American* Geography, 252, 262–73, 325–26, 18–19, 313–18.

7. Ibid., 352, 393–96, 402.

8. Ibid., 352, 387–88, 390, 413–17, 432.

9. Ibid., 457, 460–63.

10. Ibid., 469.

11. See *American Husbandry, containing an account of the soil, climate, productions and agriculture of the British Colonies in North America and the West Indies* (orig. 1775; repr., ed. Harry J. Carman, New York, 1939), quotations 61, 93, 106. For discussion of authorship see

ibid., xxxiv–xxxviii. On husbandry see Steven Stoll, *Larding the Lean Earth: Soil and Society in Nineteenth-Century America* (New York, 2002), part 1; also Benjamin Cohen, *Notes from the Ground: Soil, Science, and Society in the American Countryside* (New Haven, CT, 2009).

12. Samuel Deane, *New England Farmer, or Geographical Dictionary. Containing a Compendious Account of the Ways and Methods in which the most Important Art of Husbandry in all its Various Branches is, or may be, Practiced to the Greatest Advantage in this Country* (Worcester, MA, 1790), 6–8; also Nicholas Collin, "An Essay on those Inquiries in Natural Philosophy, which at present are most beneficial to the United States of America," *American Philosophical Society Transactions* 3 (1789): iii–xxvii.

13. Arthur Young, *Letters from His Excellency General Washington to Arthur Young, Esq. F.R.S.* (London, 1801), 2, 31; see George Washington, *The Papers of George Washington*, ed. W. W. Abbot et al., Presidential Series, 19 vols. (Charlottesville, VA, 1987–2016), 1:162; also George Washington, *Diaries of George Washington*, ed. Donald Dean Jackson and Dorothy Twohig, 6 vols. (Charlottesville, VA, 1976–79), 4:1–69 (Sept. through Nov. 1784); and the editorial note on western lands in Washington, *Papers, Confederation Series*, ed. W. W. Abbot, 6 vols. (1992–97) 2:338–56.

14. Young, *Letters from General Washington*, 127–31, followed by Jefferson's long, defensive replies comprising over nine thousand handwritten words, 136–55.

15. William Strickland, *Observations on the Agriculture of the United States of America* (London, 1801), 17, 26, 45; [John Taylor], *Arator* (Georgetown, DC, 1813), 9–11, 96–122, quotation 100. Taylor calls for "standard cart drawn by 4 oxen, and dumps a load on every 10 yard square."

16. See *Arator*, nos. 3–12. Also relevant are 13–14 on slavery, 58 on economy, 60 on rights.

17. James Madison, "Address to the Albemarle Agricultural Society, May 12, 1818," in James Madison, *The Papers of James Madison, Retirement Series*, ed. David B. Mattern et al., 3 vols. to date (Charlottesville, VA, 2009–16), 1:260–85, quotations 270–72, 282; see also editorial notes on 257–58.

18. Stoll, *Larding the Lean Earth*, 40–49.

19. George Washington to Lafayette, July 25, 1785, in Washington, *Papers, Confederation Series*, 3:151–55, quotation 152. See Andrew R. L. Cayton, *Frontier Republic* (Kent, OH, 1986), chaps. 1–3; John R. Van Atta, *Securing the West: Politics, Public Lands, and the Fate of the Old Republic, 1785–1850* (Baltimore, 2014), esp. 1–85.

20. For context see Allan Greer, *Property and Dispossession: Natives, Empires, and Land in Early Modern North America* (Cambridge, UK, 2018); for a global perspective see John C. Weaver, *The Great Land Rush and the Making of the Modern World, 1650–1900* (Montreal, 2013), esp. chaps. 4–7; Andrew R. L. Cayton, " 'Separate Interests' and the Nation-State: The Washington Administration and the Origins of Regionalism in the Trans-Appalachian West," *Journal of American History* 79 (1992): 39–67; Daniel K. Richter, *Trade, Land, Power* (Philadelphia, 2013), chap. 10.

21. Thomas Jefferson to James Madison, Oct. 28, 1785, in Thomas Jefferson, *Papers of Thomas Jefferson*, ed. Julian P. Boyd et al., 43 vols. to date (Princeton, 1950–2017), 8:681–83, quotation 682; also Jefferson to Madison, Nov. 11, 1784, in ibid., 7:503–8. On Jefferson's complex views about land see Christopher Michael Curtis, *Jefferson's Freeholders and the Politics of Ownership in the Old Dominion* (Cambridge, UK, 2012).

22. Julian Boyd's editorial notes, in Jefferson, *Papers*, 6:571–613; "Ordinance of 1784," ibid., 613–16. See Malcolm J. Rohrbough, *The Land Office Business: The Settlement and Administration of American Public Lands, 1789–1837* (New York, 1968), chap. 1.

23. See Rohrbough, *Land Office Business*, chaps. 2–14; Van Atta, *Securing the West*, chap. 3. See generally Bethel Saler, *The Settler's Empire: Colonialism and State Formation in America's Old Northwest* (Philadelphia, 2014); and Erik Hinderaker, *Elusive Empires: Constructing Colonialism in the Ohio Valley* (Cambridge, UK, 1997).

24. Gilbert Imlay, *Topographical Description of the Western Territory of North America [. . .] tending to shew the Probable Rise and Grandeur of the American Empire* (London, 1792), quotations viii, 60, 79–81, 31, 36–37, 88.

25. Imlay, *Topographical Description*, 68–70; Cayton, *Frontier Republic*, 33–50.

26. James Madison to Thomas Jefferson, Aug. 20, 1784, in Jefferson, *Papers*, 7:401–10, quotation 403; Madison to Lafayette, Mar. 20, 1785, in James Madison, *The Papers of James Madison*, ed. William T. Hutchinson et al., 17 vols. (Chicago, 1962–91), 8:251; see Jefferson, *Papers*, 4:203–4, 17:113–25, and passim through 18; Kentucky Petition quoted in Imlay, *Topographical Description*, xii–xiii.

27. See Andrew R. L. Cayton, "'Noble Actors' upon 'the Theatre of Honour': Power and Civility in the Treaty of Greenville," in Andrew R. L. Cayton and Fredrika J. Teute, eds., *Contact Points: American Frontiers from the Mohawk Valley to the Mississippi, 1750–1830* (Chapel Hill, NC, 1998), 235–69.

28. Thomas Jefferson to Robert Livingston, Apr. 18, 1802, in Jefferson, *Papers*, 37, quotation 264. See Peter S. Onuf, "Prologue: Jefferson, Louisiana, and American Nationhood," in Peter J. Kastor and François Weil, eds., *Empires of the Imagination: Transatlantic Histories of the Louisiana Purchase* (Charlottesville, VA, 2009), 23–33; also Richard White, "The Louisiana Purchase and the Fictions of Empire," in Kastor and Weil, *Empires of the Imagination*, 37–61.

29. Dumas Malone, *Jefferson and His Times*, 6 vols. (Boston, 1948–81), 4:297. See Peter J. Kastor, *The Great Acquisition: An Introduction to the Louisiana Purchase* (Great Falls, MT, 2004); and John Kukla, *A Wilderness So Immense: The Louisiana Purchase and the Destiny of America* (New York, 2003).

30. [Fisher Ames], in *Columbian Centinel* (Boston), July 13, 1803, quoted in Kukla, *Wilderness So Immense*, 291–92; see John Allen, "Geographical Knowledge and American Images of Louisiana Territory," in James P. Ronda, ed., *Voyages of Discovery: Essays on the Lewis and Clark Expedition* (Helena, MT, 1998), 39–58; Albert Furtwangler, *Acts of Discovery: Visions of America in the Lewis and Clark Journals* (Urbana, IL, 1993).

31. James P. Ronda, "'So Vast an Enterprise': Thoughts on the Lewis and Clark Expedition," in Ronda, *Voyages of Discovery*, 1–25; Thomas Jefferson's instructions to Captain Lewis (June 20, 1803) reproduced in Ronda, *Voyages of Discovery*, 31–38.

32. Gary E. Moulton, ed., *The Lewis and Clark Journals: An American Epic of Discovery*, abridged ed. (Lincoln, NE, 2003), see introduction xiii–lviii; on grizzlies, 108–10; buffalo, 113, 136, 336; spruce, 272–73; Great Falls, 129–30; boiling springs, 354; Indians, 223–24, 368–69. See also Malone, *Jefferson and His Times*, 5:196–212.

33. John Bristed, *The Resources of the United States of America* (New York, 1818), 3–4. See for example Jervis Cutler, *A Topographical Description of the State of Ohio, Indiana Territory, and Louisiana* (orig. 1812; repr. New York, 1971), 1–52, quotations 12, 15, 21, 25. See William Goetzman, *Exploration and Empire: The Explorer and the Scientist in the Winning of the American West* (New York, 1966), chaps. 1–4; James E. Lewis Jr., *The Burr Conspiracy: Uncovering the Story of an Early American Crisis* (Princeton, 2017).

34. Goetzman, *Exploration and Empire*, chap. 2; also Roger L. Nichols and Patrick L. Halley, *Stephen Long and American Frontier Exploration* (Newark, DE, 1980).

35. See F. R. Hassler, "Papers on Various Subjects Connected with the Survey of the Coast of the United States," in *Transactions of the American Philosophical Society*, new ser., 2 (1825): 232–420. By 1837 at least ten states had created "Geological Survey" projects. See Cohen, *Notes from the Ground*, chap. 5; and Forest G. Hill, *Roads, Rails and Waterways: The Army Engineers and Early Transportation* (Norman, OK, 1957).

36. Bristed, *Resources of the United States*, 1–3.

37. Mary Louise Pratt, *Imperial Eyes: Travel Writing and Transculturation* (New York, 1992); Thomas Morton, *New English Canaan* (London, 1632); *For the Colony in Virginea Britannia: Lawes Divine, Morall, and Martiall* (London, 1612), 14.

38. Thomas Jefferson, "First Inaugural Address," Mar. 4, 1801, in James D. Richardson, ed., *Messages and Papers of the Presidents*, 10 vols. (New York, 1897), 1:323; John Quincy Adams, quoted in Harlow G. Unger, *John Quincy Adams* (Boston, 2012), 129. On messianic rhetoric see Nicholas Guyatt, *Providence and the Invention of the United States, 1607–1876* (Cambridge, UK, 2007). Recent global histories have cut deeply into these claims for a unique American experience. See James Belich, *Replenishing the Earth: The Settler Revolution and the Rise of the Anglo-World, 1783–1939* (New York, 2009), chap. 3.

39. See Cayton, "Separate Interests"; Alan Taylor, *Divided Ground: Indians, Settlers, and the Northern Borderland of the American Revolution* (New York, 2006); James Merrill, *The Indians' New World* (Chapel Hill, NC, 1989); Colin G. Calloway, *New Worlds for All* (Baltimore, 1997); Theda Perdue and Michael D. Green, *The Cherokee Nation and the Trail of Tears* (New York, 2007); Laurel Clark Shire, *The Threshold of Manifest Destiny: Gender and National Expansion in Florida* (Philadelphia, 2016); and James E. Lewis Jr., *The American Union and the Problem of Neighborhood, 1783–1829* (Chapel Hill, NC, 1998).

40. See James Horton and Lois Horton, *In Hope of Liberty: Culture, Community, and Protest Among Northern Free Blacks, 1700–1860* (New York, 1997), chaps. 3–5; Alan Taylor, *The Internal Enemy: Slavery and War in Virginia, 1772–1832* (New York, 2014), 100–102; David Heidler and Jeanne Heidler, *Old Hickory's War: Andrew Jackson and the Quest for Empire*, rev. ed. (Baton Rouge, LA, 2003); Adam Rothman, *Slave Country* (Cambridge, MA, 2006); and Robert H. Gudmestad, *A Troubled Commerce: The Transformation of the Interstate Slave Trade* (Baton Rouge, LA, 2003).

41. Peter J. Kastor, *The Nation's Crucible: The Louisiana Purchase and the Creation of America* (New Haven, CT, 2004); Andrew R. L. Cayton, " 'When Shall We Cease to Have Judases?' The Blount Conspiracy and the Limits of the Extended Republic," in Ronald Hoffman and Peter J. Albert, eds., *Launching the Extended Republic* (Charlottesville, VA, 1996), 156–89; Lewis, *The Burr Conspiracy*; Walter Nugent, *Habits of Empire: A History of American Expansion* (New York, 2008), chap. 5.

42. Conevery Bolton Valenčius and Peter J. Kastor, "Sacagawea's 'Cold': Pregnancy and the Written Record of the Lewis and Clark Expedition," *Bulletin of the History of Medicine* 82 (2008): 276–309. See Annette Kolodny, *The Land Before Her: Fantasy and Experience of the American Frontiers, 1630–1860* (Chapel Hill, NC, 1984); and Amy S. Greenberg, *Manifest Manhood and the Antebellum American Empire* (Cambridge, UK, 2005).

43. George Washington to the Chevalier de Chastellux, Oct. 12, 1783, in George Washington, *The Writings of George Washington*, ed. John C. Fitzpatrick, 39 vols. (Washington, DC, 1931–44), 27:189–90.

Chapter 6

1. See various treatments of these issues in Daniel Walker Howe, *What Hath God Wrought: The Transformation of America, 1815–1848* (New York, 2007); Charles Sellers, *The*

Market Revolution: Jacksonian America (New York, 1991); John Lauritz Larson, The Market Revolution in America: Liberty, Ambition, and the Eclipse of the Common Good (Cambridge, UK, 2010); Daniel Feller, Jacksonian Promise: America 1815–1840 (Baltimore, 1995); James Henretta, The Origins of American Capitalism (Boston, 1991); and Harry L. Watson, Liberty and Power, rev. ed. (New York, 2006).

2. See John Lauritz Larson, Internal Improvement: National Public Works and the Promise of Popular Government in the Early United States (Chapel Hill, NC, 2001), esp. chaps. 1–2.

3. George Washington to Benjamin Harrison, Oct. 10, 1784, in George Washington, The Writings of George Washington, ed. John C. Fitzpatrick, 39 vols. (Washington, DC, 1931–44), 37:475; also George Washington, The Diaries of George Washington, ed. Donald Jackson and Dorothy Towhig, 6 vols. (Charlottesville, VA, 1976–79), 6:57–68. See Joel Achenbach, The Grand Idea: George Washington's Potomac and the Race to the West (New York, 2004); Ronald E. Shaw, Canals for a Nation (Lexington, KY, 1990).

4. Larson, Internal Improvement, 20–37.

5. Charles Royster, Light-Horse Harry Lee and the Legacy of the American Revolution (Cambridge, UK, 1981), chap. 5; Adam Smith, An Inquiry into the Nature and Causes of the Wealth of Nations (orig. 1776; Modern Library ed., New York, 1937), book 5; Larson, Internal Improvement, chap. 3.

6. Gerard Koeppel, Bond of Union: Building the Erie Canal and the American Empire (Cambridge, MA, 2009), 8–9, 236–46. See Carol Sheriff, Artificial River: The Erie Canal and the Paradox of Progress (New York, 1996); Nathan Miller, The Enterprise of a Free People: Aspects of Economic Development in New York During the Canal Period, 1792–1838 (Ithaca, NY, 1962); Robert G. Albion, The Rise of New York Port (orig. 1939; repr. Boston, 1984).

7. New York congressman Peter B. Porter, quoted in Miller, Enterprise of a Free People, 7. For state studies see Oscar Handlin and Mary Flug Handlin, Commonwealth: A Study in the Role of Government in the American Economy, 1774–1861 (Cambridge, MA, 1969); Louis Harts, Economic Policy and Democratic Thought in Pennsylvania, 1776–1860 (Cambridge, MA, 1948); Ray L. Gunn, Decline of Authority: Public Economic Policy and Political Development in New York, 1800–1860 (Ithaca, NY, 1988); John Majewski, A House Dividing: Economic Development in Pennsylvania and Virginia Before the Civil War (Cambridge, UK, 2006); Brian Phillips Murphy, Building the Empire State: Political Economy in the Early Republic (Philadelphia, 2015).

8. Paul B. Trescott, "The Louisville and Portland Canal Company, 1825–1874," Journal of American History 44 (Mar. 1958): 686–708.

9. Louis C. Hunter, Steamboats on the Western Rivers (Cambridge, MA, 1949); see also Andrea Sutcliffe, Steam: The Untold Story of America's First Great Invention (New York, 2004); and Robert H. Gudmestad, Steamboats and the Rise of the Cotton Kingdom (Baton Rouge, LA, 2011).

10. Allan Pred, Urban Growth and the Circulation of Information: The United States System of Cities, 1790–1840 (Cambridge, MA, 1973), 74; Albert Fishlow, "Internal Transportation in the Nineteenth and Early Twentieth Centuries," in Stanley L. Engerman and Robert E. Gallman, eds., Cambridge Economic History of the United States, 3 vols. (Cambridge, UK, 2000), 2:565; Ronald E. Shaw, Canals for a Nation (Lexington, KY, 1990), 230.

11. Hunter, Steamboats on Western Rivers, 266; see also Howe, What Hath God Wrought, chap. 6.

12. On early technology see Franz Anton Ritter von Gerstner, *Early American Railroads*, ed. Frederick C. Gamst, trans. David J. Diephouse and John C. Decker (orig. 1842–43; Stanford, CA, 1997); John Lauritz Larson, *Bonds of Enterprise: John Murray Forbes and Western Development in America's Railway Age* (Cambridge, MA, 1984), esp. chaps. 2–4.; James D. Dilts, *The Great Road: The Building of the Baltimore and Ohio Railroad* (Stanford, CA, 1993).

13. Quoted in James A. Ward, *Railroads and the American Character, 1820–1887* (Knoxville, TN, 1986), 19–21, 112; Missouri senator Thomas Hart Benton, Feb. 7, 1849, *Congressional Globe*, 30th Cong., 2nd Sess. 474. See Craig Miner, *A Most Magnificent Machine: America Adopts the Railroad, 1825–1862* (Lawrence, KS, 2010); and Zachary Callen, *Railroads and American Political Development: Infrastructure, Federalism, and State Building* (Lawrence, KS, 2016).

14. See Morton J. Horwitz, *The Transformation of American Law, 1780–1860* (Cambridge, MA, 1977); William J. Novak, *The People's Welfare: Law and Regulation in Nineteenth-Century America* (Chapel Hill, NC, 1996).

15. See Murray Rothbard, *The Panic of 1819: Reactions and Policies* (New York, 1962), 37–80; Royster, *Light-Horse Harry Lee*, 183–85; Jessica Lepler, *The Many Panics of 1837* (Cambridge, UK, 2013), chaps. 4–5.

16. Albert Gallatin, *Report of the Secretary of the Treasury on Roads and Canals* (1808), in American State Papers, Miscellaneous, 2 vols. (Washington, DC, 1832–61), 1:724–920. Gallatin's report contains example charters. See pp. 886–89 for Germantown Turnpike tolls quoted above.

17. Stanley I. Kutler, *Privilege and Creative Destruction: The Charles River Bridge Case* (New York, 1971).

18. Kermit Hall, *The Magic Mirror: Law in American History* (New York, 1989), 96–99; Horwitz, *Transformation of American Law*, 111–30; Ronald Seavoy, *Origins of the American Business Corporation* (Santa Barbara, CA, 1982), chaps. 3–4.

19. Horwitz, *Transformation of American Law*, 37, 43–47; see also Pauline Maier, "The Revolutionary Origins of the American Business Corporation," *William and Mary Quarterly*, 3rd ser., 50 (1993): 51–84.

20. See Edward Balleisen, *Navigating Failure: Bankruptcy and Commercial Society in Antebellum America* (Chapel Hill, NC, 2001), chaps. 4–5.

21. Novak, *The People's Welfare*, 90; J. Willard Hurst, *Law and the Conditions of Freedom in the Nineteenth-Century United States* (Madison, WI, 1956), chap. 1.

22. Phyllis Deane, *The First Industrial Revolution*, 2nd ed. (Cambridge, UK, 1980), 87–102; David Jeremy, *Transatlantic Industrial Revolution: The Diffusion of Textile Technologies Between Britain and America, 1790–1830s* (Cambridge, MA, 1981), chaps. 4–5; Bruce Laurie, *Artisans into Workers: Labor in Nineteenth-Century America* (New York, 1989), 15–46.

23. *One Thousand Valuable Secrets* (Philadelphia, 1795); Jacob Johnson, *Book of Trades*, American ed., 3 vols. (Philadelphia, 1807); James Smith, *The Mechanic, or, Compendium of Practical Inventions*, 2 vols. (Liverpool, 1816); George G. Carey, *The Artisan; or, Mechanic's Instructor*, 2 vols. (London, c. 1825). These and many others can be found in the marvelous collections of the Library Company of Philadelphia. See also William Rorabaugh, *The Craft Apprentice* (New York, 1986), esp. chap. 2.

24. John R. Nelson Jr., *Liberty and Property: Political Economy and Policymaking in the New Nation, 1789–1812* (Baltimore, 1987), esp. chaps. 2–5; Gary J. Kornblith, "Cementing the Mechanic Interest: Origins of the Providence Association of Mechanics and Manufacturers," *Journal of the Early Republic* 8 (1988): 355–87.

25. Bruce Sinclair, *Philadelphia's Philosopher Mechanics: A History of the Franklin Institute* (Baltimore, 1974), 2; Academy of Natural Sciences in Philadelphia, Academy Minutes, founding resolution and draft constitution, Jan. 25, 1812, ANSP Coll. 527 #1; William Maclure, "Observations on the Geology of the United States of North America," in *Transactions of the American Philosophical Society*, new ser., 1 (1818): 1–91; Franklin Institute, *Journal*, Jan., 1828, 67–68.

26. Jacob Bigelow, "Inaugural Address Delivered in the Chapel at Cambridge, Dec. 11, 1816," *North American Review and Miscellaneous Journal* 4 (Jan. 1817): 270–83, quotations 272. The twenty-nine-year-old Bigelow had just been named to the Rumford Chair for the Application of Science to the Useful Arts at Harvard. In stark contrast to Bigelow, Ben Franklin worried to the end of his days (1790) that progress *past* the agrarian "third stage" would wreck the American platform on which revolutionary republicanism was being staged. See Gordon S. Wood, *The Americanization of Benjamin Franklin* (New York, 2004).

27. Ben Wattenberg, ed., *A Statistical History of the United States* (New York, 1976), 8, 97, 106, 430.

28. See James Henretta, "Families and Farms: 'Mentalité' in Pre-Industrial America," *William and Mary Quarterly*, 3rd ser., 35 (Jan. 1978): 3–32; Michael Merrill, "Cash Is Good to Eat: Self-Sufficiency and Exchange in the Rural Economy of the United States," *Radical History Review* 4 (1977): 42–71; James Henretta, "The 'Market' in the Early Republic," *Journal of the Early Republic* 18 (1998): 289–304.

29. Paul E. Johnson, *A Shopkeepers' Millennium: Society and Revivals in Rochester, New York, 1815–1837* (New York, 1978), chaps. 1–2.

30. Ibid.

31. Sean Wilentz, *Chants Democratic: New York City and the Rise of the American Working Class, 1788–1830* (New York, 1984), chap. 3; also Howard Rock, Paul A. Gilje, and Robert Asher, eds., *American Artisans: Crafting Society Identity, 1750–1850* (Baltimore, 1995). For excellent examples of this process of change see Martin Bruegel, *Farm, Shop, Landing: The Rise of a Market Economy in the Hudson Valley, 1780–1860* (Durham, NC, 2002); Joan Jenson, *Loosening the Bonds: Mid-Atlantic Farm Women, 1750–1850* (New Haven, CT, 1986); Christopher Clark, *Roots of Rural Capitalism: Western Massachusetts, 1780–1860* (Ithaca, NY, 1990); Sally McMurry, *Transforming Rural Life: Dairying Families and Agricultural Change, 1820–1885* (Baltimore, 1995); and Seth Rockman, *Scraping By: Wage Labor, Slavery, and Survival in Early Baltimore* (Baltimore, 2009).

32. Merritt Roe Smith, *Harpers Ferry Armory and the New Technology* (Ithaca, NY, 1977), esp. chap. 8; Barbara M. Tucker and Kenneth H. Tucker Jr., *Industrializing Antebellum America: The Rise of Manufacturing Entrepreneurs in the Early Republic* (New York, 2008), chaps. 1–3.

33. See Tucker and Tucker, *Industrializing Antebellum America*, chaps. 4–7.

34. Thomas Dublin, *Women at Work: The Transformation of Work and Community in Lowell, Massachusetts, 1826–1860*, 2nd ed. (New York, 1993), esp. chaps. 6 and 8.

35. On the misattribution to Eli Whitney see Angela Lakwete, *Inventing the Cotton Gin: Machine and Myth in Antebellum America* (Baltimore, 2003).

36. See Walter Johnson, *River of Dark Dreams: Slavery and Empire in the Cotton Kingdom* (Cambridge, MA, 2013), chaps. 7–10; Edward Baptist, *The Half Has Not Been Told: Slavery and*

the Making of American Capitalism (New York, 2014), chaps. 4, 7–9; and Sven Beckert and Seth Rockman, eds., *Slavery's Capitalism: A New History of American Economic Development* (Philadelphia, 2016). For southern labor see Charles B. Dew, *Bond of Iron: Master and Slave at Buffalo Forge* (New York, 1994); Michele Gillespie, *Free Labor in an Unfree World: White Artisans in Slaveholding Georgia, 1790–1860* (Athens, GA, 2000); K. L. Merritt, *Masterless Men: Poor Whites and Slavery in the Antebellum South* (Cambridge, UK, 2018); and Robert Starobin, *Industrial Slavery in the Old South* (New York, 1970). For a discussion of "Second Slavery" and the Old South see Anthony E. Kaye, "The Second Slavery: Modernity in the Nineteenth-Century South and the Atlantic World," *Journal of Southern History* 65 (Aug. 2009): 627–50.

37. Richard R. John, *Spreading the News: The American Postal System from Franklin to Morse* (Cambridge, MA, 1995), 4, 37, 1.

38. Stephen Mihm, *A Nation of Counterfeiters* (Cambridge, MA, 2007), 180; Sharon Ann Murphy, *Other People's Money: How Banking Worked in the Early Republic* (Baltimore, 2017), 60–62; William H. Dillistin, *Bank Note Reporters and Counterfeit Detectors, 1826–1866* (New York, 1949); Rowena Olegario, *The Engine of Enterprise: Credit in America* (Cambridge, MA, 2016); Brian Luskey, *On the Make: Clerks and the Quest for Capital in Nineteenth-Century America* (New York, 2010). On credit reporting see Howe, *What Hath God Wrought*, 223.

39. Albion, *Rise of New York Port*, chap. 3.

40. Ibid., chap. 5; see also William Pease and Jane Pease, *The Web of Progress: Private Values and Public Styles in Boston and Charleston, 1828–1843* (New York, 1985).

41. Howe, *What Hath God Wrought*, 1–4, 690–99; Richard John, "Politics of Innovation," *Daedalus* 127 (1998): 187–214; Alfred D. Chandler Jr., *The Visible Hand: The Managerial Revolution in American Business* (Cambridge, MA, 1977), chaps. 3, 4, and 6.

42. Albion, *Rise of New York Port*, passim.

43. Amasa Walker, *An Address Delivered Before the Young Men of Boston, Associated for Moral and Intellectual Improvement* (Boston, 1833), 7.

44. Ibid., 10, 8, 12–13, 18–19, 27–28, 31.

45. Carl F. Kaestle, *Pillars of the Republic: Common Schools and American Society, 1780–1860* (New York, 1983); David Tyack and Elizabeth Hansot, *Managers of Virtue: Public School Leadership in America, 1820–1890* (New York, 1986); and Michael B. Katz, *Reconstructing American Education* (Cambridge, MA, 1989).

46. Catherine Beecher, *The Duty of American Women to Their Country* (New York, 1845), 33, 34, 37. See Kathryn Kish Sklar, *Catherine Beecher: A Study in Domesticity* (New Haven, CT, 1973).

47. Carl Bode, *The American Lyceum* (Oxford, UK, 1956); Lawrence Foster, *Women, Family, and Utopia: Communal Experiments of the Shakers, the Oneida Community, and the Mormons* (Syracuse, NY, 1991); Leonard Richards, *Gentlemen of Property and Standing: Anti-Abolitionist Mobs in Jacksonian America* (New York, 1971).

48. Thomas Cooper, *A Manual of Political Economy* (Washington, DC, 1833), 12. See Helen L. Horowitz, *Rereading Sex: Battles over Sexual Knowledge and Suppression in Nineteenth-Century America* (New York, 2003).

49. Orestes Brownson, "The Laboring Classes," [a review of Carlisle on Chartism] *Boston Quarterly Review* (July 1840): 358–95, quotation 370; [George Fitzhugh], *Slavery Justified* (Fredericksburg, VA, 1850), 3–4, 10. See Luskey, *On the Make*; and Jonathan A. Glickstein, *Concepts of Free Labor in Antebellum America* (New Haven, CT, 1991).

Chapter 7

1. *United States Magazine and Democratic Review* (July/Aug. 1845): 6.

2. Ibid., 5. See Robert D. Sampson, *John L. O'Sullivan and His Times* (Kent, OH, 2003). O'Sullivan usually gets credit for the phrase "manifest destiny," but evidence shows it was drafted by his assistant, Jane Casneau. See Anders Stephanson, *Manifest Destiny* (New York, 1996), chaps. 1–2.

3. See for example James Madison, "Federalist 45," in Jacob E. Cooke, ed., *The Federalist* (Middletown, CT, 1961), 308–14; on Jefferson's views see Peter S. Onuf, *Jefferson's Empire: The Language of American Nationhood* (Charlottesville, VA, 2000), chap. 5. For the expansion story generally see William W. Freehling, *The Road to Disunion*, 2 vols. (New York, 1990–2008); Walter Nugent, *Habits of Empire: A History of American Expansion* (New York, 2008); Michael A. Morrison, *Slavery and the American West: The Eclipse of Manifest Destiny* (Chapel Hill, NC, 1997); Thomas R. Hietala, *Manifest Design: American Exceptionalism and Empire*, rev. ed. (Ithaca, NY, 2003); Elizabeth R. Varon, *Disunion: The Coming of the American Civil War, 1789–1859* (Chapel Hill, NC, 2008); Matthew Karp, *This Vast Southern Empire: Slaveholders at the Helm of American Foreign Policy* (Cambridge, MA, 2016); and Paul Frymer, *Building an American Empire: The Era of Territorial and Political Expansion* (Princeton, 2018).

4. See James E. Lewis Jr., *The American Union and the Problem of Neighborhood, 1783–1829* (Chapel Hill, NC, 1998).

5. Nugent, *Habits of Empire*, chap. 5. See Pekka Hämäläinen, *The Comanche Empire* (New Haven, CT, 2008), chaps. 4–5.

6. Morrison, *Slavery and the American West*, chap. 2.

7. Ibid., chap. 1. See Robert Pierce Forbes, *The Missouri Compromise and Its Aftermath* (Chapel Hill, NC, 2007).

8. Hietala, *Manifest Design*, 30–34.

9. Daniel Walker Howe, *What Hath God Wrought: The Transformation of America, 1815–1848* (New York, 2009), chaps. 14–16.

10. Quoted in Morrison, *Slavery and the American West*, 13.

11. See Amy S. Greenberg, *A Wicked War: Polk, Clay, Lincoln, and the 1846 U.S. Invasion of Mexico* (New York, 2012). For a classic and colorful account see Bernard DeVoto, *The Year of Decision 1846* (Boston, 1943).

12. James K. Polk, "Second Annual Message to Congress," Dec. 8, 1846, and "Third Annual Message to Congress," Dec. 7, 1847, in James D. Richardson, ed., *Messages and Papers of the Presidents*, 10 vols. (New York, 1897), 4:471–95, 532–50.

13. Lansford W. Hastings, *The Emigrants' Guide to Oregon and California [. . .] with a Description of the Different Routes to Those Countries, and All Necessary Information Relative to the Equipment, Supplies, and Method of Traveling* (Cincinnati, OH, 1845). See Malcolm J. Rohrbough, *Days of Gold: The California Gold Rush and the American Nation* (Berkeley, CA, 1997).

14. Peter Knupfer, *The Union as It Is: Constitutional Unionism and Sectional Compromise, 1787–1861* (Chapel Hill, NC, 1991), esp. chap. 5; Varon, *Disunion*, chap. 6.

15. John C. Calhoun, speech in the Senate, Mar. 4, 1850, *Congressional Globe*, 31st Cong., 1st Sess. 451–55, quotations 451.

16. Daniel Webster, speech in the Senate, Mar. 7, 1850, *Congressional Globe*, 31st Cong., 1st Sess. Appendix, 269–75, quotations 269–71, 274.

17. William Seward, speech in the Senate, Mar. 11, 1850, *Congressional Globe*, 31st Cong., 1st Sess. Appendix 260–69, quotations 260, 262, 265.

18. John Lauritz Larson, *Internal Improvement: National Public Works and the Promise of Popular Government in the Early United States* (Chapel Hill, NC, 2001), chap. 4; see also Robert H. Wiebe, *The Opening of American Society* (New York, 1984), chaps. 9–11.

19. Mathew Carey, *Essays on Political Economy; or, the Most Certain Means of Promoting the Wealth, Power, and Resources, and Happiness of Nations, Applied Particularly to the United States* (Philadelphia, 1822) [reprint of *Address of the Philadelphia Society for the Promotion of National Industry* (Philadelphia, 1822), *Address to Congress Being a View of the Ruinous Consequences of a Dependence on Foreign Markets for the Sale of the Great Staples of This Nation, Flour, Cotton, and Tobacco* (Philadelphia, 1821), *Address to the Farmers of the United States on the Ruinous Consequences to Their Vital Interests of the Existing Policy of This Country* (Philadelphia, 1821)], quotations 9, 10–16, 414.

20. Henry C. Carey, *The Prospect: Agricultural, Manufacturing, Commercial, and Financial; At the Opening of the Year 1851* (Philadelphia, 1851), 83.

21. Henry C. Carey, *The Harmony of Interests: Agricultural, Manufacturing, and Commercial*, 2nd ed., (New York, 1852), 227–29.

22. See Harry L. Watson, *Liberty and Power* (New York, 1990), esp. chaps. 3–5; on political partisan praxis see M. J. Heale, *The Presidential Quest: Candidates and Images in American Political Culture, 1787–1852* (Boston, 1982).

23. See Daniel Feller, *Jacksonian Promise: America, 1815–1840* (Baltimore, 1995).

24. Orestes Brownson, "The Laboring Classes," [a review of Carlisle on Chartism] *Boston Quarterly Review* (July 1840): 358–95. See John Lauritz Larson, *The Market Revolution in America: Liberty, Ambition, and the Eclipse of the Common Good* (Cambridge, UK, 2010), 92–140.

25. *DeBow's Review* 7 (1849): 1, quoted in Amy S. Greenberg, *Manifest Manhood* (Cambridge, UK, 2005), 22; Thomas Hart Benton, speech in the Senate, Feb. 7, 1849, *Congressional Globe*, 30th Cong., 2nd Sess. 470.

26. "Memorial of Asa Whitney [. . .] Relative to the Construction of a Railroad from Lake Michigan to the Pacific Ocean," Jan. 28, 1845, House Document 72, *Congressional Globe*, 28th Cong., 2nd Sess. 218–19. On the impact of rail over animal transportation, see Wayne Austerman, *Sharps Rifles and Spanish Mules: The San Antonio–El Paso Mail, 1851–1881* (College Station, TX, 2000).

27. See Larson, *Internal Improvement*, chap. 7.

28. Thomas Hart Benton, speech in the Senate, Feb. 7, 1849, *Congressional Globe*, 30th Cong., 2nd Sess. 470–74.

29. See William E. Gienapp, *Origins of the Republican Party, 1852–1856* (New York, 1987), esp. chaps. 7–13; William W. Freehling, *Becoming Lincoln* (Charlottesville, VA, 2018); James M. McPherson, *Abraham Lincoln and the Second American Revolution* (New York, 1991).

30. See Eric Foner, *Free Soil, Free Labor, Free Men: The Ideology of the Republican Party Before the Civil War*, 2nd ed. (New York, 1995), esp. the new intro., vii–xxxix; also Morrison, *Slavery and the American West*, chaps. 7–8.

31. John Lauritz Larson, *Bonds of Enterprise: John Murray Forbes and Western Development in America's Railway Age* (Boston, 1984), chaps. 5–6, quotation 178; see George H. Miller, *Railroads and the Granger Laws* (Madison, WI, 1971), esp. chaps. 1–2. For recent reprises of

the larger railroad story see Richard White, *Railroaded: The Transcontinentals and the Making of Modern America* (New York, 2011); and William Cronon, *Nature's Metropolis: Chicago and the Great West* (New York, 1991).

32. See Tony A. Freyer, *Producers Versus Capitalists: Constitutional Conflict in Antebellum America* (Charlottesville, VA, 1994), chap. 1.

33. Abraham Lincoln and Stephen A. Douglas, First Joint Debate at Ottawa, Aug. 21, 1858, in Edwin Earle Sparks, ed., *The Lincoln-Douglas Debates*, 2 vols. (Dansville, NY, 1918), 1:277–325, quotations 289–90; *New York Times*, May 16, 1857, quoted in Foner, *Free Soil, Free Labor, Free Men*, 311. See David Hollinger, "Amalgamation and Hypodescent," *American Historical Review* 108 (Dec. 2003): 1363–90.

34. [George Fitzhugh], *Slavery Justified* (Fredericksburg, VA, 1850), 231; see also George Fitzhugh, *Sociology for the South, or The Failure of Free Society* (Richmond, VA, 1854), 46; and George Fitzhugh, *Cannibals All, or Slaves Without Masters* (Richmond, VA, 1857), 16–18.

35. Walter Johnson, *River of Dark Dreams: Slavery and Empire in the Cotton Kingdom* (Cambridge, MA, 2013), chaps. 11–14; and Edward E. Baptist, *The Half Has Not Been Told: Slavery and the Making of American Capitalism* (New York, 2014), chap. 10.

36. Sven Beckert, *Empire of Cotton* (New York, 2014), 29–82.

37. Robert Barnwell Rhett, "Address to the Other Slaveholding States," in Edward McPherson, ed., *Political History of the United States During the Great Rebellion* (Washington, DC, 1865), 12–15.

Chapter 8

1. *Scientific American* 34 (June 3, 1876): 351; *New York Times*, May 15, 1876; Joachim Miller quoted in Robert W. Rydell, *All the World's a Fair* (Chicago, 1984), 10–16, quotation 15.

2. Walt Whitman, "Song of the Exposition," in *Centennial Songs* (1876), published in *Two Rivulets*, Author's Edition (Camden, NJ, 1876), 3–11, quotations 8–9. For the period generally see Richard White, *The Republic for Which It Stands: The United States During Reconstruction and the Gilded Age, 1865–1896* (New York, 2017); and Leon Fink, *The Long Gilded Age: American Capitalism and the Lessons of a New World Order* (Philadelphia, 2018). On reconstruction itself see Eric Foner, *Reconstruction Updated Edition: America's Unfinished Revolution, 1863–1877* (New York, 2014); Edward L. Ayers, *The Thin Light of Freedom: The Civil War and Emancipation in the Heart of America* (New York, 2017); and Douglas R. Egerton, *The Wars of Reconstruction: The Brief, Violent History of America's Most Progressive Era* (New York, 2014).

3. J. S. Ingram, *The Centennial Exposition, Described and Illustrated* (Philadelphia, 1876), 21.

4. Ibid., 82–86, 89–92, 97.

5. Ben Wattenberg, ed., *Statistical History of the United States* (New York, 1976), 728. See Richard White, *Railroaded: The Transcontinentals and the Making of Modern America* (New York, 2011); Ryan Dearinger, *The Filth of Progress* (Oakland, CA, 2016), chap. 5; Mark Fiege, *The Republic of Nature: An Environmental History of the United States* (Seattle, WA, 2012), chap. 6; David Bain, *Empire Express: Building the First Transcontinental Railroad* (New York, 1999); and Alfred D. Chandler Jr., *The Railroads: The Nation's First Big Business* (New York, 1965). See George M. Smerk, "Standard Gauge" and "Standard Time" in *Encyclopedia of North American Railroads*, ed. William H. Middleton, George M. Smerk, and Roberta L. Diehl (Bloomington, IN, 2007), 999–1003.

6. Albro Martin, "The Troubled Subject of Railroad Regulation in the Gilded Age: A Reappraisal," *Journal of American History* 61 (1974–75): 339–71; John Lauritz Larson, *Bonds of Enterprise: John Murray Forbes and Western Development in America's Railway Age* (Cambridge, MA, 1984), chap. 7.

7. On pro rata pricing see Lee Benson, *Merchants, Farmers, and Railroads: Railroad Regulation and New York Politics, 1850–1887* (Cambridge, MA, 1955). For dramatic fictional critiques of railroad pricing see Frank Norris, *The Octopus* (New York, 1901).

8. See for example Maury Klein, *Life and Legend of Jay Gould* (Baltimore, 1986).

9. Richard C. Overton, *Perkins/Budd: Railway Statesmen of the Burlington* (Westport, CT, 1982), 34–46, quotation 35. On Granger cases see George H. Miller, *Railroads and the Granger Laws* (Madison, WI, 1971).

10. Alfred D. Chandler Jr., *The Visible Hand: The Managerial Revolution in American Business* (Cambridge, MA, 1977), chaps. 3–5; Richard Franklin Bensel, *The Political Economy of American Industrialization, 1877–1900* (Cambridge, UK, 2000), 307–14.

11. I rely heavily on Joseph Frazier Wall, *Andrew Carnegie* (New York, 1970).

12. Ibid., chap. 14; see also Chandler, *Visible Hand*, 258–69.

13. Chandler, *Visible Hand*, 254–58, 321–26.

14. See Ron Chernow, *Titan: The Life of John D. Rockefeller, Sr.* (New York, 1998); Ida Tarbell, *The History of Standard Oil*, 2 vols. (orig. 1904; repr. Gloucester, MA, 1963).

15. Chandler, *Visible Hand*, 250, 290–91.

16. Ibid., 302–10.

17. Ibid., chap. 7.

18. See Glenn Porter, *The Rise of Big Business, 1860–1920* (Wheeling, IL, 1973).

19. Naomi Lamoreaux, "Entrepreneurship, Business Organization, and Economic Concentration," in Stanley L. Engerman and Robert E. Gallman, eds., *The Cambridge Economic History of the United States*, 3 vols. (Cambridge, UK, 1996–2000), 2:403–34; Bensel, *Political Economy*, chap. 5; Martin J. Sklar, *The Corporate Reconstruction of American Capitalism* (Cambridge, UK, 1988), chap. 3.

20. Wattenberg, *Statistical History of the United States*, 959. See Edward W. Byrn, *The Progress of Invention in the Nineteenth Century* (New York, 1900), for a five-hundred-page celebration of technology published at the end of the century; Thomas P. Hughes, *American Genesis: A Century of Invention and Technological Enthusiasm, 1870–1970* (New York, 1989); and David A. Hounshell, *From the American System to Mass Production, 1800–1932* (Baltimore, 1985). See also Stanley Engerman and Kenneth Sokoloff, "Technology and Industrialization," in Engerman and Gallman, *Cambridge Economic History of the United States*, 2:367–402.

21. See Steven W. Usselman, *Regulating Railroad Innovation: Business, Technology, and Politics in America, 1840–1920* (Cambridge, UK, 2002), chap. 3.

22. Paul Israel, "Inventing Industrial Research: Thomas Edison and the Menlo Park Laboratory," *Endeavor* 26 (2002): 48–54; Paul Israel, *From Machine Shop to Industrial Laboratory: Telegraphy and the Changing Context of American Invention* (Baltimore, 1992); Paul Israel, *Edison: A Life of Invention* (New York, 1998); Rudolph V. Alvarado, *Thomas Edison* (Indianapolis, IN, 2002). See also Thomas P. Hughes, *Networks of Power: Electrification in Western Society, 1880–1930* (Baltimore, 1983), chap. 2.

23. Chandler, *Visible Hand*, 373–75.

24. Roger L. Geiger, *The History of American Higher Education* (Princeton, 2014), chap. 7.

25. Edward L. Ayers, *The Promise of the New South* (New York, 1992), chaps. 1, 6, 8; Sven Beckert, *Empire of Cotton* (New York, 2015), chap. 10.

26. See White, *Republic for Which It Stands*, chaps. 18, 21.

27. James C. Malin, *The Contriving Brain and the Skillful Hand in the United States* (Lawrence, KS, 1955).

28. See D. W. Meinig, *The Shaping of America: A Geographical Perspective on 500 Years of History*, 4 vols. (New Haven, CT, 1988–2004), vol. 3, *Transcontinental America, 1850–1913*.

29. Ibid., vol. 3, part 2, chap. 8; Robert N. Manley, "Samuel Aughey: Nebraska's Scientific Promoter," *Journal of the West* 6 (1967): 108–18; J. P. Harrington and Matilda Coxe Stevenson, "Anthropologic Miscellenea," *American Anthropologist*, new ser., 12 (1910): 337–43. The classic account is Walter Prescott Webb, *The Great Plains* (1931; repr. Lincoln, NE, 1981).

30. See Noam Maggor, *Brahmin Capitalism: Frontiers of Wealth and Populism in America's First Gilded Age* (Cambridge, MA, 2017); William G. Robbins, *Colony and Empire: The Capitalist Transformation of the American West* (Lawrence, KS, 1994); Andrew C. Isenberg, *Destruction of the Bison* (Cambridge, UK, 2000). For railroad colonization see Richard C. Overton, *Burlington West: A Colonization History of the Burlington Railroad* (Cambridge, MA, 1941).

31. John Wesley Powell, *Report on the Lands of the Arid Region of the United States*, 2nd ed. (Washington, DC, 1879), chaps. 1–2.

32. Ibid., 40–43; Thadis W. Box, "The Arid Lands Revisited—One Hundred Years After John Wesley Powell," Utah State University Honor Lectures, Paper 10 (1977), 9, accessed Mar. 10, 2017, http://digitalcommons.usu.edu/honor_lectures/10; Donald Worster, *A River Running West: The Life of John Wesley Powell* (New York, 2001), chap. 9. See also Robert L. Dorman, *A Word for Nature* (Chapel Hill, NC, 1998), chap. 4.

33. Hiram M. Drache, *Day of Bonanza: A History of Farming in the Red River Valley of the North* (Fargo, ND, 1964); see railroad posters such as "Millions of Acres. Iowa and Nebraska. Land for Sale on 10 years Credit by the Burlington & Missouri River R. R. Co. at 6 per ct Interest and Low Prices," 1872, Rare Book and Special Collections Division, Library of Congress; ATSF ad, Kansas Historical Society, Kansapedia, accessed Mar. 27, 2018, https://www.kshs.org/kansapedia/railroad-land-grants/16718; Northern Pacific ad, accessed Mar. 27, 2018, https://www.art-prints-on-demand.com/a/american-school/northern-pacific-railroad.html; Great Northern ad for Washington Fruit Land (n.d., in possession of the author). On cult of irrigation see John Opie, *Nature's Nation* (New York, 1998), chap. 10.

34. William E. Smythe, *The Conquest of Arid America* (1899; repr. Seattle, WA, 1969), 19.

35. Ibid., 19–29, quotations 27–28.

36. Ibid., xxvii, 284, see generally 261–93; see Patricia Nelson Limerick, *The Legacy of Conquest* (New York, 1987); Opie, *Nature's Nation*, 316–20.

37. Andrew Carnegie, *Triumphant Democracy, or Fifty Years' March of the Republic* (New York, 1886), 1–11, quotation 11; see A. S. Eisenstadt, *Carnegie's Model Republic: Triumphant Democracy and the British-American Relationship* (New York, 2007).

38. Carnegie, *Triumphant Democracy*, 18–19.

39. Russell H. Conwell, *Acres of Diamonds and His Life and Achievements* (New York, 1915), 1–59, quotations 17, 18, 21, 31, accessed Mar. 27, 2018, http://etext.lib.virginia.edu/modeng/modengJ.browse.htm.

40. Wall, *Andrew Carnegie*, 133–34. On Frick see Les Standiford, *Meet You in Hell: Andrew Carnegie, Henry Clay Frick, and the Bitter Partnership That Changed America* (New York,

2005). See also Samuel DeCanio, *Democracy and the Origins of the American Regulatory State* (New Haven, CT, 2015). For a classic study of competing economic ideologies see Sidney Fine, *Laissez Faire and the General-Welfare State: A Study of Conflict in American Thought* (Ann Arbor, MI, 1956).

41. Smythe, *Conquest of Arid America*, 3–11.

42. "Worlds Columbian Exhibition," *Century Illustrated Magazine* 43 (Dec. 1891): 312; C. C. Buel, "Preliminary Glimpses of the Fair," *Century Illustrated Magazine* 45 (Feb. 1893): 615.

43. Buel, "Preliminary Glimpses of the Fair," 654. See Erik Larson, *Devil in the White City* (New York, 2003).

44. Buel, "Preliminary Glimpses of the Fair," 661–62; Rydell, *All the World's a Fair*, 46–71, quotation 60.

45. Martin Ridge, ed., *Frederick Jackson Turner: Wisconsin's Historian of the Frontier* (Madison, WI, 1986), 26–47, quotation 26.

46. Larson, *Devil in the White City*, 247–55, 309–16, 327–33, 373–78.

47. See White, *Republic for Which It Stands*, esp. chap. 20.

Chapter 9

1. See Benjamin Herber Johnson, *Escaping the Dark, Gray City: Fear and Hope in Progressive-Era Conservation* (New Haven, CT, 2017); Dorceta E. Taylor, *The Rise of the American Conservation Movement: Power, Privilege, and Environmental Protection* (Durham, NC, 2016); Joel A. Tarr, ed., *Devastation and Renewal: An Environmental History of Pittsburgh and Its Region* (Pittsburgh, PA, 2003); Samuel P. Hays, *Explorations in Environmental History* (Pittsburgh, PA, 1998); and Samuel P. Hays, *Conservation and the Gospel of Efficiency* (Cambridge, MA, 1959).

2. See for example Ted Steinberg, *Nature Incorporated: Industrialization and the Waters of New England* (Cambridge, UK, 1991); David Stradling, *Smokestacks and Progressives: Environmentalists, Engineers, and Air Quality in America* (Baltimore, 1999); Christopher C. Sellers, *Hazards of the Job: From Industrial Disease to Environmental Health Science* (Chapel Hill, NC, 1997); Michael Williams, *Americans and Their Forests: A Historical Geography* (Cambridge, UK, 1989), esp. part 4; Andrew Isenberg, *Mining California* (New York, 2005); John F. Sears, *Sacred Places: American Tourist Attractions in the Nineteenth Century* (New York, 1989); Colin Fisher, *Urban Green: Nature, Recreation, and the Working Class in Industrial Chicago* (Chapel Hill, NC, 2015); Mark Daniel Barringer, *Selling Yellowstone: Capitalism and the Construction of Nature* (Lawrence, KS, 2002); and Carolyn Merchant, *American Environmental History: An Introduction* (New York, 2007), chaps. 6–7.

3. Ralph Waldo Emerson and Henry David Thoreau, *Nature and Walking*, intro. John Elder (Boston: Beacon Press, 1994).

4. Ibid., 7, 8.

5. Mary Kupiec Cayton, *Emerson's Emergence* (Chapel Hill, NC, 1989), 58, 76–77, 147; *Western Messenger Devoted to Religion, Life, and Literature*, Nov. 1838; *Monthly Miscellany of Religion and Letters*, Aug. 1841; *Gloucester Telegraph*, Aug. 10, 1839; *American Review: A Whig Journal of Politics, Literature, Art, and Science*, Mar. 1845; *Christian Examiner and General Review*, May 1841; *Trumpet and Universalist Magazine*, Sept. 22, 1838.

6. Henry David Thoreau, *A Week on the Concord and Merrimack Rivers; Walden, or, Life in the Woods; The Maine Woods; Cape Cod*, ed. Robert F. Sayre (New York, 1985), 28–31,

quotations 31; Laura Dassow Walls, *Henry David Thoreau, A Life* (Chicago, 2017), 186–89, 253–54.

7. Walls, *Thoreau*, 167.

8. Henry David Thoreau, "Paradise (to Be) Regained," *United States Magazine and Democratic Review*, Nov. 1843, 451–63, quotations 451, 458, 457, 452, 463.

9. See Robert L. Dorman, *A Word for Nature: Four Pioneering Environmental Advocates* (Chapel Hill, NC, 1998), chap. 2; also Lawrence Buell, *The Environmental Imagination: Thoreau, Nature Writing, and the Formation of American Culture* (Cambridge, MA, 1995).

10. Thoreau, *Walden*, chap. 1, in Sayre, *A Week on the Concord*, quotations 328–31, 363, 381–82.

11. *Universalist Quarterly and General Review*, Oct. 1949; *Literary World*, Sept. 22, 1849. For reviews of *Walden* see Joel Myerson, ed., *Critical Essays on Henry David Thoreau's Walden* (Boston, 1988), 15–47, quotations from reviews reprinted on 18, 20, 26, 31, 35–36. Additional reviews are reproduced chronologically in Raymond R. Borst, ed., *The Thoreau Log: A Documentary Life of Henry David Thoreau, 1817–1862* (New York, 1992).

12. See David Lowenthal, *George Perkins Marsh: Prophet of Conservation* (Seattle, WA, 2000); George Perkins Marsh, *Man and Nature; or, Physical Geography as Modified by Human Action* (orig. 1864; edited and with a new introduction by David Lowenthal, Seattle, WA, 2003), xv–xxxviii. See also Dorman, *A Word for Nature*, chap. 1.

13. George Perkins Marsh, *Address Delivered Before the Agricultural Society of Rutland County, September 30, 1847* (Rutland, VT, 1848), 17–19.

14. Marsh, *Man and Nature*, 3–52, quotations 3, 9, 18, 29, 36, 42–43, 52.

15. Ibid., 52–53.

16. Ibid., 36; George Perkins Marsh, "The Study of Nature," *Christian Examiner* 68 (Jan. 1860): 33–62, quotations 33–36, 56.

17. Marsh, *Man and Nature*, 442; *North American Review* (July 1864): 561; *American Presbyterian and Theological Review* (July 1864): 522; *The Independent* (July 7, 1864): 2; *The International Review* (Jan. 1875): 120–25, quotations 124–25; *Scribner's Monthly*, Nov. 1874, 119; *Historical Magazine*, Mar. 1874, 237.

18. Lowenthal, *George Perkins Marsh*, 268; Lowenthal, introduction to Marsh, *Man and Nature*, xv–xvi, xvi–xvii; William Cronon, preface to Marsh, *Man and Nature*, x. For an excellent retrospective on Marsh see David Lowenthal, "Marsh's *Man and Nature* at 150," *George Wright Forum* 32 (2015): 227–37. The final chapter of Lowenthal, *George Perkins Marsh*, offers an insightful discussion of Marsh's place among current voices in environmental history and activism.

19. I draw heavily from Donald Worster, *A Passion for Nature: The Life of John Muir* (New York, 2008), 48–122, 145. See also Dorman, *A Word for Nature*, chap. 3; and Barbara Novak, *Nature and Culture: American Landscape and Painting, 1825–1875*, rev. ed. (New York, 1995).

20. Worster, *Passion for Nature*, 170–79, quotations 174, 179.

21. Ibid., 179, 191, 195; John Muir, *Studies in the Sierra*, ed. William E. Colby (orig. 1874; repr. San Francisco, 1950), accessed Mar. 28, 2018, on Sierra Club website, https://vault.sierraclub.org/john_muir_exhibit/writings/letters.aspx; *New York Tribune*, Dec. 5, 1871.

22. Worster, *Passion for Nature*, chaps. 9–10. Worster makes the good point that John Muir was not wholly averse to agricultural life.

23. John Muir, "Treasures of Yosemite," *Century Magazine*, Aug. 1890, 483–500, quotations 487–88; John Muir, "National Parks and Forest Reserves," *Sierra Club Bulletin* (orig. 1896; repr. San Francisco, 1950), 271–84, quotation 273; John Muir, "Features of the Proposed Yosemite National Park," *Century Magazine*, Sept. 1890, 656–67. See Worster, *Passion for Nature*, chaps. 10–11.

24. John Muir, "American Forests," *Atlantic*, Aug. 1897, revised as chap. 10 in John Muir, *Our National Parks* (San Francisco, 1901). Quotations are from the revised essay pages 2, 4, 7, 8 of 10, accessed Mar. 28, 2018, https://vault.sierraclub.org/john_muir_exhibit/writings/our_national_parks/.

25. The most recent survey of these issues is Richard White, *The Republic for Which It Stands: The United States During Reconstruction and the Gilded Age, 1865–1896* (New York, 2017), chap. 22; Martin J. Sklar, *The Corporate Reconstruction of American Capitalism* (Cambridge, UK, 1988), chap. 3; also Michael McGerr, *A Fierce Discontent: The Rise and Fall of the Progressive Movement in America* (New York, 2003). Still useful is Robert H. Wiebe, *The Search for Order, 1877–1920* (New York, 1967). On corruption see Richard Franklin Bensel, *The Political Economy of American Industrialization, 1877–1900* (Cambridge, UK, 2000); and David J. Rothman, *Politics and Power: The United States Senate, 1869–1901* (Cambridge, MA, 1966).

26. Quoted in Opie, *Nature's Nation: An Environmental History of the United States* (Fort Worth, TX, 1998) 370, 378. See Merchant, *American Environmental History*, 146–53; and Douglas Brinkley, *The Wilderness Warrior: Theodore Roosevelt and the Crusade for America* (New York, 2009), chap. 15.

27. See Darrin Lunde, *The Naturalist: Theodore Roosevelt* (New York, 2016); Michael R. Canfield, *Theodore Roosevelt in the Field* (Chicago, 2015); Brinkley, *Wilderness Warrior*, chap. 14. On Pinchot see Char Miller, *Seeking the Greatest Good: The Conservation Legacy of Gifford Pinchot* (Pittsburgh, PA, 2013); and Char Miller, *Gifford Pinchot and the Making of Modern Environmentalism* (Washington, DC, 2001).

28. Theodore Roosevelt, "First Message to Congress," Dec. 3, 1901, in *Addresses and Presidential Messages, 1902–1904*, ed. Henry Cabot Lodge (New York, 1904), 292–309, quotations 308–9; see also "Second Message to Congress," Dec. 2, 1902, ibid., 347–71; and "Third Message to Congress," Dec. 7, 1903, ibid., 405–7.

29. Brinkley, *Wilderness Warrior*, chap. 19. The appendix lists all the parks and preserves set aside by Roosevelt.

30. John Muir, "Hetch Hetchy Valley," *Boston Weekly Transcript*, Mar. 25, 1873.

31. Much of this account is based on Robert W. Righter, *The Battle over Hetch Hetchy: America's Most Controversial Dam and the Birth of Modern Environmentalism* (New York, 2005); see also Kendrick A. Clements, "Politics and the Park: San Francisco's Fight for Hetch Hetchy, 1908–1913," *Pacific Historical Review* 48 (May 1979): 185–215.

32. Quoted in Clements, "Politics and the Park," 197–99, 212, 214; John Muir, "The Hetch-Hetchy Valley," *Sierra Club Bulletin*, Jan. 1908, accessed Mar. 28, 2018, https://vault.sierraclub.org/john_muir_exhibit/writings/articles.aspx; Righter, *Battle over Hetch Hetchy*, 206–12. See Roderick Nash, *Wilderness and the American Mind*, 3rd ed. (New Haven, CT, 1982).

33. Theodore Roosevelt to John Muir, Sept. 16, 1907, Theodore Roosevelt Papers, Library of Congress Manuscript Division, accessed Nov. 15, 2017, via Theodore Roosevelt Digital Library, Dickinson State University, http://www.theodorerooseveltcenter.org/Research/

Digital-Library/Record?libID = 0200320; John Muir, "The Tuolumne Yosemite in Danger," *Outlook*, Nov. 2, 1907, 486–89; John Muir, "The Hetch-Hetchy Valley," *Sierra Club Bulletin*, Jan. 1908, accessed Mar. 28, 2018, https://vault.sierraclub.org/john_muir_exhibit/writings/articles.aspx.

34. "The Hetch Hetchy Project," *Forest and Stream*, Feb. 6, 1909, 2; Robert Underwood Johnson, "Public Opinion: The Yosemite National Park," *Outlook*, Feb. 27, 1909, 506–7; and "Dismembering Your National Park," *Outlook*, Jan. 30, 1909, 252–53; Manson quoted in Righter, *Battle over Hetch Hetchy*, 90–92; James D. Phelan, "Why Congress Should Pass the Hetch-Hetchy Bill," *Outlook*, Feb. 13, 1909, 340–41; John Muir, "The Hetch-Hetchy Valley," *Sierra Club Bulletin*, Jan. 1908. See Righter, *Battle over Hetch Hetchy*, chap. 4.

35. "The Hetch-Hetchy Bill Signed," *Independent*, Jan. 5, 1914, 11. See Righter, *Battle over Hetch Hetchy*, chap. 6.

36. O'Shaugnessy quoted in Righter, *Battle over Hetch Hetchy*, 152, see generally chap. 7.

37. Compare Karl Polanyi, *The Great Transformation* (New York, 1944) with Walt W. Rostow, *The Stages of Economic Growth: A Non-Communist Manifesto* (Cambridge, UK, 1960). Both recognize that market transactions typically have been embedded in social and cultural values other than supply and demand. Polanyi sees it as a humanizing virtue; Rostow as an evil to be disabled so that modernization can proceed.

Epilogue

1. Donald Trump, State of the Union Address, accessed Feb. 4, 2018, https://www.white house.gov/sotu/. Text omits the word "beautiful" but President Trump spoke it in the video. See *Washington Post*, Jan. 31, 2018; see also, accessed Feb. 12, 2018, https://www.investopedia .com/news/how-many-people-work-coal-industry/; and see, accessed Apr. 2, 2019, https:// www.washingtonpost.com/news/fact-checker/wp/2018/01/16/fact-checking-the-trump -administrations-claims-on-saving-coal-country/?noredirect = on&utm_term = .d8195d2ba65e.

2. Donella Meadows, Jorgen Randers, and Dennis Meadows, *Limits to Growth* (Falls Church, VA, 1972). Gretchen C. Daily and Paul R. Ehrlich, "Population, Sustainability, and the Earth's Carrying Capacity," *BioScience* 42 (Nov. 1992): 761–71. See also Cathleen O'Grady, "If We Gave Everybody a Decent Standard of Living, Could We Sustain It?," *ARSTechnica*, Feb. 6, 2018, accessed Feb. 8, 2018, https://arstechnica.com/science/2018/02/a-basic-standard- of-living-could-be-environmentally-sustainable. O'Grady argues that with great efficiency improvements this might be done.

3. Constance Lever-Tracy and Barrie Pittock, "Climate Change and Society: An Introduc- tion," in Constance Lever-Tracy, ed., *Routledge Handbook of Climate Change and Society* (New York, 2010), 2–5; Intergovernmental Panel on Climate Change, press release, Oct. 8, 2018, accessed Nov. 17, 2018, https://www.ipcc.ch/site/assets/uploads/2018/11/pr_181008_P48_ spm_en.pdf; *New York Times*, Oct. 7, 2018.

4. Intergovernmental Panel on Climate Change, factsheet, "What Is the IPCC," Aug. 30, 2013, accessed Feb. 4, 2018, http://archive.ipcc.ch/news_and_events/docs/factsheets/ FS_what_ipcc.pdf.

5. "UN Conference on Environment and Development (1992)," accessed Feb. 5, 2018, http://www.un.org/geninfo/bp/enviro.html. See *Wall Street Journal*, Oct. 8, 1992, A4.

6. "UN Summary of the Kyoto Protocol," accessed Feb. 5, 2018, http://unfccc.int/ kyoto_protocol/background/items/2879.php.

7. Bjorn Lomborg, *The Skeptical Environmentalist* (Cambridge, UK, 2001); Ronald Bailey, "Why All Those Dire Predictions Have No Future," *Wall Street Journal*, Oct. 2, 2001, A17; *Economist*, Feb. 2, 2002; Nicholas Wade, "Scientist at Work/Bjorn Lomborg: From an Unlikely Quarter, Eco-Optimist," *New York Times*, Aug. 7, 2001, quotation F3. See Al Gore, *An Inconvenient Truth*, directed by Davis Guggenheim (2006); Bjorn Lomborg, *Cool It* (2010); P. J. Jacques, R. E. Dunlap, and M. Freeman, "The Organization of Denial," *Environmental Politics* 17 (2008): 349–85, quoted in R. E. Dunlap and Aaron M. McCright, "Climate Change Denial," in Lever-Tracy, *Routledge Handbook of Climate Change*, 243.

8. National Academy of Sciences, *America's Climate Choices* (Washington, DC, 2011); also accessed Feb. 8, 2018, see https://www.washingtonpost.com/news/fact-checker/wp/2017/01/11/when-did-mitch-mcconnell-say-he-wanted-to-make-obama-a-one-term-president/?utm_term=.c7fe3c43af4f.

9. See for example Rick Perry, "Remarks at the Western Republican Leadership Conference in Las Vegas, Nevada," Oct. 19, 2011, accessed Feb. 9, 2018, http://www.presidency.ucsb.edu/ws/index.php?pid=97143; Video Address by Newt Gingrich, "$2.50 per Gallon Gasoline, Energy Independence and Jobs," Feb. 22, 2012, accessed Feb. 8, 2018, http://www.presidency.ucsb.edu/ws/index.php?pid=99764; Michelle Bachman, "Address to the Commonwealth Club in San Francisco, California," Oct. 20, 2011, accessed Feb. 8, 2018, http://www.presidency.ucsb.edu/ws/index.php?pid=98452; https://www.space.com/13920-gingrich-moon-mining-republican-debate-romney.html.

10. James Inhofe, *The Greatest Hoax* (Washington, DC, 2012), iii–v, jacket blurb, 53, 86–87. In 2015 Inhofe reprised his analysis of global warming by throwing a snowball on the Senate floor—again in February. See *Washington Post*, Mar. 1, 2015. Inhofe's publisher, Joseph Farah, a self-described "conservative evangelical Christian," is a leading purveyor of conspiracy theories and an associate of radio gadfly Rush Limbaugh.

11. Pew Research Center, "Politics of Climate" (Oct. 2016), by Cary Funk and Brian Kennedy, accessed Feb. 9, 2018, https://www.pewresearch.org/science/2016/10/04/the-politics-of-climate/, 5, 16, 31, 54; *Nature Climate Change* (Apr. 2011): 1, 35–41; (July 2011): 195–96; (Apr. 2012): 236; (May 2012): 303–5.

12. Accessed Feb. 9, 2018, see https://obamawhitehouse.archives.gov/blog/2016/09/03/president-obama-united-states-formally-enters-paris-agreement.

13. See *New York Times*, Nov. 28, 2017, accessed Feb. 8, 2018, https://www.nytimes.com/2017/11/28/us/politics/donald-trump-tape.html.

14. Accessed Feb. 8, 2018, http://www.presidency.ucsb.edu/ws/index.php?pid=110306; Trump at Trump Tower, June 16, 2015, accessed Feb. 8, 2018, http://www.presidency.ucsb.edu/ws/index.php?pid=110306. See also Donald J. Trump, *The Art of the Deal* (New York, 1987).

15. For all the Trump speeches see http://www.presidency.ucsb.edu/2016_election_speeches.php?candidate=45&campaign=2016TRUMP&doctype=5000, accessed Feb. 8, 2018.

16. See https://www.politico.com/magazine/story/2016/07/2016-bill-kristol-republicans-conservative-movement-donald-trump-politics-214025; http://thehill.com/homenews/media/363995-ny-times-david-brooks-gop-under-trump-is-harming-every-cause-it-claims-to-serve; http://www.bbc.com/news/world-us-canada-37999969; https://www.washingtonpost.com/news/energy-environment/wp/2018/02/03/white-house-to-withdraw-controversial-nominee-to-head-council-on-environmental-quality/?utm_term=.cc93af5e54ae; https://

www.washingtonpost.com/news/energy-environment/wp/2018/02/07/scott-pruitt-asks-if
-global-warming-necessarily-is-a-bad-thing/?utm_term = .2eb47c808 31f, all accessed Feb 8,
2018. When Hartnett-White failed to answer in her confirmation hearing the most basic questions about science, the White House withdrew her nomination.

17. Trump on Trans-Pacific Partnership, accessed Feb. 11, 2018, https://www.washington
post.com/business/economy/withdrawal-from-trans-pacific-partnership-shifts-us-role-in
-world-economy/2017/01/23/05720df6-e1a6-11e6-a453-19ec4b3d09ba_story.html?utm
_term = .bba1d60c56c4; Trump at UN, accessed Feb. 11, 2018, https://www.politico.com/story/
2017/09/19/trump-un-speech-2017-full-text-transcript-242879; Trump at Davos, accessed Feb.
11, 2018, https://www.politico.com/story/2018/01/26/full-text-trump-davos-speech-transcript
-370861; *New York Times Sunday Magazine*, Feb. 11, 2018.

18. Stephen Macekura, *Of Limits and Growth: The Rise of Global Sustainable Development
in the Twentieth Century* (Cambridge, UK, 2015).

19. Alfred Crosby, *Ecological Imperialism* (Cambridge, UK, 1986); Clive Ponting, *A Green
New History of the World* (New York, 2007); David Landes, *Wealth and Poverty of Nations*
(New York, 1998); Kenneth Pomeranz, *The Great Divergence* (Princeton, 2000); Jared Dia-
mond, *Collapse* (New York, 2004); Ian Morris, *Why the West Rules—For Now* (New York,
2010); Donella H. Meadows, Jorgen Randers, and Dennis Meadows, *Limits to Growth: The 30-
Year Update* (White River Junction, VT, 2004).

20. Wolfgang Streeck, *How Will Capitalism End: Essays on a Failing System* (New York,
2016); Pankaj Mishra, "Great Walls," *New York Times Sunday Magazine*, Feb. 11, 2018; Thomas
Piketty, *Capital in the Twenty-First Century* (Cambridge, MA, 2014); Thomas Piketty, "Brahmin Left vs. Merchant Right: Rising Inequality and the Changing Structure of Political Conflict," accessed Feb. 18, 2018, http://piketty.pse.ens.fr/files/Piketty2018PoliticalConflict.pdf; Joel
Moykyr, *A Culture of Growth* (Princeton, 2017); Elinor Ostrom, *Governing the Commons*
(Cambridge, UK, 1990); Elinor Ostrom, *The Future of the Commons*, with contributions by
Christina Chang, Mark Pennington, and Vlad Tarko (London, 2012); Wendy Brown, *Undoing
the Demos* (New York, 2015); Robert B. Reich, *The Common Good* (New York, 2018).

21. Vaclav Smil, *Energy and Civilization: A History* [orig. title *Energy in World History*
(Boulder, CO, 1994); rev. ed. Cambridge, MA, 2017], 381–84. See Fred Cottrell, *Energy and
Society* (New York, 1955); Nicolas Georgescu-Roegen, *The Entropy Law and the Economic Process* (Cambridge, MA, 1971). The 2018 IPCC report can be found at www.ipcc.ch. For 2018
global carbon emissions see *Washington Post*, Dec. 5, 2018.

22. Steven Pinker, *Enlightenment Now: The Case for Reason, Science, Humanism, and
Progress* (New York, 2018); Gates's blurb is on the Amazon website, accessed Feb. 18, 2018.

23. See Margaret J. Wheatly, *So Far from Home: Lost and Found in Our Brave New World*
(Oakland, CA, 2012).

24. See Mark Pennington, "Elinor Ostrom, Common-Pool Resources, and the Classical
Liberal Tradition," in Ostrom, *The Future of the Commons*, 38; Ostrom's lecture of the same
title, ibid., 68–83.

25. This view has been roundly discredited by Edward Baptist, *The Half Has Never Been
Told* (New York, 2014); Walter Johnson, *River of Dark Dreams* (Cambridge, MA, 2013); and
Sven Beckert, *Empire of Cotton* (New York, 2015). See also Sven Beckert and Seth Rockman,
eds., *Slavery's Capitalism: A New History of American Economic Development* (Philadelphia,
2016).

26. Trump at the UN, accessed Feb. 11, 2018, https://www.politico.com/story/2017/09/19/trump-un-speech-2017-full-text-transcript-242879.

27. Harry L. Watson to the author, July 16, 2018.

28. See John Lauritz Larson, "An Inquiry into the Nature and Causes of the Wealth of Nations," *Journal of the Early Republic* 35 (2015): 1–23.

29. Dr. Seuss, *The Lorax* (New York, 1971), 54, 57, 59.

ACKNOWLEDGMENTS

IN THE MANY YEARS since I began this project I have accumulated debts in many directions. A Barra Fellowship from the McNeil Center for Early American Studies at the University of Pennsylvania gave me the first opportunity to explore the idea and sample the wealth of materials at hand in the Philadelphia area, especially collections of the Library Company of Philadelphia, the American Philosophical Society, the Historical Society of Pennsylvania, and the Academy of Natural Sciences of Philadelphia (now affiliated with Drexel University). Thanks to the company of McNeil Center fellows in the class 2004–5 for their lively encouragement and friendship. The McNeil Center Seminar entertained the first iteration of "Abundance" (Chapter 2), from which experience I learned far more than the audience. Two summer seminars sponsored by the National Endowment for the Humanities and hosted by the Library Company of Philadelphia gave me more opportunities to work in Philadelphia while conducting the seminar programs in 2005 and 2011.

During a sabbatical in the fall of 2013, through the good offices of Conrad E. Wright, I enjoyed a fellow's office at the Massachusetts Historical Society in Boston as well as access to their extraordinary resources. The Boston Area Environmental History Seminar worked over another draft of "Abundance" while the MHS Fellows' Brownbag Lunch seminar endured early thoughts leading to "Achievement" (Chapter 3) and "Liberation" (Chapter 4). A full year fellowship at the Charles Warren Center at Harvard in 2015–16 made it possible to finish several chapters and rough out the final shape of the book. I am especially grateful for the valuable feedback from the seminar on American Capitalism led by Sven Beckert, Christine Desan, and Michael Zakim. My colleagues at the center that year provided good company and intellectual stimulation. The Widener Library, not fifty yards from the center, remains the gold standard for academic research libraries.

Purdue University has been my academic home for thirty-five years. During that time I have enjoyed continuous support from the Department of History and the College of Liberal Arts. Special thanks are due to department head R. Douglas Hurt and deans Toby Parcel, Irwin Weiser, and David Reingold for providing research leave and financial support to supplement fellowships and sabbatical awards. Faculty colleagues and graduate students at Purdue University weighed in on drafts of early chapters at Works-in-Progress seminars and other informal occasions. The Purdue Center for the Environment hosted another presentation growing out of this project. Thanks to an exchange program with Central European University in Budapest, I was privileged to present a draft of the Introduction to an audience that had just been thrown under the bus by Viktor Orbán's Hungarian populist revolution. (I suspect global warming was far from their minds that day.)

Individuals at home and abroad have contributed in special ways to the development of this book. Daniel Richter, director of the McNeil Center showed particular interest in the idea at the outset, as did James Brewer Stewart, Michael Zuckerman, Richard S. Dunn, and Robert Lockhart. Roderick McDonald and Michelle Craig McDonald nourished mind, body, and soul whenever I resided in Philadelphia. In Boston Conrad E. Wright and Kate Viens read bits and pieces and advised my searches. I am especially grateful for conversations at Harvard with Morton J. Horwitz, Alex Keyssar, Lily Geismer, Noam Maggor, and Rebecca Marchiel. John Stauffer, Ann Jones, Martin Giraudeau, Nicolas Barreyer, and Abbey Spinak generously read drafts of chapters. My many friends in the Society for Historians of the Early American Republic listened patiently over the years as I tried to talk my way around the "culture of exploitation." At Purdue Frank Lambert provided critical advice on early chapters and James R. Farr read the entire manuscript. David Atkinson read the Epilogue and saved me from excesses there, as did my dependable spouse, Suzanne. Padraig Lawlor contributed bibliographical assistance. Daniel Richter and Harry Watson read the manuscript for the press and made essential suggestions for revision. My son, Olaf Larson, a student of permaculture and theology, scrutinized most of these chapters and saved me from any number of impulsive missteps. Nonspecialist friends provided valuable insights on drafts, especially Marguerite Trachtman and Mark Hermodson, who read the entire manuscript at least once. Robert Lockhart at Penn Press remained a critical advocate to the end. Lily Palladino and Ellen Douglas gave the manuscript the painstaking editorial attention that I find myself still incapable of doing alone. Whatever mistakes or offenses remain are mine alone, and I accept responsibility for them gladly.

Once again my domestic circle—growing smaller by the escape of grown children and the passing of esteemed canines—has endured the preoccupations of bookmaking that only those who experience it can appreciate. For probably the last time in a book I thank my spouse of forty-five years, Suzanne, for unqualified support coupled with essential demands for balance and sanity. She has experienced my lifelong preoccupation with historical explanation—something not everyone finds existentially compelling. My children, Anna and Olaf, thrive, and this gives me great hope. This book is dedicated to my ten-year-old grandson, Kevin John Nolan III—"KJ"—for whom I hope the Lorax and his friends will, indeed, return.